Russia after 2012

This book provides an overview of the state of Russia after the 2012 presidential election. It considers a wide range of domestic and international issues, examining both the run up to and the consequences of the election. It covers political, economic, and social topics. It assesses the political scene both before and after the election, and discusses the nature and likely future of democracy in Russia. The election's impact on the Russian economy is discussed in detail, as are Russia's relationships with the United States, the European Union, and other parts of the world.

J. L. Black is the Director of the Centre for Research on Canadian–Russian Relations and an Emeritus Professor of Carleton University, Canada.

Michael Johns is an Assistant Professor of Political Science at Laurentian University-Barrie Campus, Canada.

The editors were assisted by **Alanda D. Theriault**, Lecturer in Liberal Arts and Humanities at Georgian College and Humber College Business School, and Assistant Editor at the Centre for Research on Canadian–Russian Relations.

Routledge Contemporary Russia and Eastern Europe Series

1 **Liberal Nationalism in Central Europe**
   Stefan Auer

2 **Civil–Military Relations in Russia and Eastern Europe**
   David J. Betz

3 **The Extreme Nationalist Threat in Russia**
   The growing influence of Western Rightist ideas
   Thomas Parland

4 **Economic Development in Tatarstan**
   Global markets and a Russian region
   Leo McCann

5 **Adapting to Russia's New Labour Market**
   Gender and employment strategy
   Edited by Sarah Ashwin

6 **Building Democracy and Civil Society East of the Elbe**
   Essays in honour of Edmund Mokrzycki
   Edited by Sven Eliaeson

7 **The Telengits of Southern Siberia**
   Landscape, religion and knowledge in motion
   Agnieszka Halemba

8 **The Development of Capitalism in Russia**
   Simon Clarke

9 **Russian Television Today**
   Primetime drama and comedy
   David MacFadyen

10 **The Rebuilding of Greater Russia**
   Putin's foreign policy towards the CIS countries
   Bertil Nygren

11 **A Russian Factory Enters the Market Economy**
   Claudio Morrison

12 **Democracy Building and Civil Society in Post-Soviet Armenia**
   Armine Ishkanian

13 **NATO–Russia Relations in the Twenty-First Century**
   Aurel Braun

14 **Russian Military Reform**
   A failed exercise in defence decision making
   Carolina Vendil Pallin

15 **The Multilateral Dimension in Russian Foreign Policy**
   Edited by Elana Wilson Rowe and Stina Torjesen

16 **Russian Nationalism and the National Reassertion of Russia**
   Edited by Marlène Laruelle

17 **The Caucasus**
   An introduction
   Frederik Coene

18 **Radical Islam in the Former Soviet Union**
   Edited by Galina M. Yemelianova

19 **Russia's European Agenda and the Baltic States**
   Janina Šleivytė

20 **Regional Development in Central and Eastern Europe**
   Development processes and policy challenges
   Edited by Grzegorz Gorzelak, John Bachtler, and Maciej Smętkowski

21 **Russia and Europe**
   Reaching agreements, digging trenches
   Kjell Engelbrekt and Bertil Nygren

22 **Russia's Skinheads**
   Exploring and rethinking subcultural lives
   Hilary Pilkington, Elena Omel'chenko, and Al'bina Garifzianova

23 **The Colour Revolutions in the Former Soviet Republics**
Successes and failures
Edited by Donnacha Ó Beacháin and Abel Polese

24 **Russian Mass Media and Changing Values**
Edited by Arja Rosenholm, Kaarle Nordenstreng, and Elena Trubina

25 **The Heritage of Soviet Oriental Studies**
Edited by Michael Kemper and Stephan Conermann

26 **Religion and Language in Post-Soviet Russia**
Brian P. Bennett

27 **Jewish Women Writers in the Soviet Union**
Rina Lapidus

28 **Chinese Migrants in Russia, Central Asia and Eastern Europe**
Edited by Felix B. Chang and Sunnie T. Rucker-Chang

29 **Poland's EU Accession**
Sergiusz Trzeciak

30 **The Russian Armed Forces in Transition**
Economic, geopolitical and institutional uncertainties
Edited by Roger N. McDermott, Bertil Nygren, and Carolina Vendil Pallin

31 **The Religious Factor in Russia's Foreign Policy**
Alicja Curanović

32 **Postcommunist Film – Russia, Eastern Europe and World Culture**
Moving images of postcommunism
Edited by Lars Lyngsgaard Fjord Kristensen

33 **Russian Multinationals**
From regional supremacy to global lead
Andrei Panibratov

34 **Russian Anthropology After the Collapse of Communism**
Edited by Albert Baiburin, Catriona Kelly, and Nikolai Vakhtin

35 **The Post-Soviet Russian Orthodox Church**
Politics, culture and Greater Russia
Katja Richters

36 **Lenin's Terror**
   The ideological origins of early Soviet State violence
   James Ryan

37 **Life in Post-Communist Eastern Europe after EU Membership**
   Edited by Donnacha O Beachain, Vera Sheridan, and Sabina Stan

38 **EU-Border Security**
   Challenges, (mis)perceptions, and responses
   Serghei Golunov

39 **Power and Legitimacy**
   Challenges from Russia
   Edited by Per-Arne Bodin, Stefan Hedlund, and Elena Namli

40 **Managing Ethnic Diversity in Russia**
   Edited by Oleh Protsyk and Benedikt Harzl

41 **Believing in Russia**
   Religious policy after Communism
   Geraldine Fagan

42 **The Changing Russian University**
   From state to market
   Tatiana Maximova-Mentzoni

43 **The Transition to National Armies in the Former Soviet Republics, 1988–2005**
   Jesse Paul Lehrke

44 **The Fall of the Iron Curtain and the Culture of Europe**
   Peter I. Barta

45 **Russia after 2012**
   From Putin to Medvedev to Putin – continuity, change, or revolution?
   Edited by J. L. Black and Michael Johns

The Centre for Research on Canadian–Russian Relations (CRCR) was founded at Carleton University in 1990 on the basis of a generous grant from the Donner Canadian Foundation. It was re-located to the University Partnership Centre at Georgian College in the summer of 2006. The CRCR is self-financing, seeking grants and contracts for multiple projects. The *Russia and Eurasia Documents Annual*, which has subscribers in 17 countries, has been edited at the CRCR since 1987. Its monographic "Russia–Canada Series" is now in its 10th volume. The CRCR has completed contracts and arranged briefings for many government departments and private businesses, among them the departments of National Defence, Northern Affairs, Foreign Affairs, and the Security and Intelligence Service. The Centre also provides research stipends and employment for students and has an extensive list of occasional papers that it markets to libraries and other organizations. It houses a unique collection of Russian archival documents on Canada (over 20,000 pages), organizes public presentations, arranges instructors for Learning in Retirement programs, and provides research information to scholars, journalists, and other interested parties. J. L. Black is its founding director; Michael Johns and Alanda D. Theriault are members of its executive.

Russia after 2012

From Putin to Medvedev to Putin – continuity, change, or revolution?

Edited by J. L. Black
and Michael Johns
Assisted by Alanda D. Theriault

LONDON AND NEW YORK

First published 2013
by Routledge
2 Park Square, Milton Park, Abingdon, Oxon OX14 4RN

Simultaneously published in the USA and Canada
by Routledge
711 Third Avenue, New York, NY 10017

Routledge is an imprint of the Taylor & Francis Group, an informa business

© 2013 selection and editorial material, J. L. Black, Michael Johns, and Alanda D. Theriault; individual chapters, the contributors.

The right of the editors to be identified as authors of the editorial material, and of the contributors for their individual chapters, has been asserted by them in accordance with sections 77 and 78 of the Copyright, Designs and Patents Act 1988.

All rights reserved. No part of this book may be reprinted or reproduced or utilised in any form or by any electronic, mechanical, or other means, now known or hereafter invented, including photocopying and recording, or in any information storage or retrieval system, without permission in writing from the publishers.

Trademark notice: Product or corporate names may be trademarks or registered trademarks, and are used only for identification and explanation without intent to infringe.

British Library Cataloguing in Publication Data
A catalogue record for this book is available from the British Library

Library of Congress Cataloging in Publication Data
Russia after 2012 : from Putin to Medvedev to Putin - continuity, change, or revolution? / edited by J.L. Black and Michael Johns ; assisted by Alanda Theriault.
  pages ; cm. – (Routledge contemporary Russia and Eastern Europe series ; 45)
  Includes bibliographical references and index.
  1. Russia (Federation)–Politics and government–21st century. 2. Russia (Federation)–Foreign relations. 3. Russia (Federation)–Economic conditions–21st century. I. Black, J. L. (Joseph Laurence), 1937- II. Johns, Michael, 1974- III. Theriault, Alanda. IV. Series: Routledge contemporary Russia and Eastern Europe series ; 45.
  DK510.763.R855 2013
  947.086'3–dc23
  2012042508

ISBN: 978-0-415-69399-8 (hbk)
ISBN: 978-0-203-52205-9 (ebk)

Typeset in Times New Roman
by Sunrise Setting Ltd, Paignton, UK

Contents

List of figures and tables	*xi*
Notes on contributors	*xii*
Foreword	*xv*
Preface	*xvii*
Acknowledgements	*xviii*
Abbreviations and acronyms	*xix*

PART I
Domestic affairs — 1

1 The 2011–12 Russia elections: the next chapter in Russia's post-Communist transition? — 3
   JOAN DEBARDELEBEN

2 Courts, law, and policing under Medvedev: many reforms, modest change, new voices — 19
   PETER H. SOLOMON, JR

3 Centre–periphery and state–society relations in Putin's Russia — 42
   JOHN F. YOUNG

4 The challenges and prospects of reforming Russia's higher education system — 57
   ELENA MALTSEVA

5 Has the Putin–Medvedev tandem improved women's rights? — 73
   ANDREA CHANDLER

PART II
Economic and international related issues — 87

6 The economic situation in present-day Russia — 89
   V. V. POPOV

x Contents

7   Tandemology as spectator sport: the course of Medvedev's campaigns to curb corruption and encourage modernization   101
    J. L. BLACK

8   The Kremlin's future priorities in harnessing hard power: beyond the "Tandem" and "New Look"   121
    ROGER N. MCDERMOTT

PART III
Foreign affairs   137

9   Russia and the West: integration and tensions   139
    SERGEI PLEKHANOV

10 Russia–European Union relations after 2012: good, bad, indifferent?   153
    MICHAEL JOHNS

11 Russia and Central Asia: does the tail wag the dog?   167
    JEFF SAHADEO

12 Moscow's evolving partnership with Beijing: countering Washington's hegemony   184
    JACQUES LÉVESQUE

13 Defence innovation and Russian foreign policy   202
    FREDERIC LABARRE

    Concluding remarks   216
    J. L. BLACK

Appendices
1   Russian Federation parliamentary and presidential election results, 1993 to 2012   219
2   Russian Federation's international alliances, associations, and organizations   225

    Index   231

Figures and tables

Figures

4.1	The Soviet education system	60
6.1	GDP growth rates and inflation in Russia, %, 1990–2008	89
6.2	Government budget revenues and expenditure, % of GDP, Minfin data	90
6.3	Average annual GDP growth rates in CIS countries in 2000–07 (EBRD estimates)	90
6.4	Crime rate (left scale), murder rate and suicide rate (right scale) per 100,000 inhabitants	91
6.5	Mortality and life expectancy rates	92
6.6	Oil prices (Brent, $ a barrel, right scale) and GDP growth rates in Russia (%, left scale) 1990–2011	92
6.7	R&D expenditure in selected countries, % of GDP	93
6.8	Structure of Russian GDP, %	94
6.9	Real effective exchange rate (December 1995 = 100%, left scale) and year end gross foreign exchange reserves including gold ($bn, right log scale)	95
6.10	Goods exported from and imported to Russia ($bn, monthly data)	95
6.11	Real exports and imports of goods and services (national accounts statistics, 1995 = 100%)	96
6.12	Gini coefficient of income distributions in China and Russia, 1978–2006 (source: Chen, Hou, Jin, 2008; Goskomstat)	97
6.13	Balance of payments items, Russia 1992–2011 ($bn)	97
13.1	Trends of R&D and procurement, relative to defence budget (US$bn)	210

Tables

1.1	Voter preferences, presidential election 2012	7
1.2	Gap – presidential vote/party list vote in Duma election	12
13.1	Russian procurement 2005–10 (US$bn)	208
13.2	2007–12 R&D with procurement against Russian defence budget (US$bn)	209

Notes on contributors

J. L. Black, PhD (McGill University). Professor Emeritus & Distinguished Research Professor, Carleton University, Ottawa. Director of the Centre for Research on Canadian–Russian Relations, Laurentian University at Georgian College, Barrie, Ontario; Adjunct Professor in the History Department, Laurentian University, Sudbury, Ontario. Has written extensively on Soviet and Russian foreign policy, and Canadian–Russian relations.

Andrea Chandler, PhD (Columbia University). Professor in the Department of Political Science and former Director of the Institute of European, Russian, and Eurasian Studies, Carleton University. She has published research relating to Soviet and post-Soviet Russian state building, social welfare policy in post-communist countries, and gender and politics in contemporary Russia.

Joan DeBardeleben, PhD (University of Wisconsin-Madison). Began her academic career at McGill University in Montreal and is currently Chancellor's Professor in the Institute of European, Russian, and Eurasian Studies at Carleton University in Ottawa. Since 2011 she has held a Jean Monnet Chair in the EU's Eastern Neighbourhood Relations. DeBardeleben has written extensively on Russian politics, the EU's relations with its eastern neighbors (including Russia), and topics related to citizen participation, federalism, and public opinion in Russia.

Michael Johns, PhD (University of Maryland). The Vice Dean of Humanities and Social Sciences for Laurentian University-Barrie Campus and member of the Executive of the Centre for Research on Canadian–Russian Relations, he was recently an Honorary Research Fellow at Cardiff University. His work focuses on issues surrounding the European Union with specific emphasis placed on the role of the EU on issues of social cohesion.

Peter Konecny, PhD (University of Toronto). Senior Analyst at CSIS and Adjunct Research Professor at EURUS, Carleton University, and author of books on Imperial Russia.

Frederic LaBarre, PhD Candidate (Royal Military College). A freelance strategic and defense analyst, he has worked as policy adviser for the Ministry of Defence of Estonia, helping with that country's MAP process, was an International Project Manager for the Royal Military College of Canada and Advanced Distributed Learning Chair at the NATO Defense College in Rome, Italy. Formerly Head of the Department of Political and Strategic Studies at the Baltic Defence College, and lately has undertaken a string of security analysis tasks for private sector firms as well as public safety, national defense, and defense R&D of Canada. Writes on post-Soviet integration, international relations, defense and strategy in the post-Soviet and post-Socialist space, NATO–Russia relations, and on defense management

Jacques Lévesque, PhD (Sorbonne, Paris). Professeur de Science Politique, Université du Québec à Montréal (UQAM) and founding director of UQAM's Departement de science politique. Has written extensively on Soviet and Russian relations with China particularly, and with Asia generally.

Elena Maltseva, PhD (University of Toronto). After her dissertation on defense in June 2012 she assumed a position as Assistant Professor of Political Science at Nazarbayev University, Astana, Kazakhstan. She holds a Master's degree in European, Russian, and Eurasian Studies from Carleton University (Canada), and an undergraduate degree in English Literature and Political Science from Carl-von-Ossietzky University (Germany). Maltseva has published in refereed journals on comparative welfare politics, and public policy and governance in post-communist countries.

Roger N. McDermott, MA (Oxford). Senior Fellow in Eurasian Military Studies, Jamestown Foundation, Washington and Managing Editor of the Foundation's *Eurasia Daily Monitor* (EDM); Senior International Fellow, FMSO, Leavenworth; member of multiple editorial boards. Writes on Russian and Central Asian defense and strategic issues; regular contributor to the EDM and Radio Free Europe.

Sergei Plekhanov, PhD (Moscow State University). Associate Professor of Political Science, York University. Coordinator of the Post-Soviet Studies Programme at York and author of multiple studies on Russian politics and society. Teaches regularly at the University of California, Irvine.

Vladimir V. Popov, PhD (Institute of USA & Canada, Russian Academy of Science). International adviser in DESA, UN, and Professor Emeritus at the New Economic School in Moscow. He is also Sector Head at the Graduate School of International Business at the Academy of the National Economy in Moscow (on leave) and an Adjunct Research Professor at EURUS, Carleton University.

Jeff Sahadeo, PhD (University of Illinois at Urbana-Champaign). Associate Professor in the Institute of European, Russian, and Eurasian Studies (EURUS) and the Department of Political Science, and current Director of EURUS, Carleton University, Ottawa, Canada.

Peter H. Solomon, Jr, PhD (Columbia University). Professor of Political Science, Law, and Criminology, University of Toronto. Former Director of the Centre for Russian and East European Studies, University of Toronto. He has published numerous books, chapters and articles, in several countries, on Russian legal systems and practices.

Alanda Theriault, MA (McMaster University). Lecturer in Liberal Arts & Sciences at the University Partnership Centre at Georgian College, Barrie, ON. She also serves as an Assistant Editor at the Centre for Research on Canadian–Russian Relations, Laurentian University.

John F. Young, PhD (University of Toronto). Associate Professor and Chair of Political Science, University of Northern British Columbia, Prince George, BC.

Foreword

The Tandem Forever?

Peter Konecny

In May 2008, Dmitry Medvedev took over the Russian presidency and appointed former president Vladimir Putin as his premier. Many observers questioned whether Medvedev would be able to exert his authority as president, or if his mentor would continue to act as de facto head of state. Throughout his four-year presidency, Medvedev continually faced questions related to his ability to shape and follow through with a domestic and foreign policy agenda that was not being dictated by Putin. Medvedev, for his part, continually claimed that he and Putin were working together as a "tandem," and that there were no significant contradictions in their basic policy goals. Despite some apparent disagreements over foreign policy, privatization, and the treatment of opposition civic and political groups, Putin and Medvedev maintained a cohesive partnership during the latter's presidency. Ultimately, however, it was a partnership based on the understanding that Putin would dictate most of the ground rules. This reality became evident in September 2011, when Medvedev officially proposed that Putin stand again for the presidency in 2012. Despite a groundswell public backlash against this announcement and a prolonged series of demonstrations that followed (the shape and scope of which clearly took the Kremlin aback), Putin was easily elected president in the March 2012 vote. Medvedev agreed to serve as Putin's premier, ostensibly to show that the tandem would continue to pursue the basic domestic and foreign policy goals outlined in 2008.

The various contributors to this volume assess the changes that took place before and during the Medvedev presidency on such issues as the status of women, judicial reforms, anti-corruption efforts, economic "modernization," Russia's security and foreign policies, and the nature of leadership dynamics. In the sphere of domestic policy, Medvedev emphasized the need for tougher anti-corruption measures, substantial legal and political reforms, and an economic policy that focused on modernization and diversification. In the realm of foreign policy, he looked for a "Reset" with the United States while also supporting what could be called "traditional" Soviet/Russian foreign policy goals: emphasizing international collective action over unilateral action by the West; challenging perceived threats such as the US-led missile defence shield and NATO operations in the Middle East; and pushing for greater integration with the former Soviet republics. In terms of his domestic policy objectives, Medvedev proposed some bold initiatives but could not follow through with many of them. Any effort to introduce substantial privatization to state-run industries and challenge high-level systemic corruption would have acted as a fundamental challenge to the Putin system. For those reasons, Medvedev largely failed to carry through with his agenda. Although Russia did achieve a "Reset" with the United States, that relationship has now soured as traditional geo-political rivalries – manifested recently through events in the Middle East – have put Russia at odds with the West once again.

It will take some time and historical perspective to judge whether Dmitry Medvedev was merely a "caretaker" for Putin or if the kernels of some his initiatives later germinated into a reordering of the Russian government and economy. At this time (Spring 2012), however, it looks as if Vladimir Putin's agenda, driven by a desire to consolidate the statist characteristics of the Russian economy, strengthen Russia's influence over its former Soviet neighbours, and reassert Russian power globally will prevail over the next six years.

Preface

In 2009 we edited a book titled *From Putin to Medvedev: Continuity or Change?* Many of the authors in that volume had also contributed papers to briefing sessions organized by the Canadian Security Intelligence Service (CSIS) and Export Development Canada, and their analytical briefing papers formed the core of that book. For the purpose of this book, most of authors in the earlier volume agreed to update and expand on their earlier subjects, and we invited others to fill in on subjects we feel warrant examination. As a further link between the two books, we again invited Dr Peter Konecny, senior analyst at CSIS and Russia specialist, to provide us with a foreword to this collection.

We have tried to balance papers between domestic and foreign affairs, allocating a section to each, and we have placed several papers in a third section that caters to matters pertaining to both; that is, economic and societal issues that encompass both domestic and international affairs. Some papers are brief, others are long; a few offer little documentation, others include extensive referencing. All of them provide food for thought and that was our purpose.

* * *

Russian transliteration is based on a modified Library of Congress system, with common-use applications; for example, soft and hard signs are usually omitted. Endings on Russian names are simplified by using the English-language "y" instead of the more accurate "ii" or "iy," e.g. Dmitrii will be Dmitry here.

Punctuation, spelling, and referencing will vary somewhat, as the dominant style in individual papers may appear as either British or American. For the same reason, a few names and places are transliterated differently, for example, Bakiev/Bakiyev, Niiazov/Niyazov, and Kiev/Kyiv.

Acknowledgements

The authors are grateful to Peter Sowden, who took this project on for Routledge Publishers.

Thanks also to the University Partnership Centre, Georgian College, Barrie, Ontario, for providing the Centre for Research on Canadian–Russian Relations (CRCR) with valuable office space and infrastructure support.

Barrie, ON, Canada 2012

Abbreviations and acronyms

ABM	Anti-Ballistic Missile Treaty (1972–2002)
ASI	Agency for Strategic Initiatives
BRIC	Brazil, Russia, India, China, judged to be the fastest growing economies (see also BRICS and RIC); now institutionalized with regularly scheduled meetings.
BRICS	South Africa joined the BRIC in late 2010.
C^2	Operational Command Structure
C4ISR	Command, Control, Communications, Computers, Intelligence, Surveillance and Reconnaissance
CAST	Centre for Analysis of Strategies and Technologies
CBR	Central Bank of Russia
CFE	Conventional Forces in Europe Treaty
CINC	commander in chief
CIS	Commonwealth of Independent States
CMTD	Commission for Modernization and Technological Development
CPA	EU–RF Cooperation and Partnership Agreement
CPRF	See KPRF
CPSU	Communist Party of the Soviet Union
CRCR	Centre for Research on Canadian–Russian Relations
CSA	Common Space Agreement (RF and EU)
CSCE	Conference on Security and Cooperation in Europe
CSIS	Canadian Security Intelligence Service
CSTO	Collective Security Treaty Organization (CIS)
CTBT	Comprehensive Test Ban Treaty
Demokratizatsiya	Democratization
EBRD	European Bank for Reconstruction and Development
ECHR	European Court of Human Rights
EE	eastern European countries
ENP	European Neighbourhood Policy
EU	European Union
FSB	RF Federal Security Service
FSU	former Soviet Union countries

Gazprom	Gas Industry Monopoly in Russia
GDP	Gross Domestic Product
GECF	Gas Exporting Countries Forum
GIFO	Government Individual Financial Obligations
Glasnost	Publicity; Openness
GNI	Gross National Income
GOZ	State Defence Order
GPV	a state armaments programme
GUAM	Association of Georgia, Ukraine, Azerbaijan & Moldova
HDI	Human Development Index
HEI	higher education institutions
HSE	Higher School of Economics
IC	Investigative Committee (RF Procurator General's Office)
IMEMO	Institute of International Trade and International Relations, Moscow
IMF	International Monetary Fund
INDEM	Information Science for Democracy, Moscow
INF	Intermediate-Range Nuclear Forces Treaty
INSOR	Institute of Contemporary Development
Interfax	International Information Group, Moscow, with 70 international bureaus
ISKRAN	Institute of the USA & Canada, at the RF Academy of Sciences
ITAR-TASS	Russian World News Service
KGB	Committee for State Security (Soviet)
Kontrakniki	Contract Soldiers (not conscripted)
KPRF	Communist Party of the Russian Federation
LA	Latin America
LDPR	Liberal Democratic Party of Russia
LECS	Centre for Legal and Economic Research
Levada Center	Polling organization (See also VTsIOM)
MAP	Membership Action Plan (NATO)
MD	military district
MGIMO	Moscow State Institute of International Relations
MIC	Military Industrial Commission
Minfin	Ministry of Finance of the Russian Federation
MoD	Ministry of Defence
MVD	Ministry of Internal Affairs
NATO	North Atlantic Treaty Organization
NAFTA	North America Free Trade Agreement
NCO	non-commissioned officer
NGO	Non-governmental Organizations
NMD	National Missile Defence
NPPE	National Priority Project Education programme

Abbreviations xxi

NPT	Nuclear Non-Proliferation Treaty
NRU	national research universities
Nomenklatura	System of patronage within the CPSU
Oblast	Region. District
OCAC	Organization of Central Asian Cooperation
OECD	Organization for Economic Cooperation and Development
OMON	Special Purpose Police attached to MVD
OSCE	Organization for Security and Cooperation in Europe
PACE	Parliamentary Assembly of the Council of Europe
PCA	Partnership and Cooperation Agreement (with the EU)
Perestroika	Restructuring; Reconstruction
PfP	Partnership for Peace
PG	Prosecutor (Procurator) General
PJC	Permanent Joint Council
PRO	Anti-Missile Defence, in Russian
REDA	*Russia and Eurasia Documents Annual*, published by Academic International Press, Florida, since 1988.
RER	Real Exchange Rate
R&D	research and development
RF	Russian Federation
RIC	Russia, India, China, an 'axis' that had its origins in the mid-1990s and is now institutionalized.
ROE	Rosoboronexsport (RF arms export agency)
ROSNANO	Russian Corporation of Nanotechnologies
RTS	free-float capitalization-weighted index of 50 stocks traded on the Moscow exchange
SCO	Shanghai Cooperation Organization
Siloviki	People of Power, mostly with security or military backgrounds
SIPRI	Stockholm International Peace Research Institute
SORT	Strategic Offensive Reductions Treaty
Spetsnaz	Special Purpose Forces attached to Armed Forces
SSA	Sub-Saharan Africa
SSR	Soviet Socialist Republic
START	Strategic Arms Reduction Treaty
TACIS	Technical Assistance to the CIS
THE	*The Times Higher Education ratings*
UES	Russian Unified Energy System
UN	United Nations
UNSC	United Nations Security Council
UR	United Russia Party (sometimes One Russia)
USE	Unified State Exam
USSR	Union of Soviet Socialist Republics
VDV	*Vozdushno Desantnye Voyska*

VKO	Aerospace Defence
VTsIOM	All-Union Centre for the Study of Public Opinion, Moscow
VUZ	Institution of Higher Learning
WB	World Bank
WMD	Weapons of Mass Destruction
WTO	World Trade Organization
YeSU TZ	Unified Tactical Level Command and Control System

Part I
Domestic affairs

1 The 2011–12 Russia elections
The next chapter in Russia's post-Communist transition?

Joan DeBardeleben

The 2011–12 election cycle marked a potential watershed in Russian politics. At a time when many specialists had written off elections as an important political event because of their "managed" nature and almost certain outcome, Russia again surprised us. The two-part "election season" involved selection of members of the State Duma (the Russian legislative body) in December 2011, and the presidential vote that followed in March 2012. Not only was the outcome of the Duma election an unexpected blow to the ruling United Russia party, but the public activism that the election elicited suggested emerging new dynamics in the relationship between state and society. A significant element of the Russian public had apparently awakened, with tens of thousands of protesters, fed by social media contacts, pouring into the streets leading to the protest epicenter at Bolotnaya Square in central Moscow. The demonstrations erupted regularly over a period of months, beginning in December 2011 and continuing at the time of this writing in June 2012. The movement was galvanized by new figures, such as the popular anti-corruption blogger and protester, Aleksei Navalny. The Moscow demonstrations were joined by smaller protests in several cities across the country. Observers were wondering if this could mark an awakening of demands for leadership accountability, which eventually could translate into a halt or reversal of the authoritarian tendencies that had been building in the Russian political system since Putin took over the presidency in 2000. This chapter endeavors to place these events in an historical and comparative context and reflect on their significance for Russia's political development.

Leadership succession and Russian politics

As Richard Sakwa[1] has pointed out, leadership transitions have been turbulent processes throughout Russian history, a feature that has also characterized post-communist politics as well. Since Mikhail Gorbachev embarked upon *glasnost* and *perestroika* in the second half of the 1980s in his effort to reform the communist system, the newborn country, the Russian Federation, has experienced four leadership transitions involving the office of the presidency. The first, from Gorbachev to Boris Yeltsin, occurred in 1991 through the vehicle of radical systemic change, namely the collapse of the Soviet Union and formation of the

Russian Federation as its largest successor state (along with the other 14 newly independent countries that emerged from it). A pivotal point in terms of legitimizing this transition was the direct election of Boris Yeltsin as President of the Russian Republic of the USSR in June 1991, which accorded him and the Russian Republic's claim to independence in December 1991 a popular legitimacy that the former Soviet Union, headed by Gorbachev, had lacked. Yeltsin was confirmed as President of the Russian Federation in the 1996 election, which looked like a truly contested vote, despite Yeltsin's heavy marshaling of Western-style public relations techniques to polish his tarnished image. In the first round, Yeltsin outpaced his leading competitor, Communist Party leader, Gennady Zyuganov, by just over three percentage points in the popular vote, pushing the contest to a second round, in which Yeltsin won 54 percent of the vote.

Perhaps ironically, Russia's troubled democratic transition took on increasingly problematic features just as the economy began to revive after the 1998 financial crisis. Each subsequent leadership change took on a more "engineered" character, mirroring the broader depiction of Russia's electoral politics as a manifestation of what several analysts have termed Russia's "managed democracy."[2] Although elections played a role in each leadership transition, in every one of the subsequent cases the incumbent designated the "favored" successor, and the electoral outcome was unambiguous. As such, Russia has failed to pass what Samuel Huntington[3] has called the two-turnover test of democratic consolidation, namely at least two electoral transitions to new leadership groups. While the leadership changed, the process has not involved a real shift in power from one electoral group or coalition to another.

Under the 1993 Russian constitution, the president is the most powerful political institution in the Russian system, so presidential succession dynamics have commanded particular attention. The second leadership transition, from Yeltsin to Vladimir Putin, occurred in 2000. Putin was first named by Yeltsin as acting prime minister in August 1999; he then became acting president upon Yeltsin's resignation at the end of that year, less than four months before the next presidential election on 26 March 2000. Despite being a relative newcomer on the political scene, Putin won handily with 53 percent in the first round vote (see Appendix 1), strongly outpacing veteran politician Zyuganov, who received just 29 percent. The third transition followed in 2008, as a constitutional restriction prevented Putin from pursuing a third term. After much speculation, in December 2007 President Putin designated Dmitry Medvedev, one of his two deputy prime ministers and chair of Russia's state-dominated natural gas company, Gazprom, as his favored successor. Medvedev won over 70 percent of the vote in contrast to Zyuganov's distant 18 percent in the first round of the presidential vote, while Putin took over the post of prime minister and head of the government. Following the 2008 presidential election, Putin agreed to take on the post of Chair of the United Russia party, as head of the government. While the party had de facto previously been an instrument of Putin's exercise of political power in the country, until that time the leader had maintained that, as president, it was inappropriate for him to be associated with a single party;

however, as prime minister and head of the government, he considered it appropriate to head the party.

The most recent and fourth leadership transition, again "engineered" from above, went smoothly in a technical sense as it unfolded in late 2011 and early 2012. But it was surrounded by political drama. The story began to unfold after months of speculation as to whether Putin would again aspire to presidential office after a four-year hiatus (thus meeting the constitutional requirement forbidding three consecutive terms). In late September 2011, at the convention of the dominant United Russia party, President Medvedev indicated his support for Putin's presidential candidacy, and in this way removed himself from consideration as a candidate or potential competitor to Putin. Putin accepted the mandate and at the same time indicated that Medvedev should head the United Russia list in the parliamentary elections in December 2011. Putin referred to an agreement made "several years ago" regarding the future arrangement, and was quoted as saying., "the fact that we have not been disclosing our position publicly for quite a time is a matter of political expediency and conforming to the political genus in our country – I hope our citizens understand that."[4] Effectively a pre-planned "swap" of the two positions was revealed, with Putin moving into the presidency and Medvedev to be appointed as his prime minister. While this arrangement would be subject to the approval of the electorate, first in the Duma elections of December 2011 and then the presidential vote in March 2012, the dominant position of the establishment United Russia party left little doubt about the outcome.

The legislative election of December 2011 indeed maintained the majority position of Vladimir Putin's party in the State Duma. However, the results evidenced a significant decline in the party's popularity as well as its ability to manage the electoral outcome. The official results of the Duma election placed United Russia with 49.3 percent of the popular vote (down from 64.3 percent in 2007), a total that, under Russia's proportional representation electoral system, would give it a majority (238) of the 450 seats in the State Duma. The electoral system's high seven percent threshold for representation meant that over five percent of the electorate that voted for small parties would go unrepresented and that portion of the vote would be reallocated to those parties that crossed the threshold, giving United Russia the majority.

Behind this electoral "success," United Russia's popularity had been declining in the period preceding the 2011 election. While on the one hand United Russia had managed to bring into its ranks almost all of the appointed executive heads of Russia's 83 federal units, its support in elections to regional legislative bodies had already exhibited a pattern of gradual decline after 2008. Part of the pattern may have been linked to the effects of the economic crisis of 2008–09, which led to rising unemployment, wage arrears, and periodic disruptions in some public services in some localities. At the same time, earlier in the year, the party became a public target of sometimes virulent and visible political criticism; a much repeated depiction of United Russia as a party of "crooks and thieves" was coined by Aleksei Navalny in a radio broadcast in February 2011. The term resonated with elements of the attentive public who perceived the party as abusing its power and involved in the network of corruption that characterizes the Russian political system.

In addition to United Russia, the Duma election returned the same three parties that were in the out-going Duma, with the Communist Party of the Russian Federation (KPRF) increasing its share from only 11.6 percent in 2007 up to 19.2 percent in 2011. The other two parties that exceeded the seven percent threshold also gained ground, the nationalist Liberal Democratic Party of Russia (LDPR) moving from 8.1 percent in 2007 to 11.7 percent in 2011, and the moderate left party, A Just Russia (generally considered a Kremlin creation to draw support away from the Communists), rising from 7.7 percent to 13.2 percent. Despite these increased percentages, none of the other parties offered an opposition force capable of challenging United Russia's dominance. The Communist Party, considered by many to be the only genuine opposition party that routinely contradicted the government's positions, had expanded its electoral base less on account of an increase in positive support and more because of the lack of other opposition voices.

The election was marked by electoral fraud, as well as biased media coverage. Instances of ballot box stuffing were documented on the Internet, leading President Putin to command the installation of video cameras in polling places for the presidential election to follow, to protect against a repeat of these charges. The observer mission of the Organization for Security and Cooperation in Europe (OSCE) reported problems such as "denial of registration to certain political parties," "lack of independence of the election administration, partiality of most of the media, and the undue interference of state authorities at all levels." The report concluded that this mix of circumstances "did not provide the necessary conditions for fair electoral competition."[5] The public protests that followed the election demanded that the election be rerun; it was commonly believed that without interference, the vote would have left United Russia in a minority position, at least in the popular vote. Public opinion polls preceding the Duma vote indicated a significant drop in United Russia support, from a level of 52 percent in the first quarter of 2010.[6] Just before the election in 2011, about 39 percent of those surveyed indicated that they would vote for United Russia, compared to 12 percent who would vote for the Communist Party. Nonetheless, United Russia far outpaced its opponents.

In the presidential elections that followed in March 2012, Putin won easily in the first round of voting; official results gave him 63.6 percent of the vote, followed by second-runner Zyuganov at just over 17 percent. The fact that the vote for Putin fell below what Medvedev had achieved in 2008 (with 70.3 percent) was also a sign of Putin's declining, but still strong, popularity. The presidential election results left no serious doubt as to whom the public preferred or who had won; therefore, opposition calls for their reenactment met little resonance either in the broader public or the international community, unlike the situation in Ukraine in 2004. Public opinion polls preceding the vote suggested an expected level of support for Putin to be somewhat, but not dramatically, lower than the actual outcome, but far exceeding that of any of the opposing candidates, as indicated in Table 1.1.[7]

"Imagine that next Sunday the election for the president of Russia is taking place. Indicate please which of the following politicians you would vote for."

Table 1.1 Voter preferences, presidential election 2012 % of respondents

Time period	Putin	Zyuganov	Zhirinovsky	Would not vote	Hard to say
April 2011	50%	7	9	14	11
December 2011	43%	11	10	10	12
March 2012	54%	10	6	13	8

Source: Public Opinion Foundation, "Elektoral'nye reiting," Dominanty, no. 23: page 3 (Moscow, June 14, 2012), available at: http://bd.fom.ru/pdf/d23ind12.pdf.

One reason for Putin's victory was that there was no viable opposition figure or party that could seriously challenge either him or United Russia. In short, transition was successfully engineered in a formal sense; the desired outcome was achieved. But the process had generated a level of political activism and protest that was unprecedented in post-Soviet Russia. The tens of thousands of Russian citizens who took to the streets to protest the Duma election could not be quieted. The protests were laced with outspoken criticism of the president himself.

The announcement of the leadership "swap" in September 2011 apparently had not set well with significant parts of the Russian public. Furthermore, the unannounced agreement between Medvedev and Putin seemed to cross a line with critical elements of politically-aware Russians, suggesting an objectionable sense of entitlement on the part of the leadership tandem. As noted, in previous electoral cycles the "favored" candidate had been announced later, in December, after the Duma elections had been completed. However, uncertainty surrounding who would run, Putin and/or Medvedev, created an unacceptable level of speculation and rumors. The decision to announce the leadership swap so early, and in the manner in which it was done (indicating that it had been agreed on some years before), may have been a critical miscalculation, but possibly an unavoidable one; if Medvedev were to head the United Russia party list in December 2011, this would make clear that he would not be seeking re-election as president.

Furthermore, if the situation were not resolved, the latent uncertainty had the potential to nurture a split within elite circles, with some elements favoring a continuation of a Medvedev presidency and others wanting a return to Putin. Despite proclaimed unity between the two leaders, a widespread perception of fundamental differences between the two, with Medvedev associated with a more reformist orientation, fed the speculation. For example, Medvedev was purported to be more sympathetic to a minimal degree of political liberalization than Putin; Putin's strong attachment to the energy sector as a strategic resource of Russia suggested that he might be less supportive of Medvedev's concept of modernization, which would require an assertive policy of economic diversification and stronger incentives for foreign investment.

Ever since the Ukraine's Orange Revolution of 2004, the Russian leadership had been alert to the risks of an elite split, which could serve to mobilize popular discontent in a critical situation. Regional political figures could be a crucial resource in this situation, since opposition political parties did not seem to be an effective launching ground for political opposition. But the Kremlin had ensured increased loyalty of regional executives, following 2004, through the replacement of gubernatorial elections with a process in which the president had de facto appointment power. This system, by reinforcing a clientelistic dependence of the governor on the president, encouraged a "bandwagon" effect, where it is in the interest of elites to position themselves on the winning side and to demonstrate their loyalty by delivering votes in their regions.[8] By announcing the leadership decision in September 2011, both regional and national elites, as well as the public at large, were made aware of what to expect.

Understanding the public reaction to announcement of the leadership "swap" requires consideration of the manner in which the Russian public views elections. Henry Hale suggests that Russians favor a notion of delegative democracy, meaning that they are quite happy to place trust in a strong leader, but that some degree of accountability is expected. One might note that this could be distinguished from a notion of representative democracy, where the elected official would reflect the actual views of constituents. Hale's notion seems an apt diagnosis of the dynamics that galvanized discontent following the September 2011 announcement, further aggravated by the election fraud in December. As Hale writes, while on the one hand Russians "desire a strong leader who is largely unconstrained by other institutions," they also "want and expect to choose that leader through free, fair, and competitive elections and to have the right to remove that leader in a the same way should things go wrong."[9] While technically Russians could vote against United Russia and Putin, despite the Medvedev–Putin agreement announced in September 2011, in practice that pact removed the only real potential competitor, Medvedev himself, from the presidential contest. While economic issues may have played a role in specific instances (e.g. in the context of the preceding financial and economic crisis), the fundamental cause of the protest was apparently political.[10]

The protests of late 2011 and much of 2012 were of a qualitatively different nature from the demonstrations organized over the previous several years by opposition forces, primarily because they took on a mass nature and because the demands and grievances were overwhelmingly political rather than economic. Unusually large demonstrations followed the Duma election on the weekend of December 10, estimated at over 50,000 by organizers' participants. But the activism continued into subsequent weeks and months with a particularly large protest on February 4; organizers estimated over 120,000 participants, while police put the number at 38,000. Counter-demonstrations to support Putin also occurred[11] Following the presidential election, additional demonstrations took place on March 5 and March 10, as well as protests surrounding Vladimir Putin's inauguration as president on May 7, and on Russia's national day, June 12. The latter was dubbed the March of Millions.

Some prominent figures, including former finance minister, Aleksei Kudrin, expressed support for the demands of the protestors, including for new Duma elections and reform of electoral rules to promote competition.[12] The protesters included people from a range of political persuasions. Political novice, Aleksei Navalny, who galvanized youth involvement through the use of social media and

Internet blogs, reportedly described himself as a "nationalist democrat"[13] making an uneasy companion for liberals such as Boris Nemtsov and Mikhail Kasyanov. The political nature of the opposition, although diverse and lacking a clear ideological or political agenda, posed a dilemma for the leadership. The most common response to popular protest in recent years has been one of damage control, often involving limited (usually local) concessions. This was quite clear in relation to the political outcry against the monetization of social benefits in 2005, when some of the measures were at least temporarily drawn back. Similarly, the response to numerous other protests that occurred in relation to problems like wage arrears, layoffs, and service cutbacks in particular Russian cities and enterprises, in the context of the financial-economic crisis, involved concessions and redress of grievances.[14]

The responses to the demonstrations surrounding the 2011–12 election cycles were measured up until the presidential vote in March 2012. Preceding the presidential election, only minimal force was applied and Medvedev announced political concessions in his state of the union address in late December 2011: the reinstatement of gubernatorial elections and relaxed rules for political party registration.[15] This "soft" response was likely fashioned so as to avoid further aggravation of social tension and public discontent, and to maximize the effect of Putin's remaining rather large reservoir of popular support.

Although the significance of unexpected events surrounding the 2011–12 elections will only become clear after some time, several dimensions are important. Three primary factors will be discussed here: the lack of a viable opposition force, Putin's continuing level of personal support among the population at large, and the social base of the opposition movement. These three factors together will be important determinants of whether the events of late 2011/2012 mark the beginning of a return to real competitive politics and a reversal of the democratic backslide that Russia has experienced since 2004.

Opposition in Russia: why so weak?

In contrast to the Orange Revolution in Ukraine in 2004, there was no viable opposition figure to Vladimir Putin or viable opposition party posing an alternative to United Russia in the 2011–12 election cycle. The reasons for this are multiple and complex. On the one hand, the political party system of the Russian Federation has been both underdeveloped and stable over the past decade. While existing parties have not been adequate vehicles to channel public preference or opposition sentiments,[16] new parties have not been able to gain representation. On the other hand, the popular desire for strong leadership and for order and stability has bolstered Putin's personal support.

Four political parties have been represented in the State Duma since 2007. These parties are underdeveloped in the sense that they have not effectively taken on the roles normally attributed to them in political science literature. They have had weak social bases, underdeveloped linkages to civil society, and therefore have not been effective conduits for transmitting social grievances to government.

Additionally, they have not been effective as a source of political recruitment of leadership from society at large. The dominant political party, United Russia, has served as a mechanism for elite recruitment to the existing power structure, and loyalty to the party has, to a certain extent, been a prerequisite for political promotion. However, the party has served as a support for the existing authority structures.

Two of the four parties in the Duma elected in 2007 have been represented there since the first RF competitive election in 1993 – the Communist Party of the Russian Federation and the LDPR. Both still have the same leader as in 1993, despite the fact that the parties have been unable to pose a real competitive challenge to the establishment party. Neither of these parties has undergone a process of renewal that would permit them to appeal to a changing and expanded base of voters. The fourth party represented in the Duma after the 2007 election cycle, the Just Russia party, a left centrist formation encouraged by the Kremlin under the leadership of Sergei Mironov, is a relative newcomer. Many consider the Communist Party to be the only party in the Duma that poses a meaningful opposition to the Kremlin on a relatively consistent basis. However, the party has never striven to play a dominant role in the government, even in the mid- to late 1990s when it gained the plurality of the popular vote and thus could have legitimately claimed the leadership role in the parliament. Prospects for the party could improve, given its stronger showing in the 2011 Duma elections, plus an increased Russian appetite for alternatives, but it may be difficult for the party to change an image that has been largely frozen over the past two decades. Until now, the party has strongly overrepresented older segments of the population and those who have fared worse than average in the market economy of post-communist Russia. However, the prospect of a leadership change seems more likely than in the past as Zyuganov approaches the age of seventy (born June 1944). A newly visible figure, 35-year-old Sergei Udaltsev, has been active in the 2011–12 protests, and there has been some speculation about whether he could be an eventual possibility to lead the Communist Party when Zyuganov retires.[17] Such a leadership change could potentially broaden the base of the party's support to socialist elements of the younger generation.

Western-oriented (liberal democratic) forces, which did cross the five percent threshold for party representation throughout the 1990s, have not been present in the Duma since 2007 when the electoral system was changed from a mixed-member proportional system (which allowed some smaller parties to gain votes in single-member districts even if the national vote was weak) to a fully proportional system with a seven percent threshold. The failure of liberal parties has been in part a lack of resonance of their program with the Russian public, which associates these groupings with the economic decline of the 1990s; in some cases selective enforcement of electoral laws have prevented them from registering. The efforts of Mikhail Prokhorov, a prominent Russian oligarch and political newcomer, to challenge Putin in the Russian presidential race met with only minimal success, as he gained under eight percent of the popular vote. In early June 2012, following his failed campaign, he announced the formation of a new political party called

Civil Platform that would back independent candidates. His comment about his new organization is a telling commentary of the weakness of political parties in Russia. Quoted as calling it a "post-party party," to provide a vehicle for independent candidates to build support through a kind of social networking process, Prokhorov commented that "the age of parties has passed" and he announced that even he would not be joining the his new party.[18] More accurately, if Prokhorov is correct, the age of parties may be bypassed in Russia.

Opposition sentiments that take extra-parliamentary form have been largely marginalized through a combination of repressive measures, inadequate public visibility, and a popular distaste for anything that might threaten to destabilize the system. Groups such Strategy-31 and the Other Russia held periodic demonstrations and protests long before the most recent outburst of activity. Strategy-31, an initiative of the Other Russia movement, have organized monthly demonstrations since mid-2009 to demand compliance with Article 31 of the Russian constitution, which assures freedom of assembly. These demonstrations have been relatively small, and have elicited only limited public awareness. Protests associated with the economic crisis occurred sporadically around the country between 2009 and 2010, but these did not take on a unified nationwide character that could create an alternative opposition movement. Opposition figures, such as liberal politicians Boris Nemtsov, Mikhail Kasyanov, and chess champion, Garry Kasparov, do not enjoy significant support among the public at large. They are also subject to intermittent harassment and detention by police forces. Selective enforcement of election laws (e.g. relating to requirements for party registration) has often prevented these more critical forces from participating in local or national votes. Harassment of opposition figures presumably has a deterrent effect on the broader public. Whereas association with the ruling United Russia party is more likely to result in personal or career advantages, association with the extra-parliamentary opposition forces may be punished. Even association with a system-loyal opposition party, such as the Communist Party of the Russian Federation, proved to be increasingly unattractive to regional elites over time, particularly those who had fewer independent resources on which to build an independent base of political support.[19]

With the emerging protest environment in late 2011, new faces became highly visible on the political scene. Among these was the prominent journalist, Leonid Parfenov, whom 41 percent of respondents evaluated positively in a survey carried out by the Public Opinion Foundation in early June 2012.[20] Aleksei Kudrin, the former finance minister-come critic of the regime, following his resignation in September 2011, also commands relatively high levels of public regard, with 25 percent of respondents seeing him positively and 11 percent negatively (the remainder having no opinion or knowledge of him). New figures have become well-known through their role in the protest movement and through social media links connected to it. Internet blogger and corruption critic, Navalny, who was very prominent in the December 2011 protests, was less known to the public at large than Kudrin. In addition, only 20 percent of respondents were prepared to give an evaluation of Navalny, and of those 60 percent made a negative one. Kseniya Sobchak, a pop star and daughter of the late Anatoly Sobchak, a prominent reform politician of the 1990s, also took on a visible role as an opposition voice, with her apartment raided and cash savings confiscated in early June 2012. Whether any of these, or other figures, would be able to galvanize opposition sentiment in a manner to challenge the existing authorities through, or outside of, the established institutional structure remains to be seen.

Putin's support: why still so strong?

Despite the setback for both the United Russia party and Putin himself in the 2011–12 elections, a stabilizing factor lies in Putin's continuing relatively high levels of public support, even if they are somewhat lower than previously. The gap between the percentage of voters supporting United Russia in the Duma election and those supporting the party's presidential favorite is some measure of the "personal pull" that the leader has. (See Table 1.2.) In the first two elections when Putin ran for president (2000 and 2004), he got 29.3 percent more of the popular vote than did United Russia during the same election cycle for the Duma. In 2012 this difference dropped to 14.3 percent, indicating that Putin's personal strength as a candidate relative to the party he was associated with was still strong, but had waned. (In 2008, when Medvedev was the candidate favored by United Russia, Medvedev scored only six percentage points higher than the party in the Duma election, indicating that his "personal pull" was considerably weaker than Putin's.) Comparing this to the Communist Party, Zyuganov has consistently scored only slightly higher than his party, suggesting that his personal appeal has not been a significant positive asset for the party.

Despite this pattern of declining support for Putin, public approval ratings remain relatively high. According to surveys carried out by the Public Opinion Foundation, Putin's approval rating declined from a fairly consistent positive rating of 70 percent to a low of 45 percent in December 2011 and back up to 55 percent in March 2012.[21] In contrast, Medvedev's rating reached a peak of 59 percent in the first quarter of 2010 and was at 45 percent in March 2012. Indicators of vote intention before the presidential election gave Putin over 50 percent support among those who made a selection, with 18 percent undecided in February 2012. Putin far outranked the next closest candidate, Zyuganov, whom only 10 percent

Table 1.2 Gap – presidential vote/party list vote in Duma election (presidential vote percentage minus Duma list vote percentage)

Year of electoral cycle	Vote gap for United Russia (%)	Vote gap for KPRF (%)
1999/2000	4.7	29.3
2003/04	1.1	33.7
2007/08	6.1	6.0
2011/12	2.0	14.3

of respondents supported.[22] Some commentators have noted that President Putin may have attempted to shield himself from a further decline in his popularity by distancing himself from United Russia, which had come under such strong attack following the 2011 Duma elections. In May 2012, in line with the leadership swap, at Putin's suggestion Medvedev was elected chair of the faltering party, as Putin again depicted it as an inappropriate role for the president, who should represent all of the people of Russia.

These figures indicate that Putin's base of popular support remains relatively strong among the mass of the Russian population. An explanation for this strength may lie both in the political stability and the relative economic improvement that has taken place during his leadership period. The foundations of Putin's legitimacy lie in the contrast to the period of economic decline and increasing lawlessness that characterized the 1990s in Russia. More generally, drawing on Scharpf's work about democratic deficits in Europe, this base of support may be termed "output legitimacy." Scharpf argues that democracy "must be understood as a two-dimensional concept, relating to the *inputs* and to the *outputs* of the political process at the same time." The input side links policies and government actions to expressed citizen preferences, whereas the output side refers to "effectiveness of achieving the goals, and avoiding the dangers, that citizens collectively care about."[23] In line with the concept of delegative democracy, as applied by Hale to Russia, Russians may be more attuned to the output than to the input side of political legitimacy. Whereas the events of September to December 2011 may have failed to meet a minimal criterion on input legitimacy by breaching acceptable standards of accountability, for most Russians, policy outcomes are of primary importance.

Here, arguably, the Putin–Medvedev tandem has not done too badly. Despite a dip in 2009 in the face of the financial crisis, economic growth rates have been strong since 1999; even though that economic growth has been only partially the effect of policy choice and largely conditioned by high energy prices, it has still had a positive effect on public attitudes toward the regime. Furthermore, Russia weathered the economic crisis of 2008–09 relatively well because of the presence of reserve funds laid aside by the government from the energy boom. Citizens, for the most part, did not blame the Russian state for the crisis, and the government made it a priority to avoid cuts in social welfare programs. Political controversy surrounding the government's policy initiative in 2005 to replace in-kind social benefits with monetary support to the needy had sensitized the authorities to the fact that tampering with social welfare benefits could elicit popular unrest, leading the government to provide continued support for social spending despite difficult economic circumstances.[24] More generally, since 1998 the state budget was put on a more sustainable basis, also through reform of the tax system, a reform triggered in part, as Luong and Weinthal argue, by that crisis itself.[25] Thomas Remington describes the measures undertaken, particularly during Putin's first term in office, to regularize payments by businesses to support the social welfare system, in part based on solutions worked out jointly with enterprises.[26] While levels of inequality, as measured by the Gini coefficient, have increased, levels of poverty have declined (i.e. that proportion of the population falling below the minimum subsistence income). On the Human Development Index, Russia has also shown marginal improvement since 1995.[27]

No doubt long-term imbalances may challenge or undermine the stability of the Russian economy in the longer term. But the short-term ability of the government to deliver higher levels of consumption and an improved standard of living provide an important basis of legitimacy for the regime, and for Putin's continuing support, despite inadequacies in democratic processes. The success of Putin, and the Medvedev government, in assuring good economic performance with positive flows to the population, as well as visible policy successes, may be important determinants of the capacity of the opposition movement to maintain momentum. The brewing economic crisis in Europe may make it more difficult to achieve successes, particularly if it results in a drop in oil and gas export revenues. These specific policy challenges are discussed in other chapters of this book. However, linking policy outcomes and political processes is the cardinal problem of corruption, for it prevents effective and even-handed government policies from being applied, while suggesting a pervasive lack of political accountability.

A primary reliance on "output legitimacy" can be risky. Here David Easton's notions of "specific" and "diffuse" support are helpful. As Easton states, "the uniqueness of specific support lies in its relationship to the satisfactions that members of a system feel they obtain from the perceived outputs and performance of the political authorities."[28] If the public views policy outcomes as good, low levels of trust or legitimacy may be overcome.[29] However, when policy outcomes meet with general dissatisfaction, specific support may not be adequate to bolster the regime. Diffuse support is more durable. It is based in "a reservoir of favorable attitudes or good will that helps members to accept or tolerate outputs to which they are opposed."[30] In Russia, it appears that diffuse support among a significant portion of the population is low. If the legitimacy of the regime depends too heavily on specific policy outcomes rather than on an underlying sense of the legitimacy of the regime, the authorities may be undermined by poor or unpopular policy choices. But they may also be held hostage to factors beyond their control, whether it be the difficulty of reining in corruption at home or economic threats originating elsewhere.[31] In this case, systemic opposition may flourish.

Russia's discontented public: who is it and what does it mean?

Significant discontent is brewing among certain elements of the Russian public; the unrest is more marked among the young, the urban, and the affluent, but certainly not limited to these groups. The massive protests that occurred between the December 2011 Duma election and the March 2012 presidential election picked up again in early May. On May 6, 2012 (the day preceding an opulent presidential inauguration for Putin) and again on June 12 (Russia's national day) demonstrators flooded Bolotnaya Square, but this time confrontations with police occurred. Preceding the June 12 protests, the authorities detained several leading protest figures and searched apartments. Other, more innovative, forms of protest included production of an Internet-based "white album" of music supporting the protests,[32] the feminist punk-rock group, Pussy Riot, which performed an "anti-Putin prayer" in a prominent Moscow cathedral,[33] and "public strolls" that took place for a about a two-week period in May involving artists and other activists.[34] There is increasing evidence that the regime may undertake a more repressive approach in an effort to prevent the situation from having a destabilizing and self-reinforcing dynamic that could challenge the structure of power. Assertive measures taken by police against protest actions have increased, including numerous arrests and a strong presence of OMON (special forces) police. Prior to the June 12 protests, leading opposition figures were detained and their apartments searched. President Putin signed a particularly controversial measure into law on June 8, 2012, imposing heavy fines for participating in demonstrations that threaten the public or for violating the terms of the demonstration permit.[35] As repressive measures increase, the protest movement may be increasingly radicalized, and more risk-averse participants may draw back.

Nonetheless, behind the visible protests may lie the beginning of a profound societal transformation. As a new phenomenon, researchers have not yet had the opportunity to study the sociological base of the protest movement and the degree to which their actions resonate with the broader Russian public. One prominent interpretation suggests that we are observing the emergence of a politically active and increasingly assertive middle class.[36] The notion here is that now that a significant group of Russian professionals and educated young people have achieved a certain level of material security, they are demanding political accountability from the regime. Some suggest an empowering influence of the Arab Spring protests, which demonstrated the power of social media and the Internet as organizing tools beyond the easy reach of government control.

Other analysts point out that the Russian middle class is still quite limited in size and large parts of it may be conservative in orientation. Lilia Ovcharova estimates its size at 20 percent of the population, based on economic criteria, and argues that an important component consists of state employees. She observes that not only is the active middle class a relatively small group, but "even though members of the middle class have now for the first time openly shown their discontent with political developments in the country, actual reforms may clash with the economic interest of other representatives of this social stratum."[37] A preoccupation with private life could take precedence over political activism for large portions of the relatively affluent elements that make up the purported Russian middle class. This situation poses a collective action problem for critical elements in the Russian population. While political activism may, in their view, be a public good, it may be too costly for individuals involved. The 2011–12 protests are pivotal in that they represent a break-through in this collective action dilemma. Under the threat of increasing sanctions, however, the calculation could change and participants may be averse to risking personal security.

The extra-parliamentary opposition is also not characterized by a homogenous ideological approach. Nicu Popescu raises the possibility that the movement could create a new blend of nationalism and democracy, embodied in the philosophy of Navalny, whose success he describes as resting on his combination of three elements, "anti-corruption campaigning, pro-democracy activism, and a pin of moderate nationalism."[38] However, the attempt to bring together such diverse elements, while viable as an opposition strategy, may be more difficult to sustain over the longer term.

Where now?

Russia has experienced neither an Arab Spring nor an Orange Revolution. One of the fundamental reasons has to do with popular weariness with upheaval and instability. Based on Russian experience in the post-communist period, change for the sake of change is not necessarily a positive prospect. However, pressure for change is likely to continue. One mechanism through which this could occur is the reinstitution of gubernatorial elections. Provisions of the law to implement this reform, signed by President Medvedev on May 4, 2012, went into effect as of June 1, 2012, with the first elections expected in October 2012. One commentator has called this "the most important achievement of the 'Snow Revolution'."[39] To be sure, provisions of this law make it likely that these elections could be "managed." Mechanisms include a so-called "municipal filter" where potential candidates would need signatures of five or ten percent of deputies of municipal formations and/or elected municipal offices in order to run.[40] In addition, the president can request a consultation with candidates. Critics interpret these measures as an effort to assure that the political establishment will be able to exclude unwanted candidates, and note that in recent months 13 or more governors have been replaced under the current quasi-appointment procedure, pushing their election timetable back four to five years.[41] Nonetheless, we know from the various color revolutions that elections necessarily introduce uncertainty into even quite authoritarian contexts. Aleksei Titov of the Institute of Regional Politics stated the problem clearly: "the difficulty for authorities lies in the fact that they can't have elections with a single candidate, while any alternative opens the possibility for protest votes."[42] By the same token, manipulated elections can just as easily elicit discontent as can free ones allow opponents to win.

The decision to embrace this reform illustrates the dilemma facing the Russian leadership. On the one hand, too much repression and too few concessions could nurture opposition sentiments and expand the circle of citizens who feel that their trust has been abused. On other hand, as Gorbachev so bitterly learned in the late 1980s, moderate reforms can open the floodgates of increased demands. A skilled politician like Vladimir Putin may be able to chart these troubled waters, but, ironically, measures taken to avoid an Orange scenario in Russia may have unwittingly created more fertile ground for their eventual appearance. In the meanwhile, Putin must navigate between the Scylla of the presidential authoritarianism exercised by Alexandr Lukashenka in neighboring Belarus and the Charybdis of half–reforms so vividly illustrated by Soviet Union's collapse.

Notes

1. Richard Sakwa, *The Crisis of Russian Democracy: The Dual State, Factionalism, and the Medvedev Succession*, Cambridge: Cambridge University, 2011, Chapter 2.
2. Stephen K. Wengren and Andrew Konitzer, 'Prospects for Managed Democracy in Russia', *Europe–Asia Studies* 59 (2007), pp. 1025–47; T. J. Colton, *Popular Choice and Managed Democracy: The Russian Elections of 1999 and 2000, 2003*, Washington, DC: The Brookings Institution, 2003.
3. Samuel Huntington, *The Third Wave: Democratization in the Late Twentieth Century*, Norman : University of Oklahoma Press, 1991.
4. *RT News*, "Putin Agrees to Run for President in Tandem Reshuffle," September 24, 2011, http://www.rt.com/news/putin-president-medvedev-election-295/.
5. Office for Democratic Institutions and Human Rights (2012), "Russian Federation, Elections to the State Duma 4 December 2011," *OSCE ODIHR Election Observation Mission Final Report*, Warsaw, January 2, 2012.
6. Public Opinion Foundation (Fond Obshchestvennykh Mnenii), "'Reiting partii," survey of 3,000 respondents from 64 regions, November 19–20, 2011," *Dominanty*, no. 47, November 24, 2011, p. 7, available on the website of the Public Opinion Foundation, http://www.fom.ru.
7. For example, the Russian Public Opinion Research Center (VTsIOM) showed that 55.9 percent of those responding to a survey would vote for Putin on February 25, 2012, which, taking account of the 6.6 percent who indicated they would not vote, would put the percentage somewhat below 60 percent. However, it is difficult to make an estimate based on public opinion surveys, as voter intentions change and levels of non-voting are hard to predict. See the webpage of VTsIOM at http://www.wcicm.com/index.php?id=150.
8. Joan DeBardeleben and Mikhail Zherebtsov, "The Transition to Managerial Patronage in Russia's Regions," in *The Politics of Sub-National Authoritarianism in Russia*, Vladimir Gel'man and Cameron Ross (eds), Aldershot: Ashgate, 2010, pp. 85–105.
9. Henry Hale, "The Myth of Mass Russian Support for Autocracy: The Public Opinion Foundations of a Hybrid Regime," *Europe–Asia Studies*, 63, no. 8, 2011, p. 1371.
10. Joan DeBardeleben and Mikhail Zherebtsov, "Economic Crisis, the Power Vertical, and Prospects for Liberalization in Russia," in Joan DeBardeleben and Crina Viju (eds), *Economic Crisis in Europe: What it Means for the EU and Russia*, Houndsmill, Basingstoke: Palgrave Macmillan, forthcoming.
11. Ellen Barry and Andrew E. Kramer, "In Biting Cold, Protesters Pack the Center of Moscow," *New York Times*, February 4, 2012.
12. Ellen Barry and Michael Schwirtz, "Vast Rally in Moscow Is a Challenge to Putin's Power," *New York Times*, December 24, 2011.
13. Will Englund, "Russian Blogger Aleksei Navalny in Spotlight after Arrest," *Washington Post*, December 5, 2011.
14. Joan DeBardeleben and Mikhail Zherebtsov, "Economic Crisis."
15. "Medvedev Submits Bill to Reinstate Governor Elections," *RIA Novosti*, January 16, 2012.
16. On problems of party development in Russia see Henry Hale, *Why Note Parties in Russia: Democracy, Federalism, and the State*, Cambridge, New York: Cambridge University Press, 2006.
17. Michael Schwirtz, "A Russian Protest Leader Takes Center Stage," *New York Times*, May 11, 2012.
18. Will Englund, "Billionaire Mikhail Prokhorov Launches new Political Party in Russia," *The Washington Post*, June 4, 2012.
19. Ora Reuter, "The Politics of Dominant Party Formation: United Russia and Russia's Governors," *Europe–Asia Studies* 62, no. 2, 2010, pp. 293–327.
20. Public Opinion Foundation, "Otnoshenie k lideram oppozitsii i grazhdanskim aktivistam," *Dominanty*, no. 22, June 7, 2012, p. 30.

21 Public Opinion Foundation, "V. Putin: reiting doveriia," *Dominanty*, no. 22, June 7, 2012, p. 4.
22 Public Opinion Foundation, *Dominanty*, no. 22, June 7, 2012, p. 3.
23 Fritz W. Scharpf, "Economic Integration, Democracy, and the Welfare State," *Journal of European Public Policy*, 4, no. 1, 1997, p. 19.
24 Thomas F. Remington, *The Politics of Inequality in Russia*, Cambridge, New York: Cambridge University Press, 2011, p. 74.
25 P. Luong, and E. Weinthal, "Contra Coercion: Russian Tax Reform, Exogenous Shocks, and Negotiated Institutional Change," *American Political Science Review*, 98, No 1, 2004, pp. 139–70.
26 Remington, *The Politics of Inequality*, pp. 62–3.
27 International Human Development Indicators, *Human Development Reports*, http://www.hdrstats.undp.org/en/indicators/103106.html (accessed 18 June 2012).
28 David Easton, "A Reassessment of the Concept of Political Support," *British Journal of Political Science*, 5, no. 4, 1975, pp. 435–57, here p. 437.
29 Ibid, p. 438.
30 David Easton, *A Systems Analysis of Political Life*, New York: Wiley, 1965, p. 273.
31 David Easton, "A Reassessment of the Concept of Political Support."
32 See the public post "Belyi al'bom," at http://www.publicpost.ru/infographic/id/27/ or selections with video clips at http://www.avmalgin.livejournal.com/3129485.html (accessed June 12, 2012).
33 NTV, "Politsiia vozbudila ygolovnoe delo po stat'e 'Khuliganstvo' iz-za kontserta v khrame Khrista Spasitelia," February 26, 2012, http://www.ntv.ru/novosti/273232/ (accessed June 12, 2012).
34 Kanal Pik RV, "'Public Strolls' in Moscow Witness More Arrests," May 21, 2012, http://www.pik.tv/en/news/story/38057-public-strolls-in-moscow-witness-more-arrests (accessed June 18, 2012).
35 David M. Herszenhorn, "New Russian Law Assesses Heavy Fines on Protesters," *New York Times*, June 8, 2012; see also Masha Gessen, "Law and Order," *International Herald Tribune*, June 11, 2012. For revisions to the law see "Federal'nyi zakon Rossiiskoi Federatsii ot 9 iunia 2012, g. N 65-F3 g. Moskva, 'O vnesenii izmenenii v Kodeks Rossiiskoi Federatsii ob administrativnykh pravonarusheniiakh i Federal'nyi zakon 'O sobraniiakh, mitingakh, demonstratsiiakh, shesviiakh, i piketirovaniiakh'," *Rossiiskaia gazeta*, June 9, 2009.
36 See e.g. Dmitri Trenin, Maria Lipman, Alexey Malshenko, and Nikolay Petrov, "Russia on the Move," *Policy Outlook*, June 2012, Carnegie Endowment for International Peace.
37 Lilia Ovcharova, "Russia's Middle Class: At the Centre or on the Periphery of Russian Politics?," *Institute for Security Studies*, February 16, 2012.
38 Nicu Popescu, "Russia's Liberal-Nationalist Cocktail: Elixir of Life or Toxic Poison?" *Open Democracy Russia*, February 3, 2012, at http://www.opendemocracy.net/od-russia/nicu-popescu/elixir-of-life-or-toxic-poison-russias-liberal-nationalist-cocktail.
39 Vladimir Kara-Murza, "Restored Elections Spell New Trouble for Kremlin," *World Affairs*, May 3, 2012.
40 "Federal'nyi zakon Rossiiskoi Federatsii ot 2 maia 2012, g. N 40-F3, 'O vnesenii izmenenii v Federal'nyi zakon "Ob obshchikh printsipakh organizatsii zakonodatel'nykh (predstavitel'nykh) i ispolnitel'nykh organov gosudarstevnnoi vlasti sub"ektov Rossiiskoi'Federatsii" i Federal'nyi zakon 'Ob osnovnykh garantiakh izbiratel'nykh prav i prava na uchastie v referendume grazhdana Rossiiskoi Federatsii'," *Rossiiskaia gazeta*, May 4, 2012.
41 Kara-Murza, "Restored Elections."
42 Quoted by Natalia Krainova, "Tough Rules in Gubernatorial Vote," *The Moscow Times*, April 25, 2012.

2 Courts, law and policing under Medvedev

Many reforms, modest change, new voices[1]

Peter H. Solomon, Jr

Now that the Medvedev presidency is over, there is talk about the legacy of Dmitry Anatolevich, who was perceived by many to be more liberal than his partner in the ruling tandem, Vladimir Putin. One realm of policy that Medvedev embraced publically as his own was legal reform, an area of expertise for the former law professor.

Even during his electoral campaign in winter 2008, soon-to-be President Medvedev told listeners at a business forum that he felt 'like a jurist in his bones' and promised 'to eliminate unjust decisions based on the telephone and money' and to 'humanize the administration of justice'. Over his five years in office, Medvedev frequently discussed policy changes with top judges and law enforcement officials, and he also put his authority behind initiatives to soften the impact of the criminal law and to reform the police.[2]

This chapter asks: with what results? To what extent are judges in Russia more independent and accountable than five years ago? Have changes in criminal procedure improved the position of the accused or reduced accusatorial bias? Have punishments become more lenient and the use of imprisonment reduced to a level closer to European standards? What is the impact of the high profile police reform?

It is early to give definitive answers, but I argue that the full achievement of these desirable goals through the Medvedev-era reforms is unlikely (with the possible exception of the reduction of imprisonment). The reason is that most of the changes adopted represented modest or incremental steps that did not fully address underlying problems – because of flaws in design and because the normal process of bureaucratic politics ensured that the most radical proposals were discarded.

Of equal importance for the long run was the emergence in the Medvedev years of new sources of analysis and criticism of the administration of justice, and of vehicles for promoting serious reform. I will also discuss this development, including the independent assessment of the legality of the verdict in the second trial of Mikhail Khodorkovsky and Platon Lebedev.

This chapter starts with initiatives relating to the courts and criminal procedure; it then turns to crime, punishment, and policing; and finally to the matter of new voices.

Trying to fix the courts

Medvedev-supported initiatives on the courts fall into three groups – some aimed at enhancing the accountability or independence of the judiciary; others relating to court procedures; and still others relating to political concerns, like the handling of politically sensitive cases and reduction of appeals to the European Court of Human Rights (ECHR).

When the president met with top legal officials in 2008, the state of the courts had become a troubling political issue. The public had a low regard for the courts and probity of judges, whom they saw as both corrupt and responsive to powerful officials. Moreover, the carefully designed procedures for selecting and disciplining judges were not producing fair or appropriate results.[3]

Addressing the low levels of trust in courts was a central plank in the programme for improving the court system, 2007–12, already in place when Medvedev became president. That programme included the creation of the post of press secretary at all regional courts and regional judicial departments, and called as well for the publication of judicial decisions on websites or in databases. These initiatives gained wholehearted support from the new president, and a law was prepared setting out the rules for the posting of judicial decisions. Both of these measures were meant to counteract the low regard of the public toward the courts; in part a product of negative coverage of the administration of justice in the media. Press secretaries of courts could help journalists understand and appreciate the work of courts. The publication of court decisions would give interested citizens a window on what happens in the courts. The publication of court decisions might also encourage judges to write well-argued judgements, in the process contributing to their accountability.[4]

Among the new initiatives on courts adopted by Medvedev was the ending of the three-year probationary terms for newly appointed judges, which had been in place since 1993. Back then it made sense to wait a few years before giving life appointments to young inexperienced judges. But in reality judges in the probationary period felt extra pressure to deliver the decisions that the chairs and powerful outsiders (e.g. members of legislatures) wanted, so that the probationary terms represented a source of judicial dependency.[5] While their elimination could be seen as strengthening judicial independence, it was arguably premised on the relative ease of dismissing a judge with a weak record of performance.

The 1993 Law on the Status of Judges did enable judges to be fired for cause, but only with the approval of the appropriate judicial qualification commission and only for serious breaches of ethics or law. In practice, though, the powerful chairs of courts could usually have their way with the commissions and initiate the successful termination of any judge, if only for a pretext. The record showed that judges were fired whenever they displeased their chairmen, say by giving too many acquittals, by failing to take instruction in a case, or not moving their caseload quickly.[6] Certainly, it was possible to appeal such a removal to the High Judicial Qualification Commission and even then to the Supreme Court of the RF. But the whole system was stacked against judges who showed initiative or acted on principle. It was recognition of this situation that led to the decision to create a new separate body in the centre to serve as the ultimate adjudicator of alleged judicial misconduct.

The new Judicial Disciplinary Tribunal (*Prisutstvie*), established in 2010, replaced the Supreme Court as the final decision maker and body that heard appeals from judges who were dismissed by either regional qualification commissions or the high commission (for members of the higher courts). It did this not only for judges from the courts of general jurisdiction but also from judges on the arbitrazh courts (who had resented having their cases reviewed by the Supreme Court). The new tribunal was composed of three judges from the Supreme Court and three from the High Arbitrazh Court, each with at least five years experience on those courts and elected for three-year terms by their peers at the respective plenary sessions of those courts. In its first year of operation it reversed one third of the removals of judges ordered by qualification commissions, a sign that it was operating autonomously.[7] But this was not all.

In 2011, the Constitutional Court ruled that it was unconstitutional to discipline judges for mere procedural errors or any actions that fell within the scope of their discretion and did not constitute serious violations of the norms of material or procedural law. This prompted the Ministry of Justice to prepare a new version of the article in the law on the status of judges on disciplinary violations.[8] Finally, in February 2012, President Medvedev endorsed the creation of judicial disciplinary colleges at the level of a circuit (*okrug*) that embraced a number of regions, to replace entirely the regional judicial qualification commissions in disciplining judges. This proposal reflected the need to circumvent the continuing strong influence of the chairs of courts on work of the regional commissions – influence that too often led to unfair results (as the work of the Disciplinary Tribunal in the centre demonstrated).[9]

Judicial selection also received attention from President Medvedev. To begin with, early on Medvedev supported a broadening of the sources of recruitment of new judges, so that they would not be limited in the main to young jurists from the law enforcement agencies and former court secretaries, but include more outsiders, especially advocates but also jurisconsults and law teachers.[10] Putting this change into practice proved difficult. One reason was the complicated system of judicial selection, in which the chairs of courts who actually hire new judges play a crucial role. The process begins with a competition among aspirants to judgeships that includes passing examinations set by the qualification commissions.[11] But after candidates pass the exam, however fair, they will not received nominations without the support of the chair of a district or regional court. Even then, the nomination has to receive assent from the relevant high court (Supreme or High Arbitrazh) and two units within the presidential administration, one of which does a background check for criminal and political ties.[12] But as long as the chairs control appointments to their courts, they have the power to choose people they like and trust. There is no reason why they would favour more experienced jurists from outside the courts and law enforcement over people likely to be deferential and express corporate solidarity with other judges.

Protecting judges from arbitrary disciplinary measures sought by the chairs of their courts, and encouraging broader recruitment of judges, were positive steps, but by themselves insufficient to foster the independence of individual judges. For they did not supply a remedy for the roots of judicial dependence in the RF, namely the power of the chairs of court, the system of evaluating the work of judges, and the way both were used in practice. In the RF the chairs of courts were not simply judges handling administrative duties on rotation but rather bosses of their dominions, with power to manage the running of their courts, budget, staff operations, and the work of judges. Appointed to their posts by the president, with approval of the relevant high court, most of them would serve for more than 15 years, and they controlled not only the salaries of judges but also the allocation of perks, and their word on promotion or discipline was crucial. It was in the interests of the chairs to have judges who met expectations, first to cooperate with requests from the chair about particular cases (the main vehicle for outside influence on judicial decisions), and then to receive good evaluations in the system of statistical assessment that been used for 65 years. Above all, judges are evaluated on the rates of reversal, which encourages them to anticipate the actions of higher courts and act cautiously. Among other things, this means avoiding acquittals in criminal cases, even when the evidence is weak. Although acquittals are given in less than half of one per cent of cases involving state prosecution, half of these acquittals were overruled in cassation.[13] Sorry to say, the Medvedev reforms did not address the pressures on individual judges to be conformists, which were especially powerful for those seeking to move up the ranks to positions on higher courts.

While giving acquittals at trial might still be a black mark in itself, the likelihood of their cancellation in cassation represented a further deterrent for judges. It is possible that this might change with the implementation of a major change in criminal procedure that President Medvedev already approved in 2009: the replacement of cassation by a full-scale appellate review as the second instance for all court cases, civil and criminal alike. While cassation involves checking only reported violations of law (often, but necessarily, in an office setting without appearances by the sides), appellate review can include a full review of the evidence and the possibility of counsel's introduction of new evidence. In short, it represents a trial *de novo*, this time with a panel of three judges (as in cassation). Furthermore, while an overruling in cassation led to the return of a case for a new trial at the lower court (not just an embarrassment but a burden), the appellate court simply makes a new decision that replaces that of the trial court judge.[14]

Supporters of this major structural change insist that a full retrial of cases will produce better, fairer results and cut down drastically on the number of second instance court decisions that become the object of a review in supervision (*nadzor*) after the decision or sentence has gone into effect. However, a full retrial implied the need for more judges, especially at the regional courts that would handle appeals from decisions of district courts. The new law on courts of general jurisdiction of 2011 calls for the new appeals to be introduced in courts of general jurisdiction for civil cases at the start of 2012 and for criminal cases in

January 2013, and budget authorization provided for the hiring of an additional 700 judges.[15]

The intriguing question is whether the new appeals system will be fairer than the cassation it replaced. In many places cassation panels have a bad reputation, as bodies that rubberstamp the decisions of trial courts (for a long time the Moscow city courts were known as '*Mosgorshtampt*'). Certainly, the judges on cassation panels were often responsible for supervising the work of trial court judges whose quality was assessed on the basis of rates of reversal (*stabilnost prigovorov*). Operating in a conflict of interest situation, the cassation judges sent cases back for retrial only when they could not avoid it. Will this same syndrome be reproduced with the arrival of appeals? Much will depend upon the expectations imposed upon the appeals court judges, and whether they will still be held responsible for the work of judges on courts below. The introduction of appeals represents an opportunity to change the incentives and make acquittals a real possibility for trial and appellate court judges alike.

A related question is the impact of the appeals on trial by jury. In contrast to the stinginess of judges with acquittals, juries hearing serious cases at the regional courts award them in one out of every six cases that they hear. Undoubtedly, nearly half of those acquittals are reviewed in cassation at the Supreme Court and a major share sent back for a new jury trial. There have been cases with as many as three jury trials before the prosecution gave up.[16] In the new system of appellate review the three-judge panel at the Supreme Court will be in a position to simply reverse the jury's acquittal.

The other major development in the processing of criminal cases during the past five years did not represent an initiative from the top but evolved within a legislative framework established earlier. I refer to the development of a type of plea bargaining (known as 'special procedure for court hearing') that grew to become the predominant way of handling criminal cases. As of 2010, this simplified procedure where there is no review of the evidence has taken place in 63.6 per cent of cases, up from 37.5 per cent in 2006. Introduced in the Criminal Procedure Code of 2001 at the initiative of the leaders of the judiciary, and based on Italian models, the procedure soon became available to any offender charged with an offence bringing up to 10 years imprisonment.[17]

How does Russian plea bargaining work? In these cases the defendant, in consultation with an advocate and in his presence, must accept the charges in writing and petition for conviction without a full trial, also waiving the right to appeal on the facts. This usually happens at the end of the pre-trial investigation, when the defendant first sees the dossier. Both the procurator and the victim must consent to special procedure. Finally, the judge must review the motion, ensure that the defendant understands what (s)he is doing and has acted voluntarily and verify that the charges are supported by the evidence in the file (a good idea, though ironically restoring dependency on written results of the pre-trial investigation). If the judge agrees, there will no trial on the evidence (the accused will avoid embarrassment of confronting friends or family members as witnesses) and there will a hearing on sentencing alone, with the exclusion of the upper third of the normal sentencing range.[18]

Of course, the upper third of the sentencing range is not used often and some judges in practice are known to give a one-third discount to persons who plead guilty, especially in serious cases. But statistical evidence on some common charges indicates that the correlation between the use of special procedure and milder punishments is explained to a large degree by two other factors – whether the accused is a recidivist and is being held in custody before trial.[19]

While special procedure is advantageous to the jurists involved, its benefits to the accused are uncertain. It is likely that most offenders end up getting the sentences that they would have after a full trial, and that they simply give up t he opportunity to have the evidence carefully reviewed. The obligation of the judge to consider the case file is an important safeguard, but a new law from March 2012 allows investigators of crimes to cut operations when the accused admits guilt, a change that may reduce the quality of the case file.[20]

The Medvedev years also witnessed three major changes in the courts that represented responses to political concerns rather than the need for reform – the narrowing of jurisdiction for jury trials; measures to limit the independence and power of the Constitutional Court; and the provision to high courts of the power to compensate users of courts for unreasonable delays.

In December 2008, law makers moved quickly to adopt a law that removed from the purview of juries all cases dealing with terrorism, spying, treason and other serious crimes against the state. The push by law enforcement authorities and politicians alike to deprive persons accused of crimes against the state of the protection of trial by jury represented a major step backwards. In jury trials, including those involving political charges, the standards of proof were in practice much higher than in trials heard by judges alone, and juries acquitted defendants much more often than did judges. This narrowing of the jurisdiction for juries recalls similar actions taken by the Tsarist government in the 1870s that historians have qualified as 'judicial counterreform'.[21]

The attempt of political leaders to rein in the Constitutional Court (CC), far and away the most independent court within the Russian Federation, involved two initiatives. The first came in May 2009 when President Medvedev submitted to the Duma a draft law to change the system of appointing the chairman of the CC and his deputies, which was adopted in just a few weeks. Since 1990, the top judges of the CC had been elected for terms of four years by their peers on the court in a secret ballot, producing a system of rotation and surprise choices. In contrast, according to the new law, the president himself nominates both the chair and the two deputy chairs for (automatic) confirmation by the Council of the Federation, the same method already used for choosing the chairs of the Supreme and High *Arbitrazh* courts. As commentators in Russia realized, this step eliminated the only instance of authentic democracy in the management of the courts and increased the leverage of the executive and legislature over the CC.[22] The move was not based on public discussion and was barely explained. It would have been better for judicial independence in Russia had the CC's method of choosing its chair spread to other courts rather than vice versa.

As if this were not enough, in February 2011 further changes to the Law on the Constitutional Court of the RF went into effect that reduced the capacity of the court to reach as many issues as in the past and to spread its messages. The changes included: an end to court hearings by panels made up of half the judges, so that all trials would be plenary and require at least two thirds of the judges to be present; a new written procedure to produce resolutions without trial, subject to rejection by any party to a case; and, most critically, a ban on positive content in court 'determinations', the vehicle formerly used by judges to deal with cases where the legal issues were analogous to those on which the court had already spoken.[23] This change deprived the court of a way to help judges on other courts recognize the implications of the CC's earlier decisions, something advocates often attempted in vain in the face of weak and inflexible judges more devoted to the letter of the law than its interpretation by the CC.

Finally, as a response to the large number of complaints about Russian justice delivered by citizens of the RF to the ECHR, the president approved a law, in April 2010, giving Russian courts (the Supreme and High *Arbitrazh* courts and their courts at the circuit and regional levels) the right to hear claims for compensation for violation of a party's right to a trial within a reasonable time frame. Article 6, point 1 of the European Convention of Human Rights guarantees the right to a prompt trial, and a substantial share of the complaints coming from the Russian Federation have involved violations of this right. From May 2010 it became possible for Russian citizens to bring analogous complaints to domestic courts, which were in turn provided with funds to provide the kind of compensation delivered in Strasbourg. To get compensation required making timely complaints about violations of time standards for different parts of the process and also having taken the case itself through all possible instances. Courts in Russia began hearing such cases right away, and by the end of 2010 there was enough accumulated experience for the high courts to issue a resolution and a study of court practice.[24]

While the new procedure may have reduced the flow of cases to Strasbourg by as much as a quarter, it did not address the embarrassment felt by some Russian jurists and politicians of having their country's practices subject to criticism by a foreign body. The festering resentment boiled over during 2011. First, after the ECHR dared to criticize not just the practice of any ordinary Russian agency or court but a decision of the CC itself, its chair, Valery Zorkin, made the daring proposal that Russia and its CC should not always take direction from Strasbourg, but be guided instead by its own understanding of the requirements of the Russian Constitution. Zorkin cited a decision from the German CC that the lawmaker must have the right as a matter of exception to avoid international legal obligations that would violate its own constitution (and therefore sovereignty). In the case at hand (the Markin case), the Russian CC had supported special maternity leave for female soldiers because the needs of mothers and children are mentioned in the constitution; the ECHR considered this to be gender discrimination.[25] Zorkin's words aroused stern reactions from other Russian jurists, who understood that this approach violated Russia's treaty obligations. Not long after, the acting chairman of the Federation Council, 'Senator' Aleksandr Torshin, reacted to the same case by proposing legislation that would eliminate the priority Russian law gives to the court in Strasbourg, notwithstanding the fact that this would violate the Russian Constitution and expose Russia to possible expulsion from the Council of Europe. Fortunately, Torshin's draft was not adopted.[26]

Taken as a whole, the Medvedev initiatives to improve the courts were a mixed group. While some were retrogressive, others could improve the judicial process and contribute to a longer process of developing independent and accountable judiciary. However, the measures did not address the main obstacles to fair and impartial administration of justice, such as the centralized judicial bureaucracy, powerful chairs of courts and system of evaluating judges. Nor did they broaden the judicial recruitment or develop training programmes for new judges.

Humanization of criminal law and the regulation of business

In his first annual address to the Parliament in November 2008, President Medvedev announced that Russia's system of crime and punishment had become too severe and too costly, and he called for its humanization. Medvedev's public commitment to reform the criminal code came after discussions with his new minister of justice, Aleksandr Konovalov, a colleague from his days in St Petersburg, who was in turn listening closely to the arguments of retired Deputy Chair of the Supreme Court Vladimir Radchenko, made both in private and in the press.[27] With Russia's shortage of young men for the work force, it was counterproductive for it to remain number two in the world in the use of imprisonment (with 640 prisoners per 100,000 population), through which it was creating hardened criminals rather than contributors to society. Russian judges gave custodial sentences in the decade 2000–10 to 32–34 per cent of convicts; the average length of sentence to confinement exceeded five years (with the largest group receiving 5–10 years).[28]

With these arguments in mind, Medvedev commissioned the ministry to produce a draft law with measures to reduce imprisonment. Radchenko was hired as a consultant at the ministry and, under his guidance, a draft law was prepared that included the revival of non-custodial alternatives from the Soviet past (such as corrective work), decriminalization of a whole series of offences (sometimes only of the first instance), raising the minimum value of goods stolen to qualify as the crime of theft, and changes in the definition of business offences such as money laundering.[29] In spring 2009 the draft was circulated for comment by government agencies and in the summer received critical discussion at the Public Chamber, after which the ministry undertook revisions. In his November 2009 address, Medvedev criticized the pace of developing the changes as too slow, but it would take another two years for the core legislation to be passed.[30] The review of a continuing series of draft laws by the law enforcement agencies, the meetings of inter agency working groups organized by the presidential administration, and parliamentary hearings ensured substantial delays in adoption, and even so, critics claimed that the process had been rushed.

In late 2009 Medvedev also recognized the special problems posed by the overuse of the criminal law in the regulation of business activity in the RF by providing patronage to a group of jurists and economists who, for the past year, had been discussing the problem in public forums and had produced a book on the subject. This step came in response first to a year of public discussion of the issue prompted by the revelations and lobbying activities of Iana Iakovleva, a businesswoman who had herself suffered persecution by police officials, and, second, to the presentation of the group's book to the president.[31] Presidential patronage led to the formation of the Centre for Legal and Economic Research (LECS) at the Institute of Contemporary Development (INSOR), which expanded its studies, organization of hearings, and lobbying activity. The group continued to promote restrictions on the detention of businessmen during investigations, decriminalization of some offences, and changes in general principles of the criminal law connected to the application of the criminal code to businessmen.[32]

Criminal law reform under Medvedev was realized through three legislative packages, adopted respectively in March 2010, March 2011 and December 2011.[33] The first draft law dealt mainly with the crucial matter of the pre-trial detention of entrepreneurs accused of charges contained in Chapter 22 of the Criminal Code ('Business Crimes'). Unlike any other part of the code, most prosecutions according to these offences (many of which do not exist in other countries) did not reach the courts, but were stopped during the investigatory stage after payment by the accused of substantial bribes. For the police who initiated these cases, detention represented a key means of pressuring the accused. The misuse or abuse of detention of business people was a central focus of Iana Iakovleva's lobbying, as well as the proposals from the LECS group. Naturally, some law enforcement agencies (e.g. the Investigatory Committee) resisted the proposed elimination of detention in these cases, and implementation in the first year was incomplete. All the same, the number of prosecutions started for Article 22 crimes dropped by more than 30 per cent in one year.[34]

The larger package of changes to what constituted crime, the repertoire of non-custodial sanctions, the conditions for the use of custodial sanctions, and the discretion of judges was debated during summer 2010 in an interagency working group run by the Mikhail Paleev of the Presidential Administration. The opposition to parts of the package was so great that the minister of justice announced in the autumn of 2010 that he would divide the proposals into two separate pieces of legislation, so that the changes already accepted by members of the group could be introduced before agreement on the others had been achieved.[35] The first of these laws (from March 2011) featured the removal of the lower limits of the time of imprisonment for many charges, including common ones like theft, open theft and robbery, and analogous changes for non-custodial alternatives as well. By themselves these changes increased greatly the degree of judicial discretion, and to some critics the opportunities for corruption.[36] A problem in practice turned out to be the meaning of retroactivity for these changes, which became an issue because the Constitution (article 54.2) makes changes that benefit an accused person retroactive. Should everyone convicted of these articles have the right to be resentenced, or only those given the minimum at the time, or only people awaiting trial at the time the law was issued?[37]

The so-called third package of changes marking the culmination of the humanization initiative was publicized in the spring of 2011 and debated in the Duma over the next six months.[38] This law introduced a long list of changes that, taken with the elimination of lower limits of punishment, had the potential for dramatic changes in sentencing and punishment. First, as promised for a few years, the law decriminalized minor offences such as slander and defamation by converting them into administrative offences. It also eliminated criminal responsibility for importing goods into the country without paying customs duties; the crime of contraband became limited to importation of illegal goods (drugs, arms, and so on).

Second, the law enhanced the repertoire of non-custodial alternatives. This included the creation of a new punishment 'compulsory work', which could be applied instead of imprisonment for periods of two months to five years, and be served in one of 15 new special centres with dormitories, which in practice might be similar to the existing 'colony-settlements'. The option of compulsory work was added to more than 160 articles in the criminal code, so that, between the two laws, three quarters of the articles were subject to some kind of change. Provision was also made for longer periods of 'obligatory work', a form of community service performed after work, and an extension of the sanction 'corrective work' so that it would be performed without leaving one's job with a deduction from pay. Each of these additions represented a return to Soviet era practices.

Third, the use of deprivation of freedom was forbidden in sentencing of first time offenders for non-serious offences, whose definition was extended to comprise all crimes with a maximum sentence of three years imprisonment (up from two), including, for example, the common offence of 'inflicting bodily blows' (*poboi*), one of the charges that had effectively replaced hooliganism when that crime was limited to incidents involving weapons. Judges were also given new discretion to decide whether and when to send to confinement offenders who violated the probation conditions associated with suspended sentences (previously confinement was required). This change could also lead to less use of imprisonment, for more than 40 per cent of offenders received a suspended sentence. In addition, the law allowed judges to delay the implementation of punishments of all kinds for narcotics users if they pursued 'medical-social rehabilitation', a term whose meaning was not defined.

Fourth, the law provided a new mechanism for punishing businessmen whose criminal actions had caused losses or damages. Instead of a term of confinement, the convicts could be required to pay a fine of five times the estimated loss that they had caused. Critics from one side resented the idea that entrepreneurs could 'buy their way' out of prison openly and officially, but critics from the other side claimed that the punishment would mean bankruptcy for most convicts (the problem compounded by the method of computing losses) and, as a result, harm the country's economy.

The economists and jurists from the LECS centre trying to reduce prosecutions against entrepreneurs were dismayed by the third package because it failed to deliver on most of their recommendations. It was fine to have fewer businessmen in detention; good that failure to pay income tax was no longer a crime (another change introduced in a separate law); and good that contraband had been redefined and the offence of illegal entrepreneurship somewhat circumscribed. But many former entrepreneurs were languishing in prison colonies, despite the attempts by the LECS group to convince the president to grant them amnesty. And business people remained vulnerable to a wide variety of damaging charges subject to broad interpretation (such as fraud) and to principles in the general part of the code that increased their responsibility (such as the treatment of boards of directors and leadership groups as 'organized criminal groups'). As of the early months of 2012 the group was continuing its marshalling of evidence and its lobbying activity, including the writing of a brand new criminal code, so that necessary changes could be introduced into the general part.[39]

During his electoral campaign in the winter of 2012, presidential candidate Vladimir Putin promised a forum of businessmen that it was time to remove from the hands of police the tools that they used to harass and extract from businesses, 'primarily the economic articles', and he promised to create a new office of ombudsman for business. As of June 2012, according to a leader of the business group 'Delovaia Rossiia' who had spoken with both top leaders, plans were afoot for the introduction into the Duma in the autumn of a draft law that would make relevant changes in the criminal law and for an amnesty of some of the businesspeople currently in confinement.[40]

Further changes in the criminal code notwithstanding, the changes introduced under Dmitry Medvedev in the name of humanization and modernization had the potential for major impact on the sentencing practice of Russian judges and the landscape of punishment in the Russian Federation. Undoubtedly, one year into the reforms, there were signs of resentment among Russian judges and reluctance to use the new non-custodial alternatives until they had been properly organized.[41] But within a few years custodial sentences might become less frequent and shorter. Even the moderate estimates of the likely effect on the prison population of the country predicted a drop of 25 per cent, something that is rarely achieved through legal change alone.[42]

Reform of the police

During 2009, the second year of his presidency, Dmitry Medvedev faced the challenge of convincing an already sceptical public that the police in Russia could be trusted to help and protect them, instead of extracting and preying. Corruption, commercialization and abuse were known to be common traits of police work, but during 2009 a series of revelations about particularly disturbing situations involving police officers (contract killings, rapes, shooting sprees), including from police officers themselves on YouTube (starting with Dymovsky's complaints about corruption and quotas), forced the hand of the president. The death in prison of Sergei Magnitsky, who had denounced corporate raiding by MVD officers, could only have added fuel to the fire.[43]

In response to the scandals, and the negative public mood that they had generated, Medvedev issued a presidential decree that initiated reform of the MVD, calling for a 22 per cent reduction in its staff, increases in pay for the remaining officers, improvements in the ministry's systems of recruitment and training, and the centralization of the police budget, so that regional governments would no longer share in financing of the police. But this decree was only the start. The president then ordered the minister of Internal Affairs, Rashid Nurgaliev, to undertake the drafting of a new law on the police.[44]

Responsibility for drafting the new law was placed squarely in the hands of the police itself. Apart from the implementation of changes already ordered by the president, the MVD leaders emphasized organizational changes (opening and closing of units) and the specification of police powers, duties and rights rather than supply new directions in the management and conduct of policing – not to speak of dealing with its extensive commercial activity.[45] According to critics, the reform lacked a clear conceptual basis, and the drafting process itself was too closed and gave little access for human rights organizations. There were reports of an unwritten internal directive that forbade individual police officers from discussing the reform with members of the public. Moreover, the quality of discussion within the MVD was weak. The Working Group on Police Reform organized roundtable discussions in 20 regions, but only in one did the city police chief take part and discuss proposals from rights groups.[46] Once the draft law had been completed, in mid 2010, a public discussion was staged, partly on the Internet and encouraged by the president himself, through which the public, led by NGOs, offered many suggestions. Two proposals that reportedly caught the attention of the president were the idea that police officers wear name badges and the notion that people detained by the police might have a right to a phone call, and these subsequently entered the law.[47] It remained difficult for police officers to be part of the discussion – in 2010 it became a crime for an officer to criticize the decisions of his superiors.

The new law changed the name of the police in Russian from '*militsiia*' to '*politsiia*', suggesting that the reformed police would become more service-oriented and less militarized. It is not clear whether either of these goals will be realized. A centralized militarized organization had been a constant feature of police in Russia, and despite regular proposals to change this, the makers of the new law rejected decentralization, including the idea of separating local and federal policing in distinct agencies. Encouraging service to the public, as opposed to state interests, would require a transformation in the whole approach to evaluating the police, which, sad to say, did not take place.[48]

The crucial issue of the quantitative indicators used to evaluate the work of police (known as '*palochki*') did become the subject of new MVD Orders, aimed at demonstrating that police leaders were aware of defects in the incentives that they provided to their charges.[49] But the changes (for example in Order No. 25 from 2010) introduced only technical modifications and did not address the core problems caused by the longstanding insistence that police meet quotas and targets in their work. Thus, meeting expectations regarding the famous solution or clearance rate (for individual officers and unites alike) led police, especially near the end of a cycle, to neglect public complaints that did not lead to soluble cases and to push too hard with cases that they had already started to the point of fabricating evidence if confessions could not be obtained. Likewise, the need to produce cases of particular profiles regardless of local conditions also led to distortions. In one reporting period, police were asked to increase cases against narcotics users, but in one district the known narcotics users were already in confinement and there was no one to arrest, so that meeting the target could be achieved only through foul play (planting narcotics on innocent parties). At the root of this example was the paradox identified by one commentator, that succeeding in handling crime could undermine the capacity of police to show that they were uncovering it. Between 2009 and 2011 there were many attempts, by both human rights NGOs and management consultants (e.g. from the Higher School of Economics), to elaborate new ways of evaluating the performance of the police, but a comprehensive review reveals no agreement of what new system would encourage Russian police to behave in an appropriate way.[50] The year 2011 witnessed two further attempts to reform the system of evaluating police, culminating in Order 1310. Accordingly in 2012, the evaluation of police would include a public opinion component and inspections from above, as well as the usual analyses of regular crime statistics, and regional departments were given new discretion in the use of the data for management purposes. Still, the experts insisted that the measures changes did not remove the pressures on police to meet periodic targets or change the methods of police management.[51]

Nor did the law promise to make law enforcement more transparent. A good example of this problem was the conduct of the reattestation of police officers in the regions and localities. The criteria for retaining or dismissing police staff were not specified for the public, nor did public organizations have access to the process. As a result, there were suspicions that the process itself might be corrupt. The new public councils for the police did acquire increased powers of supervision, but they no longer included representatives of human rights groups that monitored the work of the police.[52]

Most important, the police reform of 2010–11 did not address the commercialization of policing that had emerged as a hallmark of police activity in the Russian Federation. Most police units, and individual police as well, were involved in some kind of police work for hire, during and after work hours, legal, semi legal and illegal. At the same time, various police officials benefited from payments for protection made by small and medium size businesses and from the extraction of rents (and even pieces of a business) in exchange for stopping criminal prosecutions against businesses. Taken together, these practices supplied the basis for the characterization of policing in contemporary Russia as 'predatory'.[53]

The start of 2012 is early to assess a reform that was still in its early stages. But it was clear that the reform was not designed to address many of the core problems of policing in the Russian Federation, such as the distorting effects of evaluation, the over commercialization of policing, and the weakness in recruitment and training. Whether the reform would reduce petty corruption (such as extraction of bribes by traffic police) remained to be seen. Raising salaries and setting out new expectations might help, but in Georgia substantial replacement of cadres and serious new training accompanied the higher salaries and noble words.[54] Technology in the form of attractive websites might also help the public appreciate the police. But as of spring 2012 there were no signs of new public trust in the police or that the police in Russia had gained legitimacy.

New sources of policy ideas

The Medvedev era was marked not only by presidential support for the reform of courts and criminal justice. It has also seen a widening of the sources of policy ideas and initiatives beyond the narrow confines of government agencies. This process built upon developments of prior years, and it was greatly facilitated by the new opportunities for communication on the Internet. But President Medvedev also made a contribution. His criticism of law enforcement and the administration of justice from the start of his term helped to make social initiatives legitimate, and in some instances he even cultivated them.

Consider two examples, both involving Russia's most famous prisoner, Mikhail Khodorkovsky, once the head of the large oil company, Yukos, whose prosecution and conviction in 2005 for tax evasion were viewed by most observers as politically motivated. Not long after Medvedev's public promises to address defects in Russia's legal institutions,[55] Khodorkovsky submitted an essay to the mainstream public affairs journal *Vlast'* in which he laid out his vision of a radical judicial reform. Rather than ignoring the voice of a self-appointed political dissident, the editors published the piece and invited scholars and top legal officials to comment. The result was a four-month debate in which the pros and cons of a range of policy options got a thorough airing.[56]

The second initiative relating to Khodorkovsky was the conduct during 2011 of a public evaluation of the December 2010 verdict in his second trial by the Presidential Council on the Development of Civil Society and Human Rights. This review reflected the general perception that, at least in the second case, the charges were both groundless and politically motivated. It also followed the dramatic revelation by the clerk to the presiding judge at the trial that the sentence he had signed had been delivered from the Moscow City Court for him to copy. This revelation came in a filmed interview that Internet users could watch on YouTube.[57] Here was concrete evidence that the practice of telephone law (instructions to judges from above or the side) was alive and well and practiced in a high profile case already seen as political. The revelation led to denials and threats of prosecution for slander, but also discussion of how to clear the air. Formally, the next step was the cassation review at the Moscow City Court, which predictably stuck to the script and did nothing more than reduce the sentences from 14 to 13 years.[58]

Even before that outcome, the leaders of the Presidential Council (which included the legal scholar, Mikhail Fedotov, and retired justice of the CC, Tamara Morshchakova) announced that they would organize a review by legal experts (domestic and foreign) of both the verdict and procedures followed at the trial. The Council of Judges denounced the move as interference in the judicial process, but the head of the CC, Valery Zorkin, and the president himself disagreed.[59] By late autumn 2011 the assessors had produced a book-length report with a set of damning conclusions. Delivered to the president in December, the report called for the granting of amnesty to convicted businessmen, including Khodorkovsky and Lebedev. When, at a meeting of the council, the president indicated that he could not grant amnesty without an admission of guilt, the council proceeded to provide him with expertise on the practice of amnesties in Russia and abroad that contradicted this position.[60]

The review of the Khodorkovsky verdict was not the first controversial step undertaken by the council. When a year earlier the scandal broke surrounding the death in confinement of lawyer Sergei Magnitsky (who had been denied needed medical attention), the council also stepped into the breach and commissioned an investigation aimed at determining fault and supplying recommendations for the reform of pre-trial detention to avoid similar calamities. The council, whose members included human rights activists as well as leading jurists, had become, under Medvedev, a place for responding to scandals and for serious contributions to public debate.[61]

Another body with presidential patronage that emerged as a source of policy initiative was the Centre for Legal and Economic Studies attached to the Institute of Contemporary Development, with sponsorship as well from the Higher School of Economics. This was the group of jurists and economists that we encountered earlier that pushed, and continue to push, for decriminalization of business offences through the conduct of research, publishing of articles and books, the holding of conferences and hearings (including at the chambers of the parliament), and through the development of draft laws.[62] The group was especially well positioned to get its messages to leadership circles. It had friends and protectors in the inner circle and operated with sponsorship from the two most often cited expert centres for economic matters in the Medvedev years, the Higher School of Economics (*Vyshka*) and INSOR.[63] When in May 2012 President Putin called for suggestions for further reform of the courts, the LECS group again came forward with proposals.

The sources of policy ideas, and evidence to support them, came to include, in the Medvedev years at least, two independent centres (think tanks) that conducted policy related research at their own initiative. The first was the INDEM Foundation, a think tank of long standing, founded by Georgyi Satarov, a former advisor to Boris Yeltsin, in October 1997. INDEM became well known for its sociological research on corruption, which included special projects on corruption in the police. It also had a track record in judicial reform, and between 2008 and 2010 it was the home for a large sociological study of the courts and the judiciary in the RF, which led to two major books, many reports and policy recommendations. In contrast to typical narrow legal scholarship in Russia, the INDEM studied informal practices and grounded its recommendations in reality. The second independent centre for policy research on the application of law was the Institute of Law and Law Enforcement at European University in St Petersburg. Founded in July 2009, the institute constituted a research centre with nine full time researchers doing socio-legal research on important topics relating to policing and the administration of justice. Not only did the institute produce innovative studies on the practice of police and courts in Russia, but it also disseminated the results in ways that could reach the world of policymakers, the publication of analytical memos (also on the institute's website) and articles in the newspaper *Vedomosti*.[64]

The Internet also facilitated the exchange of new ideas relating to courts and criminal justice during the Medvedev years. All of the bodies discussed in this chapter had impressive websites to promote their causes. In addition, prominent human rights organizations covering police and prisons (like Public Verdict, For Human Rights and the Centre for Reform of Criminal Justice) had websites with research reports and recommendations, not to speak of links to relevant journalistic writing. The best newspapers had well indexed sites (*Novaia gazeta, Kommersant, Rossiiskaia gazeta*), and there were journalistic services representing courts (RAPSI), lawyers and the Guild of Court Reporters.[65] To compete and ensure that their positions entered the public realm, the major government agencies also developed rich websites complete with press materials (the three high courts, the Judicial Department, the Procuracy, MVD, FSB, Investigatory Committee, Ministry of Justice).[66] Then, there were two excellent websites for materials on crime and criminal justice, one for the Saratov TRACCC, and the other crimpravo.ru.[67] Bodies bringing complaints from Russian courts to the ECHR had their websites (e.g. Sutiazhnik), and conservative NGOs such as the victim oriented Soprotivlenie as well.[68] To what extent people of different points of view read websites representing opposing ones is unclear, but the opportunity for dialogue is much greater than before.

Finally, one should not underestimate the potential of the Internet for whistleblowers and the creation of scandal. Just as the fury over abuses in the parliamentary elections of December 2011 mushroomed over the Internet, so too did two major scandals relating to criminal justice – the exposé of police corruption by Officer Dymovsky on YouTube (in 2009) and the revelations about the verdict in the second Khodorkovsky trial on the Gazeta.ru site (in 2011). Actions of this kind may well serve as triggers of future reforms in criminal justice.

Conclusion

As president of the Russian Federation, Dmitry Medvedev did make the reform of the administration of justice and law enforcement a matter of public priority, and he opened the door to an agenda of reform oriented policy initiatives, promoted in part by groups outside the legal agencies, whose role in policy discussions Medvedev encouraged. At the same time, the president's attachment to Russia's traditional bureaucratic pattern of law making ensured that leaders of relevant government agencies were often (but not always) able to veto measures they disliked and assume responsibility for the realization of others. There was no sign that Prime Minister Putin took positions on any of the issues, but his shadow may have given law enforcement officials added confidence to oppose presidential initiatives.

As we have seen, the result was in one area after another – judicial reform, reform of the criminal law, and police reform – the adoption of measures was not radical enough or not given sufficient political priority to produce fundamental changes. Whether the initiatives will turn out to be steps on the path to transformations of the future or half-measures without lasting impact remains to be seen.

Postscript, December 2012

The first eight months of the second presidential term of Vladimir Putin (from May to December 2012) saw the proposal and adoption of a slew of changes in criminal law that reflected the new leadership's urge to limit and control public protest, if not also civil society itself. Emblematic of the new approach was the decision in July to recreate the crime of slander (*kleveta*), whose decriminalization had been part of the Medvedev humanization law of December 2011. In its new form, slander warranted large fines rather than imprisonment and for the most part required the participation of state prosecutors, but the measure was intended as a weapon against opponents and critics of the regime bent on exposing wrongdoing on the part of officials. Not long after came another initiative from the top, this time to broaden the definition of treason (*izmena rodine*) to include giving information to representatives of international organizations or foreign NGOs, even when the perpetrator did not know that it was considered secret. In a similar vein, another law that came into force in late November made it a criminal offence for a Russian NGO that received foreign funding to fail to announce (on its website and otherwise) that it was a 'foreign agent'. Finally, plans were afoot to create the new crime of 'offending the sentiments of religious believers', an obvious response to the Pussy Riot affair, and the legal difficulties posed by the need to punish the young female singers who performed anti Putin songs in a large cathedral and spread the videotape on the web.[69]

Medvedev's concern with the plight of business people found continued expression in draft legislation redefining fraud, which included the requirement that the victim request prosecution, but opinions differed over whether some of the new provisions would also hurt business.[70] While the realization of other reforms associated with Medvedev showed no signs of abating (e.g. the reforms of police and punishment), the zeitgeist of the times had changed, and it was hard to imagine such reforms gaining momentum or the addition of further measures needed to make them effective.

Consistent with the new mood, the Supreme Court of the RF sent to the State Duma, in early November, draft legislation that would move a large part of the criminal law jurisdiction of the regional courts to that of district courts, where the option of trial by jury was not available.[71] As a result, most charges of murder and rape would no longer be eligible for jury trials and the overall number of jury trials (where the rate of acquittal was so high) stood to drop by three quarters. It was not clear, however, whether this proposed measure of judicial counterreform would be approved.

Notes

1 This chapter benefited from the assistance of Alexei Trochev and Benjamin Noble, from collaboration with members of the LECS group in Moscow, from the advice and help of Tom Firestone, and from comments by Gilles Favarel-Garriques, Matthew Light, Mary McAuley, and Benjamin Noble. I am pleased to acknowledge research support from the Centre for Human Rights and Legal Pluralism, Faculty of Law, McGill University.
2 'Prezident dostig umerennosti i ravonovesiia v sudebnykh voprosakh', http://www.ravo.ru, 2 February 2012.
3 See, for example, Anastasia Kornia, 'Sudam ne veriat', *Vedomosti*, 9 August 2007; Peter H. Solomon, Jr, 'Informal Practices in Russian Justice: Probing the Limits of Post-Soviet Reform', in Ferdinand Feldbrugge (ed.), *Russia, Europe and the Rule of Law*, Leiden: Martinus Nijhoff, 2007, pp. 79–92.
4 'Kontseptsiia federalnoi tselevoi programmy "Razvitie sudebnoi sistemy Rossii" na 2007–2011 gody', utv. razporiazheniem Pravitelstva RF ot 4 avgusta 2006, No 1082-r; 'Ob obespechenii dostupa k informatsii o deiatelnosti sudov v Rossiiskoi Federatsii', Federalnyi zakon ot 22 dekabria 2008 No262 FZ.
5 'O vnesenii izmenenii v stati 6 i 11 Zakon RF 'O statuse sudei v RF', i stati 17 i 19 Federalnogo zakon 'Ob organakh sudeiskogo soobshchestva v RF', Federalnyi zakon ot 17 iuliia 2009 g. N 157.
6 In 2009 Judge Guseva from a district court in Volgograd won her appeal in the Supreme Court against her removal by the regional qualification commission. Her 'sin' was refusing to follow an inappropriate (but not atypical) order from the chair of her court to report to him on a daily basis about the content of the cases that she was dealing with. 'Sud'ia Guseva vozvrashchaetsia na rabotu', *Novaia gazeta*, 6 April 2009.
7 Mikhail Moshkin, 'Sud dlia vnutrennego potrebleniia. Utverzhdeny reglamenty "tribunal" dlia sluzhitelei Femidy', *Vremia novostei*, 5 February 2010, and the website of the tribunal http://www.dsp,sudrf.ru.
8 Natalia Shiniaeva, 'Ditsiplinarnuiu otvetstvennost sudei konkretiziruiut v zakone', http://www.ravo.ru, 2 November 2011.
9 Vladislav Kulikov, 'Poslednoe slovo sudi', *Rossiiskaia gazeta*, 3 February 2012. Such a move would also ensure that responsibility for the selection and the disciplining of judges be assigned to different bodies, as the OECD Kyiv recommendations on Judicial Independence in Eastern Europe require 'Kyiv recommendations on judicial independence in Eastern Europe, South Caucasus, and Central Asia', 23–25 June 2010, OSCE Office of Human Rights.
10 Dmitry Medvedev, 'Vystuplenie na VII Vserossiiskom s'ezde sudei', 2 December 2008.
11 The handling of these exams has been so erratic and biased that in October 2011 another Medvedev sponsored law was introduced in the Duma to create special examination commissions for judges separate from the Judicial Qualification commissions and with jurist members from outside the judiciary; 'V Gosdumu vnesen zakonoproekt, kasaiushchiisia raboty ekzamenatsionnykh komissii po priemu kvalifikatsionnykh ekzamenov na dolzhnost sudi', 7 October 2011.
12 For details see Alexei Trochev, 'Judicial Selection in Russia: Toward Accountability and Centralization', in Kate Malleson and Peter H. Russell (eds), *Appointing Judges in an Age of Judicial Power: Critical Perspectives from around the World*, Toronto: University of Toronto Press, 2006, pp. 375–94.
13 Solomon, 'Informal Practices'; E. L. Paneakh, K. D. Titaev, V. V. Volkov, and D. Ia. Primakov, 'Obvinitelnyi uklon v ugolovnom prave: faktor prokurora', Analiticheskaia zapiska Instituta problem pravoprimenenii, March 2010, http://www.enforce.spu.ru (under analiticheskie zapiski); Peter H. Solomon, Jr, 'The Accountability of Judges in Post Communist States: From Bureaucratic to Professional Accountability', in Anya Seibert-Fohr (ed.), *Judicial Independence in Transition*, Heidelberg: Springer, 2012.

14 An appeals procedure was introduced in 1995 for the review of decisions in trials at the *arbitrazh* courts and in 2002 for decisions of the justices of the peace. The experience of these courts demonstrated the advantages of appeals over Soviet style cassation. Vladislav Kulikov, 'Sud idet. Dvazhdy', *Rossiiskaia gazeta*, 11 February 2011; 'Apelliatsiia zamenit kassatsiiu', *Advokat i zakon* (http://www.lawyer-law.ru), n.d., 2011.
15 'Chem apelliatsiia luchshe kassatsii', *Radio Svoboda*, 29 January 2010; Vladislav Kulikov, 'Kandidatskii minimum dlia raboty v apelliatsii ishchut bolee 700 sudei', *Rossiiskaia gazeta*, 5 August 2011.
16 Kristi O'Malley, 'Not Guilty until the Supreme Court Finds You Guilty: A Reflection on Jury Trials in Russia', *Demokratizatsiya*, 14:1, Winter 2006, pp. 42–58.
17 On the history of plea bargaining in Russia and inquiry into its popularity see Peter H. Solomon, Jr, 'Plea Bargaining Russian Style', *Demokratizatsiya*, 20:3, Summer 2012; see also Stanislaw Pomorski, 'Modern Russian Criminal Procedure: The Adversarial Principle and Guilty Plea', *Criminal Law Forum* 17, 2006, pp. 129–48, and Olga Semukhina and K. Michael Reynolds, 'Plea Bargaining Implementation and Acceptance in Modern Russia: A Disconnect between the Legal Institutions and the Citizens', *International Criminal Justice Review*, 19:4, December 2009, pp. 400–32.
18 Moreover, those accused who rely on defence counsel provided by the police or the courts are not required to pay for their services (the federal government assumes responsibility).
19 K. D. Titaev and M. P. Pozdniakov, 'Poriadok osobyi—prigovor obychnyi: praktika primeneniia osobogo poriadka sudebnogo razbiratelstva (g.40 UPK RF) v rossiisikh sudakh', Analiticheskaia zapiska Instituta problem pravoprimeneniia', St Petersburg, March 2010, http://www.enforce.ru (under analiticheskie zapiski).
20 'Medvedev predlozhil izmenit poriadok rassledovaniia ugolovnykh del', RAPSI, 7 March 2012.
21 Reaction to the contraction of the jurisdiction of juries in 2008 included strong objections voiced by the Public Chamber, which claimed that the move was unconstitutional, and a campaign to petition President Medvedev to veto the bill. But this short-lived protest was eclipsed by the signing of the bill by the president on the last day of 2008. Vladimir Shishlin, 'Gospoda prisiazhnye, vam zdes ne mesto', *Interfax*, 12 December 2008; 'Obshchestvennaia palata vystupaet protiv otmeny suda prisiazhnykh po delam o terrorizme', http://www.vesti.ru, 17 December 2008; Tamara Morshchakova, 'Kontrreforma: ugroza i realnost', *Sravnitelnoe konstitutsionnoe obozrenie*, 2005, no.3 (52), pp. 61–8; Peter H. Solomon, Jr, 'Threats of Judicial Counterreform in Putin's Russia', *Demokratizatsiya*, 13:3, Summer 2005, pp. 325–45.
22 See, for example, Tat'iana Skorobogatko, 'KS lishaet prava vybora', *Radio Svoboda*, 8 May 2009; and 'Nezavisimost Konstitutsionnogo suda pod ugrozoi—eksperty', http://www.baltinfo.ru/news/84516. For the text of law, see 'O vnesenii izmenenii v Federalnyi Konstitutsionnyi Zakon 'O Konstitutsionnom Sude RF', Proekt 198375-5, unpublished.
23 'O vnesenii izmenenii v Federalnyi Konstitutsionnyi zakon RF "O Konstitutsionnom Sude RF"', Federalnyi Konstitutsionnyi zakon RF ot 3 noiabria 2010 N 7, *Rossiiskaia gazeta*, 10 November 2010; 'Tamara Morshchakova: rezultatom peremen poslednikh let stalo sushchestvennoe snizhenie pravovogo statusa Konstitutsionnogo Suda', INSOR; 'Pravo i zakon', http://www.imrussia.org, 16 November 2011.
24 Ekaterina Butorgina, 'Sroki razumnogo. Prezident vanes v Gosdumu zakonoproekt ob "uskorenii" sudov', *Vremia novostei*, no. 48, 24 March 2010; Vladislav Kulikov, 'Sudite bystro, platite chestno', *Rossiskaia gazeta*, 14 January 2011; 'O nekotorykh voprosakh, voznikshikh pri rassmotrenenii del o prisuzhdenii kompensatsii za narushenie prava na sudoproizvodstvo v razumnyi srok ili prava na ispolenie sudebnogo akta v razumnyi srok, Postanovlenie Plenuma Verkhovonogo Suda RF i Plenuma Vysshego Arbitrazhnogo suda RF ot 23 dekabria 2010 no 30/64 g. Moskva', *Rossiiskaia gazeta*, 14 January 2011.

25 Valerii Zorkin, 'Predel ustupchivosti', *Rossiiskaia gazeta*, 29 October 2010.
26 Aleksandr Torshin, 'Vybor Rossii', *Rossiiskaia gazeta*, 12 July 2011; 'Torshin protiv Strasburga', *The New Times*, 7 July 2011; Andreas Gross, 'Ob ispolenenii Rossiei ob'iazatelstv pered Sovetom Evropy', *Radio Svoboda*, 19 July 2011.
27 Dmitry Medvedev, 'Poslanie Federalnomu Sobraniiu', 5 November 2008. See also Sergei Belov, 'Pod domashnii arest. Prezident shchitaet, chto ot razgovorov o gumanizatsii nakazania pora pereiti k delu', *Rossiiskaia gazeta*, 16 December 2008. For the argumentation of Radchenko see Vladimir Radchenko, 'Kak snizit chislo zakliuchennykh v Rossii', *Prestuplenie i nakazanie*, 2008, no.12; Vladimir Radchenko, 'Kak ispravit tiurmu', *Rossiiskaia gazeta*, 17 September 2009; Vladimir Radchenko, 'Obespechenie prav i interesov grazhdan pri osushchestvlenii ugolovno-pravovoi politiki v RF', Doklad Federalnoi palaty advokatov RF, n.d. (2009).
28 Radchenko, 'Kak snizit'; Criminal statistics section of the website of the Judicial Department, http://www.sudep.ru; 'Legal Reforms: Medevdev's Achievements', *Russiawatchers*, 25 April 2011.
29 'O gumanizatsii ugolovnogo zakonodatelstva' (n.d., winter 2009), Poisasnitelnaia zapiska k zakonoproektu 'O vnesenii dopolnenii v Ugolovnyi kodeks RF....' Unpublished, in possession of author; interview with Vladimir Radchenko, 30 May 2012.
30 Vladislav Kulikov, 'Ugolovnyi kodeks podobreet: Miniust vynes na obsuzhdenie variant smiagcheniia zakona', *Rossiskaia gazeta*, 9 June 2009; Kulikov, 'Ne sudimy budete', ibid., 11 June 2009; Kulikov, 'Prestupnaia rabota. Miniust predlozhil sokratit chislo arestantov za schet bolee gumannykh nazakanii', ibid., 23 July 2009; Vladimir Ovchinskii, 'Vstrechnye potoki', *Ogonek*, 25 May 2009; Ivan Rodin and Aleksandra Samarina, 'Ugolovnyi kodeks podvergnut liberalizatsii', *Nezavisimaia gazeta*, 30 September 2009: 'Poslanie Prezidenta federalnomu sobraniiu RF', *Rossiiskaia gazeta*, 12 November 2009.
31 Iana Iakovleva began her public campaign by publishing her own book, *Neelektronnye pisma*, Moscow: Praksis, 2008, and forming an organization 'Biznez—Solidarstnost' (on whose website the book may be found). The first book of the LECS group, containing transcripts of three roundtable discussions of the business crime issue, is *Verkhovensto prava i problemy ego obespecheniia v pravoprimenitelnoi praktike*, Moscow: Statut, 2009.
32 Peter H. Solomon, Jr, 'Criminalization, Decriminalization and Post Communist Transition: The Case of the Russian Federation', in William Munro and Margaret Murdoch (eds), *Building Justice in Post-Transition Europe: Processes of Criminalisation within Central and East European Societies*, London: Routledge, 2012; Peter H. Solomon, Jr, 'Sovershenstvovanie ugolovnogo zakonodatelstva v Rossiiskoi Federatsii: ekonomicheskie prestupleniia i gumanizatsiia', in *Kontsepsiia modernizatsii ugolovnogo zakonodatelstva v ekonomicheskoi sfere*, Moscow: Liberalnaia missiia, 2010, pp. 182–95. For stenograms of meetings, reprints of articles, and references to books published by LECS, see its rich website: http://www.lecscenter.org.
33 It is important to realize that the three reform packages did not constitute the only changes to the criminal law of the Russian Federation introduced in 2010 and 2011. There were a number of separate, smaller and unrelated initiatives, dealing with such matters as corporate raiding, drug offences, and paedophilia.
34 Interview with Georgii Smirnov, 4 June 2012; Viktor Diatlikovich, 'Svoboda kak politika', *Rusrep*, 19 April 2011, http://www.rusrep.ru/article/2011/04/19/freedom; V. V. Volkov, E. Paneiakh, and K. Titaev, 'Proizvolnaia aktivnost pravookhranitelnykh organov v sfere borby s ekonomicheskoi prestupnostiu. Analiz statistik', Analiticheskaia zapiska Instituta problem pravoprimeneniia, St Petersburg, 2010, at http://www.enforce.spb.ru (under analiticheskie zapiski); Olga V. Peshkova, 'Ogranicheniia arest predprinimatelei. Pervye rezultaty sudebnoi praktiki', *Sud'ia*, May 2011, pp. 30–3;

Leonid Nikitinskii, 'Gosudarstv 'silovykh struktur' mozhet postroit tol'ko 'rynochnuiu ekonomiki bez predprinimatelei', *Novaia gazeta*, 24 April 2011.
35 'Miniust predlozhil otlozhit dekriminalizatsiiu melkhikh prestupleniia', http://www.lenta.ru, 9 September 2010; Aleksandra Samarina and Ivan Rodin, 'Biznes prikazano zhdat. Dekriminalizatsiia zakonodatelstva v oblasti ekonomicheskikh prestuplenii zaderzhivaetsia', *Nezavisimaia gazeta*, 9 October 2010.
36 'O vnesenii izmenenii v Ugolovnyi kodeks RF, "Federalnyi zakon RF ot 7 marta 2011"'; Vladislav Kulikov, 'Net sroka bez dobra', *Rossiskaia gazeta*, 12 January 2011; Natalia Kozlova, 'Sud smigchitsia. Lishenie svobody budet po sereznomu povodu', ibid., 11 March 2011.
37 Vladislav Kulikov, 'Zakon obratnykh chisel', *Rossiskaia gazeta*, 12 April 2011; Fedor Bogdanovskii, 'Popravki v UK, kotorye uzhe vvedeny, eto tolko tsvetochki! Kollegi, gotovtes!' http://www.pravo.ru, 16 March 2012.
38 'O vnesenii izmenenii v Ugolovnyi kodeks RF i otdelnye zakonodatelnye akty RF', Federal zakon RF N20 ot 7 dekabria 2011, *Rossiskaia gazeta*, 8 December 2011. For examples of criticism and debate see: Vladimir Emelianenko, 'Gumanisticheskii bespredel,' *Profil*, 3 June 2011; Vladimir Panov, 'Tikhaia reforma 4', *Ekspert*, no. 28 (762), 18 June 2011; Tamara Shkel, 'Prestuplenie i nazakanie', *Rossiskaia gazeta*, 18 October 2011; Diatlikovich, 'Svoboda kak politika'; Olga Pavlikova, 'Negumannaia gumanizatsiia', *Profil*, 31 October 2011.
39 'Analiticheskaia zapiska o proekta federalnogo zakona o vnesenii izmenenii v UK RF', LECS, June 2011,http://www.lecs-center.org; Vladimir Radchenko and Alfred Zhalinskii, 'Ugolovnyi zakon: Bolshaia imitatsiia reformy', *Vedomosti*, 23 June 2011; ibid., 'Ugolovnyi zakon: politika izgnaniia biznesa', ibid., 24 June.
40 'Putin ob'iavil o vvedenii dolzhnosti upolnomochennogo po pravam biznesmenov', *Vedomosti*, 2 February 2012; 'Avtorskaia stat'ia Vladimira Putina "O nashikh ekonomicheskikh zadachakh"', ibid.; Andrei Nazarov, 'V etom godu iz tiurem mogut vyiti 13.5 tys predpriminimatelei', http://www.polit.ru, 28 May 2012; Maria-Luisa Tirmasta, Taisia Bekbulatova and Irina Granik, 'Boris Titov predlozhil amnistiiu dlia predprinimatelei', *Kommersant*, 15 June 2012; Interview with Andre Nazarov, 4 June 2012.
41 Anastasiia Kornia, 'Medvedevskaia liberalizatsiia UK ukhudshila polozhenie', *Vedomosti*, 16 May 2012.
42 The country that has recorded the most significant drop in the size of its prison population and share of prisoners in the population is Finland, where the latter fell from 250 per 100,000 to 70 between 1950 and 1990. This drop reflected not only changes in the law that encouraged fewer and shorter terms of imprisonment, but also changes in the political culture and culture of judging, as Finland sought to distance itself from the USSR and to rejoin the rest of Scandinavia. See Tapio Lappi-Seppala, 'Penal Policy in Scandinavia', in Michael Tonry (ed.), *Crime, Punishment, and Politics in Comparative Perspective*, Chicago and London: University of Chicago Press, 2007, pp. 217–96, especially pp. 228–44.
43 For a list of police scandals see Brian Taylor, 'Police Reform in Russia: A Policy Study', unpublished paper delivered at the 2011 Annual Convention of the ASEES, November 2011. The YouTube video on police corruption posted by Aleksei Dymovsky was reportedly viewed more than 700,000 times. Dymovsky now runs his own website offering help to citizens dealing with authorities. See http://www.dymovskyi.ru for background on the history of the police, and for policing in post Soviet Russia see Brian D. Taylor, *State Building in Putin's Russia: Policing and Coercion after Communism*, Cambridge: Cambridge University Press, 2011.
44 Natalia Taubina, 'Reforma: cho sdelano i chego ne khvataet,' *Obshchestvennyi verdikt*, 1 March 2012.
45 'Federal Law of the Russian Federation No.3-FZ "On the Police" of 7 February 2011', *Statutes and Decisions*, 46:4, July–August 2011. For decrees and regulations on the

implantation of the law, see 'Police in Russia: Reform or Rebranding? Responsibilities and Structure of the Ministry of Internal Affairs and the Police,' ibid., 46:5, September–October 2011; and an overview of the recertification process (attestation), ibid., 46:6, November–December 2011.
46 Sergei Poduzov, 'Is Police Reform Taking Place in Russia? A View from the Regions', *Russian Analytical Digest*, no. 84, 19 October 2010, pp. 7–9; Ilia Iashin and Vladimir Milov, 'Perestroika MVD—Ot militseiskogo proizvola k professionalnoi politsii', http://www.rusolidarnost.ru.
47 Taylor, 'Police Reform in Russia'.
48 Peter H. Solomon, Jr, 'The Reform of Policing in the Russian Federation', *The Australian and New Zealand Journal of Criminology*, 38:2, 2005, pp. 230–40; Brian D. Taylor, 'From Police State to Police State? Historical Legacies and Law Enforcement in Russia', unpublished, October 2011.
49 On the central role of indicators in the control and management of the police see V. V. Volkov, 'Ot militsii k politsii: reforma sistem otsenki deiatelnosti organov vnutrennikh del', Analiticheskaia zapiska Institut problem pravoprimeneniia, March 2011, available at http://www.enforce.ru under 'analiticheskie zapiski'. See also V. Volkov, 'Palochnaia sistema: instrument upravleniia'. *Vedomosti*, 19 February 2010.
50 Asmik Novikova, 'Sistema upravleniia v militsii: konstruirovanie virtualnoi reealnosti s realnymi postradavshimi', *Vestnik obshchestvennogo mneniia*, no. 2 (108), April–June 2011, pp. 38–46; Olga Shepeleva, 'Predlozheniia NPO po reforme sistemy otsenki deiatelnosti militsii', *Fond Obshchestvennyi verdikt*, 16 October 2011.
51 Asmik Novikova, *Upravlenie v politsiia: Biurokraticheskoe proizvodstvo prestupnosti*, Moscow: Fond Obshchestvennyi Verdikt, 2011; 'Reforma—iavnoe i skrytoe', Special issue of *Obshchestvennyi verdikt*, no. 2 (11), 2011,including four expert commentaries on MVD *Prikaz* no. 1310. These materials are reprinted on the website of Obshchestvennyi verdikt: http://www.publicverdict.org.
52 'Zaiavelnie rabochei gruppy pravozashchitnykh organizatsii po reforme MVD', 27 May 2011, *Chelovek i Zakon Marii El*, http://www.manandlaw.info.
53 Solomon, 'The Reform of Policing'; Leonid Kosals and Anastasia Duova, 'Commercialization of Police and Shadow Economy: The Russian Case', *Economic Sociology: The European Electronic Newsletter*, 13:2, March 2012, pp. 21–8; Theodore P. Gerber and Sarah E. Mendelson, 'Public Experiences of Police Violence and Corruption in Contemporary Russia; A Case of Predatory Policing?' *Law and Society Review*, 42, I, 2008, pp. 1–43.
54 Matthew Light, 'Police Reform in the Republic of Georgia: The Convergence of Domestic Policy and State Security in an Anti-Corruption Drive', unpublished paper presented at the annual meeting of the Law and Society Association, Chicago, June 2010.
55 For a comprehensive account see Richard Sakwa, *The Quality of Freedom: Khodorkovsky, Putin, and the Yukos Affair*, Oxford: Oxford University Press, 2009.
56 Mikhail Khodorkovsky, 'Rossiia v ozhidanii suda', *Kommersant Vlast*, 15 June 2009; William Pomeranz, 'Legal Reform Through the Eyes of Russia's Leading Jurists: The *Vlast* Debate on the Russian Judiciary', *Problems of Post-Communism*, May–June 2010, pp. 3–10. Khodorkovsky's goal was the development in Russia of independent courts and his choice of means included options that were in the air but probably not politically feasible, such as removing the executive from judicial selection, restricting the hiring of judges to mid career, and expanding the use of trial by jury.
57 Irina Tumilovich, 'Skandal s "otkroveniiami" po "delu Khodorkovskogo": storony vyzhidaiut', RAPSI, 16 February 2011; Ella Paneiakh, 'Extra Jus: Privychki i neprivychnoe', *Vedomosti*, 17 February 2011.
58 'Kto proverit Nataliu Vasilevu', *Radio Svoboda*, 17 February 2011; Gleb Kuznetsov, 'Sud nad Khodorkovskim: vina dokazana, nakazanie smiagcheno', RAPSI, 24 May 2011.

59 'Sudite sami', *Itogi*, no. 8, 2011, 21 February 2011.
60 'Doklad Soveta pri Prezidente RF po razvitii grazhdankogo obshchestva i pravam cheloveka o rezultatakh obshchestvennogo nauchnogo analiza sudebnykh materialov ugolovnogo dela M.B. Khodorkovskogo i P. L. Lebedeva (rassmotrennogo Khamovnicheskim raionnym sudom g. Moskvy s vyneseniem prigovora ot 27.12.2010 g.', Moscow, 2011, http://www.president-sovet,ru; 'Rekomendatsii po itogam provdeniia obshchestvennoi ekspertizy po ugolovnomu delu V. V. Khodorkovskogo i P. L. Lebedeva', ibid.; Natalia Gorodetskaia and Nikolai Sergeev, 'Mikhail Khodorkovskii i Platon Lebedev opravdany presidentskim sovetom', *Kommersant*, 22 December 2011; 'Ekspertnoe zakliuchenie v pravovom smysle instituta pomilovaniia,' i 'Dostatochno odnogo roscherka medvedskogo pera', *Osobaia bukva*, 16 March 2012.
61 'Prezidentskii sovet vnes zakliuchenie po delu Magnitskogo', *Chelovek i zakon*, 7 June 2011.
62 http://www.lecs-center.org.
63 Aleksandr Gabuev, 'Podvig sovetchika', *Kommersant Vlast*, 4 June 2012, pp. 15–23, especially 20.
64 http://www.indem.ru; http://www.enforce.ru.
65 http://www.publicverdict.org; http://www.zaprava.ru; http://www.prison.org; http://www.novaiagazeta.ru; http://www.rg.ru; http://www.kommersant.ru; http://www.rapsinews.ru; http://www.pravo.ru; http://www.sudinform.ru. There are a couple of dozen regionally based human rights groups as well, most of which report on particular incidents, but only a few of which have research capacity and take part in policy work. For a listing by region, see the website 'Rights in Russia': http://www.rightsinrussi.org.
66 http://www.supcourt.su ; http://www.arbitra.ru; http://www.ksf.ru; http://www.cdep.ru; http://www.genproc.gov.ru; http://www.mvd.ru ; http://www.fsb.ru ; http://www.sledcom.ru ; http://www.miniust.ru.
67 http://www.sartracc.ru; http://www.crimpravo.ru.
68 http://www.sutyiajik.ru ; http://www.soprotivlenie.org.
69 'Federalnyi zakon RF ot 28 iiuliia 2012 g. N 141-FZ "O vnesenii izmenenii v Ugolovnyi kodeks RF i odetelnye zakonodatelnye akty RF"' *Rossiiskaia gazeta*, 1 August 2012; 'Izmena rodine: shpionom smozhet stat kazhdyi', http://www.forbes.ru, 21 September 2012; 'Putin Signs Foreign Agent Law', http://www.en.rian.ru, 21 July 2012; Grigorii Tumanov, Aleksandr Chernykh and Pavel Korobov, 'Zakon o zashchite chuvst: oskorblenie verusiushchikh stanet ugolovnym prestupleniem', http://www.kommersant.ru, 27 September 2012.
70 Ivan Rodin and Aleksandra Samarina, 'Moshennikov razlozhat po polochkam', http://www.ng.ru, 24 October 2012.
71 Vladislav Kulikov, 'Sudit po vtoromu krugu: Verkhovnyi sud predlagaet rasshirit kompetentsiiu raionnykh sudov', http://www.rg.ru, 7 November 2012; Iana Iakovleva and Vadim Kliuvgant, 'Vse novye "novye obstoiatelstva"', http://www.vedomosti.ru, 20 November 2012.

3 Centre–periphery and state–society relations in Putin's Russia

John F. Young

Like clothing of a certain vintage, what was once dated eventually becomes fashionable again. For those who take a long-term perspective to the study of Russia, familiarity endures. This is especially so in centre–periphery relations and in the repetitive still births of local self-government. As Russia in 2012 commences another iteration of Putin as president, the dynamics of regional politics and state–society relations possess similarities with the long-standing tensions and challenges of the Russian state. We have seen this before. And while the blackmail of the single alternative offered justification for one-party centralization and the swelling of the state, both history and 2012 suggest that the consequences of hyper-statism also require reverse adjustments. All the power to the state, as both an idea and as a practice even partially pursued, was not an illegitimate response given the centrifugal forces, separatism, and the feudalism and *udel'nye kniazy* (appanage princes) of the 1990s. But an overshot mark promotes the pathologies that accompany the centralized hyper-state: corruption, bureaucratic sclerosis, and the illegitimacy of the political system. After more than a decade of Putin and Putinism, Russia is again in need of some *demokratizatsiia* and *perestroika*: a reform of already reformed reforms. That Putin 2.0 suggests his presidency will now introduce such measures requires elastic credulity among optimists. One is reminded of the dated Radio Yerevan anecdote, which inquired whether or not a man could become pregnant. Punchline: to date, not yet – but experiments continue.

Three decades ago, Gorbachev inherited a Brezhnevian sclerocracy, a centralized party-state apparatus that, in the words of Ken Jowitt, had lost its 'battle ethos'.[1] The Russian term commonly used is that of *zastoi* – stagnation or depression. This stagnation was not only a consequence of the absence of effective policy, but in large measure a predictable consequence of a centralized hyper-state. The command administrative system was overwhelmed by doing too much too often, and in too many places. *Zastoi* was manifest not only in the economy, as the state could not satisfy demands for economic production, but also in society, which had outgrown the administrative system and demanded increased opportunities for participation.[2] One response for many of these problems was the idea of self-government, which by the mid-1980s began to re-circulate with enthusiasm. Self-government was heralded not only by academics, but also by workers, community groups, and the mainstream press as a much-needed solution to many of the ills plaguing Soviet society and economic production. Self-government, it was argued, could serve as a panacea for the ills of bureaucracy and increase accountability of administration. It would increase democratic norms and behaviour in society, foster public interest and participation, and serve as a vital link between state and society.[3] The term was considered part of the greater process of *demokratizatsiia* (democratization), which, along with *uskorenie* (acceleration of economic production) and *glasnost'* (openness), became the holy trinity of early perestroika.

Gorbachev's reforms uncorked the bottle of *zastoi*. The pursuit of more effective administration and openness fostered environmental activism, national movements, worker strikes, investigative journalism, and the emergence of various political movements, factions, and parties. However, these developments, and the conflicting interests they generated, overwhelmed the unitary system of political power and quickened rather than averted economic decline. Rather than a dose of self-government to complement the leadership of the Communist Party, open competition added to the legitimacy crisis. Once the party began to face, and lose elections, a great unravelling followed. A failed push for recasting federal relations between the centre and the republics – and between republican governments and regional and local self-governments – led to the implosion of the Soviet Union in 1991. The vacuum of power that followed this implosion was hardly a victory for self-government or decentralization. It is true that, in the absence of a hyper-state, regional and local governments were less fettered by administrative control from above. Yet these regional and local governments were easily captured by particular, rather than public, interests, and typically lacked the resources and the administrative capacity to deal with the multiple demands of society. Decentralization, such as it occurred, was primarily by default – in the absence of central authority – rather than by design. Additionally, the common cause among different and disparate groups and movements against the established monopoly of the Communist Party proved insufficient to foster the continued cooperation and coordination so vital to self-government after the Communist Party lost power. Russian politics in the 1990s were divisive, confrontational, and chaotic.[4]

Efforts to recast and restructure political institutions in order to reshape the relationship between state and society were not only behind the collapse of the Soviet state, but animated many of the early tensions and conflicts in the post-Soviet Russian Federation. It is tempting to view centre–periphery relations from the perspectives of institutional development and federalism, and as a means to limit the role of the state or to help gauge the prospects for the rule of the law. Such worthy perspectives risk overshadowing the manner in which centre–periphery relations also reflect state–society relations. Admittedly, the combination of two distinct but complementary subjects will complicate any study limited to a single chapter. Yet reviewing the relationship between Moscow and its regions and cities is more than a review of which level of government does what, when, and how. Its primary relevance is what this relationship represents about the overall nature of the state and the society it rules or governs. As Paul Vinogradoff noted almost one hundred years ago, after another round of political turmoil and centralization, 'the growth of Russian society as a body distinct from the state is best illustrated by the stages in the formation of self-government'.[5]

An example of the rationale for local reform is found in the drafting and implementation of the Federal Law on Local Self-Government in 1991. Legislators and academics articulated a vision that would dismantle the unitary system of power and establish a societal model for self-government that would lie outside the reach of the state. Locally elected administrators accountable to locally elected councils would promote public participation and recast the relationship between communities and government. Exactly how these new organs of self-government would intersect with the state was unresolved, and early discussions in parliamentary committees even debated whether or not the provinces should be part of the state structure or self-governing, accountable only to society. Also debated was how to define executive–legislative relations at the local level and how local self-government would be effectively financed.[6] In short, while the concept of local self-government responded to the perceived need to limit the authority of the state and bring society in, new principles associated with both federalism and self-government invited many sorts of questions, all of which conflicted with the established practices of administrative order.

The challenge of constructing a state that incorporated principles of public participation and self-government proved to be overwhelming, not only in theory, but especially in practice. No matter how noble the vision, self-government was quickly overshadowed by other priorities. Economic reforms, for example, were also viewed by their architects as a mechanism to reshape state–society relations, and were considered more urgent. An immediate consequence of these controversial economic reforms in 1992 was the clash of executive and legislative authority between the Russian president and the Supreme Soviet. The horizontal contestation for power thus overshadowed vertical relationships between the centre and various regions, which became dominated by *ad hoc* relationships shaped by bargaining, personalities, and political strategy. Yeltsin's pyrrhic victory over parliament in October 1993 led to a new constitution that failed to resolve questions of authority and responsibility on the vertical axis with sufficient coherence, especially in terms of the allocation of resources across multi-level governments. This failure to systematize the demarcation of power on the vertical axis exacerbated, and in turn was exacerbated by, economic ruin. In this context of administrative chaos and economic decline, social forces were in disarray rather than a foundation for the construction of a coherent state.

In 2000, Putin inherited remnants of a once centralized state fused with new institutions partially and poorly designed for self-government. He also inherited a rising cacophony of political forces advocating for a recentralization of power. The weak state was recognized as an impediment not only to economic growth, but also to democracy and the future of Russia.[7] This was an odd predicament, particularly in light of the discussions and debates from only a decade earlier. How is it that limiting the power and reach of the state could shift so quickly from strategy to problem? In other terms, if the problem in 1990 was too much state, the challenge in 2000 was not enough. Yet there is a second angle for consideration: where was society in this dynamic between centre and periphery? Advocates of decentralization and democracy had earlier argued that self-government was a critical component of social and political development, yet efforts to cultivate self-government were now cast as creating impediments to Russia's future. Local politics were typically considered either fiefdoms for private interest or fractious debating chambers incapable of resolving local concerns. Journalist Leonid Radzikhovsky described the predicament of a privatized Russia in the mid-1990s:

> in such a big country as Russia there are no statesmen, and if there are no people for whom the interests of the state are more important than their own, there is no state at all. And if there are no public figures for whom the interests of society are more important than their own there is no society. There is only a place where people try 'to make money' as they can.[8]

While Russia clearly lacked a well-ordered state, it also just as clearly lacked a healthy civil society and the social requisites and experience for self-government. Trying to address both of these deficits at the same time, particularly in a country with the size and complexity of Russia, would be an impossible task. The pursuit of one risked jeopardizing the other.

In hindsight, Vladimir Putin's choices were limited. From a multitude of perspectives, without the preservation of the state there would be little rationale or opportunity to pursue economic, political or social transitions. While Putin's motivation to pursue centralization remains moot – the responsibilities of a statesman; a reflection of Russian political culture; narrow private interests; and likely a fluid combination of all three factors – the consequences of his work are clearly manifest. Over his first two terms in office, Putin reasserted the role of the state and strengthened the authority of the centre. And he found greater success in this endeavour than seemed possible at the outset of his presidency.[9] One does not have to agree with his reforms to be impressed with his accomplishments. Greater administrative control, financial monitoring, and, in many cases, financial dependency on the state were extended over non-governmental organizations. From the confiscation of Yukos to the extent to which the state influenced the media, from assertion of control over education and religion to the multiplication of bureaucrats, *ogosudarstvlenie*, or statification, of Russia was at the core of his presidency.[10] In the realm of strengthening the authority of the centre, Putin's pursuit of an ordered and systematized state is exceptionally evident. Among his reforms, Putin has:

- Asserted the territorial integrity of the state. The primary example of this assertion was the second Chechen War. This action was launched in 1999, during Putin's first tenure as prime minister. The first war had ended earlier in stalemate, coinciding with the presidential elections in 1996. The second war not only annihilated Chechnya and terminated independence, but also served

to demonstrate the lengths to which Putin would go to reassert authority and rein in the centrifugal forces of the 1990s;
- Pushed the reorganization of regional administration through a new framework of federal districts, which not only fostered more effective supervision of federal and regional administrations throughout the country, but also placed a filter between regional governors and Moscow. The seven federal districts later eroded in importance once the regions were more compliant with Moscow, but were an important step in reasserting central authority;
- Reformed the membership of the Council of the Federation, pushing regional governors and republican presidents out of the council, which neutered the influence of regional leaders in Moscow. Putin was able to accomplish this reform because he enjoyed majority support in the Duma, which overrode the council's veto. This is one of many examples that highlight the importance of parliamentary support;
- Stripped regional governors of their immunity from criminal prosecution, through which Putin gained the authority to dismiss governors who faced criminal charges, regardless of the result of those charges. Putin also claimed the right to dissolve regional legislatures if they failed to amend regional legislation that violated federal laws, and abrogated bilateral treaties that had been agreed to by his predecessor. Such moves helped set the table for the development of a *vertikal'* (vertical) system of power rather than authority premised on compromise and negotiation between equal partners of the centre and periphery;
- Streamlined and centralized the tax regime in the Russian Federation, which strengthened Moscow's hand in the allocation of transfers to the regions. This move coincided with a rapid increase in oil revenues, and a marked improvement in the fiscal health of the federal government. Putin suggested in his speech to the Federal Assembly in April 2007 that federal transfers had increased six fold since 2000;
- Demarcated powers among federal, regional, and local levels of government and between executive and legislative bodies at each level. This demarcation was tasked to one of Putin's loyal lieutenants, Dmitri Kozak. Among the original mandates of the Kozak commission was to match financial capacity with the existing authority of different levels of government, a much-needed reconciliation in Russia. Kozak, however, ended up pursuing the task in reverse: diminishing the authority of local governments to match their limited financial capacity. A new law on local government led to the creation of two tiers, effectively incorporating the higher tier of local government within the state system of power;[11]
- Strengthened the power *vertikal'* following the terrorist act in Beslan in 2004 by demanding the prerogative to appoint regional governors. Instead of popular elections, the president would nominate candidates, who would then be confirmed by the regional legislature. As regional legislatures that would not endorse the nomination could be dissolved, the change absorbed regional administration into the state apparatus;

- Altered the federal electoral system. Between 1993 and 2003, half the 450 seats in the Duma were elected by proportional representation, the other half from single member constituencies. Many deputies elected from these single member constituencies were independent and only loosely aligned to a political party or bloc; many more were representatives of regional elites. By changing the electoral system to full proportional representation, Putin consolidated the role of political parties and undermined regional and independent voices in the national parliament;
- Fostered the emergence of United Russia as the party of power. United Russia became the only coherent political organization that penetrated the whole territory of Russia. The party provided regional and local politicians with a network of colleagues and potential career opportunities. Coupled with the presidential prerogative to nominate governors, the rotation of cadres returned to Russia: mayors and governors were increasingly likely to have administrative experience from some other region rather the location of their appointment.

This recentralization is not a uniquely Russian experience. In his rough notes for a mid-nineteenth century study of France after the Revolution, Alexis de Tocqueville noted that tendencies towards decentralization in a political culture accustomed to a strong, centralized state are fleeting. He noted that the back and forth shifts between decentralization and centralization would create illusions of change, and he highlighted the repeated efforts towards decentralization in France in 1781, 1828, and 1848. In all three cases, an inevitable extension of centralization followed. 'In the beginning', wrote Tocqueville, 'we follow the logic of our principles. In the end, (we follow) our habits, our passions, power. In sum, the last word always remains with centralization, which in truth, fortifies itself in germ even when it is diminished in appearance.'[12]

To suggest that Russian culture is the primary explanation for the resurgence of the state is to ignore other powerful rationale for the return of the state. Putin surely responded with more than habit and passion. His response may also be explained by Tocqueville's third factor, the requirement of power. This requirement can be broken down further through contrasting explanations of whether the state is an ends or a means. On one hand, organizing power is part of a noble pursuit of building institutions designed to govern well. On the other hand, consolidating power is about appropriating more power as a means through which particular interests conveniently disguised as state interests could be defended and advanced. At the beginning of Putin's second term in office, it was fair to wonder whether or not the centralization of power could accurately be described as state building since, despite the flow of power to the state, Putin had rejected 'democratic state-building, with its separation of powers, free parliament, unfettered press, independent judiciary, rules of the game, and dynamic federalism'.[13] Such criticism highlighted the continuing and growing dysfunction of contemporary Russian government and society, the rampant corruption and kleptocracy, and the hollow institutions. By 2012, the return of Putin was viewed as evidence 'not of the strength, but the weakness of the system (Putin) has built'.[14]

While not without merit, such criticism tends to overlook the many significant efforts to rationalize and systematize the state apparatus noted above, even if such efforts were not in the interests of democracy. More worthy of criticism, however, is that Putin's response to the challenges of a weak state and a weak society overshot the mark. The centralization and consolidation of power undermined any capacity to promote pluralism and the competition of interests inherent to political systems with multiple levels of power open to various social forces.

The four-year Medvedev intermission continued Putin's policies. Although some early hopes for a more enlightened managed democracy surfaced at the outset of Medvedev's term, any suggestions of relaxing centralized authority failed to materialize. Yes, the financial downturn of 2008 may have diminished any wind in the sails of such suggestions. But the expected return of Putin was the most notable event of Medvedev's term of office. In terms of centre–periphery relations, Medvedev continued the consolidation of central authority through *varyagi*: regional and municipal executives appointed by Moscow without loyalties to the region or its elite. So, for example, the new governor of Arkhangelsk was previously the mayor of Yakutsk, six time zones away. Such a rotation undermined the influence of local and regional elites, strengthened loyalty and accountability to the Kremlin, and was occasionally defended as a countermeasure against local corruption. The rotation of cadres was also connected with the further development of United Russia (UR), otherwise known as the party of power, and UR-dominated executive and legislative leadership throughout the country. By 2010, 78 of 83 governors were members of UR, and the party had a majority in 81 of 83 regional legislatures.[15] In essence, the practice of rotating cadres suggests that Moscow entertained little confidence in the ability of local voters to hold mayors or governors accountable. The state would do so instead, even if it caused violence to the principles of self-government. And the struggle against corruption saw no real progress. Medvedev started his term as president with significant fanfare, convening an Anti- Corruption Council and introducing new legislation to monitor the income of state bureaucrats. But the elimination of executive elections in the regions had already undermined what limited influence the public had to hold officials accountable, and the state proved to be inept at monitoring itself. Even Medvedev admitted that, despite the efforts, there were only very modest returns. By 2012, outgoing President Medvedev's new anti-corruption strategy focused on deregulation and privatization – in short, shrinking the state rather than expanding it. Sergei Guriev, rector of the New Economic School in Moscow explained, 'government interference in the economy through state ownership and excessive regulation is the main way a corrupt official increases control over society and business'.[16]

Joel Moses has correctly pointed out that centralization and the rotation of cadres began to backfire.[17] The more power concentrated in the centre, the greater the risk of backlash against Moscow in the regions. If state building is characterized by the development of a *vertikal'*, it must be pointed out that the results have not been warmly embraced by local elites or the public at large. Neither has it improved public perceptions of corruption in public administration. This is why any growing opposition to the *vertikal'* is most clearly manifest in the regions and municipal governments. In Murmansk, for example, incumbent Mayor Mikhail Savchenko was soundly defeated for re-election in 2009. He was the UR candidate and was backed by the national party leadership. His victorious opponent was Sergei Subbotin, who had been endorsed by the regional governor, Yuri Yevdokimov, and ran as a local candidate loyal to Murmansk. In the aftermath of the Murmansk insurrection against Moscow and UR, President Medvedev removed Yevdokimov, a fourteen-year governor, from his position. His replacement was Dmitry Dmitrienko, a *varyag* from a federal ministry in Moscow.[18] One year later, Subbotin was unanimously dismissed from his post as mayor by the UR-dominated city council and Governor Dmitrienko.[19] Yet in January 2012, Dmitrienko resigned from his position as a consequence of the abysmal election results for UR in Murmansk during the December 2011 Duma elections. UR gained only 32 per cent of the vote, compared to 56 per cent in the previous elections of 2007, which led to Putin singling out Murmansk for its 'very, very poor effort'.[20] In Murmansk and other cities, local communities have rejected perceived interference from the party of power and Moscow and supported the elections of local opposition candidates.[21]

Thus, it is fair to suggest that Russia in 2012 has, to one degree or another, overshot the mark regarding centralization. Just as the centralized and bloated Brezhnevian state was characterized by *zastoi*, the accumulation of power and *ogosudarstvlenie* risks the dwindling of legitimacy, vitality, and accountability. Nikolay Petrov characterizes the contemporary Russian state as 'big but weak':

> Its weakness is related to its internal ineffectiveness and omnipresent façade, given the inadequacy of its legal institutions, the functions of which have become 'privatized' and are used to further individual, group, or corporate interests. Finally, the state is weak because of overcentralization, whereby the center of gravity during all important decision making processes rests at the top and the entire system becomes sluggish.[22]

Does this mean Russia is back where it started prior to Gorbachev? No. One must recognize the role that economic change, the convertible rouble, the incorporation of technology and social media, foreign travel, the flow of information, and elections (even with limited choices) now play in distinguishing contemporary Russia from its Soviet past. Likewise, comparing Russia of 2000 with 2012 reveals a revitalized yet excessive state, improved standard of living, and economic growth. At the same time, state–society relations have not matured in any significant way. The centralization and consolidation of power notwithstanding, there remains a pronounced conflation of private with public interest, and societal influence over the state is limited by the limited pluralism of Putin's network of power. In this regard, while there are marked differences between the contemporary Russian state and Russian past, the challenges and weaknesses of too much state have returned. Putin's *vertikal'* carries with it the shades of the hyper-state.

Tensions between state and society and between centre and periphery were revealed during the latest parliamentary election cycle. Leading up to the election, critics of the party of power – or the party of swindlers and thieves, in the words of Aleksei Navalny – encouraged voters to vote for any other option or to destroy their ballots, and to get involved in election monitoring. On the day of election, allegations of vote rigging and malfeasance by the governing party put into question even the disappointing returns for UR. Putin's party gained a narrow majority with 49 per cent of the popular vote and 53 per cent of the 450 seats in the Duma. These results represented a decline of 15 per cent in the popular vote from 2007, and a decline from the 70 per cent seat majority UR enjoyed in parliament prior to the election. Beyond the numerical results, however, was the very limited degree to which the election served to legitimate the government. Some placed the actual vote for UR as low as 40 per cent.[23] And the level of disdain for the results and the government was demonstrated by the large protests in cities around the country, the largest since the 1990s. Putin was publically booed, and Russian society seemed to re-engage in the public square with enthusiasm after more than a decade long hiatus.[24] Disdain was also manifest in the jokes and social media that circulated: 'Breaking news: Vladimir Churov, head of the central elections commission of Russia, has been badly injured in a fire. He has sustained burns over 146 per cent of his body'.[25] In the aftermath of this election questions arose concerning Putin's prospects for the March presidential election and the legitimacy of the Russian state.[26]

The state's response to this social and political ferment indicates its defensiveness. Outgoing President Medvedev attempted to salvage his reputation by proposing a return to elections for regional governors and revised the statutes concerning the registration of political parties and which parties could contest elections. The registration of political parties was made less onerous, requiring only 500 members rather than 40,000, and another bill ended the obligation of parties to petition for inclusion on election ballots beyond the presidential election. Medvedev's proposal to elect rather than appoint regional governors to five-year terms was also a concession to public frustration against *varyagi* and the Kremlin's unitary *vertikal'*. While the proposal for elected governors was eventually watered down by a 'filter' that would require the nomination of candidates by members of the corresponding legislature, the shift away from direct executive appointment was a clear concession to voter frustration with the minimal capacity to influence their political leaders. These proposals were approved by the Duma in March 2012.

While Medvedev's final months in office were marked by modest reversals, what of Mr Putin? In the first two months of 2012, Vladimir Putin was listed as author of four essays published over consecutive weeks in four different newspapers. Collectively, these essays reflect Putin's perspectives towards the past 20 years and constitute both an explanation for his actions and an electoral platform for the election that followed.[27] For Putin, the post-Soviet era is over: the economic, social, and political chaos of the 1990s has been resolved. The self-identified 'humble servant' formed and led a team of like-minded individuals that heroically delivered Russia from the blind alley of civil war, restored constitutional order, and sparked economic growth. The authority and power of the state was restored. At the same time, Putin suggested that society was still underdeveloped, and he devoted two essays to the challenges of a multi-ethnic state and state–society relations. As the signed author of these essays, Putin articulated an allegiance to statism only thinly veiled by multiple references to civil society and democracy:

> The self-determination of the Russian people is to be a multi-ethnic civilization with Russian culture at its core. ... Russian people are state-builders ... Their great mission is to unite and bind together a civilization ... a type of state civilization where there are no ethnicities but where 'belonging' is determined by a common culture and shared values. This kind of civilizational identity is based on preserving the dominance of Russian culture, although this culture is represented not only by ethnic Russians, but by all the holders of this identity, regardless of their ethnicity.[28]

He then went on to suggest that a multi-ethnic state had little room for national self-determination or Russian chauvinism, both of which would threaten Russian statehood. In an almost Mussolini-esque manner, Putin clearly identified the interests of the state as the greatest priority. The interests of the state thus supersede democracy, and society must become mature enough and capable of channelling democracy in the interests of the state. The maturity level for self-government was not yet evident:

> Our society consisted of people who had been freed from communist dogma but had not yet learned to be the masters of their destinies, who still waited for benefits from the state, often yielded to the temptation of illusions, and had not yet learned to stand up against manipulation.[29]

Putin referenced Pavel Novgorodtsev, an early twentieth century legal scholar, to suggest that mere liberty and universal suffrage would not be enough to develop Russia's future. And Putin's one directional understanding of the relationship between state and society was demonstrated by his conflation of rights with entitlements. Rights are things the state bestows on society:

> In terms of which rights people consider to be their priorities, the right to employment (and with it the right to earn an income), the right to free healthcare and education for children are a long way ahead at the top of the list. Restoring and guaranteeing people these rights have been the key objective of the Russian state, which Dmitry Medvedev and I have worked to achieve during our terms as president of Russia.[30]

And in the first of the four essays, Putin stated:

> I see our goal in years to come as sweeping away all that stands in the way of our national development, completing the establishment in Russia of a political system, a structure of social guarantees and safeguards for the public, and an economic model that together form a single, living, ever-changing organism of state that is, at the same time, resilient, stable, and healthy.[31]

Collectively, these essays identify Putin as an unapologetic statist, with democracy, culture, self-government, and economic development as the means to preserve and promote the state, rather than the other way around. This explains why political accountability, corruption, and legitimacy take a back seat to the state and its sovereignty: first comes the state, and then come endeavours to moderate the consequences. Russia is a cause and the state is an end in itself, rather than a means for society to pursue its goals and aspirations. His position begs the question whether or not his return to power will lead to a recasting of state–society relations in any meaningful way. His rationale is not indefensible, particularly in light of the circumstances of the Russian state since 1990. But it is evident that Putin's efforts to moderate any pathologies of statism will be limited by the interests of the state rather than society.

Putin's electoral victory in March was greeted with the same level of disdain that met the parliamentary elections the previous December. Allegations of vote rigging and manipulation circulated widely, and the results – almost a two-thirds majority for Putin on the first ballot – led to public demonstrations and arrests. Although Putin was sworn into office in May, it is clear that his rule will suffer from a diminution of legitimacy compared to his two earlier terms of office. As with the parliamentary elections, the regional breakdown of the vote reveals significant variation across the country. Among the regions with the lowest levels of support for Putin were Moscow City, Moscow Oblast, some 'heartland' regions such as Kostroma, Orel, and Vladimir, and major Siberia regions, such as Novosibirsk, Irkutsk, Omsk, and Khabarovsk. Official results have these regions' support for Putin at between 48 and 58 per cent. The top ten regions for Putin were ethnic enclaves, where electoral violations are often routine: Chechnya, Dagestan, Karachai-Cherkassia, and Tuva all reported 90 per cent or higher. Opposition to Putin, then, is not limited to economically depressed areas or ethnic republics. In light of these electoral results, it seems likely that Putin's power *vertikal'* will not find future opposition from an alternative *vertikal'*. Instead, opposition is most likely to emerge from an assortment of different regional and local coalitions of interests. This predicament helps explain the frustration of many voters. With limited opportunity to make significant choice, either in the parliamentary or presidential election, they vented their animosity. Putin's tendency towards the hyper-state has little room to accommodate pluralism. This is why regional and local politics are likely to be revitalized, and once again animate Russian politics.

A few contrasting scenarios might be worth identifying for the near future. A Putin optimist would examine the prospects for Russia through the lens of stability and expect continued economic and social development. The avuncular state, led by the able and astute President Putin, will supervise the gradual maturation of society. Regional and local governments will evolve as schools of sovereign democracy, where society will harmonize their interests with the interests of the state. Civil society will thus emerge gradually, in collaboration and cooperation with the government. The academic, Leonid Polyakov, writing in *Nezavisimaia gazeta,* suggests that Putin's leadership thus personifies the hopes for a new stage of democratic development, even misattributing Tocqueville's phrase 'schools of democracy' to President Putin.[32] Such optimism might be admirable, but it fails to explain the apparently increasing frustration with the status quo and the limited opportunities for effective participation in the political process. It is highly unlikely that the state that has consolidated and centralized power can now begin to cultivate and promote pluralism. Formally, Putin is back in power, but he does not enjoy the same latitude as he experienced in his earlier terms in office. His majority in parliament has diminished, new political parties will contest elections in the regions, and there is likely to be increased activity of political opposition in the regions and municipal governments and greater public scrutiny of the affairs of the state. Even more surprising, given the centralization of power, is that the city of Moscow appears to reject Putin with the loudest voice. When polls compare respondents who support Putin against those who oppose him, the gap has declined from a plus 60 rating throughout 2010 to a steady 30 by June 2012.[33] While many Western politicians would love to have such positive support in the polls, there are few transparent reasons such as economic turmoil for the decline. Instead, Putin may have passed his best-before date, and Russian society may have already begun to outgrow the Putin state.

A second scenario provides a realist's perspective on the next decade under Putin. Rather than a conflict-free, gradual merging of state and society, a cacophony of interests will be expressed at all levels of society. These interests will multiply, and will increasingly pressure the state and seek accommodation.[34] State–society relations will be marked by confrontation and compromise, not unlike the latter years of the Gorbachev era. This is not a suggestion that Putin's state will implode, but that society will find its many voices and push the contestation of values and policies on a state poorly designed to accommodate such pluralism and increasingly limited in its power. Society will chip its way back in from the cold. In this scenario, regional and local politics will be the primary battlegrounds, and the bloated state will require additional reforms and concessions. Rather than society conforming to the state, the state will be required to address the varied interests of society – hardly a pretty picture, but a realistic vision of pluralist politics.

A third scenario is much more fatalist. In such a scenario, Putin will resist any fracturing of power and will maintain the consolidation of authority. Managed democracy will continue, despite any rhetoric to the contrary, and civil society (such as it exists) will continue to be monitored, regulated, and influenced by the state. The centralized state will retain its influence throughout the regions, inhibiting pluralism and protecting the interests of those who control the state. Corruption and inertia will continue to erode the legitimacy of the state and eventually lead to a more protracted political crisis, directed against the network of power and private interests that can no longer disguise itself as the state.

Yes, the Russian state is bloated and over-centralized. Putin the state-builder has restored some semblance of order to the institutions of government. But the principles of self-government are almost as lacking as they were 30 years ago, and society has been marginalized again. Justified or not, this marginalization invites the pathologies of old. Political platforms aside, it is unlikely that Putin's leadership will promote any meaningful development of self-government, which will require autonomous power and authority, and confidence in society. Instead, limited political pluralism will emerge from local and regional governments, but such developments are likely to be obstructed rather than promoted by the overwhelming power of the central state. In this matter, centre–periphery relations highlight the limited influence that society has had over the state, and will be a harbinger of any change to come.

Notes

1 Jowitt suggested that bureaucratic sclerosis was the consequence of the Soviet regime's loss of its 'combat ethos' and its organizational integrity. See Ken Jowitt, 'Soviet Neotraditionalism: The Political Corruption of a Leninist Regime', *Soviet Studies* 35:3, July 1983, pp. 275–97. See also Jan Pakulski, 'Legitimacy and Mass Compliance: Reflections on Max Weber in Soviet-Type Systems', *British Journal of Political Science*, 16:1, January 1986.

2 See, for example, D. D. Tsabriia, *Sistema Upravleniia*, Moscow, 1990, and Ron Hill, 'Party–State Relations and Soviet Political Development', *British Journal of Political Science*, 10:2, April 1980, pp. 149–65.

3 See, for example, discussions of self-government in the Soviet press: *Moskovskaia Pravda*, 6 and 9 October 1987, and 20 November 1987; *Sovetskoe Zaural'e*, 25 October 1987; and *Sovetskaia Sibir'*, 11 June 1987.

4 For a revealing perspective, see Vladimir Shlapentokh, 'Early Feudalism: The Best Parallel for Contemporary Russia', *Europe–Asia Studies*, 48:3, May 1996, pp. 392–411. See also the same author's 'Hobbes and Locke at Odds in Putin's Russia', *Europe–Asia Studies*, 55:7, November 2003, pp. 981–1007.

5 Paul Vinogradoff, *Self-Government in Russia*, London: Constable and Company Ltd, 1915.

6 See, John F. Young, 'Russia's Elusive Pursuit of Balance in Local Government Reform', in Cameron Ross and Adrian Campbell (eds), *Federalism and Local Politics in Russia*, London: Routledge, 2009, pp. 248–62; and Young, 'Parallel Patterns of Power? Local Government Reform in Late Imperial and Post-Soviet Russia', *Canadian Slavonic Papers*, 42:3, September 2000, pp. 269–94.

7 Vladimir Gel'man discusses these forces in 'Leviathan's Return: The Policy of Recentralization in Contemporary Russia', in Ross and Campbell (eds), *Federalism and Local Politics in Russia*, pp. 1–24. See also Kathryn Stoner-Weiss, *Resisting the State: Reform and Retrenchment in Post-Soviet Russia*, New York: Cambridge University Press, 2006; and Anastasia V. Obydenkova, 'A Triangle of Russian Federalism: Democratization, (De-)Centralization, and Local Politics', *Publius*, 41:4, April 2011, pp. 734–41.

8 Leonid Radzikhovsky, *Novoe Russkoe Slovo*, 18 August 1995, as cited in Shlapentokh, 'Early Feudalism', p. 399.

9 See John F. Young, 'What Putin has Wrought: Centralization and the State in Contemporary Russia', in J. L. Black and Michael Johns (eds), *From Putin to Medvedev: Continuity or Change?*, Manotick: Penumbra Press, 2009, pp. 38–52.
10 Gerald M. Easter, 'The Russian State in the Time of Putin', *Post-Soviet Affairs*, 24:3, July–September, 2008, pp. 199–230.
11 See John F. Young and Gary N. Wilson, 'The View from Below: Local Government and Putin's Reforms', *Europe–Asia Studies*, 59:7, November 2007, pp. 1071–88.
12 Alexis de Tocqueville, in Francois Furet and Francoise Melonio (eds), *The Old Regime and the Revolution, vol. II: Notes on the French Revolution and Napoleon*, translated by Alan S. Kahan, Chicago: University of Chicago Press, 2001, p. 261.
13 John B. Dunlop, 'Backsliding in Moscow', *Hoover Digest*, no. 1, 2005. Easter also references some of these concerns in 'The Russian State in the Time of Putin'. Stephen Skowronek defined the task of state building as an 'exercise in reconstructing an already established organization of state power'. With the noted exception of revolution, the success of state building 'hinges on recasting official power relationships within governmental institutions and on altering on-going relations between state and society', Stephen Skowronek, *Building a New American State: The Expansion of National Administrative Capacities, 1877–1920*, Cambridge: Cambridge University Press, 1982, p. ix.
14 Stephen Holmes, 'Fragments of a Defunct State', *London Review of Books*, 34:1, January 2012.
15 See Robert Orttung, 'Center–Periphery Relations', in Lipmann and Petrov, *Russia 2020*, p. 339. See also, Aleksandr Kynev, 'Political Systems in the Russian Regions', in Lipmann and Petrov, Russia 2020, pp. 417–34; Joel C. Moses, 'Russian Local Politics in the Putin–Medvedev Era', *Europe–Asia Studies*, 62:9, November 2010, pp. 1427–52; and John F. Young, 'What Putin has Wrought'.
16 Masha Charney, 'Dmitry Medvedev's New Assault on Corruption in Russia', *Russia Now*, 2 April 2012. See also Gulnaz Sharautdinova, 'Subnational Governance in Russia: How Putin Changed the Contract with His Agents and the Problems it Created for Medvedev', *Publius*, 40:4, 2010, pp. 672–96.
17 Joel C. Moses, 'Russian Local Politics in the Putin–Medvedev Era'.
18 Ibid.
19 Trude Petterson, 'Unanimous Vote for Murmansk Mayor's Dismissal', *Barents Observer*, 3 June 2010.
20 Alexei Druzhinin, 'Two Russian Governors to be Sacked', *RIA Novosti*, 24 January 2012.
21 In 2012, the hunger strike of mayoralty candidate Oleg Schein in Astrakhan, the stunning victory of Evgeny Uralshov in Yaroslavl as a result of a united opposition against UR candidate Iakov Yakushev, and the victory of Sergei Andreev in Togliatti are further examples.
22 Nikolay Petrov, 'The Excessive Role of a Weak Russian State', in Lipmann and Petrov, *Russia 2020*, p. 303.
23 http://www.vybory.izbirkom.ru. On allegations and analysis, see Dmitri Trenin, Maria Lipman, Alexey Malashenko, Sergei Aleksashenko, Natalia Bubnova and Nikolay Petrov, 'Duma Elections: Expert Analysis', http://www.carnegieendowment.org/2011/12/13/duma-elections-2011/8kkf. Allegations of vote-rigging were buttressed by wonky results: in Rostov, 140 per cent of registered voters took part in elections, and in Chechnya, there was 99.5 per cent turnout with over 99 per cent in favour of United Russia.
24 Trenin, *et al.*, 'Duma Elections: Expert Analysis'.
25 Alexey Kovalov, 'Russians Express Their Frustrations with Explosion in Political Satire', *The Guardian*, 22 December 2011.

26 See, for example, Ariel Cohen, 'Russian Elections: The End of an Era?', *National Interest*, 6 December 2011; and Walter Rodgers, 'After Russia's Elections, Public Anger at Putin: Can He Fix Corruption?', *Christian Science Monitor*, 8 December 2011.
27 Vladimir Putin, 'Russia in Focus: The Challenges We Must Face' was published first in *Izvestiia*, 16 January 2012; 'The Ethnicity Issue' was published in *Nezavisimaia gazeta*, 23 January 2012; 'Economic Tasks' in *Vedomosti*, 30 January 2012; and 'Democracy and the Quality of Government' in *Kommersant*, 6 February 2012. The essays were also published in translation on the website of the Office of the Prime Minister. Quotations here are from the translated versions.
28 Putin, 'The Ethnicity Issue'.
29 Putin, 'Democracy and the Quality of Government'.
30 Ibid.
31 Putin, 'Russia in Focus'.
32 Leonid Polyakov, 'Puti rossiiskoi demokratii', *Nezavisimaia gazeta*, 5 July 2012.
33 Kirill Rogov, 'Itogi politicheckogo sezona: granitsy vlasti Putina', *Vedomosti*, 11 July 2012.
34 Rogov notes that while roughly 1 per cent of the Moscow population participates in demonstrations, more than 50 per cent are sympathetic or loyal to the protestors and two-thirds condemn any tightening of constraints against demonstrations. Such claims indicate that the latent power of society is much stronger than otherwise manifest.

4 The challenges and prospects of reforming Russia's higher education system

Elena Maltseva

It is often argued that a close correlation exists between the quality of a country's higher education and its democratic performance and economic development.[1] Seymour Martin Lipset, for example, stated that 'education presumably broadens men's outlooks, enables them to understand the need for norms of tolerance, restrains them from adhering to extremist and monistic doctrines, and increases their capacity to make rational electoral choices'. In other words, 'if we cannot say that a "high" level of education is a sufficient condition for democracy, the available evidence does suggest that it comes close to being a necessary condition'.[2]

Economists also confirmed the important role of education in promoting positive political and economic changes. They argued that, although the relationship between education and economic growth could vary over time, and although the direction of causal mechanisms was not always clear, education did contribute to economic growth.[3] There is thus some consensus among scholars that without quality education, a country's population is less competitive economically and lacks the necessary skills to engage in the complexities of the contemporary world and to check the country's governing powers.

Numerous studies suggest that good-quality higher education is an important factor in facilitating positive economic, political and social changes in societies.[4] For example, many observers attribute India's leap onto the world economic stage to its decades-long, successful efforts to provide high-quality, technically oriented higher education to a large number of its citizens.[5] In other words, higher education leads to a more prosperous, entrepreneurial and civic society.

Following the breakup of the Soviet Union, many post-Soviet governments needed to re-examine the principles of Soviet education and to adjust their education systems to new democratic realities, while simultaneously maintaining the quality of their educational services, scientific research and innovation. Yet despite the determination with which the education reforms were pursued and the governments' optimistic views of possible reform outcomes, in many post-Soviet countries the reforms in fact failed to achieve the desired results. For example, in Russia the education reform launched in the early 1990s, and conducted simultaneously with liberal economic reforms, resulted in a rapidly deteriorating quality of higher education and in significant brain drain. The country's financial difficulties and wide-ranging political decentralization contributed to the establishment of numerous private institutions of dubious quality and with weak credentials.

Even at nationally recognized universities, payments became an essential part of student life, thus defying the principle of free and accessible education for all. This process was accompanied by growing demoralization among the remaining academic staff and within the student body, resulting in growing corruption and poor ethical standards. As a result, the quality of academic research also declined: by the early 2000s, of more than 600 state higher education institutions (HEIs) operating in Russia, only a dozen could be classified as research oriented, with the prestige of the Russian Academy of Science also dwindling.[6]

This period also saw significant changes in student preferences: the majority now chose market-oriented fields of study, such as economics, business administration and law, whereas programmes in the social or applied sciences witnessed dramatic declines in enrolment. At the same time, however, little has changed in the academic curricula or in teaching methodologies (which remain Soviet in style), especially in the humanities and social sciences.[7] These kinds of negative developments undermined the quality of Russian higher education, leaving policy makers with sensitive and painful questions regarding the future of Russian education and the country's ability to compete with such education powerhouses as the USA, the UK and Japan.

An attempt to improve the state of Russia's higher education system occurred under the leadership of Vladimir Putin. In 2002, the government passed 'The Concept for the Modernization of Russian Education until 2010', and it went on to introduce several changes in Russia's system of higher education.[8] In 2003, Russia joined the Bologna Process and moved to the bachelor's-master's (or four-plus-two-year) system. It also introduced the Unified State Exam (USE), akin to the North American SAT, meant to replace entrance exams to state universities. In 2006, the government chose education as one of its four major national projects, alongside support for agriculture, the provision of accessible housing and the development of healthcare.[9] Within the framework of this project, the government created seven federal universities and several national research universities (NRU), increasing their funding. It also announced its intention to improve the hiring process at Russian HEIs, to invest in research and innovation and to attract international specialists to raise the prestige of Russia's higher education system.[10] Furthermore, the government claimed it would promote the modernization of teaching methods and curricula at Russian universities, especially in the social sciences and the humanities. Speaking to the heads of Russian universities in the summer of 2011, Prime Minister Putin urged the further modernization of Russia's higher education system and stated that 'our next steps should be aimed at modernising the entire network of higher education institutions in Russia, to make it so that the honourable title of university, academy or institute indeed means in practice modern quality and ample education, contemporary education'.[11]

While many of these initiatives deserve praise, the government might better focus on promoting greater competitiveness and openness in the academic hiring process and on improving the training, working conditions and remuneration of Russian academics, offering them greater opportunities for travel, research and language training. By raising the wages of Russian academics and improving the overall environment in higher education and on the academic job market, the government will be able to attract some bright young minds and to revive the dynamism at Russian universities, which will gradually facilitate the successful integration of the Russian academy into the global education market. In addition, Russia's HEIs should promote active learning techniques as a method of instruction and should encourage greater cooperation between academic staff and students. Together, these initiatives would offer academics and students both more freedom and greater opportunities for participation in the education process, eventually contributing to the further democratization and modernization of Russian society and the country's economy.

The Soviet system of higher education

The origins of the Soviet system of higher education date back to the Great October Revolution. The upheavals of World War One, of the revolution and of the ensuing civil war had all thinned the ranks of the Russian intelligentsia and of the labouring classes, so that the Soviet government faced the problem of how to rebuild the country quickly from the ruins of the Russian empire. It recognized the need for an effective education reform, because the country required more scientists, engineers and skilled workers of all kinds.[12] Bolshevik Russia's first constitution in 1918, and all subsequent Soviet constitutions (1924, 1936, 1977), therefore proclaimed the right to an education, including a higher education, made possible by free access to schools and universities, a wide network of educational institutions and stipends for students.[13]

By the mid-1970s, following a series of reforms introduced by the Soviet government during the 1950s and 1960s, the Soviet education system had stabilized and taken on its most distinctive features, which all former Soviet republics inherited following the collapse of the Soviet Union (see Figure 4.1). In brief, a child would usually begin his or her educational journey in a pre-school establishment, such as a nursery or a kindergarten, which accepted children from the age of two or three months to seven years. These pre-school establishments were often run by farms and industrial plants and factories, though local departments of education operated some.[14]

The next step in the Soviet education system was the secondary school, which was divided into three stages: elementary school (grades 1–3), incomplete secondary school (grades 4–8) and complete secondary school (grades 9–10).[15] As is evident from Figure 4.1, compulsory schooling ended after the eighth grade, when students could decide what to do next. They had several options: The majority went on to complete two more years of schooling, during which they studied general subjects such as Russian, mathematics, history and the like, and also had the opportunity to specialize in a particular subject. At the end of the tenth grade, students received a secondary school certificate known as the Attestation of Maturity (*Attestat Zrelosti*), which entitled them to apply for admission to institutes of higher education. But it did not guarantee them entry: a preliminary examination had to be taken by all applicants, and only applicants with the best grades were accepted.[16]

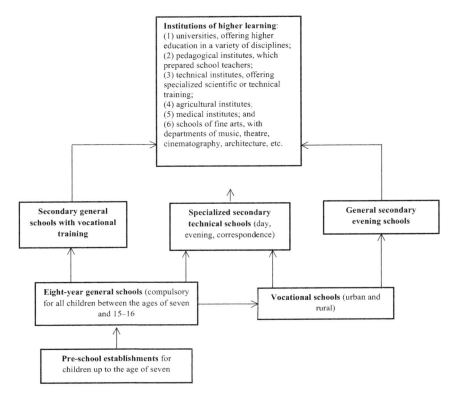

Figure 4.1 The Soviet education system

Source: N. P. Kuzin, M. I. Kondakov, P. V. Zimin, M. N. Kolmakova, V. I. Lubovsky, G. V. Berezina, and A. I. Foteyeva, *Education in the USSR* (Moscow: Progress Publishers, 1972), 18 and 121.

A smaller percentage of the students went on to attend secondary specialized schools, which offered a combination of general and vocational education. Two types of secondary specialized schools were known: *tekhnikumy*, with courses in electronics, engineering, textiles, metallurgy, transport and the like, and *uchilishcha*, which offered medical (e.g. for nurses or pharmacists), artistic or pedagogical training. The students who finished these specialized secondary schools also had the chance to apply for admission to HEIs. The majority of youngsters, however, went straight into jobs after the completion of their education.

Perhaps one of the most remarkable aspects of the Soviet education system was a spectacular rise in the number of institutions of higher education, spread equably across the country. If in 1914 there were 105 such institutions, including eight universities, concentrated primarily in major Russian cities, by 1959 there were already 766, 40 of which were universities. The number of men and women in higher education also increased: in 1914 there were 127,400 students, but in 1976, total enrolment reached nearly five million.[19]

Competition for entry into institutions of higher learning in the Soviet Union was fierce, with only a tiny proportion of applicants accepted to institutes and universities following the examinations.[20] Once accepted, students' performance was continually checked with the help of essays, laboratory assignments, homework, exams (usually a combination of written and oral testing) and final diploma work. On graduation, if a student wanted to continue his or her education, two higher degrees existed – the Candidate of Sciences (*Kandidat Nauk*) and the Doctor of Sciences (*Doktor Nauk*). The degree of Candidate of Sciences required at least three years of further study after graduation, during which candidates (*aspiranty*) had to conduct a piece of original research for publication in their own fields, and then to defend it at a public hearing before an examining board appointed by the appropriate institution. The degree of Doctor of Sciences was awarded much more rarely and was regarded as extremely distinguished. To qualify for this honour, a specialist had to hold the Candidate degree, have done several years of active work in his or her field, and have conducted and published major independent research, defended before an academic council.[21]

The Soviet system of education was highly centralized and rigid. Each institution had a *rector* at the top, who was assisted by a *deputy rector* or *prorector*. Both were appointed and dismissed by the USSR Ministry of Higher Education, to which they were responsible. Planning and administration were the responsibilities of the Academic Council (*Uchonyi Sovet*), chaired by a *rector* and composed of *deputy rectors*, heads of faculties and departments, some of the professors and representatives of the Communist Party, the trade union, and the ministry. Among its duties were the planning of teaching and research, the confirmation of the appointments of lecturers and assistants, the nomination of senior lecturers and professors, and the awarding of higher degrees.[22]

Each HEI was divided into faculties, such as the faculty of chemistry, biology, history and so on, which were headed by a dean (*dekan*). Faculties were divided into departments (*kafedry*). Departmental staff varied in numbers and composition, but it generally included up to five professors with doctorates; readers or senior lecturers (*dotsenty*), mostly with Candidate degrees; lecturers (*prepodavateli*, or instructors) and assistant lecturers (*assistenty*). The institute's Academic Council usually made appointments after advertising in the press, and they required confirmation by the Ministry of Higher Education for the posts of reader or professor. All academic staff formally gave up their posts every five years, and although their appointments were in practice almost always renewed, the fixed terms were meant to prevent staff from becoming academically inactive.

Overall, the Soviet educational system served well the objectives of the Communist Party and conformed to the requirements of raising loyal and obedient experts in narrow fields. According to the Basic Law on Education, which came into effect in 1974, the Soviet education system aimed to prepare 'highly educated, well-rounded, physically healthy and active builders of a communist society, brought up on the ideas of Marxism–Leninism and in the spirit of respect for Soviet laws and socialist legality, capable of working successfully in various areas of socioeconomic cultural construction, actively participating in social and state activity, and ready to defend selflessly the socialist homeland and to preserve and increase its material and spiritual wealth and protect and preserve nature'. In line with this philosophy, students were expected to passively absorb and then repeat without analysis what instructors said in lectures, a practice that encouraged memorization rather than critical thinking, and one that privileges abstract theory over practical details.[23] Built on the example of the lecturer-centred system of continental Europe and inherited from the tsarist era, the Soviet education system emphasized hierarchy and encouraged a rather passive acceptance of knowledge.

The education system of the Soviet Union achieved remarkable results and illustrated both a high degree of accessibility and a remarkable degree of efficiency in attracting and promoting bright and promising students.[24] Outside observers and many émigrés who moved to the West between the 1970s and 1990s often praised the Soviet system, pointing out that Soviet immigrants excelled in science and mathematics and generally had much broader knowledge of theories, facts and events. The critics of the system, however, argued that even though the Soviet graduates absorbed a lot of information during their studies, many of them had problems with applying their knowledge and with using it in unanticipated settings. Besides, the emphasis on maths and applied science meant that other disciplines, such as the humanities and social sciences, were perceived as less prestigious and often suffered underfunding. Some even questioned whether the Soviet curriculum for social sciences could and should be classified as science at all, given its emphasis on Marxism–Leninism and on a dogmatic teaching style.[25] In conclusion, alongside its many positive aspects, the Soviet system's major drawbacks were thus related to lacking analytical skills and critical thinking among Soviet students. Such was the system largely inherited by the Russian Federation following the collapse of the Soviet Union.

Reforming Russia's higher education system, 1992–2000

The debate about the rigidity and over-centralization of the Soviet education system began as early as late 1980s, when a team of reformist professional educators within the Ministry of Education, led by Edward Dneprov, started criticizing the bureaucratic tyranny and the dictatorial regime of uniformity in the Soviet education system. They advocated the end of the state monopoly on education, de-politicization and the humanization of the education system.

In July 1990, the Supreme Soviet of the Russian Federation appointed Dneprov as Minister of Education. The appointment set off a liberal education reform, which continued well into the post-Soviet era. Until the end of the 1990s, the education reform was largely driven by two state agencies – the Ministry of Education and the Ministry of Finance. The latter pressed the Ministry of Education to move forward with liberal cost-cutting measures, allowing very little preparation and analysis of how these changes would affect the quality of education in the Russian Federation. In July 1992, the Supreme Soviet passed the Law on Education, which ended the state monopoly on education, legalized the establishment of private schools and HEIs by individuals and organizations and promised state funds to those educational establishments that passed accreditation. The law also provided greater freedoms for public schools and HEIs to change curricula and to engage in instructional and pedagogical innovation.[26]

The law opened the door for the establishment of numerous private universities and colleges, whose number by 1995 had reached 208; yet only 10 per cent of these private institutions were registered and accredited in that year. According to Valeri Meshalkin, then chair of the licensing and accreditation section of the State Committee on Higher Education (*Goskomvuz*), the main problem with these institutions was 'the absence of the guarantee of the degree's quality'. For example, in 2003, when some 700 private schools and universities were inspected, it was found that 90 per cent of them did not comply with the relevant articles of the Law on Education. As a result, many of them were closed.[27]

The government generally presented decentralization in education as a process that would increase productivity, efficiency and accountability, and give more control to local communities regarding educational decision-making. In practice, however, decentralization increased inequalities in educational performance between the poorer and richer regions of Russia. The situation was further exacerbated by the fact that decentralization unfolded within the context of deepening economic crisis and was accompanied by a significant decline in federal support for education. According to various accounts, by 1997, the Russian state spent only one-third of the amount spent per student in 1989.[28] Federal funds were barely enough to cover salaries and stipends, and they did not include costs for research, maintenance or utilities. In some regions, such as the Krasnoiarsk region, the situation became so desperate that the regional power company shut off electricity to all universities and institutes because of their outstanding debts.[29] Often, however, even paying off salaries and stipends was problematic. In 1998, for example, the state's debt to instructors amounted to 15.8 billion roubles. In some cases, such as in Barnaul, instructors were paid in toilet paper and vodka.[30] And even if paid in cash, they received barely enough money to buy food: for instance, in September 1997, the salary of a Russian professor belonging to one of the highest wage categories – the seventeenth – amounted to only 961,650 roubles, roughly equivalent to US$165 per month. The salaries of junior academic staff were even lower.[31]

The desperate financial situation of the Russian education sector becomes especially evident when compared to the level of expenditures on education during the Soviet times. For example, in 1970 the Soviet Union allocated 7 per cent of its GDP to education, well above the average level of expenditures reported by Western countries, where it amounted to 5.3–5.5 per cent. In 1994, the Russian government allocated to education only 3.5 per cent of the GDP, and by 1998, real expenditures on education had collapsed.[32] Such dramatic spending cuts hurt many state institutions and forced them to seek alternative sources of financing. In search of revenue, many state institutes and universities started to accept students for financial reasons, rented university facilities to commercial organizations and began to charge students for access to technology, services and information. This led to a rapid deterioration in the quality of the educational services, as well as in their accessibility, causing widespread protests by angry and disappointed teachers, academic staff and students.[33]

It is thus small wonder that many Russian professors chose to leave academia for the business sector or to accept academic positions abroad during this period. Those who stayed had to seek additional sources of income, often offering private tutoring and/or accepting bribes and other payments for their services.[34] The Russian education reform consequently created numerous opportunities for corruption, making the Russian education system known for widespread payments to instructors and deans to secure the passing of entry exams or regular tests.[35]

The reform also failed to democratize the Russian education system and integrate it into the global academic community. Although many universities introduced new disciplines and courses into their curricula, the organizational and ideational framework of the Russian education system has remained unchanged. The new courses are often taught by former specialists in Marxism–Leninism who changed little in their approach to teaching and who expected students to passively absorb information. In addition, the decentralization process has contributed to the formation of a corporatist structure, which has prevented open competition and has resulted in patronage and growing stagnation within the Russian academy, as well as in its continuing isolation from the West and a lack of international experience.

The challenges and prospects of modernizing Russian higher education

When Vladimir Putin came to power, the nature and dynamics of the Russian education reform changed. An improved economic environment and a new parliament compliant with the wishes of the president meant that no fundamental obstacles existed to launch another attempt at reforming the Russian education system. In October 2000, the government passed the 'National Doctrine of Education in the Russian Federation 2000–2025', which emphasized the role of education as a major factor in the country's economic development and transition to a truly democratic state, outlined the government's priorities in the education sector and promised a gradual increase in federal spending on education, with the goal of bringing Russia's education expenditures on par with those in the developed world within the coming 25 years.[36]

The government's intention to fundamentally reform the Russian education sector was confirmed in August 2001, when the president opened the session of the State Council (a consultative body that includes governors from all Russian regions) stating that 'the development of the education system is a goal of national importance' and that the Russian education system had considerable advantages over many of its counterparts abroad, but was in urgent need of modernization.[37] Emphasis was thus placed not on *reforming* Russian education but on *modernizing* it. In December 2001, the government approved the 'Concept of the Modernization of Education in Russia until 2010', which has become the framework for all innovations, experiments and reforms enacted in Russia in the area of education since that time.[38] In essence, both the National Doctrine and the Concept declared that education should reflect the needs of the labour market and the nation's socio-economic growth. For the first time, education has thus been defined in economic terms as a 'long-term investment' and 'the most effective capital investment'.[39]

Modernization began with an attempt to fight corruption, increase the efficiency and transparency of the system and offer students a targeted mechanism of social support. In 2001, the government announced the development of a USE, which would assess school graduates' knowledge in Russian, maths and a number of other subjects, and whose results would be used for the application to and enrolment in the HEIs.[40] The first test of the exam was conducted in five Russian regions in 2001. The exam then spread to other regions, and in 2009 it became the only extant graduation examination in schools and the main form of preliminary examinations in universities.

In the beginning, the government planned to introduce the USE simultaneously with a system of budget funding for tertiary education based on Government Individual Financial Obligations (GIFO), which would be issued to students based on any individual's performance in the exam.[41] In theory, the GIFO offered a great alternative to the existing system of direct budget funding for HEIs, because in the new system, budget funds would follow the student, hypothetically helping eliminate, or at least reduce, corruption and encouraging universities to compete for the best students. In 2005, however, the experiment was temporarily suspended, because the USE's effectiveness required further fine-tuning.[42]

As in any reform, the introduction of the USE and targeted financial assistance for students became the subjects of heated debate. Opponents argued that the exam did not allow the assessment of a student's entire knowledge, that it would be difficult to guarantee the confidentiality of the materials and the security of the test's administration and that it would not prevent corruption, among other things. These concerns were not groundless. There were numerous cases in which teachers wrote the exam for their students.[43] However, the advantages of keeping the new exam system were greater than the disadvantages, and they included a lower level of corruption, greater transparency and objectivity in assessing students' knowledge, better chances for students from poorer or rural regions to be accepted into larger universities and a smoother transition to a modernized education system in line with the model of the Bologna Process.[44] As MP Vladimir Burmatov summarized the results of the USE implementation: 'overall, the introduction of the Unified State Exam was an experiment and a reform, which, despite all the criticism, paid off. [...] Nevertheless, there is still a lot to be done'. His latter statement referred to the need for improved objectivity for the test in assessing students' knowledge, for fighting corruption and for upgrading the technological infrastructure of the exam.[45]

The next step in the modernization of the Russian higher education system occurred in 2003, when Russia joined the Bologna Process and started transforming its higher education system to make it compatible with Bologna principles. The transformation process has presupposed a replacement of the old system of preparing specialists during five years of studies with a two-tier, bachelor's-master's education system. The government's decision was met with fierce opposition from many prominent university leaders, including from the rector of Moscow State University, Viktor Sadovnichy.[46] Despite the opposition, the process continued: the final move was made in October 2007, when the universities introduced a BA/BSc diploma in the middle of their standard specialist programmes.[47] The rationale behind the reform was to raise the quality of Russian education to international standards and to make it compatible with international degrees, increasing academic mobility and competitiveness, thus also expanding the export of education services. Critics of the move pointed out that the new system would destroy the cultural traditions of Russian national education, as well as threaten the Russian 'free-of-charge' education: as programmes of study increased in length of time, the government would find it difficult to finance all master's students, which would likely result in a reduction of degree candidates.[48] Others worried that the Russian job market was not yet ready to consider holders of bachelor's degrees as full graduates, jeopardizing their prospects.[49]

Yet many of these concerns seem unreasonable. As some education experts have pointed out, once the Bologna system becomes more commonplace, employers will start accepting the bachelor's degree as a full one. In addition, in comparison to the Soviet model of higher education, the Bologna Process is better adapted to the realities of the contemporary world, one characterized by uncertainty and dynamism. In this world, it makes more sense to give students at the undergraduate level broader skills and to teach them how to analyze information, form and defend an argument, and how to conduct independent research. The master's degree, on the other hand, should be viewed as a specialized degree for mature professionals, who already know what they want to learn. In other words, the transition to the Bologna Process will make Russian higher education more competitive on the international educational market and offer Russian students greater job and learning opportunities. To address other criticisms, the Russian government has significantly increased its funding of higher education and has continued supporting both undergraduate and graduate students. And besides, as some education experts have noted, there would be nothing wrong if the government decided to support mostly undergraduate education. In the end, the decision to enrol in a master's programme is a conscious one, made by adults who know exactly what they need to learn and why. To assist them, however, the government should develop a system of student loans to help them finance their degrees.[50]

This said, it would be wrong to assume that the adoption of the two-tier system alone would make Russian higher education competitive and attractive to international and domestic students. Rather, it marked the first step in the right direction, with additional measures needed to modernize the Russian system, including better and more efficient funding strategies, a more competitive and open academic job market, attractive working conditions for academic personnel, and better infrastructure and research opportunities.

Another step in the modernization of Russian higher education occurred in 2005, when the government launched the National Priority Project Education (NPPE). As part of this programme, the government significantly increased its federal spending on higher education and launched a complete shake-up of Russia's university system with the establishment of a network of new, high-status federal institutions, created through the amalgamation and restructuring of existing HEIs in seven federal districts. These new universities were expected to provide effective teaching and to concentrate research in particular priority areas identified as strategically important for the region. They were also expected to develop close links with international universities.[51] In 2008, the government also came up with the idea of granting NRU status to some Russian universities on a competitive basis. The first two NRUs were created in May 2008 in a decree signed by President Medvedev. In 2009, a special commission selected 12 winners from among 110 applicants, which secured the winners' additional funding through the federal budget to finance their research programmes (in volume up to 1.8 billion roubles each).[52] The establishment of federal and national research universities was expected to strengthen the research and teaching profile of Russian universities and to raise them to the status of supposedly world-class institutions with a good international reputation.

The government also came up with an initiative to support research and innovation by offering young researchers individual research grants, and it announced its intention to attract foreign professors and students to Russian universities.[53] In February 2012, the government promised to significantly raise the stipends and salaries of Russian students and academic staff. It also called on universities to streamline the ratio of instructors to students, leaving and promoting only the best academics and teachers: currently, the majority of Russian universities have one-to-four or one-to-five professor-to-student ratio, whereas the normal ratio is one professor to ten students. The government also asked the country's universities to better support young researchers and instructors and to provide them with better housing conditions. Finally, in April 2012, Russian President-elect Putin announced government plans to offer grants to Russian students to enable them to study abroad at the world's top universities; if they returned to Russia on graduation and worked in their fields for at least three years, he added, they would not have to pay back the loan.[54]

As these developments illustrate, the Russian government has taken seriously its task to modernize Russian higher education. While it is still too early to adequately assess the success of these measures, the outlook appears rather promising, even if Russian universities dropped significantly in *The Times Higher Education* (THE) ratings of 2012. The editor of the THE rankings, Phil Baty, attributed this drop to Russia's 'appalling brain drain' and to the continuing isolation of its scholarly community.[55] In response, the Russian education minister, Andrei Fursenko, questioned the quality and objectivity of the THE rankings, perhaps correctly so,[56] and stated that his ministry would develop its own rating system for universities. And yet, Baty's words do indicate a key problem that the Russian government needs to address if it wants to improve the academic ranking of Russian universities in the future.

In particular, to raise the quality of Russian higher education and to make it competitive on the international market, the Russian government should concentrate not only on attracting foreign professors but also on supporting Russian researchers, promoting the best ones and offering them greater opportunities for academic travel, English-language training and the possibility for developing collaborative research projects. The reality is such that only by developing and supporting cutting-edge research projects and by increasing the number of publications in international scientific journals will Russian universities be able to raise their prestige and the international profile of Russian higher education. The example of China illustrates the possibility of raising the international profile of a country's education system within a short period of time. One of the prerequisites for a successful academic career in China is having papers accepted in peer-reviewed English-language publications, and this system has already had a positive impact on the international ranking of Chinese universities.[57] A similar procedure could be implemented in Russia.

Part of the problem is that the majority of Russian academics have a poor command of English, are not accustomed to working in an open international environment and have no incentives to change this practice. The reason is simple: the only thing required of Russian academics to keep their posts is to publish one or two articles in Russian academic journals per year. English-language publications are not required for the professorship contests mandatory for the academic staff of all Russian universities every three to five years, nor are they needed to defend doctoral or post-doctoral theses. Thus, the issue is bigger than simply a poor command of English and relates to the problem of a stagnant academic environment, which lacks open competition and dynamism. To address this problem, the government should invest in training Russian professors and students to write academic articles in comprehensible English by offering various language courses. In addition, it should change the incentives structure for Russian academics and make the Russian academic environment more competitive, motivating professors to learn English and publish in international scholarly journals.

To be fair, some Russian universities have already begun to respond to this alarming situation. For example, the Moscow State Institute of International Relations (MGIMO) was among the first Russian universities to establish a competitive internal ranking for its academic staff. The latter was based on the number and quality of their publications, conference communications and other academic achievements. Another example is the Higher School of Economics (HSE), which started differentiating academic salaries based on academic achievement. Both schools also seem to understand the importance of publishing in English-language journals; the MGIMO even established rector's grants for the preparation of publications in English.[58] Yet these are rather isolated examples, not yet indicating a general trend.

Conclusion

Attempts to reform or modernize the Russian system of higher education are not new. The question is whether the most recent government initiatives will have a positive impact on Russian higher education. Larger injections of funds, the introduction of the USE, accession to the Bologna Process, the establishment of several flagship universities and various grant and fellowship programmes offered to Russian and international scholars doubtlessly constitute important steps toward a modernized and internationally competitive Russian higher education system. Similarly, by inviting international specialists to its universities, Russia will be able to not only boost its research profile but also engage further in the internationalization of its higher education. The Russian government thus should now concentrate on improving the financial situation of academic staff and on making Russian universities more competitive and dynamic. Whether the proposed plans for Russian higher education will become reality will depend on the consistency and determination with which the reforms are implemented, as well as on Russia's overall economic situation and the government's willingness to further invest in education. So far, the outlook seems positive.

Notes

1 On the relationship between democracy and education, see, for example, John Dewey, *Democracy and Education*, New York: Macmillan, 1916; Seymour Martin Lipset, 'Some Social Requisites of Democracy: Economic Development and Political Legitimacy', *American Political Science Review*, 53, No. 1, 1959, pp. 69–105. See also Robert J. Barro, 'The Determinants of Democracy' *Journal of Political Economy*, No. 6, 1999, pp. 158–83; Adam Przeworski, Michael Alvarez, Jose A. Cheibub and Fernando Limongi, *Democracy and Development: Political Institutions and Material Well-Being in the World, 1950–1990*, New York: Cambridge University Press, 2000.
2 Lipset, 'Some Social Requisites of Democracy: Economic Development and Political Legitimacy', pp. 79–80.
3 For example, Amartya Sen pointed out that education produces positive externalities to human capital that can help an economy overcome (or at least delay the appearance of) diminishing returns and therefore generate long-term economic growth. See A. K. Sen, 'No School, No Future', *Economist*, 27 March 1999, p. 45. See also Kartik C. Roy and Anatoly V. Sidenko, 'Institutional Failure and the Delivery of Education in Russia', in *Russia: Economic, Political and Social Issues*, Charlie Patel and Oliver J. Dhesi (eds), New York: Nova Science Publishers, 2008, p. 64; and Mark Blaug, *An Introduction to the Economics of Education*, London: Penguin, 1970.
4 David E. Bloom, Matthew Hartley and Henry Rosovsky, 'Beyond Private Gain: The Public Benefits of Higher Education', in *International Handbook of Higher Education*, James J. F. Forest and Philip G. Altbach (eds), Springer: Berlin, 2007, pp. 293–308.
5 David Bloom, David Canning and Kevin Chan, 'Higher Education and Economic Development in Africa', *World Bank Report*, 20 September 2005.
6 Ben Eklof, 'Introduction: Russian Education; The Past in the Present', in *Educational Reforms in Post-Soviet Russia: Legacies and Prospects*, Ben Eklof, Larry E. Holmes and Vera Kaplan (eds), London and New York: Frank Cass, 2005, pp.13–14.
7 Ibid., p. 14.
8 OECD Thematic Review of Tertiary Education, 'Country Background Report for the Russian Federation', February 2007, http://www.oecd.org/dataoecd/22/10/40111027.pdf, p. 7.
9 Vladimir Putin, 'Remarks at State Council Meeting on the Development of Education', 24 March 2006; Russian Federation Presidential website, *Russia and Eurasia Documents Annual, 2006*. Vol. 1: *Russian Federation*. Gulf Breeze, FL: AIP, 2006, pp. 365–7.

70 *Elena Maltseva*

10 Sophia Kishkovsky, 'Russia Moves to Improve Its University Rankings', *New York Times*, 25 March 2012.
11 'Putin Urges Modernization of Russian Higher Education', *RIA Novosti*, 24 August 2011.
12 Nigel Grant, *Soviet Education*, Middlesex, UK: Penguin, 1979, p. 22.
13 N. P. Kuzin, M. I. Kondakov, P. V. Zimin, M. N. Kolmakova, V. I. Lubovsky, G. V. Berezina and A. I. Foteyeva, *Education in the USSR*, Moscow: Progress Publishers, 1972, pp. 120–1.
14 Grant, *Soviet Education*, pp. 84–6.
15 Kuzin *et al.*, *Education in the USSR*, p. 19.
16 Grant, *Soviet Education*, pp. 95–6.
19 Ibid., pp. 123, 96–7.
20 In the majority of higher education institutions, the proportion of applicants accepted varied from one in three to one in eight, with some extreme cases, such as the Leningrad Mechanics and Optics Institute, where only one in thirty was accepted. Grant, *Soviet Education*, p. 134.
21 Ibid., pp. 144–5, 142.
22 Grant, *Soviet Education*, pp. 146–7. For explication in next two paragraphs see ibid., pp. 148, 25.
23 Michael V. Deaver, 'Democratizing Russian Higher Education', *Demokratizatsiya*, Vol. 9, No. 3, 2001, p. 351.
24 See, for example, Joseph Zajda, 'The Politics of Education Reforms and Policy Shifts in the Russian Federation', http://www.springerlink.com/content/rh30631t23h2n57k/fulltext.pdf.
25 Eklof, 'Introduction: Russian Education; The Past in the Present', p. 6.
26 Linda J. Cook, *Postcommunist Welfare States: Reform Politics in Russia and Eastern Europe*, Ithaca and London: Cornell University Press, 2007, pp. 70–3.
27 Zajda, 'The Politics of Education Reforms', p. 187.
28 Deaver, 'Democratizing Russian Higher Education', p. 353.
29 'Voina protiv vyshchei shkoly: Vlasti ne nuzhen intellect natsii', *Pravda*, 10 July 1998.
30 Deaver, 'Democratizing Russian Higher Education', p. 354.
31 'Rossiiskii professor deshevle amerikanskogo chernorabochego', *Nezavisimaia Gazeta*, 16 April 1998; Marina Ivaniuchshenkova and Iuliia Fukolova, 'Utsenka plodov prosvechsheniia', *Kommersant-Vlast'*, 29 April 1998. Other sources suggest even lower salaries. So, for example, according to *Nezavisimaia Gazeta*, in 1998, the average salary of an academic instructor at the Moscow Aviation Institute was approximately 700 roubles, a professor without administrative duties earned about 1,000 roubles, a *pro-rector* about 1,500 and a *rector* 2,000 roubles. 'Vse prilichnye liudi okanchivali MAI', *Nezavisimaia Gazeta*, 5 June 1998.
32 'Voina protiv vysshei shkoly: Vlasti ne nuzhen intellekt natsii', *Pravda*, 10 July 1998.
33 See, for example, Cook, *Postcommunist Welfare States*, p. 73. To read more on the declining quality and accessibility of the Russian education system, review Valery Kornev, 'Sistema obrazovaniia povergla prokuraturu v stolbniak', *Izvestiia*, 25 July 1997; 'Propala zarplata 4 mln. Chelovek: U kogo zavalialos' 2,5 trilliona?', *Argumenty i Fakty*, 18 February 1998. See also 'Terpelivye razbushevalis'', *Moskovskii Komsomolets*, 21 May 1998.
34 Marina Ivaniuchshenkova and Iuliia Fukolova, 'Utsenka plodov prosvechsheniia', *Kommersant-Vlast'*, 29 April 1998.
35 Iuliia Ul'ianova, 'Rektory vuzov ne khodiat na zabastovki', *Segodnia*, 29 May 1998; Deaver, 'Democratizing Russian Higher Education', *Demokratizatsiya*, p. 354.
36 V. I. Korotkevich, *Istoriia sovremennoi Rossii 1991–2003*, Saint Petersburg: Saint Petersburg State University, 2004, http://www.edu.tltsu.ru/er/er_files/book346/book.

pdf, 60; 'Natsional'naia doktrina obrazovaniia v Rossiiskoi Federatsii', http://www.dvgu.ru/umu/zakrf/doktrin1.htm.
37 Vladimir Isachenkov, 'Russian Government Moves to Improve Declining Education System', *Associated Press Writer*, 29 August 2001; 'Putin Hopes for Governors' Support of Modernization of Education System', *Interfax Presidential Bulletin*, 29 August 2001.
38 See 'Kontseptsiia modernizatsii rossiiskogo obrazovaniia na period do 2010 goda', *Rossiiskoe obrazovanie federal'nyi portal*, http://www.edu.ru/db/mo/Data/d_02/393.html#1.
39 Tatiana Gounko and William Smale, 'Modernization of Russian Higher Education: Exploring Paths of Influence', *Compare: A Journal of Comparative and International Education*, Vol. 37, No. 4, 2007, pp. 540–1.
40 E. V. Mishukova, 'Edinyi gosudarstvennyi ekzamen: Ideia, sushchnost', printsipy', December 2001, http://bank.orenipk.ru/Text/t19_141.htm.
41 OECD Thematic Review of Tertiary Education, 'Country Background Report for the Russian Federation', p. 19.
42 For an overview of factors that slowed down the implementation of the GIFO, see 'Eksperiment po vvedeniiu GIFO nuzhdaetsiia v novoi otsenke', *RIA Novosti*, 9 July 2009.
43 'V Rostovskoi oblasti zaderzhany 70 uchitelei, sdavavshie EGE za uchenikov', *Fontanka.ru*, 3 June 2010, http://www.fontanka.ru/2010/06/03/084/; Olga Khrustaleva, 'To Cheat or Not to Cheat?', *Moscow News*, 4 July 2011.
44 On the advantages and disadvantages of the new Unified State Exam, review 'Eksperiment po vvedeniiu GIFO nuzhdaetsiia v novoi otsenke', *RIA Novosti*, 9 July 2009; Anna Semenova, 'Plus odin: V Rossii nachinaetsiia draka za dopolnitel'nye bally po EGE', *Chastnyi Korrespondent*, 28 November 2008, http://www.chaskor.ru/p.php?id=1428; Lev Sirin, 'Andrei Fursenko: "EGE umen'shil vziatki"', *Fontanka.ru*, 26 October 2009, http://www.fontanka.ru/2009/10/26/050/; Mariia Krivoviaz, Tatiana Tkacheva and Elina Trukhanova, 'Poslednii Shans: Vuzy podozhdut abiturientov do kontsa avgusta', *Rossiiskaia Gazeta*, 28 August 2009; 'Chto nado znat o EGE 2009', *Pedsovet.su*, http://pedsovet.su/publ/35-1-0-478; Sergei Kara-Murza, 'V otlichie ot EGE, sovetskoe obrazovanie zastavlialo podrostkov dumat', *KM News*, 21 September 2011, http://www.km.ru/bez-kupyur/2011/09/20/problemy-ege/v-otlichie-ot-ege-sovetskoe-obrazovanie-zastavlyalo-podrostkov-du; Vladimir Dolotov, 'Ekzamen na korruptsiiu', *Kommersant: Den'gi*, 9 March 2009; Irina Ivoilova, 'Verkhovnyi Sud EGE ne sdal', *Rossiiskaia Gazeta*, 18 May 2009; Sophia Kishkovsky, 'U.S.-Style College Exams Take Hold in Russia', *New York Times*, 6 February 2011; 'Putin Signs Law on Two-Tier Higher Education System-1', *RIA Novosti*, 25 October 2007.
45 'Poka shkol'niki sdaiut EGE, deputaty dumaiut, kak ego reformirovat', *Katalog*, 30 May 2012, http://ndce.edu.ru/news/index.php.
46 Nick Holdsworth, 'Europe Is "Threat to Russian Excellence"', *Times Higher Education*, 17 October 2003.
47 'Bologna Process', St Petersburg State University of Service and Economics, http://service.in.spb.ru/Mission.html.
48 Galina Telegina and Hermann Schwengel, 'The Bologna Process: Perspectives and Implications for the Russian University', *European Journal of Education*, Vol. 47, No. 1, 2012, p. 44; Yulia Shumilova, 'Implementation of the Bologna Process in Russia: Tomsk Polytechnic University as a Case Model', MA thesis, Department of Management Studies, University of Tampere, May 2007, http://tutkielmat.uta.fi/pdf/gradu01892.pdf, p. 25.
49 Sergei Guriev, 'How Will Russia Handle the Bologna Process?', *Moscow Times*, 6 October 2010.
50 On these judgements, see Ibid.

51 See 'Creation of New Universities in Federal Districts', *National Training Foundation*, http://eng.ntf.ru/p96aa1.html.
52 '12 Russian Universities Will Receive a Status of National Research Universities', *Ministry of Education and Science of the Russian Federation*, 7 October 2009, http://eng.mon.gov.ru/press/news/4183/.
53 For example, in September 2011, the Putin government announced that it had launched a 12-billion-rouble (US$415 million) project to attract the best international specialists to its universities. 'Medvedev Suggests Inviting Foreign Engineering Professors to Give Lectures in Russia', *Interfax*, 30 March 2011; 'RF Government Allocates $175 on Grants on Science Research', *SKRIN Newswire*, 28 September 2011; 'Putin Urges Modernization of Russian Higher Education', *Education News*, 1 September 2011. See also 'Prime Minister Vladimir Putin Meets with Rectors of Russian Universities', *Government of the Russian Federation*, 14 February 2012, http://premier.gov.ru/eng/events/news/18086/.
54 Sara Custer, 'Putin Plans to Fund Top Students Abroad', *PIE News*, 4 April 2012, http://thepienews.com/news/putin-plans-to-fund-top-students-abroad/.
55 'Russian Universities Drop in 2012 Ratings, Fursenko to Explore Own Rating System', *Modern Russia*, 2 April 2012. See also Oleg Barabanov, 'Putin's Challenge: Can Russian Universities Join the World Education Leaders?', *Valdai Discussion Club*, 17 May 2012, http://valdaiclub.com/culture/42880.html.
56 See Marina Murav'eva, 'Reforma obrazovaniia: 10 let kompromissa', *Nauka i tekhnologii RF*, 24 May 2011, http://www.strf.ru/material.aspx?CatalogId=221&d_no=39921.
57 Barabanov, 'Putin's Challenge'.
58 Ibid.

5 Has the Putin–Medvedev tandem improved women's rights?

Andrea Chandler[1]

Vladimir Putin and Dmitry Medvedev have now dominated the Russian political system for years, and stand to do so for years to come. Vladimir Putin, the most popular leader in Russian history, easily won presidential elections in 2000 and 2004. His presidency ended in 2008, because the constitution allows a president to serve only two consecutive terms. Dmitry Medvedev, Putin's former deputy prime minister, served as president from 2008–12, while Putin became Medvedev's prime minister. Following Putin's successful presidential election bid in March 2012, the two leaders were poised to switch roles in May 2012. Have they encouraged the inclusion of women in Russian social and political life? As powerful leaders in a resource-rich, centralized state, they presumably have the capacity to pursue strong social policy initiatives. Can this system, where two men hold such concentrated power, promote gender equality?

When communism collapsed in the Soviet Union, Russia had a new opportunity to achieve democratization. One of the ways that we measure a country's progress towards democracy is the degree to which women and men are treated equally. Indeed, one of the great changes in politics in the last century is the acceptance of the idea that men and women should have equal rights.[2] Equality can be understood as having the same rights and opportunities, such as the ability to vote, to own property, to hold a paid job or a profession, and to run for office. Feminists often define equality as requiring not just formal rights, but tangible proof that women are able to realize these rights in practice. Therefore, in evaluating women's equality, feminist researchers look for various benchmarks: how prominent are women in a country's political leadership? Are women's incomes catching up to those of men? Do government policies on matters such as day-care availability enable women to make the same kinds of choices that men make, and do they allow men and women to share their family responsibilities equitably?

During Soviet times, women had enjoyed formal legal rights with men. The vast majority of women worked outside the home; levels of women's literacy and access to higher education greatly increased. Women enjoyed substantial participation in elected bodies, such as the Soviet parliament. Women had a third of the seats in the Soviet parliament, the Supreme Soviet.[3] However, in practice, women were rarely included in the Communist Party's top decision-making bodies, nor did women have access to the full range of employment options available to men.[4] In the 1980s, under *glasnost*, women began to voice more openly some of the problems of Soviet life. These problems included a lack of access to contraception, the uneven quality of social welfare services (such as day-care and maternity hospitals), and the chronic shortages in food and consumer goods.[5] Because of such shortages, many women spent long hours on housework and food preparation, in addition to their full-time jobs outside the home. As communism collapsed, activists in the nascent Russian women's movement took initiatives to advance the cause of gender equality, organizing conferences and building networks with Western organizations.[6]

Despite the hopes for democratic improvement, experts became concerned in the 1990s that there seemed to be an inverse relationship between democracy and women's rights in Russia. Legislatures became open to competitive elections where citizens had real choices, but the number of elected women parliamentarians dramatically dropped.[7] Market economic reform ended the state's monopoly over production, but the majority of the new unemployed were women.[8] Some individuals – the so-called 'oligarchs' who benefited from state privatization policies – became wealthy, but the most visible wealthy oligarchs were all men. Finally, and tragically, as the 1990s ended, domestic violence and human trafficking became recognized as serious problems that had jeopardized the safety of unknown numbers of Russian women and girls.[9] How had this happened? Had the post-communist transition to democracy left women behind? One of the most powerful criticisms launched at the relatively liberal period of Boris Yeltsin's presidency, was the idea that democracy had been accompanied by economic insecurity, even impoverishment, for many citizens.[10] Vladimir Putin, upon coming to power, declared stability and improvement in the living standards of the Russian population to be key goals. Insofar as women were the majority of the Russian population, women stood to benefit from the social stability promised by Putin. Were these promises fulfilled?

The status of women in Russia

How can we determine whether there have been advances in gender equality? One way to evaluate improvements in the status of women is to examine statistical trends. Unfortunately, it is difficult to find statistics on gender issues in Russia that provide comparable kinds of data over the past 20 years. International organizations, such as the United Nations, provide a wealth of statistics on gender and society in a broad range of countries. However, their methods of analysing gender-related social trends have become more differentiated over time, meaning that it is difficult to establish trends with precision over a long period. At the same time, Russian official sources tend to make less statistical information available on gender-related trends today than they did in the 1990s. As a result, we should take caution not draw the conclusion that the position of women was worse in the 1990s, simply because at that time the subject was discussed more frankly by the Russian authorities. That being said, statistical information does give us insight into the status of women in Russia.

Employment trends

By the end of Putin's second term as president, fewer women were active in Russia's paid workforce than a decade earlier. While in 1995, the percentage of women working was only six percentage points lower than men, by 2011 the gap had grown to 17 per cent.[11] To some extent, this may reflect the choice to opt out of the workforce, an option that women did not have in Soviet times, when full employment was the norm. However, the declining rate of working women may also reflect the challenges in finding family-friendly employment faced by mothers of young children, combined with the considerable difficulty that Russian parents have in finding affordable day-care. By 2007, although more men were unemployed than women, it took unemployed women on average longer to find work than unemployed men.[12]

Income levels

Another important indicator of gender equality is whether men and women receive equal pay for their work outside the home. According to figures from the United Nations Development Programme for 2004 (the most recent statistics available), women's earnings in Russia are only about 64 per cent of those of men.[13] This figure shows a slight improvement over 1999 levels (60 per cent).[14] A survey conducted in 2001 suggested that in the country's rural areas the disparity was even greater, with women reporting earning less than half of the wages of men.[15] Although rates in the 60 per cent range are not unusual even for Western industrialized countries, these levels are striking for a country like Russia, which had high female employment throughout the twentieth century. The income disparity between men and women cannot be explained by factors such as education or literacy: generally speaking, Russian women show levels of education higher than those of men, and their literacy rates are close to 100 per cent.[16] Furthermore, although on the whole fewer women are employed than men in Russia, the disparity between the percentage of men working compared to the percentage of women working is still not great. The majority of Russian women work outside the home.[17] So the equalization of pay for men and women ought to be one of the key objectives in the advancement of Russian women's rights. The issue of pay equity has not, however, been a priority for Russian leaders, and is rarely addressed in the political arena.

Property ownership and business

According to the Organization for Economic Cooperation and Development (OECD), women in Russia face more difficulty in practice getting bank loans than men, even though the law does not permit discrimination.[18] This finding was confirmed in a 2001 study, in which the author of a public opinion survey found that men formed a disproportionately large number of Russia's new property owners. In the researcher's opinion, this was because women were less likely to receive credit and less well connected to the close networks that have formed between government officials and businesses in the new Russia.[19] Russian women clearly have entrepreneurial initiative: many became small-scale traveling businesswomen soon after the collapse of communism. Such 'shuttle traders' often earned enough to support their families.[20] Still, for the most part, it is difficult for women to enter the Russian economy's 'big leagues'. According to the online business magazine, *Forbes.ru*, Russia's 101 richest individuals included only one woman (Elena Baturina, wife of the former mayor of Moscow).[21]

Representation in political parties, decision-making bodies and government

Women are not well represented in political institutions, although there were some modest gains in the past decade. During Putin's presidency, women's representation in the lower house of parliament, the Duma, increased from 7.5 per cent in 1999 to 14 per cent in 2007.[22] (However, as will be discussed below, the representation of women declined after 2011 elections.) In the Federation Council (Senate) as of 2011, only 4.7 per cent of deputies were women.[23] During his second term as president, Vladimir Putin established the Public Chamber, a largely appointed body, whose purpose was to air the views of select members of society on matters of public policy and legislation. In theory, the Chamber's formation could have been an excellent opportunity for Putin to consult members of groups who were largely excluded from elected bodies, but even in this body women formed only a small minority. In fact, the percentage of women in the Chamber declined from 25 per cent in its first year (2006), to 23 per cent in 2010, to its current (2012) level of 20 per cent.[24] In Russia, women hold a large proportion of government staff positions, but very few women reach the top levels of government.[25] As of the end of Putin's term as prime minister, in April 2012, all of Russia's first deputy prime ministers and deputy prime ministers (seven individuals) were men, and only three of the 19 federal ministers in the cabinet were women.[26]

Some of Russia's most influential politicians have been women. Valentina Matviyenko, the former governor of Saint Petersburg, became speaker of the Federation Council (Senate) in 2011. Two women (Ella Pamfilova and Irina Khakamada) have run for president.[27] A prominent opposition leader, Galina Starovoitova, was a rising political star until she died of gunshot wounds in 1998.[28] Two women have been deputy speakers of the lower house of parliament (Duma).[29] Despite their political talents, women in politics are often sidelined. For example, Ella Pamfilova, appointed to head the Presidential Council on Human Rights, resigned in 2010 after eight years. She told an interviewer that she felt that her efforts were ignored, and that there was political interference in her work.[30] One of the hallmarks of the Putin presidency was the rejection of all forms of affirmative action to increase women's representation. For instance, female deputies proposed legal amendments to guarantee a minimum quota of seats for women in the Duma (lower house of parliament), but the legislature defeated those amendments.[31] Putin and Medvedev did little to include women's voices in political structures, or to provide women with the wherewithal to become successful economic entrepreneurs.

Government policies

While the Putin–Medvedev 'tandemocracy' did not directly acknowledge gender equality as a goal in itself, the two leaders did fairly explicitly call for government intervention as a way to improve the social position of women. Indeed, the two leaders saw women as playing a central role in the modernization of Russia. However, their view of women was based on a paradox: in their vision, women's most important role in the new Russia would be as mothers of the new generation of youth. Mothers of two or more children would now be valorized by the state.

Since 2006, Russia's government has been encouraging women to have more children in an attempt to halt the country's population decline. The government adopted a package of policy incentives intended to make life more affordable, and simpler, for women with family responsibilities. Women who bore and raised a second child would be rewarded with a large lump-sum bonus that could be applied to investments in new housing, retirement savings, or education costs. The Russian government also established new programmes to improve prenatal health and obstetrical facilities.[32] These policies began while Putin was still president. Once in the presidential office, Dmitry Medvedev introduced some new initiatives of his own, including the awarding of medals for exemplary parenthood, and spearheading an initiative to move children out of orphanages and into the care of loving families.[33]

It was hoped, at the time, that the new pronatalist policies would help to create a Russian middle class. Putin, Medvedev, and United Russia ushered in the policies with great fanfare, and the policies seemed designed to attract political support. Were the policies successful? The government claimed that its policies to increase the birth rate had worked, especially in the first two years after the policies were introduced. According to the Ministry of Health and Social Development, between 2007 and 2011, the birth rate had increased 21.1 per cent, and that the birth rate per woman of childbearing age had risen from 1.3 to 1.6.[34] However, according to one economist, the birth rate had already begun to increase before the policies were adopted, because of the fact that the children of the Soviet-era baby boom of the early 1980s were having children of their own. By 2011, she argued, the overall birth rate had already fallen.[35] Furthermore, there were concerns that the government had planned for the births of babies, but had not sufficiently forecasted the needs of an expanded cohort of older children. According to the Ministry of Education, as of 2012, about 2 million children aged 7 and under were on the waiting list for spaces in a day-care system that accommodates only 5.9 million children.[36]

Like many other countries, Russia has been affected by the global recession that began in 2008, which, even considering Russia's oil and gas resources, creates pressures for fiscal restraint. Such pressures may affect the government-funded social benefits upon which many men and women depend. Russian women assume much of the responsibility for the care of children and elderly relatives, so women are especially affected by changes in the level of state social services.[37] In 2011, for the first time, Russia's leaders seriously considered raising the pension age, which since Soviet times has been 55 for women and 60 for men.[38] While unusually low by international standards, the low retirement age for women is deeply valued by Russia's older generation. Early retirement is often regarded as a just reward for the difficult lives of Russian women, many of whom raise children alone. Any attempt by the authorities to raise the pension age is likely to be unpopular with Russian citizens, male and female. Other post-communist countries that raised their pension ages – such as Latvia in 1999 – faced significant political backlash.[39]

Women's activism

The women's rights movement has been generally weak in the Russian Federation. In the 1990s, a women's party, Women of Russia, did well in 1993 Duma elections and gained a substantial number of seats in parliament. Even after the party lost its prominence, women deputies were able to influence the adoption of some progressive legislation, such as a 1997 Duma resolution on gender equality.[40] However, since the late 1990s, the influence of the women's movement has declined. There are many reasons for this. In the first place, as market economic reform declined in popularity by the late 1990s, anti-Western sentiment increased, and Putin's rhetoric drew increasingly upon nationalist themes. In this environment, Russian women's activists were criticized for the close networks they had formed with Western feminists and funding organizations based outside Russia.[41] Second, Russian women's movements are weak because civil society, and social movements in general, are weak. The communist order in the Soviet Union tolerated no independent citizens' organizations. Although citizens' groups mushroomed in the Yeltsin era, since Putin became president new obstacles have been imposed on such organizations. Still, some analysts, pointing to the exceptional initiative shown by the human rights movement and the environmental movement, are optimistic that autonomous social movements will gain strength in the coming decades.[42] Finally, it is hard for many women to find the time for participation in social activity. Many women are single parents; many grandmothers are actively involved in the care and rearing of their grandchildren. After the hours spent earning a living, caring for children and other relatives, politics may be very far from the minds of many women.

The Dmitry Medvedev presidency was a turning point for women in Russia. Unlike Putin, Medvedev was a politician who often met with women, was photographed with them, and who appeared to enjoy their company. Medvedev presented an image of a more woman-friendly president. Political scientist, Joel Moses, argued that under the presidency of Dmitry Medvedev, the appointments of women in top positions in regional and local governments considerably increased. This was partly because of a desire to increase women's inclusion in the elite, but also because of an emerging perception that women are highly qualified for positions of administrative responsibility, and are relatively untainted by corruption.[43] Medvedev's annual addresses to parliament, especially his 2011 address, paid more attention to social policy and family policy than Putin did during his eight years in the same office. Medvedev's more open style, and his incomplete efforts to lift some aspects of authoritarianism, raised expectations for democratic reforms within the citizenry as a whole. But Medvedev also faced the aspirations of women, who showed signs of wanting something in return for the contributions they were making to society.

In 2010–11, women showed unprecedented activism. In 2010, women in some Russian cities marched with their babies in strollers, demanding improved access to day-care.[44] In 2011, women staged demonstrations in Moscow protesting planned cuts to maternity leave benefits. The protesters, at least one of whom was in her ninth month of pregnancy, claimed that the cutbacks were inconsistent with the plan to increase the birth rate.[45] The demonstrations led parliament to amend the legislation in order to soften the cuts. As another example of women's activism, in 2012, Russian environmental activist Lidia Chirikova won a major award, the Goldman prize, for her efforts to preserve the Khimki Forest outside Moscow.[46]

The desire for change among women was reflected also in public opinion surveys. A 2011 public opinion survey, conducted by the All-Russian Centre for the Study of Public Opinion (VTsIOM), suggested that women were developing distinct voting preferences and an appetite for change. Forty-five per cent of women, as opposed to 26 per cent of men, thought that there should be more women in politics, and 24 per cent of women 'definitely' supported quotas for women in politics (as opposed to 12 per cent of men). Women were also more than twice as likely as men to favour a woman president. These numbers showed increased rates for these preferences from 2005–11.[47] In light of the growing interest of women in politics, the elections of 2011–12 could have been an opportunity for women to express themselves and for politicians to court the women's vote. Was this opportunity realized?

Women and the 2011–12 elections

Elections for the lower house of parliament (the State Duma) took place in December 2011, and presidential elections were held in March 2012. Until a month or so before the parliamentary elections, the results of the election were widely assumed to be highly predictable. The party that supported Putin and Medvedev, United Russia, has been the dominant political party in the legislature since 2003, and had a parliamentary majority from 2003 to 2007. However, when the elections occurred, the ruling party, United Russia, lost support and retained only a narrow majority of seats. (The only other opposition parties to gain seats in the election were the Communist Party of the Russian Federation (KPRF), the Liberal Democratic Party of Russia (LDPR) and a centre-left party, A Just Russia.) The elections, and the Central Electoral Committee (the body responsibility for conducting the elections and for issuing the results), were widely criticized for alleged violations and irregularities. Among the bodies that raised questions about the conduct of the elections were the Organization for Security and Cooperation in Europe (OSCE), the Parliamentary Assembly of the Council of Europe (PACE), and the Russian non-governmental organization *Golos* (which means 'voice' in Russian).[48] Large protests on 5, 10 and 24 December and 5 February featured growing calls for reform of the electoral system and for new elections.

The elections did not accommodate the desire among women to be heard. As a result of the December 2011 elections, the representation of women in the Duma declined substantially. After the 2007 elections, the Duma was 14 per cent female.[49] However, after the allocation of seats from the 2011 election, only 11 per cent of deputies were women.[50] This is substantially below the world average for women's representation in parliament (19.5 per cent).[51] The decline reverses two cycles of increases in women's representation in parliament in the previous two elections.[52] The party which showed the least regard for gender parity was the Communists, in which women gained only four of the party's 92 seats, while the ruling United Russia gave 12.6 per cent of its seats to women.[53] Parties are not required by law to put quotas of women on their party lists, and the numbers suggest that parties are not putting enough women in top places on the party lists.

After the December 2011 elections, as opposition politics developed, women were prominent as activists and leaders. As a sign of a new trend, younger women (such as the TV personality, Ksenia Sobchak, and the environmental activist, Evgeniia Chirikova)[54] became visible in the protest movement. However, as opposition influence increased following the protests in Moscow's Bolotnaya Square on 10 December, women were less prominent. Media attention focused primarily on the utterances of male activists such as Aleksei Navalny and Sergei Udaltsov. President Medvedev met with opposition leaders on 20 February 2012, and only one woman was visible in the photographs of the 10 invited leaders at the table (Galina Khavraeva, of 'Za zhenshchin Rossii').[55]

Even during the week of the presidential election (4 March 2012), several women's protests attracted front-page attention from the news media. Activists from the radical feminist group, FEMEN, took their tops off in the polling station where Putin had voted revealing anti-Putin slogans on their bare chests (and were arrested).[56] Controversy continued over the prosecution of the all-female punk rock group, Pussy Riot, who were arrested on 26 February after some of them were alleged to have donned hoods and begun to sing an anti-Putin song in Moscow's Cathedral of Christ the Saviour on 21 February.[57] Activists such as Aleksei Navalny called for the release of the young women, noting that two of them were mothers of small children.[58] The 4 March 2012 presidential elections confirmed Putin as president by a strong majority, but again there were serious concerns about the validity of the election results, and protests continued. In Putin's first press conference as president-elect a few days after his election, one of the first questions from reporters was about his reaction to the 'manifestations of women's collectivism' that had taken place in recent days. (He apologized to believers and clerics for the incident in the cathedral, which he said he hoped would not be repeated).[59]

Why is it so difficult for women to gain influence in the Russian political arena? One hypothesis is that Russian politicians take women's votes for granted. The conventional wisdom was that women were more likely either to vote for Putin, or to vote Communist. In an early study, political scientist, Vicki Hesli, found that compared to men, women were less likely to vote nationalist, slightly more likely to vote communist, and that social welfare issues were important in women's votes.[60] More recent research has called for a more sophisticated interpretation of women's voting behaviour. Although women are slightly more likely than men to vote for the incumbent (be he Putin or Medvedev), this may reflect the fact that women are less likely than men to vote for extreme nationalist, Vladimir Zhirinovsky (of the LDPR).[61]

A survey published by the respected survey research institution the Levada Centre following the December 2011 elections confirmed this trend. According to the study, men were more likely than women to vote for the Communist Party and Zhirinovsky, and women were more likely than men to vote for United Russia and A Just Russia. Interestingly, the Levada Centre found that these tendencies were more pronounced in 2011 surveys than in 2007 surveys, suggesting that a gender gap in voting is increasing.[62] In this light, the Communist Party's loss of women's support is striking. One might expect the country's largest opposition party to make a greater effort to court a group that represents the majority of voters. The findings suggest that women are increasingly rejecting the political extremes of nationalism and communism. Instead, one can draw the conclusion, therefore, that they constitute a strong potential base for moderate and centrist political views, and Russian politicians would be well advised to take note.

The composition of Dmitry Medvedev's new government, confirmed in May 2012, showed a weakened commitment to the inclusion of women in positions of responsibility. Neither of the two women in the previous cabinet was invited to stay on in the government's inner circle. Instead, they moved to Putin's presidential administration, where they may continue to hold substantial influence, but are likely to have less public visibility and less autonomy.[63] The new cabinet did include two women, one of whom was a deputy prime minister, and the other the minister of health.[64] Since the previous government had no female deputy prime ministers, this may be seen as a positive change for women. However, whereas the previous cabinet allocated one of the prestigious economic ministries to a woman (Elvira Nabiullina), both of the women in the new cabinet held social policy portfolios. As critical as social and health policies are to the functioning of government, these policy domains tend to receive less attention from the top elite than matters relating to industry, trade, or security.

Conclusion

One of the most important goals of the Putin–Medvedev tandem was the improvement of social conditions. As one of the groups adversely affected by the Yeltsin reforms, women stood to benefit from the stability promised by the Putin–Medvedev tandem. However, the government failed to devote sufficient attention to women's equality, even when signs emerged of women's growing interest in politics. There are signs that the position of women may be improving, not because of government policy, but because of the advances of a path-breaking new generation of women leaders. According to a recent article in the newspaper, *Moscow News*, women occupy 50 per cent of positions in the top strata of accountants, financial managers and lawyers.[65] If correct, those statistics indicate that women are becoming highly competitive in the business world. In 2012, radio station, *Echo Moscow*, published its first ever list of the 100 most influential women in Russia, a sign that such a list can be compiled. The list included politicians, writers, government ministers and leaders of organizations, among others.[66] If women's situation is improving in Russia, it is largely because of their own initiative. Sociological research suggests that Russian women have been remarkably resilient in the face of the challenges of the post-communist transition, sustaining a much higher life expectancy than men, and demonstrating lower levels of preventable illnesses, while men suffer disconcertingly high rates of alcohol-related deaths. Evidently, while some men have thrived in the post-communist environment, others have found it difficult to cope with a rapidly changing society.[67] Although Russian policymakers should address the conditions that make life challenging for women, they should also address the serious health problems that have affected the male population, and should strive to create more opportunities for all citizens.

Has the tandem improved women's rights? Since 2008, there has been little change in women's rights: they have not improved, but nor have they dramatically worsened. Promoting equality has been a low priority for the Russian government since the 1990s. Pronatalist policies, while they have provided some material support to mothers, have done little to improve the position of women in the workplace or in public life. Given the propaganda value that the Soviet Union attached to the advancement of the status of women, it is somewhat puzzling that Russia has missed its opportunity to be a world leader on gender equality issues. Women in Russia face many challenges that will not be fixed by a photo-op or a presidential message on International Women's Day (8 March). For their lives to improve, they need anti-discrimination legislation, better access to good day-care, and a stronger voice in parliament. Still, women can send the message that their votes can really make a difference – and that they will be scrutinizing politicians' statements for firm commitments on the issues that matter to them. The next step – electing Russia's first woman president – might not be so far away.

Notes

1 Author's note: Some of the ideas in this chapter were first presented at a seminar at the Department of Political Science at Carleton University on 20 March 2012. I am grateful for the comments that I received.
2 Ann E. Towns, *Women and States: Norms and Hierarchies in International Society*, Cambridge, UK and New York, NY: Cambridge University Press, 2010.
3 R. A. Vardanian and E. V. Kochkina, 'Elections: the Gender Gap', *Russian Social Science Review*, vol. 49, no. 3, May–June 2008, p. 61.

4 Joel C. Moses, 'Women in Political Roles', in Dorothy Atkinson, Alexander Dallin and Gail Warshofsky Lapidus (eds), *Women in Russia*, Stanford, CA: Stanford University Press, 1977, pp. 333–53; in same source, Janet Chapman, 'Equal Pay for Equal Work?' pp. 235–6.
5 Mary Buckley, *Redefining Russian Society and Polity*, Boulder, CO: Westview Press, 1993, pp. 116–35, 298–303.
6 Julie Hemment, *Empowering Women in Russia*, Bloomington: Indiana University Press, 2007, pp. 3–4, 9–11.
7 Carol Nechemias, 'Democratization and Women's Access to Legislative Seats: the Soviet Case, 1989–1991', *Women and Politics* vol. 14, no. 3, 1994, pp. 1–18; Linda J. Cook and Carol Nechemias, 'Women in the Russian State Duma', in Marilyn Rueschemeyer and Sharon L. Wolchik (eds), *Women in Power in Post-Communist Parliaments*, Washington, DC: Woodrow Wilson Centre Press, 2009, p. 25.
8 Linda Racioppi and Katherine O'Sullivan See, 'Organizing Women before and after the Fall: Politics in the Soviet Union and Post-Soviet Russia', *Signs*, vol. 20, no. 4, summer 1995, pp. 825–6.
9 Janet Elise Johnson, *Gender Violence in Russia: the Politics of Feminist Intervention*, Bloomington, IN: Indiana University Press, 2009; Mary Buckley, 'Public Opinion in Russia on the Politics of Human Trafficking', *Europe–Asia Studies*, vol. 61, no. 2, March 2009, pp. 213–48.
10 See Vladimir Popov, 'Russia Redux?' *New Left Review*, vol. 44, March–April 2007, pp. 50–2.
11 United Nations Development Programme, *Human Development Report 1998*, New York: Oxford University Press, 1998, p. 188; *Human Development Report 2011: Sustainability and Equity: a Better Future for All*, Jeni Klugman, lead author, New York: UNDP and Palgrave Macmillan, 2011, p. 140.
12 United Nations, Committee on the Elimination of Discrimination against Women. Combined Sixth and Seventh Periodic Reports of States Parties. Russian Federation. CEDAW/C/USR/7, 9 March 2009, pp. 61–2. Online at http://www.unhcr.org/refworld/publisher,CEDAW,,RUS,4a1fa06c2,0.html.
13 United Nations Development Program (UNDP). *Human Development Report 2004: Cultural Liberty in Today's Diverse World*, New York: UNDP, 2004, p. 222.
14 United Nations Development Program (UNDP), *Human Development Report 2001: Making Technologies Work for Human Development*, New York: Oxford University Press, 2001, p. 211.
15 Stephen K. Wegren, David J. O'Brien and Valeri V. Patsiorkovski, 'Russian Agrarian Reform: the Gender Dimension', *Problems of Post-Communism*, vol. 49, no. 6, November–December 2002, p. 52.
16 UNDP, *Human Development Report, Cultural Liberty in Today's Diverse World*, New York: UNDP, 2004, p. 218.
17 According to the UNDP, in the year 2010, 57.5 per cent of Russian women worked, as opposed to 69.2 per cent of men. *Human Development Report 2011: Sustainability and Equity: a Better Future for All*, Jeni Klugman, lead author, New York: UNDP and Palgrave Macmillan, 2011, p, 140.
18 Organization for Economic Cooperation and Development, *OECD Social Institutions and Gender Index. Results 2009*, http://genderindix.org/sites/default/files/pdfs/RUS.pdf.
19 Marina Liborakina, 'The Social Consequences of Privatization for Women', *Problems of Economic Transition*, vol. 43, no. 9, January 2001, p. 42.
20 Irina Mukhina, 'New Losses, New Opportunities: (Soviet) Women in the Shuttle Trade, 1987–1998', *Journal of Social History*, vol. 43, no. 2, winter 2009, pp. 341–59.
21 http://www.forbes.ru/rating/rossiiskie-biznesmeny-v-mirovom-reitinge-forbes/2011#pages-1.

84 *Andrea Chandler*

22 Inter-parliamentary Union (Geneva, Switzerland), '*Parlin' Database on National Parliaments*, 1999 data: http://www.ipu.org/parline-e/reports/arc/2263_99.htm; 2007 data: http://www.ipu.org/parline-e/reports/arc/2263_07.htm.
23 Inter-Parliamentary Union (Geneva, Switzerland), '*Parline' Database on National Parliaments*, http://www.ipu.org/parline-e/reports/2264_A.htm.
24 Chandler's calculations, based on the numerical lists of Public Chamber members listed at the website of the Public Chamber of the Russian Federation http://www.oprf.ru/about/chambermembers.
25 United Nations, Committee on the Elimination of Discrimination against Women. Combined Sixth and Seventh Periodic Reports of States Parties. Russian Federation. CEDAW/C/USR/7, 9 March 2009, pp. 22–3, online at http://www.unhcr.org/refworld/publisher,CEDAW,,RUS,4a1fa06c2,0.html.
26 http://www.government.ru/gov/.
27 R. A. Vardanian and E. V. Kochkina, 'Elections: the Gender Gap', *Russian Social Science Review*, vol. 49, no. 3, May–June 2008, p. 60.
28 Masha Gessen, *The Man without a Face: the Unlikely Rise of Vladimir Putin*, London, UK: Granta, 2012, pp. 3–7.
29 Cook and Nechemias, p. 29.
30 Maria Morozova, trans. Robert Coulson, 'Former Presidential Rights Advisor Says Russian System Turned into "Rock-Solid Insult to All of Us"', *Radio Free Europe-Radio Liberty*, 5 May 2011.
31 R. A. Vardanian and E. V. Kochkina, 'Elections: the Gender Gap', *Russian Social Science Review*, vol. 49, no. 3, May–June 2008, p. 61.
32 Andrea Chandler, 'Gender, Political Discourse and Social Welfare in Russia: Three Case Studies', *Canadian Slavonic Papers*, vol. LI, no. 1, March 2009, pp. 3–24.
33 Dmitry Medvedev, 'Address of the President to the Federal Assembly of the Russian Federation', 30 November 2010, online at http://www.kremlin.ru/transcripts/9637.
34 [n.a.] 'Rozhdaemost' v Rossii vyrosla na 20 protsentov', *Rossiiskaia gazeta*, 7 March 2012.
35 Ekaterina Shcherbakova, 'Chislo rodivshikhsia stalo sokrashat'sia, obshchii koeffitsient rozhdamosti v pervom polugodi 2011 goad snizil'sia do 11.9 protsent', *Demoskop Weekly*, no. 475:6, 29 August–11 September 2011, Institute Demografii Natsional'nogo Issledovatel'skogo Universiteta "Vyshaia Shkola ekonomiki"', http://www.demoscope.ru/weekly/2011/0475/print.php.
36 Irina Taradanova, deputy director of the Department of General Education of the Russian Federation Ministry of Education, interviewed by Kseniia Larina, on the show 'Roditel'skoe sobranie: ochered' v detskie sady. Kak vyiti iz situatsii', *Echo Moscow* radio, 12 February 2012. http:///www.echo.msk.ru/programs/assembly/857728-echo/.
37 See for example Jennifer B. Barrett and Cynthia Buckley, 'Gender and Perceived Control in the Russian Federation', *Europe–Asia Studies*, vol. 61, no. 1, January 2009, pp. 41–4.
38 [n.a] 'Shuvalov Rejects Pension Age Hike Proposal', *RIA Novosti*, 23 April 2012, http://www.en.ria.ru/society/20120423/172992603.html.
39 Andrea Chandler, 'Globalization, Social Welfare Reform and Democratic Identity in Russia and Other Post-Communist Countries', *Global Social Policy*, vol. 1, no. 3, 2001, pp. 310–37.
40 Amy Caizza, *Mothers and Soldiers: Gender, Citizenship and Civil Society in Contemporary Russia*, New York: Routledge, 2002, pp. 51–83.
41 Janet Elise Johnson, *Gender Violence in Russia: the Politics of Feminist Intervention*, Bloomington, IN: Indiana University Press, 2009, pp. 52–4, 149–50; Julie Hemment, *Empowering Women in Russia*, Bloomington: Indiana University Press, 2007.
42 For example, Laura A. Henry, *Red to Green: Environmental Activism in Post-Soviet Russia*, Ithaca, NY and London: Cornell University Press, 2010; Elena Chebankova,

'Evolution of Russia's Civil Society under Vladimir Putin: A Cause for Concern or Grounds for Optimism?', *Perspectives on European Politics and Society*, vol. 10, no. 3, September 2009, pp. 394–415.
43 Joel C. Moses, 'Medvedev, Political Reform and Russian Regions', *Problems of Post-Communism*, vol. 58, no. 1, January/February 2011, pp. 25–7.
44 [n.a.] 'Russian Parents Protest Lack of Preschools', *Radio Free Europe-Radio Liberty*, 13 July 2010, http://www.rferl.org/articleprintview/2098400.html.
45 Svetlana Pleshakova, '2011: poslednii god rozhdaemosti', *MK*, 18 January 2011, http://www.mk.ru/print/articles/558749-2011-posledniy-god-rozhdaemosti.html.
46 http://www.goldmanprize.org/recipient/evgenia-chirikova.
47 'Zhenshchiny vo vlasti', Vse-Rossiiskii Tsentr dlia Izucheniia Obshestvennogo Mneniia (VTsIOM) 17 July 2011. http://www.wciom.ru/index.php?id=581.
48 'Organization for Security and Cooperation in Europe. Office for Democratic Institutions and Human Rights. Russian Federation. Elections to the State Duma. 4 December 2011', *OSCE/ODIHR Election Observation Mission, Final Report*, Warsaw: OSCE, 12 January 2012. Council of Europe, Parliamentary Assembly, 'Document 12833, 23 January 2012', *Observation of the Parliamentary Elections in the Russian Federation (4 December 2011)*, Tiny Kox, rapporteur http://www.assembly.coe.int.
49 2007 figures: International Parliamentary Union. IPU PARLINE database, Russian Federation, http://www.ipu.org/parline_e/reports/arc/2263_07.htm.
50 Organization for Security and Cooperation in Europe, Office for Democratic Institutions and Human Rights, *Russian Federation. Elections to the State Duma, 4 December 2011. Final Report*, Warsaw, Poland: OSCE, 12 January 2012, p. 14.
51 'Women in National Parliaments. World and Regional Averages', Inter-Parliamentary Union, http://www.ipu.org/wmn-e/world.htm.
52 Andrea Chandler, 'Women, Gender and Federalism in Russia: A Deafening Silence', in Melissa Haussman, Marian Sawer and Jill Vickers (eds), *Federalism, Feminism and Multilevel Governance*, Surrey, UK: Ashgate Publishing, 2010, p. 150.
53 Organization for Security and Cooperation in Europe, Office for Democratic Institutions and Human Rights, *Russian Federation. Elections to the State Duma, 4 December 2011. Final Report*, Warsaw, Poland: OSCE, 12 January 2012, p. 14.
54 Evgeniia Chirikova blogged on 8 March about the protest on 5 March and the importance of maintaining unity among the leadership. 'Ne fontan', *Echo Moscow*, 8 March, 2012, http://www.echo.msk.ru/blog/chirikova/866486-echo/.
55 http://www.kremlin.ru/photo/2043?page=2. The 10 leaders were named at http://www.news.kremlin.ru/ref_notes/1157/print.
56 [n.a.] 'Odna iz aktivistok Femen, razdevshaiasia na uchastke, gde golosoval Putin, deportirovana v Kiev', *Gazeta.ru*, 9 March 2012, http://www.gazeta.ru/news/lenta/2012/03/09/n_2235077.
57 'V Rossiiskom obshchestve aktivno obsuzhdaetsia posledstviia skandal'naia aktsii v khrame Khrista Spasitel'ia, ustroennoi devushkami pank-gruppy Pussy Riot', *Echo Moscow*, 7 March 2012, http://www.echo.msk.ru/news/866292-echo.html, accessed 7 March 2012. Evgeniya Chaykovskaya, 'Feminist Punks Perform in Christ the Saviour Cathedral', *Moscow News*, 21 February 2012.
58 Aleksei Navalny, 'Pro Pussy Riots', 7 March 2012, http://www.echo.msk.ru/blog/navalny/86616-echo/
59 Vladimir Putin. Press Conference, 7 March. Transcript, in Russian, online at Website of the Prime Minister of the Russian Federation, http://www.premier.gov.ru/events/news/18379/print/. The quotation is Chandler's translation.
60 Vicki Hesli, Ha-Lyong Jung, William M. Reisinger and Arthur H. Miller, 'The Gender Divide in Russian Politics', *Women in Politics*, vol. 22, no. 2, 2001, pp. 41–80.
61 Timothy J. Colton and Henry Hale, 'The Putin Vote: Presidential Electorates in a Hybrid Regime', *Slavic Review*, vol. 68, no. 3, Fall 2009, pp. 486, 502.

62 L. D. Gudkov, B. V. Dubin, N. A. Zorkaia and M. A. Plotko, *Rossiiskie parlamentskie vybory: elektoral'nyi protsess pri avtoritarnom rezhime*, Moscow: Analyticheskii Tsentr Iuriia Levady/Levada Centre, 2012, http://www.levada.ru/books/rossiiskie-arlamentskie-vybory-2011-goda.
63 Svetlana Bocharova and Ol'ga Kuz'menkova, 'Rokirovka v storonu pomoshchnikov', *Gazeta.ru*, 22 May 2012.
64 [n.a.] 'Sformirovano novoe pravitel'stvo', *Rossiiskaia gazeta*, 21 May 2012.
65 Natasha Doff, 'Women: The Hidden Face of Russian Business', *Moscow News*, 30 January 2012.
66 http://www.echo.msk.ru/blog/echo_rating/838907-echo/.
67 See for example Pamela Abbott and Claire Wallace, 'Talking about Health and Well-being in Post-Soviet Ukraine and Russia', *Journal of Communist Studies and Transition Politics*, vol. 23, no. 2, June 2007, pp. 181–202.

Part II
Economic and international related issues

6 The economic situation in present-day Russia

Vladimir Popov[1]

The Russian economy lost 45 percent of output during the transformational recession of 1989–98, income inequalities increased greatly, the crime rate doubled, and life expectancy went down from 70 to 65 years. The short-lived stabilization of 1995–98 (when the rouble was pegged to the dollar and inflation subsided) ended up in the spectacular currency crisis of August 1998 – the rouble then lost over 60 percent of its value in several months, inflation got out of hand again, and crime, suicides, and mortality increased once more.

However, after the 1998 currency crisis the Russian economy started to grow – the average annual growth rate totaled about 7 percent in 1999–2007. Real incomes and personal consumption increased even faster – they more than doubled in 1999–2007 – and have already surpassed the pre-recession level of the late 1980s. The major push was given by devaluation of the rouble in 1998 and by higher world prices for oil and gas later, but the government could have at least taken the credit for not ruining this growth. Inflation fell from 84 percent in 1998, when prices jumped after the August 1998 currency crisis and dramatic devaluation of the rouble occurred, to 10–12 percent in 2004–07 (see Figure 6.1).

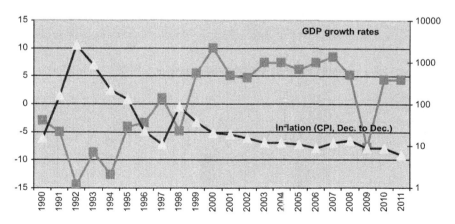

Figure 6.1 GDP growth rates and inflation in Russia, %, 1990–2008 (right axis, log scale)

Economic growth and high world fuel prices helped the government to collect more tax revenues, so the government budget moved from a deficit to surplus, and government spending as a proportion of GDP increased from 1999 (see Figure 6.2), allowing it to restore partially the institutional capacity of the state that was lost in the 1990s. Moreover, high oil and gas prices in the world markets allowed Russia to enjoy high foreign trade surpluses and to accumulate foreign exchange reserves – they increased from less than US$15 billion right after the 1998 currency crisis to nearly $600 billion by August 2008.

True, in comparative perspective Russian performance was not that impressive. Many other former Soviet republics – Armenia, Azerbaijan, Belarus, Estonia, Kazakhstan, Latvia, Lithuania, Turkmenistan, and Uzbekistan, not to speak about central European countries – in 2007 well surpassed the pre-recession level of output, whereas Russian GDP was still only 99 percent of the 1989 level. Russian growth rates in 1999–2007 were high (7 percent), but still lower than in other fuel exporters in the former Soviet Union region, such as Azerbaijan, Kazakhstan, and Turkmenistan (over 10 percent in 1999–2007). Even some fuel importers, such as Armenia and Belarus, showed higher growth rates than Russia (see Figure 6.3).

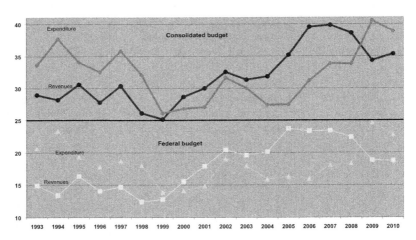

Figure 6.2 Government budget revenues and expenditure, % of GDP, Minfin data

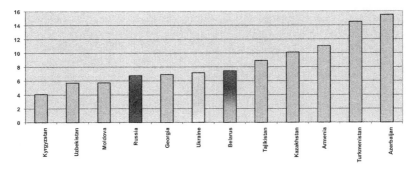

Figure 6.3 Average annual GDP growth rates in CIS countries in 2000–07 (EBRD estimates)

Besides, the world economic recession of 2008–09 hit Russia harder than other countries. Russia's GDP for 2009 fell by about 8 percent on account of the collapse of oil prices and the outflow of capital caused by world recession – more than USA, European, and Japanese GDP (2, 4, and 5 percent, respectively) and considerably more than the GDP in most emerging market economies that did not experience a recession (China registered growth of 8 percent, India 6 percent, Middle East 2 percent, and Sub-Sahara Africa (SSA) 2 percent). Now, after 4–5 percent growth in 2010–11, pre-recession 1989 GDP will be surpassed in 2012. In sum, therefore, for over two "lost decades" (since 1989) there has been no increase in output.

Russian HDI – Human Development Index (accounting not only for GDP per capita, but also for life expectancy and the level of education) – is still below the USSR level and even below that of Cuba with life expectancy of 77 years against 66 years in Russia. China with a life expectancy of 72 years is rapidly approaching the Russian level of HDI. But at least there is more stability in Russia today than in the rocky 1990s.

Economic growth and gradual restoration of the government's ability to provide public goods led to the improvement in the social sphere – since 2002–03 the murder rate, suicide rate, and mortality rate started to fall, albeit very slowly, the birth rate and marriage rate increased, the decline of the Russian population (it fell from 148.6 million in 1993 to below 142 million by mid 2008) slowed down. The number of murders reached a peak in 2002 and fell in 2003–08; the suicide rate decreased in 2001–08 (see Figure 6.4); the mortality rate stabilized and fell in 2004–08, life expectancy increased slightly (see Figure 6.5); the birth rate, after reaching a 50-year minimum in 1999, started to grow, the marriage rate increased, and the divorce rate fell. On the other hand, a more than 50 percent increase in the crime rate in 2002–06 is most likely the sign of better registration of crimes because the number of violent crimes (these are always registered better than others) continued to decline.

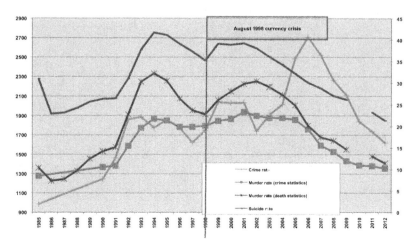

Figure 6.4 Crime rate (left scale), murder rate and suicide rate (right scale) per 100,000 inhabitants

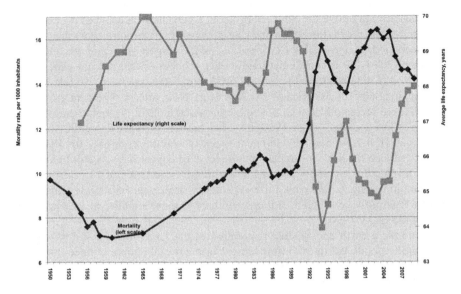

Figure 6.5 Mortality and life expectancy rates

Russia was unable to cope properly with the growing stream of petro-dollars. In fact, the right question to ask about the recent performance of the Russian economy is why Russian growth rates lagged behind the growth rates of other countries and were not growing in 2001–08 despite a nearly fivefold rise in average annual oil prices (see Figure 6.6). The answer may be disappointing, but is hardly disputable – Russia did not manage to use its growing resource rent in the best possible way.

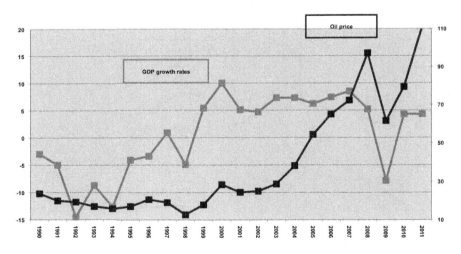

Figure 6.6 Oil prices (Brent, $ a barrel, right scale) and GDP growth rates in Russia (%, left scale) 1990–2011

The economy is too dependent on oil and gas exports, which account for between one-half and two-thirds (depending on world fuel prices) of total Russian exports. And the prosperity of recent years was mostly based on growing world fuel prices. The simple calculation shows the importance of the windfall oil revenues. Russian GDP at the official exchange rate was about $1 trillion in 2007, whereas the production of the oil and gas sector, which employs less than 1 million workers, is valued at about $500 billion at world prices of $80 per barrel of oil. When oil was priced at $15 a barrel in 1999, Russian oil and gas output was valued at less than $100 billion. The difference, $400 billion, is the fuel windfall profit that literally fell on Russia from the skies.

Few specialists would call the USSR a resource economy, but Russian industrial structure changed a lot after the transition to the market. Basically, the 1990s were the period of rapid deindustrialization and "resourcialization" of the Russian economy, and the growth of world fuel prices since 1999 seems to have reinforced this trend. The share of output of major resource industries (fuel, energy, metals) in total industrial output increased from about 25 percent to over 50 percent by the mid 1990s and stayed at this high level thereafter. Partly, this was the result of changing price ratios (greater price increases in resource industries), but also the real growth rates of output were lower in the non-resource sector. The share of mineral products, metals, and diamonds in Russian exports increased from 52 percent in 1990 (USSR) to 67 percent in 1995, and to 81 percent in 2007, whereas the share of machinery and equipment in exports fell from 18 percent in 1990 (USSR) to 10 percent in 1995, and to below 6 percent in 2007. The share of R&D spending in GDP amounted to 3.5 percent in the late 1980s in the USSR, but fell to 1.3 percent in Russia today (China = 1.3 percent; US, Korea, Japan = 2–3 percent; Finland = 4 percent; Israel = 5 percent) (see Figure 6.7). So, today, Russia really looks like a "normal resource abundant developing country."

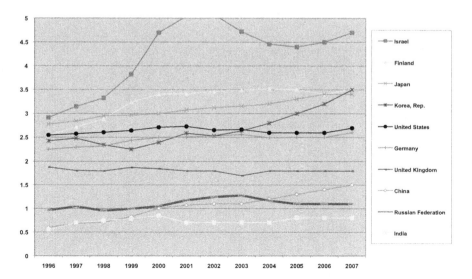

Figure 6.7 R&D expenditure in selected countries, % of GDP

The government failed to channel the stream of petro-dollars to repair the "weakest link" of the national economy – provision of public goods and investment into non-resource industries. Investment and government consumption amounted to about 50 percent of GDP in the early 1990s, fell to below 30 percent of GDP in 1999, right after the 1998 currency crisis, and recovered only partially afterwards – to about 40 percent of GDP in 2007 (see Figure 6.8). Wages and incomes in recent years have been growing systematically faster than productivity.

Tax collection fell dramatically over 1992–98, from over 50 percent of GDP to about 30 percent, whereas GDP itself nearly halved. The efficiency of the government in the 1990s deteriorated greatly: low spending levels meant that the state simply could not provide enough public goods. The shadow economy, which the most generous of estimates placed at 10–15 percent of the GDP under Brezhnev, grew to 50 percent of the GDP by the mid 1990s. In 1980–85, the Soviet Union was placed in the middle of a list of 54 countries rated according to their level of corruption, with a bureaucracy cleaner than that of Italy, Greece, Portugal, South Korea, and practically all the developing countries. In 1996, after the establishment of a market economy and the victory of democracy, Russia came in forty-eighth in the same 54-country list, between India and Venezuela.

Since 1999, revenues and expenditure increased as a percentage of GDP, but by far too little to restore the provision of public goods to the levels of the late USSR. As a result, education and healthcare, public utilities, and law and order continue to be dramatically underfinanced. Instead of using windfall petro-dollars to repair the weakest link – state capacity to provide public goods – the government, on the one hand, decreased tax rates, allowing petro-dollars to leak into personal incomes, and on the other hand maintained a budget surplus that expanded to nearly 10 percent of GDP and was used to finance the accumulation of foreign exchange reserves in the Central Bank of Russia (CBR) and the Stabilization Fund.

The share of investment in GDP increased marginally after 1999, but again, far too little to compensate for the fall of the 1990s. This share remains at a level of

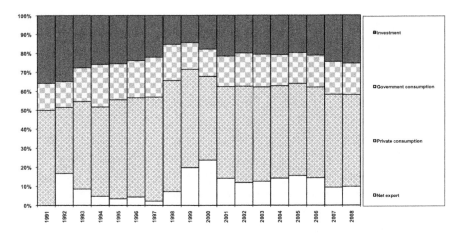

Figure 6.8 Structure of Russian GDP, %

25 percent as compared to 36 percent in 1990–91 (see Figure 6.9), whereas the real volume of investment in 2007 barely reached 40 percent of the 1990 level. It means that Russia was literally "eating up" its capital stock at a time, when the stream of petro-dollars created better conditions for repairing this stock than ever before.

In recent years, Russia has developed a typical "Dutch disease" – dramatic appreciation of the real exchange rate of the rouble (see Figure 6.10) that undermined

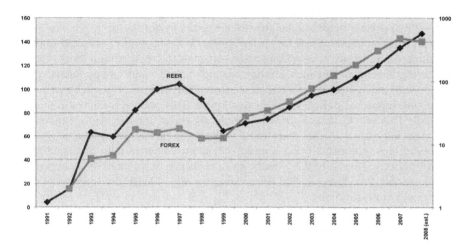

Figure 6.9 Real effective exchange rate (December 1995 = 100%, left scale) and year end gross foreign exchange reserves including gold ($bn, right log scale)

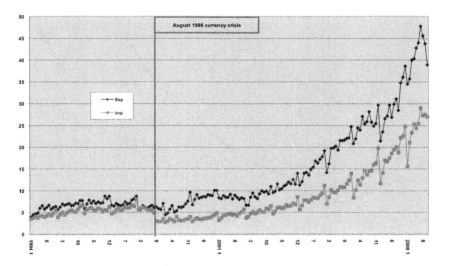

Figure 6.10 Goods exported from and imported to Russia ($bn, monthly data)

growth of all tradable-goods industries except for resource-based. The Russian Central Bank was doing the right thing going against the grain – accumulating foreign exchange reserves to prevent the appreciation of the rouble, but not fast enough to prevent real appreciation of the rouble (growing ratio of Russian prices to foreign prices). As a result, Russian non-fuel industries became non-competitive as compared to foreign goods, so imports in real terms grew faster than anything else in the national economy. As Figures 6.11 and 6.12 suggest, the growing trade surplus of recent years is mostly on account of constantly increasing fuel prices, whereas the growth of the physical volume of imports (fivefold in real terms over 1999–2008) greatly outpaced the growth of exports in real terms.

True, Russia maintains low fuel prices in the domestic market via export taxes and direct administrative restrictions on exports, which create stimuli for the manufacturing industries. But such a policy has high costs – huge energy intensity of GDP, one of the highest in the world. It is theoretically possible to switch to a more promising industrial policy – undervaluation of RER and high domestic prices for fuel. This would have a growth-stimulating effect for the whole economy, and especially for high tech industries, without the misfortunate energy waste. However, there are virtually no resource-abundant countries with this combination of policies. Normally these countries, like Russia, have exactly the opposite combination – low domestic fuel prices and overvalued RER, not to speak of the poor quality of institutions.

Income inequalities increased greatly – Gini coefficient (changes from 0 to 100, the higher the number the higher are inequalities) increased from 26 percent

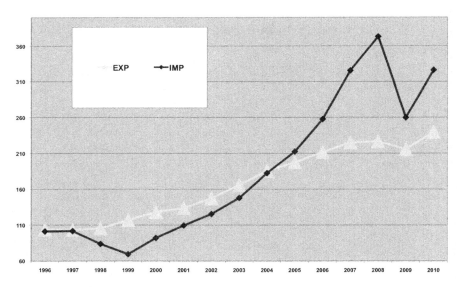

Figure 6.11 Real exports and imports of goods and services (national accounts statistics, 1995 = 100%)

The economic situation in present-day Russia 97

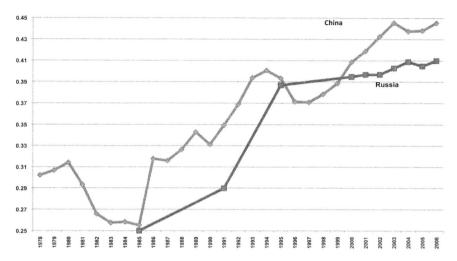

Figure 6.12 Gini coefficient of income distributions in China and Russia, 1978–2006 (source: Chen, Hou, Jin, 2008; Goskomstat)

in 1986 to 40 percent in 2000, and 42 percent in 2007 (see Figure 6.13). The decile coefficient – ratio of incomes of the wealthiest 10 percent of the population to incomes of the poorest 10 percent – increased from 8 in 1992, to 14 in 2000, to 17 in 2007. But the inequalities at the very top increased much faster: in 1995 there was no person in Russia worth over $1 billion; in 2007, according

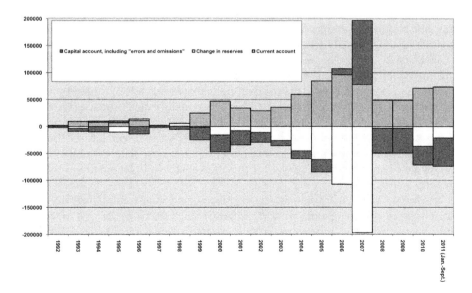

Figure 6.13 Balance of payments items, Russia 1992–2011 ($bn)

to Forbes, Russia had 53 billionaires, which propelled the country to the second/third place in the world after US (415) and Germany (55). Russia had two billionaires less than Germany, but they were worth $282 billion ($37 billion more than Germany's richest). In 2008, the number of billionaires in Russia increased to 86 with a total worth of over $500 billion – one-third of GDP.

The described weaknesses – overvalued exchange rate and lack of diversification of the economy and exports, low spending for investment and public goods, and high income inequalities – were partially concealed by high oil and gas prices in 2003–08, but were not in late 2008 to early 2009, when oil prices fell. From May to November 2008 Russian stocks (RTS index in dollar terms) lost three-quarters of their value. The decline was driven partly by the world financial crisis and partly by declining world oil prices (from a maximum of nearly $150 in June 2008 to below $50 by the end of the year). There was an outflow of capital starting from August 2008, so the foreign exchange reserves dropped from 600 billion in August 2008 to $426 billion by the year end. Seasonally adjusted index of industrial output was not growing since May 2008 and fell by over 10 percent by the year end. The national currency had already gone down from 23 roubles per dollar in July 2008 to 36 by mid 2009. Later the rouble appreciated to 30–33 roubles a dollar in 2010–12, but capital flight continued and only relatively high oil prices and large foreign exchange reserve were preventing the ruble from devaluation (Popov, 2011).

Conclusion

Wassily Leontief (1974) noted once that an economy using the profit motive without planning is like a ship with a sail but no rudder. It may move rapidly, but cannot be steered and might crash into the next rock. A purely planned economy that has eliminated the profit motive is like a ship with a rudder but no sail. It could be steered exactly where one wants it to go, if only it moved. To move forward while avoiding dangerous pitfalls, an economy needs both some reliance on the profit motive and some planning, a sail and a rudder.

Similarly, Holmes (1997) claims that the major lesson to be learned by western democracies from recent Russian developments is exactly the one about the crucial importance of the state institutions. Whereas the Soviet Union has proven that a non-market economic system with the strongest state cannot be efficient, Russia today is proving that the market without strong state degrades to the exchange of unaccountable power for the untaxable wealth leading to economic decline.

In Popov (2000, 2007), various explanations of the transformational recession are discussed and the alternative explanation is suggested: the collapse of output was caused primarily by several groups of factors. First, by greater distortions in the industrial structure and external trade patterns on the eve of the transition. Second, by the collapse of state and non-state institutions, which occurred in the late 1980s–early 1990s, and which resulted in chaotic transformation through crisis management instead of organized and manageable transition. Third, by poor economic policies, which basically consisted of bad macroeconomic policy and import substitution industrial policy. Finally, fourth, the speed of reforms (economic liberalization) affected performance negatively at the stage of the reduction of output because enterprises were forced to restructure faster than they possibly could (because of limited investment potential), but positively at the recovery stage.

This second reason – the institutional collapse – is largely responsible for the extreme depth of the transformational recession; here differences between eastern European (EE) and former Soviet Union (FSU) countries are striking. The adverse supply shock in this case came from the inability of the state to perform its traditional functions – to collect taxes and to constrain the shadow economy, to ensure property and contract rights, and law and order in general. Naturally, poor ability to enforce rules and regulations did not create a business climate conducive to growth and resulted in the increased costs for companies.

The trick of transition, as is evident *post factum*, was not to carry out economic liberalization, but to carry it out in such a way as not to throw away the baby with the bathwater, not to squander the precious achievements of the previous communist period in the form of strong institutions. China generally did not squander this heritage, even though government spending fell, income inequalities rose and crime rates increased, whereas Russia and most other Commonwealth of Independent States (CIS) did.

Reforms that are needed to achieve success are different for countries with different backgrounds. Manufacturing growth is like cooking a good dish – all needed ingredients should be in the right proportion; if only one is under- or over-represented, the "chemistry of growth" would not happen. Fast economic growth can materialize in practice only if several necessary conditions are met simultaneously. Rapid growth is a complicated process that requires a number of crucial inputs – infrastructure, human capital, even land distribution in agrarian countries, strong state institutions, economic stimuli, among other things. Once one of these crucial necessary ingredients is missing, the growth just does not take off. Rodrik *et al.* (2005) talk about "binding constraints" that hold back economic growth. Finding these constraints is the task of "growth diagnostics." In some cases, these constraints are associated with the lack of market liberalization; in others with the lack of state capacity, or human capital, or infrastructure.

Why economic liberalization worked in central Europe, but did not work in Sub-Saharan Africa and Latin America (LA)? The answer, according to the outlined approach, would be that in central Europe the missing ingredient was economic liberalization, whereas in SSA and LA there was a lack of state capacity, not the lack of market liberalization. Why did liberalization work in China and central Europe and did not work in the CIS? Because in the CIS it was carried out in such a way as to undermine the state capacity – the precious heritage of socialist past – whereas in central Europe, and even more so in China, the state capacity did not decline substantially during transition. The reduction of government expenditure as a share of GDP did not undermine significantly the institutional capacity of the state in China, but in Russia and other CIS states it turned out to be ruinous.

Note

1 The views expressed in this chapter reflect the opinions of the author and not that of organizations with which the author is associated.

References

Chen, Jiandong, Wenxuan Hou and Shenwu Jin (2008). *The Effects of Population on Income Disparity in a Dual Society: Evidence from China*. 2008 Chinese (UK) Economic Association annual conference at Cambridge, UK and the 2008 Hong Kong Economic Association Fifth Biennial Conference at Chengdu, China.

Holmes, S. (1997). "What Russia Teaches Us Now," *The American Prospect*, July–August, 1997, p. 30–9.

Leontief, Wassily (1974). "Sails and Rudders, Ship of State," in Leonard Silk (ed.) *Capitalism, the Moving Target*. New York: Quadrangle Books, 1974, pp. 101–04.

Popov, V. (2000) "Shock Therapy versus Gradualism: The End of the Debate (Explaining the Magnitude of the Transformational Recession)," *Comparative Economic Studies*, 42(1): 1–57.

Popov, V. (2004). "The State in the New Russia (1992–2004): From Collapse to Gradual Revival?", *PONARS Policy Memo* No. 342, November 2004.

Popov, V. (2007) "Shock Therapy versus Gradualism Reconsidered: Lessons from Transition Economies after 15 Years of Reforms," *Comparative Economic Studies*, 49(1): 1–31.

Popov, V. (2009). *"Lessons from the Transition Economies. Putting the Success Stories of the Postcommunist World into a Broader Perspective,"* UNU/WIDER Research Paper, No. 2009/15.

Popov, V. (2009). "Memories about the Future: The Second Edition of the 1998 Crisis," *Russian Analytical Digest*, No. 54, February 3, 2009.

Popov, V. (2010). "Mortality Crisis in Russia Revisited: Evidence from Cross-Regional Comparison," *MPRA Paper*, No. 21311, March 2010.

Popov, V. (2011). "To Devaluate or not to Devalue? How East European Countries Responded to the Outflow of Capital in 1997–99 and in 2008–09," *CEFIR and NES Working Paper*, No. 154. January 2011.

Rodrik, D., R. Hausmann, and A. Velasco (2005). "Growth Diagnostics, 2005." Available at: http//www.ksghome.harvard.edu/~drodrik/barcelonafinalmarch2005.pdf.

World Bank (1997), *The State in A Changing World. World Development Report*, New York: Oxford University Press, 1997.

7 Tandemology as spectator sport

The course of Medvedev's campaigns to curb corruption and encourage modernization

J. L. Black

A new version of Russia's National Strategy for Countering Corruption and the National Plan for Countering Corruption in 2010–2011 was introduced with great fanfare by the Kremlin in April 2010. These two integrated anti-corruption documents fine-tuned a similar plan and strategy signed into law by President Dmitry Medvedev early in his first year as president. At that time he made curbing corruption a personal crusade, warning then, and in the 2010 edict, that corruption threatened Russian security, handicapped economic development, and damaged the country's image abroad.

The upgraded assault on corruption followed, by about six months, Medvedev's pronouncement that economic modernization was vital to Russia's future and could no longer be delayed. With two years of apparently unproductive struggle against corruption already behind him, and facing a wave of scepticism washing over his newer scheme for the modernization of Russia, in 2010 Medvedev intensified the battle on both fronts.

Though they have much deeper roots, the economic, political, or social implications of Medvedev's anti-corruption and modernization campaigns are treated here as current phenomena worthy of description and comprehension – with reference mostly to Russian opinion. 'Corruption' and 'modernization' are words with very broad manifestations, but the targets for this chapter are corruption within the bloated Russian bureaucracy and modernization as a pragmatic means to tie Russia efficiently and productively to the global economy. A dilemma for Medvedev from the beginning was the fact that his first crusade, curbing corruption, had to succeed before the second battle, modernization, could be won. Characterizing them as crusades is not unreasonable given the importance he attached to them in his rhetoric.

During the final two years of Medvedev's term as president, the election of March 2012 loomed large over every statement and decision made by him or by Prime Minister Vladimir Putin. Since 2008 these two men governed Russia in what came to be called a Tandem, a name coined to convey a new system in which the president, constitutionally by far the most powerful person in Russia, and the prime minister governed Russia together as equals. Although bloggers and pundits predicted the end of the Tandem from the moment of its inception, and sought frantically for any nuance that might yield a clue to one or the other's political demise, few substantive distinctions between them were found. The tendency to exaggerate subtle differences between the two leaders provided useful talking points – called here Tandemology – for public and even learned discourse. These discussions brought subjects into the public eye that might not otherwise have been broached.

Although Putin was also well aware of the debilitating consequences of corruption,[1] it was Medvedev who forced the issue to the forefront. His lengthy Strategy called on the Public Chamber, the Chamber of Commerce and Industry, the Association of Lawyers of Russia, political parties, public organizations, and other bodies to help turn popular opinion against bribe taking and bribe offering. 'An atmosphere of strict intolerance to corruption' must be created, the document intoned.

By April 2010 few people would deny that corruption was a nationwide problem. Corruption perpetuated long-standing mistrust of government agencies and officials at all levels, served as an almost insurmountable hindrance to small business growth, rendered the judicial system impotent, and embarrassed Russia abroad. Sporadic and enthusiastic public drives against individual corrupt officials had not altered the overall situation to any great degree, and Russian non-government commentary on the new plan and strategy was subdued, at best patronizing, at worst outright scornful.[2]

Attempts to modernize Russia were nothing new either. From Peter the Great to M. S. Gorbachev, scattered leaders pushed Russia to modernize, under the rubrics of Westernization, from the eighteenth to early twentieth century, and a Marxist–Leninist *perestroika* in the 1980s. Putin reintroduced the need for modernization as early as December 1999 in a speech often referred to as the 'Putin Manifesto'.[3] Circumstances, history, habit, and officialdom slapped them all down mercilessly.

During the USSR's final half-decade, Gorbachev was faced with a huge and cumbersome ruling elite that neither wanted nor understood the need for change. Membership in the Communist Party was almost the sole avenue for upward career movement, and members perceived any challenge to the system as a threat to their mobility. The Communist Party of the Soviet Union (CPSU) provided entrée to local and national political and social power, and special privilege: access to dachas, special healthcare facilities, rare consumer goods, mutual protection, and bribes of all kind. In effect, the CPSU was the institutional framework for a giant *krysha*, a 'roof' for millions of members for whom quality of work and efficiency were of only secondary concern. David Remnick's characterization of the CPSU *apparat* as 'the most gigantic mafia the world has ever known' was well founded.[4]

It did not take long for Gorbachev to discover that efforts to reform the system would be wasted if the public were left out of the equation. Urging the population to work harder with neither incentive nor purpose quickly proved pointless and forced him to adopt a 'democratization' programme in the workplace. When that failed to bring the public onside, he had no choice but to introduce *glasnost* (openness, publicity), to demonstrate precisely why citizens should be working harder.

This first small step towards transparency backfired in that the concomitant shattering of the CPSU's monopoly on the dissemination of information proved fatal to the USSR itself. The public suddenly took up the cause of re-shaping Soviet society, but instead of more productive labour they put their hammers and sickles down and took up pen, politics, and strikes.

The Soviet Union dissolved in a flurry of promised democratic changes, most of which faded from sight in the 1990s as re-shaped state agencies continued to serve the interests of the individuals and groups who ran them. Corrupt officials and a small class of acquisitive entrepreneurs combined to shift state assets to a handful of newly-minted capitalists, usually referred to as 'oligarchs', i.e. holders of great wealth and influence over the country's political arena, its media, and its economy.[5] A new and powerful non-party faction also emerged within government. Dubbed the *siloviki*, the group included former and even serving members of intelligence agencies, the armed forces, and other uniformed institutions. They consolidated and strengthened their positions during the post-Soviet first decade when, Constitution of 1993 notwithstanding, no one was truly in charge.[6] Public office was, as before, the wellspring of privilege and perquisite, and now also a potential source of enormous personal wealth.

Every prime minister in the 1990s knew the truth of Sergei Stepashin's statement to the Federation Council in May 1999 that, no matter how much progress there was, 'crime and corruption reduce the best ventures to nothing'.[7] Putin faced this dilemma himself after he replaced Stepashin as prime minister in August and during his first four years as president. Early in 2001 he handed the Security Council a special mandate to fight corruption and, a little more than a year later, created a Council for Combatting Corruption responsible directly to him. The State Duma formed a commission of its own to fight corruption in 2003. But Putin had far more pressing business with which to deal, and the Duma's enthusiasm for ending corruption was feeble to begin with. Thus, there was little pressure on these bodies to curb bureaucratic corruption, which in turn was abetted by the relentless growth of the bureaucracy itself.

The super-bureaucratization of present-day Russia was not Putin's invention. It had its first spurt during the chaotic Gorbachev years, as the Brezhnev system was broken apart in the name of *perestroika*. It was under Gorbachev and Yeltsin that the *krysha* system took its current form; that is, the 'roofs' were privatized along with the national assets.[8] Oligarchs who controlled key sectors of the economy sometimes had prior association with organized crime, and together they provided complimentary legal and illegal forms of protection for huge economic complexes. To wrest economic power from the oligarchs and shift it to the state apparatus, Putin launched operations against a few select targets. Several fled the country and at least one, Mikhail Khodorkovsky, still languishes in prison. The remaining billionaires agreed to avoid opposition politics and pay their taxes. In return, the threat of re-nationalizing former state assets was removed. Putin's policies provided an answer to the 'who is in charge?' query that dominated public conversation during the unstable Yeltsin era: officialdom and mandarins – just as they had during much of Russian history.

Shifting economic power back to the state did not resolve the corruption problem. In the year before Medvedev became president, evidence suggested that corruption had spread more widely than even in the 1990s. Some analysts believed that bribery and kickbacks were so integrated into the system that the general population saw them as part of a normal way of life. They provided a perverse sort of order that the public understood and with which they could live.[9]

The new president also had to deal with international disapproval generated by widely cited international corruption ratings. In 2007, the Corruption Perception Index produced annually by Transparency International placed Russia one hundred and forty-third out of 180 countries.[10] The next year there was some slight improvement in score (one hundred and twenty-sixth of 154 countries listed), but the new ranking was still horrific for Russia's international prestige and attractiveness to foreign investors.

Corruption and modernization came together as themes in Medvedev's annual address in November 2009. Although the bulk of the speech was taken up with modernization and the means to achieve it, corruption was pinpointed as a 'social evil' to be fought 'on all fronts'. Complaining of Russia's 'chronic backwardness, dependence on raw materials export, and corruption', the president outlined domestic problems with candour and laid out a blueprint for a new type of *perestroika*. He defined modernization as a matter of developing the four 'i's – investment, innovation, infrastructure, and institutions. In the latter case, Medvedev highlighted the values and institutions of democracy.

Bringing the population on side was a daunting task. A public opinion survey on modernization conducted in November 2009 revealed that a clear majority of Russians were doubtful about prospects for its success. Nearly 60 per cent believed that a transition to an innovative economy, if it was to occur at all, depended almost entirely upon government intervention, and only about 12 per cent believed that it depended on the people themselves. That said, there were no uniform ideas on how the government should behave as the engine of change.[11]

Inculcating 'intolerance' to corruption was an equally imposing challenge. Medvedev was the first Russian leader to grant the reduction of corruption priority in practice as opposed to merely in speeches. Adopting modernization as a co-priority expanded the enormity of his ambition. These two causes marked Medvedev then as more than Putin's parrot, though not necessarily his competitor.

Where to go for help was a first consideration in the modernization campaign. Yeltsin turned to foreign advisers when he tried to overhaul Russia's economy in the nineties, with well-known disastrous results. In his turn, Putin made a point of ignoring foreign advice, often – and usually rightly – referring to it as unwelcome and unhelpful preaching. He protected designated 'national champions' and strategic industries from foreign ownership. Obsessed with re-establishing Russia as a major player in world politics and economics, and buoyed for nearly a decade by high-energy prices, Putin lent credence to a new unofficial state ideology, vaguely termed 'sovereign democracy'. Expressed first by Vladislav Surkov, deputy head of the Kremlin administration, the doctrine is above all a 'doing it our own way' approach to transition. The aggressive Eurasianism pushed by Putin therefore persuaded some observers in Russia that Medvedev's appeal to international participation in his modernization campaign was an early challenge to Putinism.

The modernization campaign was institutionalized in May 2009 when a Commission for Modernization and Technological Development (CMTD) was formed. Its mandate was 'to promote the sustainable technological development of Russia's economy and to improve public administration by promoting modernization programmes in priority economic fields'.[12] Shortly thereafter, priority sectors were broadly defined as those with existing momentum, parts of the economy that could serve as a catalyst for modernization in related industries, spheres related to defence and security, and projects with social benefits for Russia's people.

Over the next three years the commission met on sites all around the country, entertained briefs from large and powerful companies, such as Gazprom, discussed modernization partnerships with the European Union, and issued press releases on proposals ranging from energy-saving light bulbs to the creation of Russia's own computer games industry.

The most ambitious project was announced just two weeks after Medvedev's new anti-corruption programme was signed into law. At the end of April 2010 he outlined the legal framework for a major innovation project announced already in March, a Russian version of the Silicon Valley at Skolkovo, in the Moscow Region. No room was left for doubt that Skolkovo was Medvedev's project.[13] The idea was to build a new technology town (innogorod) from scratch, in an area that was already the site of Moscow's International School of Management.

Anatoly Chubais, former chief of the Russian Unified Energy System (UES) and currently general director of the Russian Corporation of Nanotechnologies (ROSNANO), was placed in charge of seeding the project with money from Russia's modernization and innovation budget, and US$500 million in investments. Other sources of funding were sought aggressively.

Billionaire Viktor Vekselberg, head of the Renova group of companies and major shareholder in BP's Russian subsidiary, TNK-BP, was named coordinator of the Russian part of the Skolkovo Innovation Centre. The aim was to attract young scientists for work on priorities set earlier by the president and narrowed even further to energy efficiency, strategic information technology, telecommunications (space technology), medical technology, and nuclear technology. More appointments were named to Skolkovo's board of directors, steps were taken to attract top foreign scientists, and grants were established for young researchers in the defence industry. Two management bodies were put in place: a council to oversee everyday operations and an advisory board for issues related to science.

In light of Putin's relatively insular approach to economic development, Medvedev's appointments as co-chairs of the scientific advisory board and its sub-units were quite extraordinary. These were two Americans and a Russian communist: Craig R. Barrett as co-chair of the supervisory board to manage the project's companies; Roger Kornberg and Zhores Alferov as co-chairs of the organization's research council. Kornberg and Alferov are both Nobel Prize winners, in Chemistry and Physics respectively. Barrett is a former CEO of Intel Corporation. Medvedev explained his choices as follows: 'I am absolutely certain that the involvement of these two exceptional people will spur international interest towards our project. We need exactly these kinds of well-known people'.[14] Several Russian pundits remarked wryly that there was an additional reason for such choices – Russian government officials at the top might be susceptible to corruption.[15]

To attract potential innovators to Skolkovo, Medvedev offered a ten-year 'privileged' tax regime for Russians (no property or land taxes, exemption from VAT, and so on), special entry and exit rules for foreign scientists and entrepreneurs, state grants for research projects in priority sectors of the national economy, and substantial funding for relevant research at Russian universities. Plans were put forward to send up to 500 Russians who were part of a programme titled 'Managers in the Innovation Sphere' abroad for a period of managerial internship. To qualify, candidates for the programme had to be under 40 years of age, prepare a specific project to work on, have completed some higher education, and speak a foreign language. The Ministry of Education concluded bilateral agreements for specific courses of study with seven countries in Europe, plus the United States and Kazakhstan.

In addition to financial incentives to lure foreign scientists and business to Skolkovo, immigration laws were changed to make it easier for foreign workers to bring their skills to Russia. The Federal Migration Service may now override previously set quotas to provide work permits for highly qualified foreigners on the basis of written requests by a Russian employer. Residence permits will be available without preconditions and workers hired under the modernization programme will pay less than half of the taxes previously required.[16]

Skolkovo will have a special form of local self-government. Though as yet undefined, it is conceivable that the shape that governing body takes on will itself represent an innovation that may prove useful as a model for other parts of Russia. Arkady Dvorkovich, presidential aide and executive secretary of the CMTD, hinted as much in the spring of 2010, long before the flurry of changes brought on by the election crises of December 2011 and March 2012.[17]

Desperate to bring the US on board, in May 2010 Medvedev met personally in Gorki with visiting heads of American venture capital funds to discuss prospects for joint projects in such areas as biomedical technology, energy efficiency, space and nuclear industries, and the commercialization of new technology at Skolkovo. Special Aide to the US President on national security, Michael McFaul – named ambassador to Russia a year later – and Surkov participated in the meeting. To sustain its call for help from North America, the Russian government launched an English-language website specifically to tout the merits and progress of its modernization campaign.[18] The appeal was but a part of a flurry of Russian diplomatic overtures to the West in which the Kremlin tied its modernization campaign to foreign policy. A EU–Russia Partnership for Modernization established in late 2009 still tends to be long on promise and short on accomplishment, but serves as a useful sounding board for Medvedev's ideas.

At home, Surkov urged Russia's largest business associations, Business Russia and the Russian Union of Industrialists and Entrepreneurs, to participate in innovation projects.[19] They responded by demanding that the government stop harassing business. Nonetheless, over 50 Russian companies had applied to the CMTD for funding in support of various projects by mid-summer 2010.[20] Russian Railways and the Alfa Group were the first domestic companies to set up offices at Skolkovo.

Two important foreign companies signed on in early June 2010: Nokia, the world's largest manufacturer of mobile phones, and General Electric (GE). Nokia agreed to help coordinate research in software development; GE reached an agreement on a joint venture within the energy and health care sectors.[21] Medvedev drew support from other large American firms during a quick visit to the Silicon Valley in 2010. CISCO Systems, for example, announced that it would invest $1 billion over the next decade in high-tech innovation in Russia, and maintain a physical presence in Skolkovo.[22] Google decided to invest and construct a research centre at Skolkovo. Microsoft and Siguler Guff, a huge US private equity investment firm, also came on board.

In both his crusades, Medvedev appeared to switch direction from that of his immediate predecessor. This was true early on in his fight against corruption, which was on the front burner almost from the day of his election as president in 2008. Speaking that year to an All-Russian Civic Forum in Moscow, for example, Medvedev insisted that a full-scale national assault had to be launched against corruption. He was the first Russian leader to recognize openly that corruption is a long-standing part of Russian culture itself. Calling this home grown phenomenon 'legal nihilism', he added that no other European state has a similar level of disdain for the law.[23] In contrast to Putin, who tended to blame foreign influences and oligarchs for his country's ills, Medvedev did not hesitate to place a large part of the blame on Russia's own 'people in power'.[24]

The president knew that he had to get the Russian public involved in the war against corruption for the modernization plan to succeed. But surveys tended to confirm the opinion of Stanislav Belkovsky, president of the National Strategy Institute and no friend of the administration, who insisted that the 'universal acceptance of corruption' within Russia's population would prove impossible to change in the 'foreseeable future'.[25] Doubt about the president's ability to rein in corruption was rooted in reality and history. Public criticism of the National Strategy portrayed it as a way of putting the old *apparatchiki* in charge of implementing a programme purported to protect the country from – the *apparatchiki*, i.e. the foxes guarding the henhouse.

Hoping to persuade the public that something was being done to curb corruption, Prosecutor General Yury Chaika reported in January 2010 that over 800 senior officials were charged with crimes related to corruption in the previous year. A new spate of arrests and trials of corrupt officials from all walks of bureaucratic life were highlighted in the Russian media, implying that no one was inviolate. But these were only the tip of the iceberg. In the case of charges against highly placed officials, the question seemed always to be whether the fight against corruption was real, or merely a weapon wielded in an on-going war between powerful cliques within the inner circles of Russian politics and economics.

The fact that in many such cases charges were eventually dropped tended to confirm public cynicism.

Particularly depressing was the news from the military. Defence Minister Valery Serdyukov's widespread dismissals and forced retirements of senior officers, and purge of his entire procurement section, notwithstanding, Chief Military Investigator Aleksandr Sorochkin told an interviewer in March 2010 that 'the dimensions and scope of corruption of individual officials [in the military] is mind-boggling'.[26] Equally discouraging was the news from the educational sector, where systemic corruption was found at both ends of the spectrum: bribes to secure places in kindergarten classes and to gain university admission. As late in Medvedev's term as March 2012, corruption in the education system remained systemic.[27]

Foreign investors have not helped. In March 2010, for instance, the US Justice Department charged German carmaker, Daimler, with bribing Russian officials to purchase its cars over the years 2000 to 2008. The Russian Ministry of the Interior was accused of taking nearly half of this amount, and six other Russians businesses or official agencies, including the military, were charged with the remainder.[28] At that time, Germany's Siemens and America's Hewlett-Packard were also under investigation for allegedly offering millions in kickbacks in return for business opportunities in Russia.

An odd consequence of the hardly shocking revelation that foreign companies provided Russia officials with bribes was a public pledge in April by some multinationals that they would offer no (further) bribes in Russia. Initiated by the Russian–German Chamber of Commerce in Moscow, the pledge was taken by 56 companies, mostly German, including Daimler, Siemens, and Deutsche Bank. Several large Russia-based companies, such as St Petersburg's Lenergo and TNK-BP, signed on and more followed. Russian cynics suggested that this would merely force corporate bribers to pay higher amounts and guard their secrets more closely.

The public at large was more sceptical about Medvedev's campaign to end corruption than it was about modernization. A poll of some 2,000 Russian citizens conducted in January 2010 found that 79 per cent believed that the level of corruption in Russia was high, and 58 per cent said that in a year's time it would be higher than it was at the time the question was asked.[29] These and other surveys also demonstrated that a majority of Russians believed that the state was the only agency capable of ensuring modernization. On the other hand, analyst Leonid Grigoriev cautioned as early as 2007 that, whereas a strong state is the essential engine of development in Russia, it must still prevent state regulation from 'cutting off oxygen' to innovation.[30] The potential for contradiction between state intervention and the independence needed for innovation has been a centuries-long dilemma for Russia.

For Medvedev, this was particularly the case within the political sphere. Whereas most Russian authorities believed that modernization could be achieved without major political change, the bulk of Western analysts assume that loftier goals, such as greater transparency, supremacy of law, and political democracy are necessary prerequisites to modernization. This conundrum made it likely that the foreign companies would stick to the comfortable special regime at the Innogorod and not venture much further into the Russian economic morass.

Even as the question of corruption hovered as a gloomy shadow over the quest for modernization, a few early signs of a desire for change emerged in the summer of 2010. Medvedev's chances of bringing the citizenry on side in the struggle against corruption were bolstered by emerging public fury over government and business officials claiming special privilege and getting away with blatant acts of injustice, some as extreme as hit-and-run crimes and mysterious in-prison deaths. One sign of the growing outrage was a 'blue bucket' campaign against the flashing blue lights (*migalki*) used by wealthy and powerful drivers to ignore traffic and other rules. Another was a detailed poll conducted in June by the Academy of Sciences that showed that the public was far more interested in social fairness than they were in modernization. These respondents believed that modernization would succeed only if corruption was checked first.[31] The newly focused popular anger might have been a cause for the other telling change: opinion polls in the spring and summer of 2010 found Medvedev was running nearly neck-and-neck with Putin in popularity, and *Nezavisimaia gazeta*'s quarterly ranking of the most influential people in Russia placed Medvedev slightly ahead of Putin for the first time. That lead was short-lived but nonetheless significant. In July, surveys suggested that the number of Russians who had confidence in Russia's ability to modernize rose slightly, to 17 per cent from 12 per cent in November 2009; 32 per cent saw the chances of his success as poor, a drop from 38 per cent the earlier survey.[32] Not a great leap forward, to be sure, but a sign that Medvedev's campaigning may finally have found an audience – an audience that was to erupt on to the streets two years later.

As for the modernization file, Putin suddenly became a target in the spring of 2010. One analyst placed him and Surkov among 'conservatives' who feared that modernization on the Medvedev model would ensure renewed chaos like that which came with *perestroika* and *glasnost*.[33] Another political writer predicted that 'Putin officialdom' would stifle innovations started at Skolkovo.[34] Analogies with Gorbachev's *perestroika* grew more common, put forward at first by writers who thought Medvedev's campaigns were whimsical and probably fatal politically. References to Potemkin Villages popped up in connection with Skolkovo.[35] Gorbachev himself chimed in, warning in July that the elites would 'talk' the idea of modernization (which he supports) into irrelevance. Belkovsky took up the theme of a renewed *perestroika* as well, reminding readers in a series of bitterly sarcastic essays of the 'chaotic processes, that accompanied Gorbachev's failed attempts to modernize'.[36] Chubais, an old *perestroikite* now involved heavily in the modernization process, insisted that political transformation was necessary for that campaign to succeed. Another Russian pundit believed that modernization would be possible only if Medvedev fired Putin.[37] There was never much chance of that.

Not many Russian analysts saw the struggle for modernization as a matter of competing visions for Russia's future offered by Medvedev and Putin, but a few political people did. For instance, Olga Kryshtanovskaia, prominent among members of United Russia's (UR) Liberal Club, proclaimed that her own party's conservatism was a barrier to modernization. Because the UR is better known as Putin's party, the charge could not help but reflect on him.[38] If there was a serious dichotomy within the ruling Tandem over Skolkovo, however, it remained well hidden. The rationale for the Tandem all along had been that the two men were 'like-minded' and shared the same visions for their country. They merely had separate portfolios. Medvedev confirmed their political unity of mind at a modernization forum convened in September at Yaroslavl. Promising that there would be no major changes in the political structure of Russia, he warned that 'parliamentary democracy' – as opposed to centralized presidential democracy – would prove ruinous. Here was unequivocal accommodation with Putin and Russia's conservative elites.

The modernization campaign was energized in October 2010 when California's governor, Arnold Schwarzenegger, arrived at the head of a large team of American venture capitalists and enthusiastically touted cooperation between the Silicon Valley and Skolkovo. Executives from Google, Microsoft, and Oracle were with the delegation and were plainly interested. Microsoft pledged millions in support of Skolkovo, and a few weeks later the South Korean government joined the enterprise. But these encouraging words about one of Medvedev's campaigns were tempered by almost simultaneous discouraging words on the corruption front. Chaika told a meeting of the heads of law enforcement agencies that the size of average bribes had surged by a third as the government's campaign against corruption faltered, and complained that law enforcement agencies had slacked off in their anti-corruption efforts.

One Russian authority responded to Chaika's remarks with the prediction that the 'Christian crusade against corruption' will fail because corruption 'is part of the Russian mentality'.[39] That is precisely what Medvedev complained about in the first place. Adding insult to injury, in October, Transparency International ranked Russia one hundred and fifty-fourth of 178 countries for 2010 – on a par with Laos, Cambodia, Congo, Papua New Guinea, and Tajikistan – and WikiLeak exposés caught foreign diplomats privately referring to Russia as a 'virtual mafia state'.[40] Perhaps that is why Medvedev's crusade against corruption was almost frantic in 2011 as he dismissed dozens of generals from both law enforcement and the military, replaced governors, and ordered senior government officials to give up their seats on boards of major companies.

Although their success or failure depended on systemic change at home, the anti-corruption and pro-modernization campaigns had serious international ramifications for Russia. Towards the end of March 2011, Medvedev outlined the so-called 'Ten Commandments of Investing' in Russia so as to attract further Russian and foreign investments. These rules, in which he again highlighted the debilitating factor of corruption, were delivered in Magnitogorsk at a meeting of the CMTD. Among other things, he created a mechanism to deal with corruption complaints, promised to launch a direct investment fund, and broadened the powers of the Ministry of Economic Development.

The Skolkovo Innovation Centre grew apace in 2011, with about 300 companies signed up as residents by the end of the year.[41] The link-ups were not all one-way; for example, in March 2011 ROSNANO opened an office in the Silicon Valley. When it came to popular appeal at home, however, even Medvedev acknowledged in April 2011 that few Russians had any idea what Skolkovo was all about.[42] As it was one of the defining pillars of his presidency, this revelation must have been dispiriting.

When Medvedev remarked in the spring of 2011 that he would consider running for president again, Russian bloggers and mainstream journalists had a field day. Some said the president was merely posturing, others insisted that he was making a pre-emptive strike before Putin gained the initiative; some said that the Tandem was as strong as ever, others said that it was doomed. Belkovsky predicted that in July Medvedev would hand in his resignation and Putin would 'return to the Kremlin'.[43] Putin added to the confusion, telling reporters that it was too early for him to say if he would run again, or even if Medvedev would seek a second term. He reasoned aloud that if either of their decisions were known 'half the presidential administration and more than half the government would stop working in expectation of some kind of change'.[44]

The excited Tandemologists pounced in a flood of journalistic probing, pondering, and pandering: the Tandem was obsolete; the Tandem was plotting to provide sinecures for themselves and run a third candidate in their stead; conflict within the Tandem was growing; the Tandem is the only source of stability for Russia, and so on.[45] A more tangible event came in late April when Gleb Pavlovsky, head of the influential Foundation for Effective Politics and contractual adviser to the presidential administration, resigned that latter post. Clearly supportive of Medvedev, he called the fact that neither potential candidate for president wanted to speak openly about it 'absurd' and said that he had to be free to speak his mind on the subject.[46] A mainstream newspaper termed Medvedev and Putin 'liberal' and 'conservative' respectively in their approaches to economic modernization, and the modernization project figured more prominently in the public discussion about presidential qualifications.[47]

This may have been why Putin suddenly jumped on the modernization bandwagon – though in general terms only – and acknowledged that corruption needed to be 'reined in'. In his 2011 report on the government's performance during the previous year, Putin expressed a desire for modernization in the military and Russia's economic infrastructure while avoiding any reference to Skolkovo or any change in political institutions. Russia 'requires decades of steady, uninterrupted development. Without sudden radical changes in course or ill-thought-through experiments based in ... unjustified economic liberalism', he intoned.[48] Bloggers and journalists seized on this remark as an oblique backhand to Medvedev's brand of modernization, though it was more likely a reference to the ill-fated shock therapy of the 1990s.

Fault lines were spotted both in the Tandem and within the *siloviki* by the spring of 2011. Though minor, there was always the danger that such divisions could expand exponentially like a crack in an automobile's windshield. Whether these perceived differences of opinion were substantial or not, and many saw them as greatly exaggerated,[49] it was clear that some visible progress in his two pet projects were necessary if Medvedev hoped to return as president. He crossed a line himself by telling an interviewer for *The Financial Times* in June that 'any leader, who holds a presidential office, is simply obliged' to run for a second term.[50]

In China for a BRICS (Brazil, Russia, India, China, South Africa) summit, Medvedev added a sub-text. Russia's only path to a strong future lay with the 'modernization of the economy and modernization of [Russia's] political life', he told an interviewer for Chinese television. Accompanied by a delegation of 100 Russian business people, he visited Hong Kong a day after the BRICS meetings and urged the business community there to participate in Skolkovo. Putin fired back by announcing a new Agency for Strategic Initiatives (ASI), to promote business by curbing bureaucratic impediments, recruiting and training young professionals, and encouraging innovation. Putin's plan focused on training and recruiting Russians, whereas Medvedev internationalized his scheme by relying on foreign expertise. Whether intended or not, the ASI had the potential of derailing Medvedev's modernization campaign.

The anti-corruption dossier was expanded in 2011 too. The tax service opened a hot line and e-mail address in January for citizens to report corruption offences without having to leave their name. The Public Chamber followed suit in February with its own phone hotline and website, calling on citizens to report corrupt officials. At about the same time an announcement that more than one-third of the people who committed corruption-related crimes in 2010 were policemen confirmed a commonly held opinion.

Medvedev took accusations against law enforcement officials seriously. Senior policemen and ministry of interior personnel began dropping like flies. The head of Moscow's traffic police was fired in January 2011 and a month later the deputy head of the FSB was fired for 'ethics violations'. Between then and June over 60 more police generals, three colonels, and two deputy ministers were dismissed from the MVD. Another one-third of the senior police officers did not pass the screening test established in 2010 (119 of 335) and lost their jobs.[51] The extent of corruption within law enforcement, including former policemen, prosecutors, tax inspectors, customs agents, and even judges was such that Medvedev had to create a prison system for them alone – to protect them from other inmates. Ten such 'police prisons' have been mandated, using old prison colony facilities.[52]

Among the new anti-corruption rules was a bill to increase fines for both commercial kickbacks and the taking and offering of bribes. Following up his earlier judgement that financial penalties were more effective than the threat of prison terms, Medvedev's amendments to the criminal code and code of administrative offences set penalties at multiples up to 100 times the bribe amount.[53] He then ordered the immediate dismissal of any state official implicated in schemes to siphon off funds allocated to regional communal and housing services. This latter decision was made shortly after the head of the Kremlin's control department, Konstantin Chuichenko, told Medvedev in a televised meeting that the equivalent of nearly $900 million allocated to such services had been stolen over the previous two years.

The public seemed finally to take notice after Police Major-General Aleksandr Nazarov told *Rossiiskaia gazeta* that the average kickback amount had more than doubled since 2010 and that large bribes were up by 30 per cent since 2009. Tens of thousands of violations were recorded within officialdom in both the federal and regional spheres of government.[54] And, in May 2011, reports demonstrated that property prices in Moscow were inflated by about 60 per cent as a result of rampant corruption.[55]

Corruption watchers in Moscow had their day as senior police officers, city tax officials, and the former head of the Moscow Metro system were arrested and charged with various crimes. The president and vice president of the Bank of Moscow, and Yelena Baturina, wife of ex-Moscow Mayor Yuri Luzhkov, were all caught up in corruption investigations. The condition of municipal services in Moscow was such that Luzhkov's replacement, Sergei Sobyanin, told journalists that every sphere in his municipal services was corrupt, and that he had to use lie-detector tests to weed the miscreants out.[56]

Officially sanctioned separate demonstrations against corruption on the streets of Moscow led by the pro-government youth movement, *Nashi*, and liberal oppositionist People's Freedom Party were described by detractors as interesting but unlikely to break the everyday opinion that corruption is not evil, rather it is part of Russia's reality.[57] But even this old assumption was frayed at the edges by 2011. Public anger in May over reports of wide-ranging acts of nepotism on the boards of major companies, as the children of prominent officials were handed executive positions, and seats in local legislative assemblies were taken by members of the *siloviki*, displaced much of the old 'so what' attitude.[58] New anti-corruption websites began attracting large audiences. Among these was a website owned by political activist, Aleksei N. Navalny; http//www.RosPil.info has thousands of daily visitors. The Communist Party created a website of its own specifically to expose corruption on the part of officials, indelicately naming the agency and website the Anticorruption Committee in the Name of J.V. Stalin (http://www.beyvora.ru).

Perhaps driven by surveys that showed that more Russians than previously believed that the level of corruption among officials had risen over the previous year (proving the accuracy of predictions made in polls taken the previous year), Medvedev returned to his original thesis, telling a meeting of young parliamentarians that the only way to reduce 'unbridled' corruption was to create a completely new political culture.[59] As it happened, the same surveys showed that the percentage of Russians who condemned bribe taking had also increased, a small step toward the healthy 'intolerance' of corruption that Medvedev had called for in 2009.

In May 2011, an impatient Russian media went on the attack. The president was called a 'political corpse' in one paper, experts debated his 'lame duck' status in another, and a prominent website cast his National Plan to Counter Corruption in 2010–2011 as a complete failure. Medvedev's two crusades received further body blows as the founder of Hermitage Capital, William Browder, once Russia's largest foreign investor, continued to warn investors off because Russia's attempt at modernization was compromised by unshakeable corruption.[60] Oddly, the growing criticism from within Russia came in contrast to increasing appreciation from international investors for Medvedev's efforts both to innovate and to curb corruption. Their worry, in fact, was that if he did not run for the presidency again, or ran and lost, his economic projects would fade away and their investments would be jeopardized.[61] No such luck at home – the financial daily *Vedomosti* dubbed Medvedev's modernization agenda 'castles in the sky' and suggested that this particular campaign had become little more than presidential electioneering rhetoric.[62] After two years of seemingly valiant effort on his part, and general sympathy from the Russian media, the sudden turn on Medvedev from almost all sides seemed mean-spirited – or perhaps contrived.

A lot rode on Medvedev's anti-corruption and modernization projects and how the Russian public perceived them. The president displayed a sense of urgency in a speech to a large audience of Russian and foreign business and political leaders at the annual St Petersburg International Economic Forum. Noting that the dominant role of the state in the economy was needed after the chaos of the 1990s, he firmly rejected the idea of state capitalism for the future. Further decentralization and privatization were now necessary, Medvedev insisted, making it plain as well that the entire plan for modernization would work only if 'we put a relentless stranglehold on those guilty of corruption'.[63] This link had been drawn previously, but seldom as directly: curb corruption or we may never modernize.

Two days later, Putin also rejected state capitalism and both members of the Tandem insisted that there were no differences between them.[64] But the reality of corruption was still there to muddy the waters. An investigation of 35 ministries by experts close to government found that whereas the ministry of defence was the most corrupt, it was followed closely by the ministries of transport, economic development, health and social development, and finance, most of which were central to Medvedev's modernization ambitions.[65] Nearly a year after Chaika complained about bribes growing larger, both a spokesman for the MVD's Economic Security Department and Transparency International's Russia office reported that the average bribe had risen still further.[66] After four years and a wellspring of legislation, corruption on the part of predatory bureaucrats was flourishing almost unabated, even as more big names were openly under investigation.

As the summer of 2011 progressed, the president set out indirect challenges to the *siloviki* and other vested interests by forcing the pace and extent of government privatization and submitting a bill to the State Duma to return the threshold for seats in that body to five per cent of votes cast in an election. Stepping away from his earlier accommodation with the power brokers usually associated with Putin, he told a television audience that 'centralized power, even in as complex a federal state as Russia, cannot continue forever'.[67]

There was some noticeable resonance in July to Medvedev's initiatives: the Public Chamber allocated a large sum of money in support of roundtables, conferences, and forums designed to 'activate civil society', in part by encouraging modernization and discouraging corruption; and some 20 intellectuals signed an open letter favouring Medvedev over Putin precisely because of his two crusades and apparent belief in more democratic institutions.⁶⁸ By that time, their roles seemed reversed when Putin appeared to quote Medvedev, telling a worker in Magnitogorsk that '[w]e need new instruments, new people and deep modernization and an innovation process to secure a speedier growth of the economic and social sectors and to reinforce the political basis of our society'.⁶⁹ No one believed that Medvedev and Putin would run against each other; indeed many Russian observers, frustrated that neither man would commit himself, assumed that the Tandem would remain intact after the election and that Medvedev's campaigns would merely flutter along as before.⁷⁰

Such assumptions apparently were proven true on 24 September 2011 when Medvedev addressed a UR Congress. Emphasizing yet again that Russia must curb corruption so as to modernize its economy and denying vigorously that there were ever any 'splits' within the Tandem, he went on to nominate Putin as the UR's candidate in the next presidential election. While accepting that proposition, Putin named Medvedev as the ideal person to take up his spot as prime minister when it became vacant. Putin claimed that this decision was reached 'years' earlier. Talking heads popped up everywhere on Russian and Western television channels feverishly analysing the 'surprise'. But there was not much surprise on the streets of Moscow where Putin's dominant place in the Tandem had long been assumed.⁷¹ That said, whatever Putin's behind-the-scene role really was, the extraordinary energy Medvedev put into his two crusades was not a charade. Medvedev's activity on the modernization and corruption files suggests that the decision to reverse order in the Tandem was reached much more recently than the 'years' earlier that they claimed. As a matter of fact, in March 2012 Putin claimed that the decision was based on who was leading in the popularity polls, i.e. which of them had the best chance to win.⁷²

The president put on a brave face as his now truly lame duck period wound down. In late November and early December, the latest Transparency International report card placed Russia at 143 among 154 of the world's most corrupt countries, with China being the worst for offering bribes when doing business abroad.⁷³ The president gave up on plans to force officials to declare their expenditures, temporarily, and in January 2012 Russian economists expressed concern that corruption within Russia's large companies would offset any advantages Russia might gain from this year's entry into the World Trade Organization.⁷⁴

The CMTD continued to meet and, even though Medvedev's own influence seemed to fade, Russian and foreign business concerns showed a readiness to take up the modernization campaign – but in their own interest. It was not clear at all whether the Russian bureaucracy and the huge energy monopolies, such as Gazprom, were going to allow economic favouritism – and therefore political power – to shift to a mixture of Russian and foreign high-tech companies at Skolkovo. On the other hand, Skolkovo's research potential came in for high praise from Edward F. Crawley, Russian-speaking director of MIT's Engineering Leadership Program in February 2012.⁷⁵

Responding to a question in 2009, Medvedev said that his form of modernization would be based on 'people's internal desire for change'.⁷⁶ Although the one-term president's subsequent efforts to nurture change appeared to run up against the unassailable fortress of the status quo, the uproar following the Duma election in December 2011 revealed unexpected breaches in the fortress walls. In January 2012, Putin produced a long election campaign-related article on the 'new' Russian economy in which he co-opted Medvedev's modernization approach. Putin urged Russians to adopt a new competitive economy based on technological leadership and innovation, move away from reliance on energy exports, accelerate the privatization of state assets, and embrace competition. These were themes touted by Medvedev, and practically ignored by Putin, over the previous few years.[77] The decision in April 2012 that Skolkovo would host the G8 in 2014 may serve as a game-saver.

Beating the anti-corruption drum over an even longer period may also have inculcated a more internal, intuitive desire for change among Russia's citizenry. Moreover, as Medvedev's National Strategy for Countrering Corruption came up for review in the winter of 2012 there were some grounds for optimism. No one, least of all Chaika, pretended that there was significant improvement. Yet the legislative framework demanded in the earlier Strategy is now in place, monitoring bodies exist, and training programmes for officials are underway. Inspections have increased. New proposals by Medvedev are part of the Strategy for 2012–13. To be sure, polls conducted in March show that most Russians still believe that the level of corruption has remained the same or is increasing. Plainly, more 'waiting and seeing' is in store for anti-corruption advocates.[78]

As early as February 2012, the Russian media began raising doubts that Medvedev would stay in politics and warning that his modernization projects would not survive his departure of the presidency. Still, amid solemn pronouncements that Putin's dominance meant the end of the Tandem in practice, if not yet in name,[79] the astonishing breadth of post-Duma election protests throughout Russia was clearly a manifestation of Medvedev's hoped-for 'internal' desire for change. If that desire, now external, remains a force in Russian society, then Medvedev's unfaltering campaigns warrant much of the credit for it. Given that public outrage over corruption is the only unifying factor among Russia's widely disparate opposition, Medvedev may also have created his own handicap as Russia's newly-minted prime minister.

Conclusion

In late April, Medvedev won a few victories as most of his bills reforming the political process were passed. But in his final major interview as president he acknowledged again that his anti-corruption campaign was a failure to date and made it clear that a long-promised overhaul of the Interior Ministry was only just getting underway. He formally accepted the position as head of the UR party after a 27 April meeting at his residence in Gorki with leaders of the party, and the next day told an audience at Skolkovo that modernizing the economy would still rank high on his agenda as prime minister. As Putin's inauguration loomed, he and Medvedev marched together in the May Day parade. To some this was mere 'tandemonstration'; to others it appeared that the Tandem was rising shakily to its feet.[80] The test will be the degree to which Medvedev's anti-corruption and pro-modernization campaigns are part of their mutual agenda during Putin's third term as president, or merely castles in the sand.

Notes

1 Responding to a journalist's question about the most difficult issue he had to solve during his first eight years as president, Putin answered 'corruption', http//www.Kremlin.ru, 14 February 2008.
2 See, e.g. 'Bor'bu s korruptsiei raspanirovali na dva goda', *Kommersant,* 15 April 2010, and Aleksandra Samarina, 'Medvedev ob'viavil voinu "krysham"', *Nezavisimaia gazeta,* 15 April 2010.
3 Putin, 'Rossiia na rubezhe tysiacheletiia', *Rossiiskaia gazeta,* 31 December 1999.
4 David Remnick, *Lenin's Tomb. The Last Days of the Soviet Union,* New York: Vintage, 1994, p. 183.
5 On Oligarchies generally, see Jeffrey A. Winter, *Oligarchy,* New York: Cambridge University Press, 2011.
6 For a detailed explication see Ian Bremmer and Samuel Charap, 'The Siloviki in Putin's Russia: Who They Are and What They Want', *The Washington Quarterly,* 2006–07, vol. 30, no. 1, pp. 83–92; and Vladimir Pribylovsky, *Vlast'-2010: 60 biografii,* Moskva: Tsentr Panorama, 2010.
7 Stepashin's speech to the Federation Council, ITAR-TASS, 17 May 1999.
8 For a detailed analysis of *krysha* and its consequences, see 'Russian Organized Crime', *Task Force Report,* Washington, DC: Center for Strategic & International Studies, 1997.
9 Sergei Kanev, 'Kak ustroeny "kryshi" v Rossii', *Novaia gazeta,* 22 October 2007; *Fond Obschestvennoi mnenie,* 11 November 2007.
10 Transparency International, *Corruption Perception Index,* Berlin, 2007.
11 Anastasiia Bashkatova, 'Prizyvy k modernizatsii ne ubedili Rossiian', *Nezavisimaia gazeta,* 9 December 2009. The survey was conducted by the Levada Centre.
12 http://www.Kremlin.ru, 15 and 21 May 2009.
13 http://www.Kremlin.ru, 30 April 2010. See also *Nezavisimaia gazeta,* 14 May 2010.
14 http://www.Kremlin.ru, 30 April 2010. The council's official title is the Foundation for the Development of the Centre of Research and Commercialization of New Technologies at Skolkovo. Medvedev approved the appointment of six prominent Russian scientists, three Germans, and two other Americans to the council on 24 August 2010.
15 See e.g. 'Silikonovye yaitsa faberzhe', *Moskovskaia komsomolets,* 16 April 2010.
16 On this see Tal Adelaja, 'Foreigners' Paradise', *Russia Profile,* 6 May 2010.
17 Dvorkovich, 'the simplified [regulatory] rules for Skolkovo are a test of the ideas we have for the country as a whole …', *Vedomosti,* 20 June 2010.
18 The initial website was opened in July 2010 as http://www.modernrussia.com, and a second site was created in March 2011 as http://www.i-Russia.ru.
19 http://www.Politkom.ru and *Kommersant,* 30 May 2010.
20 *Vedomosti,* 20 June and 1 July 2010.
21 ITAR-TASS, 4 June 2010. General Electric (US) and Nokia (Finland) both have long histories of doing business in the USSR and Russia.
22 For a description of this tour, which was part of Medvedev's state visit to the USA, see Irina Aervitz, 'High Tech and Vekselburgers', *Russia Profile,* 29 June 2010. See also Igor Tsukanov, 'Ploshchadka dlia Cisco', *Vedomosti,* 1 July 2010.
23 See 'Dimitry Medvedev: Glavnoe dlia nashei strany – eto prodolzhenie spokoinogo i stabil'nogo razvitiia', *Rossiiskaia gazeta,* 15 February 2008.

24 'Kandidat v prezidenty Dimitry Medvedev oglasil svoi predvybornye tezisy', http://www.NEWSru: V Rossii, 22 January 2008; 'Dimitry Medvedev: Rossiia budet razvivat' grazhdanskoe obshchestvo ...', *Interfax*, 22 January 2008.
25 Interview with the *Svobodnaia pressa*, 19 April 2010, http://www.svpressa.ru, a well-known Moscow oppositionist website, and *Moskovskiy komsomolets*, 15 April 2010.
26 *Komsomolskaia Pravda*, 1 March 2010. See also *Nezavisimoe voennoe obozrenie*, 17 April 2010, for specific 'kickback' cases uncovered by the chief military procurator Sergei Fridinsaki, and *RIA Novosti*, 30 April 2010. For continuing problems *NVO*, 30 August 2010, and *Komsomolskaia Pravda*, 28 October 2010.
27 Anna Vasileva and Natalia Sergeeva, 'Ekzamen na korruptsiia,' *Kommersant*, 15 March 2012; For an overview, Eduard Klein, 'Corruption and Informal Payments in Russia's Educational System', *Russian Analytical Digest*, 30 May 2011, no. 97, pp. 5–9.
28 *Moscow Times*, 25 March 2010.
29 'Indikator "Korruptsiia v Rossii"', *Fond Obshchestvennoe mnenie* (n.d.). The questions were asked on 16–17 January 2010, in 100 populated areas of 44 components of the Russian Federation.
30 On this generally, see Leonid Grigoriev, 'Russian Modernisation: Interests and Coalitions', *Pro et Contra* (Moscow), 2007, no. 11, pp. 4–5. This essay re-appeared in *Russia in Global Affairs*, 2008, no. 1.
31 Daria Nikolaeva, 'Grazhdane predpochitaiut innovatsiiam bor'bu s korruptsiei', *Kommersant*, 10 June 2010. On the 'Blue Buckets', see Roland Oliphant, 'A Bucket of Fury', *Russia Profile*, 2 June 2010.
32 'Vse bol'she rossiian veriat v modernizatsiiu', *Fond Obshchestvenno mnenie*, 10 July 2010.
33 See e.g. *Nezavisimaia gazeta*, 5 June 2010.
34 Aleksandr Golts, 'K voprosu o vyrashchivanii kukuruzy v Skolkovo', *Yezhednevyi zhurnal*, 28 June 2010.
35 See e.g. *Moskovskiy komsomolets*, 27 July 2010, and *Novaia gazeta*, 21 June 2010. Andrei Kulesnikov, http://www.Gazeta.ru, 22 June 2010, wrote that modernization would undoubtedly fail on the political side; and an editorial in *Nezavisimaia gazeta*, 28 June 2010, named Skolkovo a mere 'state of mind' on the part of Medvedev, his officials and Russian businessmen. See also E. A. Pain in *Nezavisimaia gazeta*, 3 September 2010, and Sergei Aleksashenko in *Voenno-promyshlennyy kuryer*, 24 June 2010.
36 For the first issue of Belkovsky's series, see *Moskovskiy komsomolets*, 27 July 2010, and for Gorbachev's comments, *Ezhednevnyi zhurnal*, 14 July 2010.
37 *Svobodnaia Pressa*, 21 September 2010; *Interfax*, 18 September 2010.
38 See Kryshtanovskaia, 'Al'ternativy modernizatsii strany ne sushchestvuet', http://www.Kreml.org, 31 May 2010, and 'Modernization as Liberalization', ibid., 4 June 2010. D. Ye. Furman, 'Posledniaia modernizatsiia', *Nezavisimaia gazeta*, 25 August 2010.
39 Olga Radko, 'V Rossii prodolzhaet protsvetat' korruptsiia,' *Novyi Region*, 22 October 2010.
40 *RIA Novosti*, 1 and 2 December 2010. Transparency International, *Corruption Perception Index, 2010; Vedomosti*, 27 October 2010.
41 *Moscow Times*, 19 August 2011; Olga Razumovskaia, 'Skolkovo Innovation Hub Braving the Waters', *The Moscow Times*, 16 June 2011; http://www.Kremlin.ru, 24 February 2011.
42 See Medvedev's opening address to a joint meeting of the Modernization Commission and the Skolkovo Board, http://www.Kremlin.ru, 25 April 2011.
43 Stanislav Belkovsky, 'K vozvrashcheniiu Vladimir Putina', http://www.Slon.ru, 1 April 2011; see also Yuliia Latyniia, 'Twitter-prezident i vostorzhennye liberally', *Yezhednevnyi zhurnal*, 4 April 2011; 'Tandem konets?' *Kommersant*, 28 March 2011.

44 *Interfax*, 14 April 2011. For an example of doomsday punditry from a Russian oppositionist journalist often featured in Western journals, see Pavel Felgenhauer, 'The Putin–Medvedev Ruling Tandem Disintegrates', *Eurasia Daily Monitor*, 14 April 2011.
45 On the Tandem's alleged plot, see Aleksandr Mukhin in *Argumenty i fakty*, 20 April 2011, and on the Tandem as obsolete, http://www.Gazeta.ru, 19 April 2011; on the Tandem as a natural system for Russia, Yuri Kondratov, 'Ravenstvo v tandeme', *Nezavisimaia gazeta*, 29 July 2011, and too many more to list here.
46 Aleksandra Samarina, 'Gleb Pavlovskii: "Ya narushal molchalivuiu distsiplinu tandem"', *Nezavisimaia gazeta*, 28 April 2011.
47 Igor Naumov, 'Mezhdu liberalom Medvedevym i konservatorom Putinym', *Nezavisimaia gazeta*, 25 April 2011.
48 http://www.premier.gov.ru, 20 April 2011; *Rossiiskaia gazeta*, 21 April 2011.
49 See especially Andrew Monaghan, 'The Russian *Vertikal*: the Tandem, Power and the Elections', Chatham House, Russia and Eurasia Programme Paper REP 2011/01.
50 *Interfax*, 20 June 2011.
51 *The Moscow Times*, 31 May 2011.
52 On this, see an interesting article with interviews by Andrew E. Kramer, 'Russian Prisons for Police Thrive, but Some See Politics', *New York Times*, 5 June 2011.
53 The bill was signed into law on 4 May 2011.
54 *Rossiiskaia gazeta*, 1 March 2011.
55 *Moscow News*, 4 May 2011.
56 *Interfax*, 22 April 2011.
57 Denis Belikov, 'Moskvu perekroiot dlia bor'by s korruptsieu', *Moskovskiy komsomolets*, 17 April 2011.
58 See *Vedomosti*, 12 and 16 May 2011.
59 http://www.kremlin.ru, 13 May 2011. This meeting was held in Kostroma. For the surveys, see *Fond Obshchestvennoe mnenie*, 13 May 2011.
60 In March 2012, Browder spoke at a hearing of the US House Committee on Foreign Affairs titled 'Russia 2012: Increased Repression, Rampant Corruption, Assisting Rogue Regimes'. He told the already extraordinarily biased panel that Russia was 'akin to a criminal enterprise'. Press release from the Hermitage Fund, 21 March 2012.
61 See Tai Adelaja, 'Impudence and Impunity. Russia's Investment Climate Becomes Murkier as Entrenched State officials Resist the Fight Against Corruption', *Russia Profile*, 30 May 2011; Narasha Doff, 'Investment Whisperers', *Russia Profile*, 7 June 2011; http://www.URA.ru, 28 May 2011; *Russia Profile*, 27 May 2011; *Svobodnaya Pressa*, 29 May 2011.
62 'Ot redaktsii: Predvybornyi zhanr', *Vedomosti*, 20 June 2011.
63 http://www.kremlin.ru, 17 June 2011.
64 *Interfax*, 21 June 2011. Putin was speaking at a news conference with the French prime minister in Paris.
65 'Reiting korrumpirovannosti ministerstv i vedomstv Rossii ot "Novoi gazety"', *Novaia gazeta*, 7 June 2011.
66 *Interfax*, 10 August 2011.
67 http://www.kremlin.ru, 27 June 2012.
68 'Vybor est'. Obrashchenie k grazhdanam Rossii', *Novaia gazeta*, 25 July 2011; http://www.Gazeta.ru, 13 July 2011.
69 *Interfax*, 15 July 2011.
70 See e.g. Aleksei Gorbachev and Aleksandra Samarina, 'Tiani-tolkai-tandem', *Nezavisimaia gazeta*, 9 August 2011.
71 This author was in Moscow on 24 September 2011.
72 *Interfax*, 2 March 2012.
73 *Novaia gazeta*, 22 November 2011; Transparency International, *Bribe Payers Index*, 2 November 2011, and *RIA Novosti*, 1 December 2011.

74 See e.g. Oleg Nikiforov, 'Korruptsiia kak ekonomicheskii faktor', *Nezavisimaia gazeta*, 17 January 2012. Medvedev resurrected a bill to force officials to declare expenditures in February 2012.
75 'Skolkovo – chast' natsional'noi sistemy nauki', *Kommersant*, 29 February 2012; 'State–Business Relations and Modernization', *Russian Analytical Digest*, no. 105, 5 December 2011. See also 'Modernization is Becoming a Meaningless Term', *Svobodnaya pressa*, 5 October 2011.
76 'The Results of the Year with the President of the Russian Federation Dmitry Medvedev', Embassy of the Russian Federation in Canada Press Release, 14 December 2009.
77 Vladimir Putin, 'Nam nuzhna novaia ekonomika,' *Vedomosti*, 30 January 2012.
78 'Problema korruptsii v Rossii', FOMnibus, 17–18 March 2012. For Chaika's report on the National Strategy, see *Kommersant*, 2 March 2012. Medvedev signed the new Strategy into law on 13 March 2012. See also Anna Sulimina, 'Tackling State Corruption', *Moscow News*, 6 March 2012.
79 See e.g. 'Konets tandem,' *Nezavisimaia gazeta*, 30 December 2011; Ivan Rodin, 'Medvedev ostaetsia reformatorom', *Nezavisimaia gazeta*, 7 February 2012; Andrew Roth, 'The Vanishing President,' *Russia Profile*, 16 February 2012; and Brian Whitmore, 'The Unravelling. The Tandem's Slow Death', RFE/RL, 2 April 2012.
80 On the not very optimistic view that the parade solidarity was mere 'tandemonstation', see *Moskovskiy komsomolets*, 30 April 2012.

8 The Kremlin's future priorities in harnessing hard power

Beyond the "Tandem" and "New Look"

Roger N. McDermott

Any effort to define the Kremlin's future military priorities in support of its foreign policy agenda, extending over the next decade and beyond, must necessarily begin by recognizing the huge importance of Vladimir Putin in terms of his grip on power since 2000, and his relationship with Russia's armed forces. Indeed, for many analysts and commentators, Russian or non-Russian, the name of Putin evokes mixed reaction or even controversy.[1] Before exploring the type of military challenges facing the Russian presidency following the presidential elections in March 2012, it is crucial to place Putin and his legacy to the armed forces in its broader context and offer some observations about his role in the reform of the conventional armed forces launched in the latter part of 2008 and the specific challenges arising from that process.[2]

First, when Putin became the Russian President in 2000, the situation facing the country and the military were similarly challenging. Following the time of troubles in the 1990s, when Russia was economically and politically weak, especially in the international arena, a new type of leadership sought to reverse or address many of these trends. The armed forces had numerous problems and systemic weaknesses, mainly related to their Soviet past and the failure to address the question after the collapse of the Soviet state as to what kind of military Russia really needed. Senior officers remembered the debacle of the first war in Chechnya, 1994–96, and they quickly understood that Putin was a different type of leader from either Gorbachev or Yeltsin. For the armed forces, over Putin's first two presidential terms, the sense of stability was restored. The author takes this achievement by Putin, restoring stability to the Russian armed forces, as argued by the US analyst, Dale R. Herspring, to be axiomatic. It is the key to understanding Putin's legacy to the military from this period.[3]

Moreover, there are other important points to bear in mind in assessing the possible contours for the military of a Putin presidency that may last into the next decade. The first is that Putin, and no one else, was the initiator of the current reform of the armed forces. Yet, in his public statements he has remarkably little to say about it; that task is left to others. He may be characterized as the "quiet man" of the reform. Equally, many of the weaknesses in the Russian military system that the reform was intended to address, or the previous failed efforts to conduct reform during 2000–08 have been carefully disassociated from Putin. This is hardly surprising as no politician wants to be associated with failure of any kind. But if many of the reform aims or aspirations are to be realized, Putin will have a lot of sorting to do. In pole position is the issue he has known about for several years: a large portion of the defense budget gets "lost" or stolen. That will have serious implications for the effort to modernize Russia's strategic nuclear deterrence or achieve its ambitious aims to re-equip the conventional armed forces. Indeed, tackling corruption in the defense ministry was certainly one of the reasons behind Putin's decision in February 2007 to appoint Anatoly Serdyukov as the defense minister. Serdyukov's background in the finance ministry, combined with his tasking to manage the impending reform, indicate that Putin was well aware of the sorrowful pre-reform condition of the armed forces.[4]

This chapter argues that the reform of the armed forces, albeit initiated by Putin and on the cards certainly since 2007 and most likely earlier, was poorly planned, hurriedly executed, and resulted in confusion and a policy planning mess. Signs of this were evident in implementing the plan to form the new brigade-based structure of the army in 2009, subsequently testing it during operational-strategic exercises only to discover that different brigade sizes were needed; or, in the declared aim of the officer downsizing to reach a total of 150,000 officers, then three years later "adjusting" the target to 220,000; or, in the manifold reversals concerning many reform initiatives. Undoubtedly the reform process has affected much change in the armed forces since 2008, but no one really knows its precise aims or agenda, let alone the path to its realization. Those serving in the military can only really guess as to what it is all about, and lament its lack of clarity in private since, by presidential decree, they are banned from criticizing it. Above all, given the tendency during the early stages of a new Russian presidency to promise better times ahead for the military, it is likely that there will be some re-statement of the goals and tasks ahead in reforming and modernizing the armed forces.[5]

To reform or not to reform?

There is little doubt that, unlike the previous failed experiments or efforts to instigate genuine reform in Russia's armed forces, the "new look" initiated in the fall of 2008 was very real. It did result in real change, and broke the mould of the post-Soviet legacy forces by, for instance, finally abandoning "mass mobilization" and with it the cadre units. Conceptually, the search for its roots leads to how such new thinking was emerging in the defense ministry and the general staff, which largely seems to lie in the capacity to examine and learn from foreign military experience. Thus many of the reform initiatives find their roots predominantly in western militaries, and indeed no attempt was made to deny or disguise this by the Russian leadership. But the task of dismantling the old system was arguably much simpler than defining precisely how to construct its replacement.[6]

Politically, support for unleashing this reform on the armed forces began prior to the ruling tandem emerging as a brief interlude in the rule of Vladimir Putin. Statements from Putin concerning the need for an "innovative army" precede the reform by several years, and speed at which the "new look" was mooted after the Five Day War with Georgia in August 2008 further attests to the longer term approach to commencing the process.[7]

However, the reform was conceived and planned in secret and in its early phase little attention was given to adequately setting its agenda. Much of the task fell on the defense minister and the chief of the general staff, both to attack the pre-reform condition of the armed forces by reference to the flaws exposed during the Five Day War. An early indication of the problems associated with defining the nature of the reform was provided in *Nezavisimoe voyennoe obozrenie* in January 2009; the editor had to trawl countless sources and statements in order to cobble together any meaningful overview of what the reform envisaged. Despite Serdyukov's claims in late 2011 that the first phase of the reform, mainly organizational, had been successfully completed with the key future focus placed on modernizing the weapons and equipment, few observers lent such assessments any credibility.[8]

In December 2011, a Russian television report reflected on the first four years of the reform and its starting point was an attempt to outline what the agenda may have been in 2008. It noted that Serdyukov had been appointed as defense minister and brought with him a cohort of "efficient managers" and "professional economists" to shake up the military's financial system and make it accountable and transparent, while concentrating on making the armed forces more compact, "professional," and well-equipped. The report noted that much had been done since 2008, including providing more money to the military, outlining ambitious rearmament plans, and making an effort to promote professionalization. But it went on to suggest the reform had aimed at a "mobile, professional army of contract servicemen," well paid, with no bullying, and accommodation and pensions provided to discharged officers and apartments for serving officers and their families. For many, the description appeared to border on fantasy, and the broadcast quickly exposed this by interviewing a number of Russian experts who highlighted some of the drawbacks involved in the reform.[9]

Vladislav Shurygin criticized the defense ministry for its failure to provide apartments to discharged officers, as well as the manner in which these personnel were treated during the ruthless downsizing of the officer corps in 2008–11. He also raised questions about terms and conditions of service. Shurygin believed the reform had intended an army of professional personnel and instead offered only an unprofessional lumpen mass. Plans to introduce new high standard non-commissioned officers (NCOs) had come unstuck, were subject to several revisions, and exposed difficulties in recruitment and in organizing courses, let alone producing adequate numbers of such key personnel. Viktor Baranets noted that, in the financial laws passed aimed at raising officers' pay, important social benefits had also been taken away. He was scathing about Serdyukov infamous Order 400, a bonus system to reward outstanding commanders, which had become a notorious source of corruption. "These bonuses caused mayhem among officers. They provoked a lot of grievances, whistle blowing, and corruption, and divided the officer corps into those who were in favor and those who were not. In short, a huge number of criminal investigations were launched," Baranets explained.

The report ended by saying that, according to the Audit Chamber, the defense ministry is the leader in the corruption stakes and asked if the "team of reformers" would fulfill their promises.[10]

Although the "reform critics" did not form any cohesive opposition to the reform that served to impair or derail its pursuit, it would be misleading to characterize such critics as either representing communist die-hards or those opposed to any form of change whatsoever. Respected retired military officers offered several critiques of the reform, ranging in seriousness from Anatoly Tsyganok casting the "new look" as "plastic surgery," to Vladimir Dvorkin raising objections about how it was carried out. One critical factor appears to be the inability of the defense minister to carry the officer corps with him as the reform unfolded. Moreover, while the reform progressed rapidly in terms of actual implementation, and avoided becoming weighed down by experiment, there is a sense in which the whole process evolved into an experiment writ large.[11]

Aspiration and shifting reform priorities

In Orenburg on 26 September 2008, President Medvedev outlined the five priorities in the reform, going as far as to state that these would determine the future combat capability of the armed forces:[12]

1 Improving the organization and structure of the forces by converting all divisions and brigades to permanent readiness brigades, abolishing the mass-mobilization principle and abandoning the division-based system.
2 Enhancing the overall efficiency of C^2 and improving its effectiveness in the armed forces (which was later interpreted as opting for a three-tiered structure: operational, command-military, district-brigade).
3 Improving the personnel training system, including military education and military science.
4 Equipping the armed forces, the army and the navy, with the latest weapon systems and intelligence assets, primarily high-technology, in order to "achieve air superiority, deliver precision strikes on ground and maritime targets, and ensure operational force deployment."
5 Improving the social status of military personnel, including pay and allowances, housing, and every day living conditions as well as a broad range of support packages.[13]

As a statement of intent it appeared impressive and clear. It might even be construed as a useful tool in measuring the level of success or progress in implementing the reform, but such logic defies analysis of Russian defense planning. The trouble is that no other statement by the president, prime minister, defense minister or the top brass either matched this criteria or offered similar clarity. Prior to examining the extent of confusion present in Russian defense reform planning, it is worth using Medvedev's list as a means to reflect on what the transformation has thus far achieved. Certainly, there has been an improvement of the structure, particularly in abolishing the notional mass-mobilization present in the old system, and with it jettisoning the cadre or skeleton units. This has resulted in a largely brigade-based structure (exception to this is the *Vozdushno Desantrye Voyska* (VDV)) that the defense ministry claims to model on "permanent readiness."[14]

Nonetheless, there are a number of problems suggesting that this is a work in progress. Quite apart from top-brass statements failing to agree on the actual number of brigades in the ground forces, or plans to remodel the brigade types, from a one-size-fits-all approach to "heavy," "medium," and "light" (with differing requirements for firepower and rearmament), to extending this to "Arctic" and "mountain" brigades (though the latter exist in small numbers), there are deeper issues to be resolved. The brigades are not all fully manned and, more to the point, they are mixed: *kontraktniki* and conscripts serve in the same units, which restrict their combat readiness or deployment options.[15] Equally, a careful reading of the 2010 Military Doctrine, as well as interviews with senior officers, indicates some continued adherence to at least a type of "mobilization" within the system, though no one has explained for what type of conflict such mobilization would be required (with "permanent readiness" brigades at the disposal of the general staff) or addressed the absence of a sufficiently well-trained reserve.[16]

The four-tiered and overly-complex C^2 structure has in fact given way to a more simplified and potentially stronger three-tiered C^2 (Joint-Strategic, Command-Military, District-Brigade); the Military Districts (MDs) have been reduced and resized from six to four, which in wartime function as Joint-Strategic Commands harnessing all military and paramilitary assets in the MD under a single command. However, after more than ten years in developmental stage and intensification since the reform began in 2008, the automated C^2 (*Yedinaia Sistema Upravleniia v Takticheskom Zvene* (Unified Tactical Level Command and Control System) YeSU TZ) still awaits introduction (while the VDV will have its system).[17]

The training, education system, and condition of military science are long-term projects, and hardly likely to yield instant results; while there has been some intensification of combat training its achievements have been limited by relying on large numbers of 12-month serving conscripts being rotated out of the brigades every six months. Senior officers and defense officials reflecting on the results of the 2011 training year noted that "firing" and "driving" were the two main weaknesses, while commanders at tactical level complain that, on account of the high level of paperwork, the time spent on training is limited. Rearmament is proceeding more slowly than political promises in 2010–11 would have implied, and the problems related to the 2011 State Defense Order (*Gosudarstvennyi Oboronnyi Zakaz* (GOZ)), disputes among the political leadership on the level of defense spending, as well as the continued chronic weakness of the Russian defense industry suggest grounds for caution in achieving the set target of "70 percent" new by 2020.[18]

Social packages have seen progress with significant pay increases for the officer corps introduced on 1 January 2012, though even Russian military commentators are uncertain how this will improve standards or limit corruption among officers.

The idea of writing and introducing a "code of professional conduct" for Russian officers seems to have been kicked into the long grass, and reportedly corruption among officers is a booming industry. Without changes to the recruitment or promotion policy for officers, or redefining their training and professional development, it is likely that officer reform will be subject to serial experimentation.[19]

Tracing the nature of the confused statements on the reform from the Russian political-military leadership reveals deeper problems with a reform all too reliant upon aspiration rather than substance. In an important study of the reform in its wider context of previous failed efforts since the 1990s, the Dutch analyst, Marcel de Haas, collated such statements over a three-year period in a highly informative appendix.[20]

By December 2009, both Serdyukov and Chief of General Staff Nikolai Ye. Makarov claimed the downsizing target of 150,000 had been achieved, which was later contradicted by each official as early as March 2010 when they claimed an additional 35,000 officers must be discharged in order to achieve the stated goal. The senior political and military statements on the number of ground forces brigades consistently failed to agree on the actual number; and by March 2011 the unified air defense plans and improving border security and military infrastructure in the Russian Far East had crept into the list of "top five" priorities, without any explanation. Following the fanfare in 2009 about creating "permanent readiness" brigades, Medvedev stated in May 2010, that he hoped that all military units would achieve "permanent readiness" status by 2015. In January 2012, a member of the Duma Defense Committee noted that the under-manning of private posts in the military was around 30 percent, and in the army and navy it was as high as 35 percent. Indeed, the comparison of statements on the permutations of the future structure of military manpower also followed this pattern of reversal and implied policy planning on the hoof.[21]

Reflecting the difference of style and approach within the duumvirate, the defense tandem has also displayed similar "nuances." Addressing the Defense Ministry Public Chamber on 17 November 2011, Serdyukov claimed that the main tasks in the reform had been accomplished. He then highlighted the seven main priorities facing the future development of the armed forces:

1 To fulfill the 2011 GOZ and overcome problems in pricing and transfer the functions of the ordering body to the Federal Procurement Agency.
2 Improve combat training, particularly at tactical level.
3 Test the new YeSU TZ in the operational-strategic exercise Kavkaz 2012.
4 Continue the development and equipping of the newly formed aerospace defense *Vozdushno Kosmicheskaia Oborona* (VKO).
5 Introduce military police, establishing training systems and organizational structure in military bases.
6 Extend the outsourcing of catering on military bases throughout the armed forces, and ensure that commanders work with directors of these companies to promote high quality service.
7 Switch to a new system of contract personnel and NCOs.[22]

Some of these tasks reflected problems experienced in the reform and modernization processes in 2010–11, and inadvertently highlght where the weaknesses are found. Continued bickering between the defense ministry and the defense industry over pricing and procurement contracts, resulted in numerous issues of conflict during the implementation of the 2011 GOZ; exercises had shown the top brass that, despite intensifying combat training at tactical and individual level, there was still plenty of scope for improvement; the new C2 system was subject to many setbacks in 2009–11, mostly linked to the overly-complex nature of the software design used in the YeSU TZ resulting in additional delays to planned introduction within the brigades; forming the VKO not only produced pressure for additional officer posts in the manpower structure but raised fresh challenges for the defense industry to meet the demands of modernizing air defense and ballistic missile defense systems; as discipline reportedly declined, several initiatives aimed at improving discipline were trialed – introducing military police represents the latest effort; outsourcing of catering in the brigades was given much publicity but also revealed its own weaknesses and many retired officers still question if these civilian entities would be deployed during operations; the minister offered little detail on what he meant by a "new system" of contract personnel and NCOs, while both proved to major hurdles in the reform process.[23]

General Makarov offered much more in the way of substance during his lengthy presentation, beginning by outlining the "threat" environment facing the Russian Federation and then proceeding to describe some of what the defense reform had achieved during its first three years. The chief of the general staff was realistic concerning the scale of the challenges ahead in vastly increasing the numbers of serving contract personnel, or *kontraktniki*, which aims at raising the numbers from 186,400 in 2012 to 425,000 by 2016 by recruiting "50,000" *kontraktniki* annually. This process would prioritize NCO posts, naval units, with emphasis to begin with on the Southern Military District because of instability in the North Caucasus and the potential re-ignition of conflict with Georgia or a crisis over Karabakh. Special forces would also be boosted, as would drivers of military vehicles and other specialist positions that "determine combat capability."[24]

Despite the ambitious plans to shift military manpower towards greater reliance upon contract personnel, previous efforts to achieve such targets ended in failure. During Putin's first presidential terms, similar grand schemes were mooted in an effort to professionalize the armed forces. In that case, the general staff successfully restricted this planning to an experimental basis in certain key formations, mainly in the airborne forces, while a number of factors coalesced to undermine the experiment. By February 2010, the top brass, in a rare moment of honesty, admitted that the *kontraktniki* targets had failed, and some commanders went so far as to say they could not actually distinguish between *kontraktniki* and conscripts serving for only twelve months. In the interim, it appears the defense ministry and general staff ignored or underestimated the need to recalibrate the recruitment system or formulate coherent plans to revitalize the image of the military among the wider public. In short, like painting by numbers, the approach was rooted in setting certain benchmarks and not paying too much attention to whether these may prove to be realistic. Moreover, the main recruitment pool for the *kontraktniki* is the serving conscripts, and paradoxically the numbers of conscripts drafted into the armed forces was reduced in the 2011 fall draft. At a time when the numbers needed to be maintained, the reduction will make the recruitment of *kontraktniki* from this resource pool more difficult. Three years after launching the reform, the key issues facing the future of manpower remain mostly undecided, subject to reversal, or consigned to a "hope for the best" attitude in planning that served to expose underlying limited planning capacities.[25]

Makarov concluded his presentation by defining the seven priorities facing Russian defense transformation:

1 Creating a new and modern system of automated command and control.
2 Developing and equipping the VKO.
3 Re-equipping the armed forces with modern weapons and equipment in line with the GOZ to 2020.
4 Introducing new types of approaches in operational and combat training, including new advanced combat training centers.
5 Organizing the structure of the armed forces, improving support systems, and *increasing* the number of units.
6 Forming an optimal basing system and building modern military towns.
7 Creating military police.[26]

Again, it is worth noting how new features or aims were creeping into such statements of reform targets, particularly on forming military police, new approaches to combat training, the high priority attached to the aerospace defense forces, or pole position assigned to the automated C2 system. Perhaps most puzzling was Makarov's passing reference to increasing the number of combat units, since in late 2008 their reduction was high priority. Since these numbers have been significantly culled (from 1,890 to 172 units), Makarov may have been indicating some need for future revision, suggesting the optimum number had not yet been established. Correcting the ratio between teeth and tail is one clear illustration of the absence of overall systemic planning in the reform agenda.[27]

An alternative interpretation of the recalibration of the priorities in the reform would note the increasing emphasis on technology and air and space defense as drivers of the process (automated C^2, aerospace defense forces, missile defense systems, and German procured combat training simulators), with lower priorities centered around structure, or efforts to improve discipline.[28] What is clear is the reform launched in late 2008, simply in terms of its key aims and aspirations, is difficult to trace in more recent statements, while confusion is the order of the day. Aleksei Arbatov, the head of the International Security Centre at the World Economy and International Relations Institute summarized the underlying sense of chaos in the latest reform effort:

> The reform was designed behind the scenes, behind closed doors, without broad discussion, without the involvement of external experts. Usually,

in such cases there are committees or commissions that work on specific issues – there was nothing. Accordingly, when they began to carry out such drastic measures, it transpired that everything was going not the way it had been planned but it was going wrong, so they began to change things as they went.[29]

According to Serdyukov, by far the most controversial aspect of the reform proved to be the initial plan to reduce the officer corps from 355,000 to 150,000, though the actual target was later adjusted to 220,000.[30] However, take as a hypothetical example, an officer with a wife and young children, and someone not engaged in benefitting from corruption. At the outset of the reform, he naturally began to worry if he would be dismissed from service, which did nothing for his morale and family security. Then, as it progressed, some of his colleagues were dismissed, often without explanation or reason, all in the interests of "downsizing." Others were "placed at the disposal of the commander" a kind of legal limbo meaning they were neither out nor fully in the armed forces. Still others in this insecure environment would return home from work, receive a telephone call from the defense ministry, strip off their epaulets, and return to work the following day doing the same job but "civilianized."

In addition to possible family pressure to find an alternative more stable career path to pursue, he is told conflicting things, such as there will be a written code of professional conduct for officers and an assembly held in Moscow to discuss this; the assembly is later postponed and actually never takes place. He is also told the top brass think the vast majority of officers have poor leadership skills and are incapable of performing command duties, so they must be re-trained. Moreover, when he reads the Russian military press, he comes across information about the introduction of high-tech gadgets and systems and the need to develop network-centric warfare capabilities, and he is unsure what all this really means. Then he begins to ask what happens with the relationship between army chaplains and educational officers? If there is a crime on the base in future, who should be informed about it, the military police? But he learns from an interview with Serdyukov that the military police will have no powers to investigate, so how does that work? In short, in the absence of any one single source, document, or official statement that clearly elaborates what this reform is about, how can he know whether he wants to remain part of this system and develop a career or pack up and move on?

Enter: Vladimir Putin

While Putin has been cautious in his public statements about the reform agenda, he has aligned himself very closely with certain aspects of the modernization aims, including supporting the plans to spend 19.4 trillion roubles on rearmament by 2020 to achieve the target of 70 percent modern or new in the table of organization and equipment. Although this close association with rearmament plans faces deep challenges relating to an ailing and corrupt defense industry, Putin has taken the risk of lending public support to this drive to modernize the Russian armed forces. In particular, Putin stresses the need to modernize the navy, and has offered full support for the 700 billion roubles program for the development of the civilian and military shipbuilding industry to 2020 (450 billion roubles of which is earmarked for military shipbuilding). This is hardly surprising given the consistent eagerness he has displayed since 2000 for photo opportunities with the navy, but Putin understands that naval rearmament will be no easy task and much will depend, like the rest of the ambitious rearmament plans, on the performance and accountability of the defense industry. Noting in passing that spending 19.4 trillion roubles by 2020 is "frightening," Putin appointed Dmitry Rogozin as deputy prime minister and in charge of the defense industry in December 2011 and tasked him with tackling corruption and ensuring that these ambitious procurement plans bear fruit. However, the challenges of corruption, non-transparent pricing, and the inefficiencies of the defense industry are likely to mitigate the success of such plans. Rogozin's reputation for courting controversy is equally sure to constantly bring the tension between the defense ministry and the defense industry to the surface and perhaps more into the public glare. It remains unclear as to how these character-dependant initiatives will work out.[31]

Another aspect of the generic reform "plans" that Putin has proven keen to promote is the increases to pay and allowances for servicemen. In November 2011, Putin boasted that such increases in pay and allowances had not been seen on this scale in the "history of modern Russia." He stressed that, from 1 January 2012, lieutenants, for instance, would receive 50,000 roubles.[32] Such increases were no doubt a long-overdue attempt to address the standing of officers in Russian society and improve their pay conditions, which may also have reflected the need to boost Putin's popularity among the military electorate ahead of the March 2012 presidential election. The extent to which this measure alone may curb corruption or help to develop a new type of officer in the reformed armed forces is unclear, especially in the absence of change to the system of recruitment or promotion. Moreover, the increase to pay for contract and conscript personnel also means that more money will be sloshing around a system that functions on the basis of institutionalized bullying, or *dedovshchina*.

Beyond populist measures, untangling the much deeper complex knot of policy planning confusion, offering some clarity simply beyond a re-statement of the reform aims, would depend ultimately on the quality of advice offered to the Kremlin. If it results in the leadership having sufficiently clear insight into the weaknesses and errors in that process to date, there may be scope for a level of consistency to emerge following a re-assessment of the reform. This will be subject to a number of variables, mainly linked to personalities placed in key posts, maintaining a strong working relationship between the defense minister and the chief of the general staff, the extent to which there may be progress towards reforming the ailing defense industry, stemming the tide of corruption, or indeed whether these processes are subject to unforeseen correction in the aftermath of any involvement of the Russian armed forces in an unexpected armed conflict.[33]

Moreover, Putin's approach is likely to be cautious and gradual, rather than flamboyant or offering speedy remedies. As the commander in chief, the questions he asks of both the defense ministry leadership and the top brass will be as important as the quality of advice he receives. There are some potentially useful questions he may ask: if there is a real crisis, how many of the ground forces brigades are in a condition to deploy? What steps are being taken to reform the officer corps? Why does Russia need to maintain brigades at all, in theory, in the state of readiness? Equally, if Putin simply offers nebulous aims for the reform and modernization process and leaves to others the task of working out its implications, then their roles will be pivotal in gauging any level of success. Putin may follow the pattern of recent presidencies and offer a re-statement of the principle aims of the reform. Observers may consequently rush to use such a statement as a means against which to measure the success or failure of this complex process, but perhaps first there needs to be consistency in similar statements from other political and military officials.

In terms of the broad military priorities facing the new Putin presidency, these will mainly relate to modernizing the strategic nuclear deterrent and developing the capabilities of the VKO. However, making good the claims surrounding Russian foreign policy will involve some credible progress in conducting both reform as well as modernization of the conventional armed forces. If one theme that gained prominence during Putin's first term in office, 2000–04, linked to addressing the weaknesses in the conventional forces can be identified, it is the experimental policy to professionalize the manpower structure. While this political commitment has fluctuated and arguably failed to materialize in any tangible progress, paradoxically it is likely to resurface in another guise driven by the much deeper and less obvious effort to adopt and develop network-centric warfare capabilities.[34]

Although many features of the reform planning were proven to be susceptible to experiment, reversal, or even failure, with a sense of near chaos present in its presentation and implementation, the adoption of what the late General Vladimir Slipchenko referred to as sixth-generation, or non-contact warfare capabilities is an underlying guiding theme that will prove crucial over the next decade and beyond. Indeed, numerous aspects of the new look can only be explained by identifying the uniting factor of developing network-centric warfare capabilities, inter alia, the emphasis upon the introduction of automated C^2, optimizing the C^2 structures, greater reliance on high-technology integrated weapons systems, and, crucially, the brigade structure itself: the brigade is the fundamental organic unit in network-centric operations.[35]

General Makarov and other leading senior officers promote the automated C^2 and the adoption of network-centric warfare capabilities as central to the reform and modernization of Russia's Armed Forces. The future capability to conduct non-contact warfare utilizing C4ISR (Command, Control, Communications, Computers, Intelligence, Surveillance, and Reconnaissance) is a long way off, but has become a guiding principle among the leading advocates of reform. The commander in chief (CINC) of the ground forces, Colonel-General Postnikov, has staged conferences on network-centric warfare in the Combined-Arms Academy in Moscow and also places great emphasis on the capacity of the YeSU TZ to revolutionize decision-making and enhance C^2. This would enhance the algorithm of battle management and allow a brigade commander to transmit his decisions in real time to his battalion commander displayed on his personal computer. Resolving design flaws in the system has taken time and resulted in recrimination between the defense ministry and defense industry. In the fall of 2010, Dmitry Kandaurov, a Moscow-based expert on automated C^2, examined design problems related to the YeSU TZ in a series of articles in *Nezavisimoe voyennoe obozrenie*. He noted flaws in the development of high-intensity graphics in the software, but the author placed these complexities in a wider context of improving the overall efficiency of C^2. Yet, by August 2011, Kandaurov questioned whether the existing plans for introducing automated C^2 would result in any real improvement.[36]

The Russian defense ministry arguably places unrealistic emphasis on the future impact on the armed forces resulting from the automated C2 system. Without adequately trained personnel, the improvement would be of only marginal value. In addition to retraining personnel, as well as retaining them within units, the general staff would need to successfully develop a Russian network-centric doctrine that maximizes the interface between personnel and new technologies. If network-centric approaches to operations, or even the plans to modernize the equipment and weapons inventory, are to succeed at any level, a new officer culture of innovativeness will also be necessary. This would facilitate the capacity to use new means and methods of performing missions. Such innovativeness denotes a military culture that quickly and efficiently absorbs new weapons and equipment into its units.[37] Without managing these complex tasks adequately, there is in fact great potential for the state to expend a great deal of money with minimal or no benefits to show as a result. This will also involve resolving a "debate" over manpower that has persisted in Russia since even before the dissolution of the USSR; namely whether to prioritize contract personnel or retain large numbers of conscripts.

None of this should be viewed as a panacea for the Russian armed forces, and they will encounter numerous problems and setbacks as this process unfolds, but at the highest levels of the defense ministry and general staff there is an awareness, most likely understood to some extent in the Kremlin, that this will be essential in retaining Russia's ability to act in future as a security actor within Eurasia. Its conventional forces' weakness presents few options in an escalating local or regional conflict other than to ultimately resort to sub-strategic nuclear weapons in order to de-escalate such a conflict. The path towards greater options in such scenarios is deemed by the political-military leadership to revolve around avoiding being left out of what Moscow considers a growing trend among other actors to possess or develop their own network-centric capabilities. In this area the challenges are likely to prove acute, and the leadership provided by the Kremlin will be important in harnessing the future of hard power through this modern means of warfare. There are skeptics within Russia and beyond, and what emerges in its final form as some type of networked capability may be unlike western approaches, but somehow the Russians must try to make sense of this "post-modern" and high-technology information-based shift in the use of military power.

Perhaps, in the midst of the many reform setbacks and challenges, it is worth highlighting its greatest achievement: introducing real change in the Russian armed forces and breaking the institutional inertia that long contributed to preventing overdue reform and modernization. However, this has given rise to a sense of confusion and uncertainty for the military that may require the type of stability Putin once worked hard to bring about after its years of turbulence. Putin's ability to oversee real reform and deliver a modernized Russian military that can meet the future threat environment may be hampered by the aftermath or damage from the domestic political crisis, but it is certain that this type of stability, coupled with long-term vision and consistent political commitment, will be required in order to shepherd the Russian armed forces though a difficult and prolonged period of institutional convulsion.

Notes

* Unless otherwise noted, English-language titles in Russian journals are transliterations from the Russian.
1 This chapter was presented at the Glasgow University Centre for Russian and East European Studies, 9 February 2012, "Putin 2.0: Repackaging Russia's Conventional Military Priorities." The author wishes to thank participants and, more importantly, a colleague in Almaty for advice and support.
2 See Thomas Gomart, *Russian Civil–Military Relations: Putin's Legacy*, Washington, DC: Carnegie Endowment for International Peace, 2008.
3 Dale R. Herspring, *The Kremlin and the High Command: Presidential Impact on the Russian Military From Gorbachev to Putin*, Lawrence: University Press of Kansas, 2006.
4 "Putin Sets Army Tasks for Period Until 2020," *Agentstvo voennykh novostei*, 15 February 2008; Vladimir Putin, "Speech at Expanded Meeting of the State Council on Russia's development Strategy through to 2020," 8 February 2008, http://www.kremlin.ru/eng; Sergei Ivanov, "Military Reform as Part and Parcel of Transformation in Russia," *Krasnaia zvezda*, 25 April 2001; "Urgent Tasks of the Development of the Russian Federation Armed Forces, White Paper," Moscow: Ministry of Defense, October 2003, p. 1–68, online at http://www.psan.org; "Press Conference on Military Reform with Sergei Karaganov, Andrei Kokoshin, Nikolai Mikhailov and Vitaly Shlykov," *RIA Novosti*, 6 October 2003; Dale Herspring, "Vladimir Putin and Military Reform in Russia," *European Security*, 14:1, March 2005, pp. 137–55.
5 Yury Gavrilov, "The Officer Corps of the Armed Forces Will Reach 220,000," *Rossiiskaia gazeta*, 4 February 2011; Vladimir Mukhin, "Military Space Reform," *Nezavisimoe voennoe obozrenie*, 3 February 2011; "Russian Defense Minister Says Number of Officers in Army to Increase from 2012," *Zvezda Television*, 2 February 2011; "Russian Pundit Dismisses Medvedev's Proposal to Increase Number of Officers," *Ekho Moskvy*, 2 February 2011; "Russian Army Chief Cancelled Reduction," http://www.dni.ru/society.2011/2/2/206781.html, 2 February 2011; "The Reform of the Russian Army Has Turned Back," http://www.news.rambler.ru/8908959/, 2 February 2011.
6 Aleksandr Belkin, "And Still an Unsolved Problem. Who Could Protect the Country from Military Attack: Conscript or Contractor?", *Voenno promyshlennyy kuryer*, 10 November 2010; Dale Herspring and Roger McDermott, "Serdyukov Promotes Systemic Russian Military Reform," *Orbis*, Spring 2010; *Voennoe stroitelstvo i modernizatsiia Vooruzhennykh sil russiy*. SVOP: Moscow, April 2004.

7 Nikolai Poroskov, "President Dmitry Medvedev's Army Modernization Plan, Transition to Brigade Composition," *Vremya Novostei*, 8 October 2008; "Russia Will Have an Innovative Army by 2020," *Agentsvo voennykh novostei*, 23 June 2008.
8 Vadim Solovev, "Military Reform 2009–2012," *Nezavisimoe voennoe obozrenie*, 1 January 2009.
9 "Russian TV Takes a Dim View of Four-Year Military Reform," *RenTV*, 24 December 2011.
10 Ibid.
11 Anatoliy Tsyganok, "Plastic Surgery: Triumphant Reports About the Success of the Formation of the Army's New Look Are Far From Reality," *Vremya novostei*, 3 December 2009; Nikolai Poroskov, "The Courageous Accountant: The Experts on Army Reform," *Vremya novostei*, 15 January 2009.
12 Viktor Baranets, "The Army Will be Getting the Latest Weapons and Lodgings and Will Be Rid of Hazing: Dmitry Medvedev Has Formulated Five Principles of Development of the Armed Forces," *Komsomolskaia pravda*, 1 October 2008.
13 Nikolai Poroskov, "Military Arrangement," *Vremya novostei*, 8 October 2008.
14 Daniyal Ayzenshtadt and Yelizaveta Surnacheva, "The Abkhaz-Israeli Reform of the Russian Armed Forces," http://www.gazeta.ru, 19 November 2008; "Russian Defence Minister Announces Overhaul of the Armed Forces Structure," *Zvezda Television*, 14 October 2009.
15 "CINC Ground Troops Press Conference on New Brigades, Armament Plans," *Rossiiskaia gazeta*, 26 February 2010; "Will Have to Serve Without Contract," Izvestiia, 26 February 2010; "Military Board," *Ekho Moskvy*, 20 February 2010; Major-General (Ret.) Ivan Vorobev and Colonel Valeriy Aleksandrovich Kiselev, "Ground Troops Transition to Brigade Structure as a Phase of Improving their Maneuverability," *Voennaia mysl*, no. 1, 2010; Irina Kuksenkova, "Expert Opinions on MoD Reform, Need for Brigade, New Brigade Structure Shown," *Moskovsky Komsomolets*, 11 November 2008.
16 2010 Military Doctrine, http://www.kremlin.ru, 5 February 2010.
17 "Russian Military Source Reviews Commanders' Role in Combat Training After Reform," Interfax, 17 August 2010.
18 Vasiliy Burenok, "Where's the Logic?", *Vremya novostei*, 22 April 2010; "Russian Armed Forces Need to Replace 10 Per Cent of Weapons Annually – Official," Interfax, 19 April 2010; Ivan Kornovalov, "Sergei Ivanov Requested the Addition of Only One Trillion above the New State Programme for Rearmament," *Kommersant*, 25 March 2010.
19 "Russian All-Army Conference in 2010 to Seek Officer Code of Honour," Interfax. 30 December 2009.
20 Marcel de Haas, "Russia's Military reforms: Victory After Twenty Years of Failure?," Clinginendael Papers, no. 5, November 2011.
21 Ibid.; "Russian Military is 30 Per Cent Short of Privates," Interfax-AVN, 12 January 2012.
22 Report on Defense Ministry Public Chamber Meeting, Defense Ministry Website, 18 November 2011.
23 Roger McDermott, "Is Anybody There? Russian Military Command and Control," *Eurasia Daily Monitor*, vol. 8, issue 182, 4 October 2011.
24 Aleksandr Sadchikov, "They Are Calling Artificial Intelligence Into the Army," *Moskovskiy Novosti*, 8 November 2011; Author discussions with Moscow-based western defense attachés.
25 Yury Barsukov, "Formation of Contract Army Postponed," http://www.infox.ru, 7 April 2010.
26 Author interviews with western defense attachés and retired Russian officers, December 2011, January 2012.

27 Ibid.
28 Ibid.
29 "Russian Pundit Says Army Reform Theory Not Matched by Practice," *Ekho Moskvy*, 7 September 2011.
30 Yury Gavrilov, "Interviews with Anatoliy Serdyukov," *Rossiiskaia gazeta*, 23 December 2011.
31 Pavel Felgenhauer, "Russia's Former Permanent Representative to NATO Appointed as Deputy Prime Minister," Eurasia Daily Monitor, vol. 9, issue 13, 19 January 2012; "Russia to Allocate 700 Billion Rubles for Shipbuilding by 2020 – Putin," Interfax, 5 December 2011.
32 "Russian Premier Pledges Higher Pay for Military, Law-Enforcement Personnel," Channel One TV, 29 November 2011.
33 Author discussions with NATO military specialists, January 2012.
34 See Roger N. McDermott, Russian Perspective on Network-Centric Warfare: The Key Aim of Serdyukov's Reform, FMSO, December 2010, and "Putin's Military Priorities: The Modernization of the Armed Forces," in Russian Military Reform 1992–2002, London: Frank Cass, 2003, pp. 259–77.
35 McDermott, Russian Perspective on Network-Centric Warfare.
36 Dmitry Kandaurov, "Tanks Do Not Wash," Zavtra, 3 August 2011; Dmitry Litovkin, "Defence Programme Failed the Internet War," Izvestiia, 1 August 2011.
37 Vasiliy Burenok, Aleksei Kravchenko and Sergei Smirnov, "Direction to the Network System of Arming," Vodushno kosmicheskaia oborona, http://www.vko.ru/DesktopModules/Articles/ArticlesView.aspx?tabID=320&ItemID=328&mid=2892&wversion=Ataging, May 2009.

Part III
Foreign affairs

9 Russia and the West
Integration and tensions

Sergei Plekhanov

As the world's biggest state incorporating most of Northern Eurasia, Russia has an unusually wide and diverse set of foreign policy interests. It has more neighbours than any other country – 13 in all, including the United States and China. Since the early eighteenth century, Russia has been involved in most key issues of international politics – a role that culminated in the Cold War when the Soviet Union was for, almost half a century, one of the two superpowers whose competition and cooperation affected every aspect of global politics. Post-Soviet Russia does not claim such a status in world affairs, but it does remain one of the world's most influential powers.

Russia's post-Soviet rulers officially characterize their foreign policy as 'multi-vector' – that is, focused on all areas around Russia. Indeed, four geographic vectors – Western, Southern, Eastern and Northern – are easily discernible in the complex network of Russia's interactions with the world at large.

Relations with the West – by far the most important vector – include Russia's relations with the US, the EU, processes of Russia's continuing integration in the global capitalist economy, issues of the systemic transformation of Russian society under heavy influence of Western ideas and practices, as well as numerous and multilevel societal links which have grown between Russia and Western countries in the past two decades.

The most important elements of the Southern vector are Russia's relations with the belt of Muslim countries south of Russia, including the Middle East, as well as with Israel and India.

The Eastern vector at the current stage is predominantly focused on China, although Russia is also developing relations with Japan and other East Asian and Southeast Asian countries.

The new Northern vector has emerged in response to the melting of Arctic ice and the start of international competition for control of the Arctic Ocean. As the country with the longest Arctic shoreline, Russia is asserting its interests in the region's natural resources and in the terms of access to the opening Arctic sea-lanes.

The Cold War legacy

During the Cold War (1946–91), Russia, governed by communists in the form of the Soviet Union – the fifth historical form of the Russian state – was ideologically opposed to the West as the world's first anti-capitalist country committed, since the Russian Revolution of 1917, to the spread of socialism around the world. The Russia–West conflict over the fate of capitalism, however, never led to an all-out war between the entire West and the Soviet Union. Anticommunism was one of the ideological rationales of Hitler's war against Russia in 1941–45, but the main goal of Nazi Germany's attempt to conquer the communist state was geopolitical rather than ideological – to establish German global hegemony at the expense of Russia and rival Western powers. The challenge mounted by Germany and its allies was defeated by the Grand Alliance formed by Western democracies and the communist Soviet Union.

Within a year after the defeat of Nazi Germany and Japan, Russia and the West were facing each other off in the new global conflict – the Cold War. If in World War II, ideology (communism v. capitalism) and geopolitics (competition between major powers) were not in sync, in the Cold War the ideological and geopolitical lines of conflict merged in a historically unprecedented pattern: the main division in global politics became the issue of capitalism v. communism, while the US and the Soviet Union rose to the status of two superpowers locked into a global East–West conflict. Neither the US nor Russia had ever been in such global roles before: America in the role of defending the capitalist world system from the socialist challenge, Russia in the role of the main base of support for this challenge. The fact that both powers built up arsenals of nuclear weapons gave the global conflict another unprecedented characteristic: if it had ever been brought to the level of all-out war, human civilization would have perished.

But the Cold War remained cold in the sense that the numerous local wars, revolutions and counterrevolutions that it consisted of were never allowed to escalate to a nuclear war. The unique fusion of ideology and geopolitics that led to the Cold War in the late 1940s gradually dissipated. Europe, divided into the capitalist West and the communist East, experienced a long period of peace and prosperity on both sides of the divide. The million-strong armies of East and West remained in their barracks, while East–West cooperation in economic, political and cultural spheres widened. In Asia, communist China broke with the Soviet Union and aligned itself with the anti-communist United States against communist Russia. From the early 1960s, the two superpowers were constructing a stable relationship, underpinned by their national interests, to prevent nuclear war, enhance international security and promote East–West cooperation and convergence.

By the 1980s, the Soviet Union no longer represented an ideological threat to the West. Its stagnant, authoritarian bureaucratic system gave a bad name to socialism, while global capitalism was booming, despite its structural problems – and, associated with the idea of 'freedom', capitalism challenged the communist world through the minds of people living there, who were increasingly attracted to the Western model of society associated with freedom and prosperity. In 1985–91, led by Mikhail Gorbachev, the Soviet leadership attempted to revitalize the communist system through market reforms and democratization. These reforms required an end to the Cold War conflict between Russia and the West, and in May 1988, following a series of agreements between Moscow and Washington, such an end was officially declared during President Reagan's visit to Moscow. The ideological axis of the Cold War collapsed in 1989–91, when governments committed to Western-type democratic capitalism replaced East European and Soviet communist regimes.

The three post-Cold War periods

The two decades since the end of the Cold War can be divided into three distinct periods.

The first period, 1991–2001, can be characterized as the time of Western triumph. The collapse of the socialist alternative was proclaimed capitalism's historic victory. Globalization was integrating formerly closed markets of communist countries with the capitalist world system. Neoliberal ideology, asserting the advantages of minimal government regulation of markets, reigned supreme. The United States was now the only superpower in what came to be called 'the unipolar moment' – a fleeting historical situation when one country towered over all others in terms of its power to influence world events. Meanwhile, Russia, led by strongly pro-Western President Boris Yeltsin, shrank both territorially and economically, seeking Western help in its extremely difficult and painful transition to capitalism, retreating from its Cold War geopolitical positions, and barely holding its new state form – the Russian Federation – together. Most remarkably, the United States and other Western countries got deeply involved in Russian politics, guiding Russia's market reforms and shoring up Yeltsin's failing presidency. Post-Soviet Russia integrated with the West as a country on the West's periphery, with all the consequences of a peripheral status.

By 2001, global winds shifted, and the second post-Cold War period began. In 1999–2000, a new political regime headed by President Vladimir Putin emerged from Russia's protracted economic and political crisis. Putin's policies represented a form of market authoritarianism – a mix of neo-liberal economics and reassertion of the power of the state over society. A more stable state meant less democracy, but at a time when Russian citizens, the markets and, indeed, the world community were impatient for an end to dangerous chaos in Russia and restoration of some kind of order there, Putin's market authoritarianism was accepted as a realistic alternative to the turbulent 1990s. If the only way to stabilize new Russian capitalism was to put Russian democracy on hold that was a trade-off the West could live with.

In the meantime, the United States came under attack from the international Islamist insurgency – a new force in global politics. The response of the Bush Administration was to declare the Global War on Terror, which the US was determined to wage by means of military interventionism with scant respect for international law or the opinions of other countries. This unilateralist thrust aroused opposition in many quarters of the world. In Europe, Asia and in Russia, US actions against terrorist bases were met with understanding and support, but the 2003 invasion of Iraq, carried out under the false pretence of eliminating weapons of mass destruction there, became a turning point after which sympathy for the American case against 'world terrorism' began to wane, as did the US's overall ability to lead globally.

In the 2000s, Putin's Russia, experiencing a rapid economic recovery, began to act more independently in foreign policy, strengthening partnerships with Europe and China, continuing to integrate Russia with Western-dominated economic institutions and, at the same time, increasingly criticizing US unilateralism, the eastward expansion of NATO, and Western support of 'colour revolutions' in post-communist states – Serbia, Georgia, Ukraine, Kyrgyzstan and Moldova.

Despite Western pressures, the second post-Cold War period was mostly favourable for the Putin regime: the Global War on Terror enabled Putin to portray his suppression of secessionist rebellion in Chechnya as an anti-terrorist and anti-Islamist struggle, while the booming world economy and tensions in the Middle East drove up oil and gas prices, enabling Russia, as a top producer of both, to post record economic growth rates in 2001–08. By the end of the decade, Russia was seen as experiencing a 'resurgence' as one of the world's four fastest growing economies, including China, India and Brazil. Russian incomes were rising, the government was paying its bills and Russia's external debt was dwindling.[1]

The second post-Cold War period came to an end in 2008, when a third period, characterized by surging global instability, was ushered in through a series of dramatic events. In August 2008, a small-scale war erupted between Russia and neighbouring Georgia, sparked by Georgia's attempt to re-conquer its breakaway regions of South Ossetia and Abkhazia. The war quickly brought Russia and the US, which was heavily aiding Georgia, treating it as an ally and preparing the ground for its accession to NATO, to the brink of direct military conflict. The war, brought to an end through effective mediation by France and the EU, served as a dramatic warning of deterioration of relations between Russia and the West. The war showed the danger of US and Russian clients locked into their own conflicts provoking a major Russian–Western clash, as well as the danger of further NATO expansion into regions Russia has traditionally regarded as vital for its security. The urgent need to repair Russia–West relations became manifest.

In October 2008, while diplomats were still grappling with the consequences of the Russia–Georgia war, the world financial crisis reached its peak, with the potential of an unprecedented global economic catastrophe. As major Western financial institutions faced bankruptcy, the world economy was screeching to a halt in an open-ended Great Recession, the causes of which could easily be traced to the practices of neo-liberalism in the previous decades.

The economic crisis dealt the final blow to the floundering Bush Administration, and in November 2008, Americans elected Democrat Barack Obama as a new president who promised changes in both foreign and domestic policies. Among its top foreign policy priorities, the Obama Administration moved to improve US relations with Russia. In contrast to the Bush Administration which did not consider relations with Russia an important area of US foreign policy, expecting Moscow to accept whatever decisions the US would choose to make, the Obama Administration recognized the dangers of such neglect and the fact that the US and its allies, now that 'the unipolar moment' was over, needed Russia as an effective partner. The joint statement signed by US President Obama and Russia's President Dmitry Medvedev in London on 1 April 2009 contained the following pledge:

> Reaffirming that the era when our countries viewed each other as enemies is long over, and recognizing our many common interests, we today established a substantive agenda for Russia and the United States to be developed over the coming months and years. We are resolved to work together to strengthen strategic stability, international security, and jointly meet contemporary global challenges, while also addressing disagreements openly and honestly in a spirit of mutual respect and acknowledgement of each other's perspective.[2]

The statement then listed in detail a remarkably wide agenda for joint action by the two countries. In particular, Moscow and Washington decided to resume the process of strategic arms reductions, and within a year, a new Strategic Arms Reduction Treaty (New START) was signed. Apart from the importance of new nuclear arms cuts, the Treaty also signalled the restoration of the substantive US–Russian process of arms control, which was neglected in the Bush years.[3]

> The 'Reset' in US–Russian relations proclaimed by the Obama Administration found its reflection in positive changes in relations between Russia and NATO. Further NATO expansion into the post-Soviet space was put off. Taking Russian views into account, President Obama changed US policy on the construction of a European missile defence system and launched a new dialogue with Russia on possible cooperative efforts in this area. The work of the NATO–Russia Council, established a decade earlier and playing a largely ceremonial role, received a boost. At the Council's meeting held during NATO's Lisbon Summit in November 2010, NATO and Russia committed themselves, in a stronger language than ever before, to building a better relationship:

> We recognized that the security of all states in the Euro–Atlantic community is indivisible, and that the security of NATO and Russia is intertwined. We will work towards achieving a true strategic and modernised partnership based on the principles of reciprocal confidence, transparency, and predictability, with the aim of contributing to the creation of a common space of peace, security and stability in the Euro–Atlantic area.[4]

Afghanistan became a major area of closer security cooperation between NATO and Russia. Sharing with NATO the goal of ensuring a viable and stable state in Afghanistan and defeating the radical Islamist insurgency in South and Central

Asia, Moscow has provided the alliance with air corridors and railway routes for carrying supplies to and from landlocked Afghanistan, rendered military and economic assistance to Kabul, and allowed NATO to use an airbase in the Russian city of Ulyanovsk for logistical purposes. The two sides also cooperated in suppressing piracy off the Somali coastline and in such areas as anti-terrorism, counter-narcotics and search and rescue at sea.[5] Even on such a thorny issue as Iran's nuclear programme, which has divided Russia and the West for years, there was progress in reaching common positions aimed at the peaceful resolution of the dispute.

In the economic sphere, the process of Russia's accession to the World Trade Organization, started in 1993, finally resulted in Russia's accession to the world's trading body, a major factor for this development being strong support from the US Government, motivated by US business interest in the full integration of the world's sixth largest economy into global markets.

The fact that Dmitry Medvedev served as Russia's President in 2008–12 facilitated the positive trends in Russia–West relations. Even though Vladimir Putin retained most of his political power as Medvedev's Prime Minister, the Medvedev Presidency was marked by increased influence of liberal ideas on Russia's foreign and domestic policies and an emphasis on improving Russia's relations with the US and the EU.

Toward a balance of interests

In 2011–12, progress in relations between Russia and the West slowed down to a halt, creating an impression that the Reset was over and that it had been a failure.

In Washington, Republican Congressman John Boehner, Speaker of the US House of Representatives, addressed a conservative audience at the Heritage Foundation in October 2011. He presented a picture of Russia having been for two and a half years:

> the beneficiary of American outreach and engagement. During that time, Russia has continued to expand its physical, political, and economic presence ... under the guise of what's strangely called a 'sphere of influence.' Within Russia, control is the order of the day, with key industries nationalized, the independent media repressed, and the loyal opposition beaten and jailed. Russia uses natural resources as a political weapon. And it plays ball with unstable and dangerous regimes. In Russia's use of old tools and old thinking, we see nothing short of an attempt to restore Soviet-style power and influence.[6]

Comparing the results of the Reset with its original goals declared in the 2009 Obama–Medvedev joint statement, it is easy to conclude that the Reset has fallen short of expectations. But the fact remains that relations improved, new cooperative arrangements were established and the two sides came closer than ever before.

The Reset was not expected to remove all sources of differences and conflicts; rather, its goal was to *normalize* relations – to enhance cooperation in the areas of common interest and to make it possible to manage the differences and tensions in a more peaceful manner. A new balance between cooperation and competition has been achieved. Whether this balance can be maintained in an increasingly unstable international environment remains to be seen.

In 2011–12, massive debt crises in the US and Europe became the latest manifestation of the continuing decline of the neo-liberal model which has shaped the processes of globalization since the 1980s. The ailing global economy, combined with the failures of governments in Washington and Europe to work out effective remedies, is creating an impression of a seminal 'decline of the West' and of a seemingly unstoppable shift of global power and influence from West to East. In the words of a Canadian author:

> Within the last few decades, the world centre of gravity has moved from the Atlantic to the Pacific. By virtually any metric, whether it is economic power, military power, political power, or global influence, the world centre of power has come to reside in the Pacific – with China at the heart of this profound transition ....[7]

Given the realities of the integrated global economy, the deepening Western malaise exacerbates Russia's own problems, such as the excessive dependence of its economy on the exports of oil and gas, the extraordinary social inequality, the unstable political system plagued with authoritarianism, corruption and lawlessness, and so on. As a country on the periphery of the West, Russia is bound to suffer the consequences of Western crises more painfully than countries of the Western core, such as the United States, Britain or Germany.

For two decades, the main idea of post-communist reforms in Russia has been to *westernize* the country by putting in place institutions of capitalism and liberal democracy. In the words of a prominent Russian scholar:

> Since Yeltsin's times, the contemporary Russian elite has been sincerely convinced that Russia must become part of 'the civilized world', that is, of the West broadly understood – if not politically, then at least economically and culturally. The most important forces pushing in this direction are private commercial interests which often have more ties with Cyprus, London and southern regions of France and Spain than with Moscow, since those are the places where they invest money and buy real estate.[8]

Trade and investment links with the West are the overwhelming part of Russia's economic relations with the world at large. The European Union, the US and Japan account for 57 per cent of the total volume of Russia's foreign trade. Russia's trade with the Netherlands alone, Russia's biggest Western trade partner, has the same volume (US$6bn) as its trade with China.[9] Western banks are the biggest creditors of Russian companies.

A recent survey of Russian elite preferences on foreign policy concludes:

> A 'West-centric' picture of the world remains dominant, based on the notion that it is still Western Europe and the US that determine the course of world political and economic events, while the alternative centres of power like China or the Muslim world are viewed as hard to understand and, as a result, potentially dangerous. The main tangible result of participation in international activities remains economic interaction or exchange of experience enabling Russia to gain modern technologies (including managerial ones).[10]

It is not surprising, then, that signs of the West's decline are viewed in Russia with dismay. In a major policy speech to Russia's ambassadors in July 2012, President Putin said:

> The traditional Western economic powers are being weakened by the crisis, which has exacerbated social and economic problems in the developed economies, and by the multi-vector nature of global development today. We can already see this for a fact now. Colleagues, this is no cause for joy. We should not take delight in this turn of events, and much less feel malicious glee. On the contrary, we cannot but worry over these developments, because the consequences of these tectonic shifts in the global economy are not yet clear, nor are the inevitable shifts in the international balance of power and in global policy that will follow.[11]

Russians have always regarded the West with mixed feelings – as a model for emulation, but also as a source of threats. Since the seventeenth century, when they first became aware of their country's lagging behind the West in terms of socioeconomic and technological development, Russian rulers have made several forceful efforts to modernize Russia along Western lines. The main motive of modernization drives was usually a concern that Russia's backwardness presented a threat to its security and undermined its positions in international competition. Viewing Western powers as stronger competitors easily tempted to take advantage of Russia's failures and weaknesses is a deeply embedded tradition in the Russian worldview; the need to learn from the West in order to feel secure vis-à-vis the West has been a major Russian policy priority under all kinds of regimes.

The Putin Presidency is associated with Russia's success both in terms of deepening integration with the West and in terms of restoring to some extent Russia's power and ability to pursue its national interests. Maintaining this success has turned out to be increasingly difficult.

Deeper integration with the West does not guarantee harmonious relationships. In 2008, Pierre Morelle, a high-ranking EU diplomat, pondered over a paradox:

> I am struck by the contrast between our interdependence and the problems in our relations, which remain unresolved. It is a contrast between practical cooperation and psychological confrontation. Ties between the two worlds

are strengthening on a scale, which was unthinkable in the past – and yet psychological tensions remain. Even though experience implies that it is better to learn together – and even if we experience disappointments, we will achieve a lot if we move forward working together.[12]

The impact of psychological factors is not to be underestimated, but the problem lies deeper: closer integration between Russia and the West not only creates webs of cooperation, but also may, and does, generate new sources of conflict stemming from the existence of competitive interests. A stronger Russia better capable of asserting its own interests, be it the terms of its energy exports to the West or the status of contested sectors of the Arctic, will almost inevitably be met with a stronger Western pushback. A Russia self-confident enough to oppose concerted Western political actions, such as sanctions against Iran or Syria, could be ignored in the time of Western triumph, while in the period when Western positions are slipping it is likely to provoke Western irritation and anger.

In the time of global disorder, anxieties in Russia and Western countries may have the same basic sources and call for joint efforts to deal with the mounting global problems. But in practice, the on-going crisis of globalization has boosted nationalist sentiments everywhere, including Europe, North America and Russia, privileging assertion of national interests over steps toward greater international cooperation.

In Russian politics, this trend has translated into a surge of zero-sum thinking about Russia–West relations, when any Western gain is assumed to lead to Russia's loss, and vice versa. In the nationalist narratives, the West is suspected of being opposed to Russia's resurgence and wanting to undermine the current regime and thereby to push Russia back into chaos. The West is portrayed as determined to control Russia, motivated primarily by Western appetites for Russia's rich natural resources. NATO's eastward expansion pursued in the face of strong Russian objections and NATO's plan to build a continental ballistic missile defence system, which could at some point be used against Russia's nuclear deterrent, are offered as proof of continued Western hostility to Russia. It follows from this type of thinking that Russia needs to be strong and vigilant; even though confrontation with the West is not desirable, Russia must be adequately prepared to defend its interests.

Zero-sum narratives are gaining adherents in the West, too. Among Western concerns are the revival of Russian authoritarianism under Putin's leadership, Russia's stepped-up efforts to reintegrate with post-Soviet new independent states, its use of force against Georgia which resulted in the effective secession of Georgia's two regions, its use of energy exports as tools of foreign policy leverage and its maintenance of friendly relations with countries perceived as enemies of the West – Iran the most important among them. In the US, an anti-Russian perspective has become part of the outlook of the ultra-conservative-dominated Republican Party whose 2012 candidate for presidency, Mitt Romney, called Russia 'without question our number one geopolitical foe'.[13] In many countries of Eastern Europe, hard-line attitudes to Russia are maintained by nationalist political forces that keep urging the West to counter 'the Russian threat'. Such postures call for a return to policies of containment of Russia, utilizing the West's economic and military superiority over the Russian Federation.

A counterrevolutionary Russia

From 1917 to the end of the Cold War, Russia positioned itself in world politics most of the time as a supporter of revolutions, whereas the West generally held on to a posture of defending the existing order from radical challenges. In the twenty-first century, a new wave of revolutionary upheavals aimed at overthrowing authoritarian regimes in post-communist states and in the Muslim world (some of them successful, others not) is once again generating tensions between Russia and the West. This time, however, Russia and the West have traded places: it is the West that tends to support opposition forces in Eurasia and the Muslim world (unless they are socialist-oriented), while Russia tries to protect those beleaguered regimes which it considers important partners, or argues for gradual peaceful change. Russia shares this posture with another former revolutionary state – the People's Republic of China.

Allergy to the very idea of revolution reflects a sense of insecurity in the minds of Russia's new rulers. Putin came to power in 1999–2000 at a time when Russia's very existence as a state was in question after a stormy decade when the Yeltsin regime he worked for faced a number of situations where it might well have been overthrown. The goal of restoring and maintaining state capacity by whatever means possible has always been central to his presidency, and a decidedly negative attitude to any forceful attempts at overthrowing an existing government characterizes his worldview. The new conservatism that has become the dominant ideology in the country reflects the interests of Russia's ruling class, which has accumulated enormous wealth in the two post-communist decades, and the mindset of broad segments of the population.

From this point of view, the West's policies with regard to matters of political change look decidedly dangerous. Armed with the ideologies of responsibility to protect human rights around the world and global promotion of democracy, relying on transnational civil society networks and the global media, employing covert and overt use of force in some cases, the US and the EU have been supporting and encouraging political challenges to existing regimes – mostly, if with some exceptions, in the countries considered unfriendly to the West. Every time Russia has tried to follow the West's suit and go along with regime change (as in Georgia in 2003 or Libya in 2011), Russia's business and/or political interests suffered as a result. Criticizing the Western inclination to foment regime change, Moscow refuses to accept Western concern about human rights at face value, seeing these policies as mere means to advance Western interests: to weaken states, reduce them to dependent status, and take over their resources and markets.

Since the December 2004 Orange Revolution in Ukraine, in which part of the ruling elite successfully mobilized popular protest – and Western support – to confront the state and effect regime change, the Putin government has been seriously concerned about the possibilities of a similar political turn in Russia. In winter 2011–12, this fear materialized in the form of the so-called 'Russian awakening'.

It is both ironic and revealing that Putin's September 2011 decision to return to the presidency, expected to strengthen the Russian state at this turbulent moment in world affairs, triggered a period of the most serious political instability in Russia since the 1990s – the political revolt of a significant part of Russian society against election fraud and Putin's return. Surprised at the scale and vigour of protests against the regime in December 2011–May 2012, Putin and his supporters resorted to nationalist rhetoric, portraying the opposition as a subversive force financed by the West and serving Western interests. The first months of Putin's new presidency were marked by the adoption of a series of repressive laws aimed at undermining the opposition.

One of those laws, an amendment to existing legislation, established a requirement for Russian non-profit organizations receiving funding from abroad and engaging in political activities (vaguely defined) to register as 'agents of foreign states'. Since many Russian NGOs working in various areas of public policy, including defence of human rights and fight against corruption, have for years been receiving grants from various Western sources, the new law was a blow not only at the financial base of their activities, but also at the public perception of opposition groups: many of them would now be branded as 'foreign agents'. As testimony to Putin's success at this linkage between domestic opposition and Western intrigues, the law received almost unanimous support in the State Duma, including votes of most opposition MPs, while opinion polls registered overwhelming public approval of the measure, seen as necessary for preventing Western interference in Russian domestic affairs.

While the notion of foreign meddling was inflated by pro-government propaganda, it is a fact that Putin's return to the Kremlin was not the outcome of the Russian 2011–12 electoral season preferred by Western leaders. The Obama Administration, in particular, personalized its Reset policy, regarding it as a way of boosting the standing of President Medvedev in the Putin–Medvedev tandem and thereby encouraging liberal pro-Western trends in Russian politics. In March 2011, Vice President Joseph Biden, visiting Moscow to promote the Reset, left no doubt in his public statements that the US would like to see liberal reforms in Russia and that such reforms were associated with the figure of President Medvedev. In the winter of 2011–12, during the peak of anti-Putin protests, newly appointed US Ambassador, Michael McFaul, met with a group of leaders of the protest movement, an episode which was immediately publicized by pro-Putin groups citing the meeting as evidence that the protests were being orchestrated from Washington.

Aleksei Pushkov, a lawmaker from the ruling United Russia Party and Chairman of the International Affairs Committee of the State Duma, blasted President Obama in a radio interview:

> We have nothing to expect from the so-called 'reset' except polite smiles ... Imagine that you are the President of the United States. For half a year, you

have been systematically criticizing Russia, your Secretary of State Hillary Clinton questions the legitimacy of the Russian parliamentary elections. You send Michael McFaul to Moscow as your Ambassador, and on the second day of his stay he meets with representatives of the radical opposition that loudly calls for a 'Russia without Putin'. Then you question, at least to some extent, the legitimacy of the presidential election in Russia. After that, you criticize the actions of Russian authorities against protesters. When the police disperse Occupy Wall Street demonstrators and 120 people are arrested, it is considered the normal democratic way, while events in Moscow are portrayed as bloody repression … So, when Putin cancelled his visit to the US, he was sending a message that if this is the way the US is going to proceed in our relations, there will be no agreement on Syria, no agreement on missile defence, no agreement on anything.[14]

As the global recession threatens to damage the Russian economy, and thereby weaken the mass base of his regime, Putin's room for political manoeuvre is increasingly limited, and the conflict between the regime and the new protest movement may involve wider sections of the Russian society and lead to a serious political crisis. To pre-empt such developments, and faced with the new reality that the younger and more liberal-minded Russians are no longer willing to support him, Putin has been cultivating his conservative constituency, which still includes a majority of the electorate. A key element of that strategy is to project the image of Russia that is under threat and therefore needs national unity and strength.

Need for realism

The truly nightmare scenario for Putin's Russia would be to face a united West hostile to Russia's existing regime and determined to undermine it. But, while such an idea may be popular with some neo-conservatives in the US and ultranationalists in Eastern Europe, it does not attract the attention of dominant Western elites or broad sections of population of Western countries, if only because it runs counter to the realities of the post-Cold War world.

Relations between Russia and the West did enter into a stagnant phase in 2011–12, and disappointment with the results of the Reset was evident on both sides. Neither in Moscow nor in Western capitals was there evidence of serious interest at this stage in mounting any new efforts at closer cooperation as governments' attention everywhere turned inward, and reconciling divergent interests was becoming more difficult.

Facing a West increasingly absorbed in its own predicaments and expecting little prospect for progress in Russia's relations with US and Europe in the near future, Moscow was not willing to invest significant political capital in any new initiatives in that area of its foreign policy, especially at multilateral levels (NATO and EU). Instead, it was prioritizing other projects, such as stepping up efforts for re-integration of the post-Soviet space and deepening the Russia–China partnership. This 'Eastern trend' in Russian foreign policy may produce tangible results, stemming from shared interests and concerns of the ruling elites in Russia, China and many post-Soviet states. And it may encourage Putin to bargain somewhat harder in negotiations with the US and EU on issues such as missile defence and energy trade.

At the same time, Russia is not likely to shift its attention eastward at the expense of its relations with Europe and the US, continuing to regard these relations as vital to its security and economic interests and to be wary of dangers of significant deterioration. For Russia, China is not an alternative to the West, but an addition to it. In America and Europe, too, there is no interest in pushing Russia into isolation. Europe, in particular, needs Russia just about as much as Russia needs Europe. Relations between Russia and the West have reached a plateau at which tensions and cooperation are in a state of an uneasy balance. But in the increasingly unstable world, and in the absence of concerted political will from both sides for upgrading and consolidating cooperative projects, the dynamics of tension and conflict may gain an upper hand.

Concerned about the danger of such scenarios and taking issue with the revived notion that Russia is still a global enemy of the West, E. Wayne Merry, a former State Department and Pentagon official and a highly respected Western expert on Russia, writes:

> Russia is not a major international player in finance, commerce or innovation. Even in energy, Russia depends as much on its customers as they do on it. Russia can obstruct international initiatives if it feels challenged or disadvantaged, however. This is why China, Europe, India and Turkey maintain better relations with Russia than we do; as Eurasian neighbours, they want to keep the neighbourhood civil. They also have more commerce at stake. An abiding failure of American policy has been to attempt too much with Moscow, to search for partnership without a shared agenda and not to comprehend that Russia will not accept junior-partner status. We need to work on building something resembling normal relations with a Russia that is no longer a global or ideological competitor. More trade and investment would help, as will Russian membership in the World Trade Organization. Serious progress in Russian rule of law would do even more. With Mr Putin back in the Kremlin, we should maintain perspective and recognize that Russia today is a great regional power like Indonesia, India and Brazil, but no longer a global rival. Washington does not need a special agenda with Moscow, but rather balanced and realistic normal relations.[15]

Such a pragmatic approach to Russia is agreeable to Russian policymakers. It is also more in tune with the sentiments in most European capitals. The challenge to both sides is to work harder to cultivate their *shared* interests, while learning to deal with their *conflicting* interests in such a way as to avoid their escalation and militarization.

Notes

1 See Sergei Plekhanov, 'Russia – A Resurgent Power?', in J. L. Black and Michael Johns (eds), *From Putin to Medvedev: Continuity or Change?*, Manotick: Penumbra Press, 2009.
2 'Text: Statement from Obama, Medvedev'. *CBS News*, 1 April 2009, http://www.cbsnews.com/8301-503544_162-4909175-503544.html.
3 *Treaty between The United States of America and the Russian Federation on Measures for the Further Reduction and Limitation of Strategic Offensive Arms (New START)*, Nuclear Threat Initiative: http://www.nti.org/treaties-and-regimes/treaty-between-the-united-states-of-america-and-the-russian-federation-on-measures-for-the-further-reduction-and-limitation-of-strategic-offensive-arms/.
4 'NATO-Russia Council Joint Statement at the meeting of the NATO–Russia Council held in Lisbon on 20 November 2010', NATO, Brussels, 2010, http://www.nato.int/cps/en/natolive/news_68871.htm
5 'NATO's Relations with Russia', NATO, Brussels, 2012, http://www.nato.int/cps/en/natolive/topics_50090.htm
6 'Congressman Boehner on Reasserting American Exceptionalism in the U.S.–Russia Relationship', Washington, US House of Representatives, 25 October 2011.
7 'Shifting Our Guns to the Pacific', in David S. McDonough (ed.), *Canada's National Security in the Post-9/11 World: Strategy, Interests, and Threats*, Toronto: University of Toronto Press, 2012.
8 Boris Kozlovsky and Pavel Lukin, 'Ot aktivnosti k effektivnosti. Kogda vneshnyaya politika izbavitsya ot sovetskogo naslediya' (From activism to efficiency. When foreign policy will part with Soviet legacy), *Russia in World Affairs*, 30 June 2012.
9 'Federal'naya tamozhennaya sluzhba', Federal Customs Service, Moscow, 6 March 2012, http://www.customs.ru/index2.php?option=com_content&view=article&id=15685&Itemid=1981.
10 Mikhail Vinogradov, 'Vzglyad za okolitsu. Vneshnyaya politika glazami rossiyskoy elity za predelami profil'nykh vedomstv'(A look beyond the fence. Foreign policy as seen by the Russian elite outside main government institutions), *Russia in Global Affairs*, 30 June 2012.
11 'Meeting With Russian Ambassadors and Permanent Representatives in International Organizations', President of Russia, Moscow, 9 July 2012: http://www.eng.kremlin.ru/news/ 4145.
12 Pierre Morelle, 'Po odnu storonu stola' (On the same side of the table), *Strategiya Rossii*, March 2008 http://www.sr.fondedin.ru/new/admin/print.php?id=1206353430&archive=1206354399.
13 'Romney: Russia is "without question our No.1 geopolitical foe"', *ThinkProgress*, 26 March 2012, http://www.thinkprogress.org/security/2012/03/26/452202/romney-russia-geographical-foe/?mobile=nc.
14 Interview with Aleksei Pushkov, Russkaya sluzhba novostei, 17 May 2012, http://www.pda.rusnovosti.ru/interviews/202747.
15 E. Wayne Merry, 'Retire The "Reset" With Russia', *The Washington Times, 16* March 2012.

10 Russia–European Union relations after 2012

Good, bad, indifferent?

Michael Johns

Russia and the European Union (EU) have one of the most unique geo-political relationships in the world today. In many ways they are like binary stars constantly rotating around one another, never able to be in the same place at the same time, never able to get away from one another. Remarkably, this continual push and pull has been going on for centuries and shows no signs of ending anytime soon. Russia (and the Soviet Union) has fascinated, confused and periodically terrified Europe. It represents the great unknown, a country so similar to Europe but in other ways completely foreign. The feeling in Russia is similar, with both the people and the government often striving to be seen as European but always leery of their Western neighbours. From the time of Peter the Great this mistrust and cooperation has continued. It continued through two World Wars, a Cold War and the break-up of the Soviet Union. Every time the two sides get close, they inevitably push each other away. Unlike binary stars who are always attracted and repelled at the same time equally, the relationship between Russia and Europe has never been one of equals. The power dynamics are always shifting between them, when one side thinks it has an advantage over the other it quickly finds that the reality is turned on its head. In previous work I have described their relationship as that of 'reluctant dance partners', and if this image is to hold true we have to accept that they have spent their entire history arguing over who should lead.[1]

The song may be coming to an end however. After years of focusing attention on one another, there appears to be a growing rift between Europe and Russia. While the EU may continue to hope to keep Russia at arm's length but engaged, the feeling in Moscow may not be entirely mutual. With the re-election of Vladimir Putin, the distancing of Russia away from Europe, a move that began during his first presidency and was accelerated by Dmitry Medvedev, could, and in all likelihood will, continue. This would have ramifications for both Russia and the EU on a variety of issues politically, economically and socially. This chapter will trace the relationship between Russia and the EU from the immediate post-Soviet period through to today. It will outline the key areas of dispute between the two continental powers and illustrate how Putin is slowly moving Russia away from looking west for its economic and political future and instead looking elsewhere. The chapter will conclude with a discussion of where the relationship is heading and what it would mean for Russia and the EU if the two sides slowly drift away from one another.

The history of the Russian–EU relationship is characterized by starts and stops, two steps forward and then one or two steps back. In the immediate aftermath of the end of the Soviet Union in 1992, the EU saw an opportunity to bring the newly independent Russia into the fold of the rest of Europe. Russia's first post-communist president, Boris Yeltsin, saw an opportunity to work with Europe and fast track the Russian economy. He and the then European Commission signed the Partnership and Co-operation Agreement (PCA). On paper the PCA was an agreement between two equal powers. It called for bilateral trade and political cooperation. It also put Russia on par with Europe by agreeing to hold semi-annual meetings to keep dialogue open and free flowing. While the PCA was agreed to in principle by 1994, it took until 1997 for all 15 member states to ratify it. The agreement was to last 10 years and allows Russia to develop its economic and political institutions while working on issues of human rights in order to allow for potential membership (an idea more popular with the European states than Russia) in the organization at a later date. While the PCA was writing to promote the idea of equality, the reality was much different. Russia was a relatively poor, still unstable state and Europe was enjoying the economic boom that corresponded with the success of the European Community. Because of internal crises, most notably the first Chechen War, Russia under Yeltsin became less concerned with foreign policy and was forced to turn inward. In the face of criticism from Europe over Chechnya and other issues, both the member states of the EC and Russia quickly became disenchanted with their working agreements and the PCA. In 1999 Yeltsin abruptly resigned and left a crumbling relationship with Europe in the hands of Vladimir Putin.

Under Putin, during his first term as president, the relationship with the EU was altered radically. While Yeltsin was constrained by Russia's weak post-Soviet economy and hampered by internal strife, Putin was able to capitalize on Russia's improving economy and stability to better enforce greater equality between the EU and Russia. Putin's goal was to instil pride in the Russian population and one way to do that was to stand up against the EU on issues such as Chechnya, Kosovo and other matters of foreign policy. In many ways Putin was Janus-faced as on one hand he worked to distance Russia from the West and on the other he continued to build economic partnerships. His interaction with the EU could be described as 'competitive but not antagonistic'.[2] He also set out to move the relationship away from the PCA, which in practice was much more hierarchical and paternalistic toward Russia than it appeared in theory. In 2003, with the expiration of the PCA looming in the future, Putin was able to negotiate the EU–Russia Common Space Agreement (CSA). Unlike the PCA, which had specific benchmarks Russia had to meet to better integrate into Europe, the CSA was quickly followed in 2005 with the Road Map for the Common Spaces. The two powers agreed on four Common Spaces:

1 Common Economic Space
2 Common Space on Freedom, Security and Justice

3   Common Space of External Security, and
4   Common Space on Research and Education, Including Cultural Aspects.[3]

Rather than a binding treaty (like the PCA) the Common Spaces are just areas where both sides agree to work. They set goals and objectives in all four areas and then work collaboratively to achieve those that are possible or politically viable.

After the expiration of the PCA, the entire Russia–EU relationship rests on the two sides' ability to work within the Road Map to achieve common objectives. Under President Medvedev, Russia moved further away from the EU. While the trade relationship remained strong and the two sides continued to follow the Road Map, Medvedev's interests were more to the East than the West. He saw opportunities to build a relationship with states in the near abroad and to turn to China as a potential trading partner. With the high price of oil and gas during his time as president, Medvedev was able to better dictate where he was willing to place emphasis economically and the terms in which he would trade. Medvedev saw the future of Russia's economic stability as better ties with the growing economies of China and India and their increasing thirst for energy. As a result of this lack of interest, the relationship stalled and numerous issues and areas of contention remain. Now that Vladimir Putin has returned to the position of president he will need to address both the issues that confront the relationship today and the ramifications of previous issues still unresolved between Russia and the EU.

Energy

Of all the aspects of the EU–Russian relationship, none are as important today, and in the immediate future, as energy. Russia's ability to provide oil and natural gas to Europe, and the EU's increasing dependence on it, has turned the entire relationship on its head. Energy is shaping Russia's decisions surrounding the Shanghai Cooperation Organization and it has helped to re-establish Russia as a major world player.[4] The dependence of the EU on Russian energy cannot be overstated. In 2007 Russia supplied over 30 per cent of the EU's oil and 50 per cent of its natural gas. The situation in Eastern Europe is even more dramatic where nine states receive over 90 per cent of their oil from Russia and six Eastern EU states are entirely dependent on Russian oil and gas.[5] While the dependence on Russian oil is a concern for the EU, the amount of natural gas supplied by Russia may eventually become more problematic. Unlike oil, that can be transported in numerous ways (for example in both pipelines and by oil tanker), natural gas can only be shipped by established pipes. Therefore, it is very difficult to change suppliers, meaning the EU is now forced to continue to use Russian gas or pay an immense cost to change distributers and risk interruptions in supply.

The EU's reliance on Russian energy has allowed Russia to use the idea of energy security to its advantage. It now knows that if the EU crosses a line in negotiations on other issues, it can simply cut off the taps. Europe got a taste of this possibility in 2006 when a long-standing disagreement over revenue sharing of pipeline profits between Russia and Ukraine led to Russia shutting off the supply. As most of the European gas and oil travel through Ukraine they suffered as well. This show of force surrounding energy accomplished two goals. It brought Ukraine more in line with Russia's goals and it scared the states of the EU to try to secure their own long-term energy future. During Putin's first term as president he consolidated the government's influence on Russia's major energy company, Gazprom. This allowed the government to better dictate the price for Russian energy and where the supply goes. Recently, the Nord Stream pipeline, that links Russian gas fields and Germany, became operational with plans for a second pipeline to become operational very soon. The South Stream pipeline that would travel under the Black Sea, through Serbia and Bulgaria, and provide gas to Italy, Austria and Greece, is expected to start construction during the beginning of Putin's new term. While it is true that Russia uses its energy resources as a tool in negotiations with the EU, it must be careful not to overplay its hand. As Proedrou correctly notes, the energy relationship is interdependent in that the EU needs Russian energy but they are also willing to pay the highest price for it. While Russia may look elsewhere for demand, they may already have their best customer in the EU.[6]

Georgia conflict

The damage done to the EU–Russian relationship as a result of the five-day conflict between Russia and Georgia in August of 2008 simply cannot be ignored. To briefly review: as a result of a civil war in 1992 in the de facto independent territory of South Ossetia, much of the region was left under the control of a government that had declared itself independent from Georgia. Only Russia recognized this breakaway region of Georgia as an independent state. A similar situation played out in the Georgian territory of Abkhazia as well, again with Russia recognizing the government but the rest of the international community denying such claims. To protect the 'fledgling Republics' Russia sent Peacekeepers (with Georgia sending their own Peacekeepers to protect ethnic Georgians) to the region, where they had remained when the 2008 conflict began. Georgia, in an attempt to end the long-standing dispute, and claiming that the Russian military was acting in an aggressive not a peacekeeping capacity, invaded South Ossetia. They came into direct conflict with the Russian Peacekeepers and this resulted in the introduction of more Russian troops into the region and airstrikes into the region. Shortly thereafter the Russian Army, along with troops from Abkhazia, opened a second front against the Georgian military. The conflict continued until 12 August 2008 when a ceasefire was signed. While the majority of Russian troops left Georgia, the peacekeepers remain.

During the conflict the EU was adamant that the fighting needed to end and was instrumental in negotiating the terms of the ceasefire. As the major power-broker in the region, the EU was the logical political body (Russia being a member of the United Nation's Security Council eliminated it as a potential negotiator) to take the lead on negotiations and was careful not to lay blame during the conflict. However, Russia was alarmed afterward when the EU, led by the Baltic States and Poland, released an assessment of the conflict on 1 September 2008. In this analysis Russia was found to be solely responsible for the conflict, going so far as to refer to Russia's actions as disproportionate and unacceptable. For Russia, this assessment was completely unacceptable. They argued that their peacekeepers were under attack as were citizens of the region by Georgian forces and that they had no choice but to protect themselves from attack. Russia viewed the EU's analysis as simply old hatreds, particularly from some of the EU's new Eastern members. Worse, it emphasized how quickly the states of the EU could fall back into old stereotypes about Russia. During the Cold War the Soviet Union was portrayed in the West as aggressive and eager to start conflicts. By so quickly laying complete and total blame at the feet of the Russian government, Russia was reminded that they were still not trusted throughout the region. Beyond the damage the EU did to its relationship with Russia, it faced the embarrassment a year later of having to admit that the 2008 report was incorrect when an independent investigation carried out on behalf of the Council of the EU found that Georgia was completely responsible for the start of the war and that its actions did not meet the standards of international law. While it did argue that the Russian response of attacking deep into Georgia was excessive (including the use of the Russian Navy in the Black Sea, airstrikes and other military activity far away from the region) the fact remained that despite the EU's (and the rest of the West) claim, Georgia, not Russia, started the war.[7] The EU's initial stance not only helped sour relations with the Russian government, but also, more importantly, it further proved to the Russian people that they were not trusted in Europe.

Neighbourhoods

As Russia has never been an official candidate country for EU membership it has always found itself on the periphery of the EU specifically and Europe generally. In that Russia is not alone. While there has been eastward expansion in 2004 (which included the former Soviet Republics of Estonia, Latvia and Lithuania bringing the EU to Russia's border) and 2007, which has incorporated much of the former communist bloc into the EU fold, there remains numerous countries that are nearby but do not qualify for EU membership. While not EU-candidates, the Union has tried to reach out to many of them to establish better trade opportunities and to shape these states to better mirror EU policies and governance structures. To accomplish this goal the EU introduced the European Neighbourhood Policy (ENP) in 2004. The ENP, according to the EU, has as an objective 'of avoiding the emergence of new dividing lines between the enlarged EU and our neighbours and instead strengthening the prosperity, stability and security of all'.[8] Moreover, the EU contends that through the ENP it offers,

> neighbours a privileged relationship, building upon a mutual commitment to common values (democracy and human rights, rule of law, good governance, market economy principles and sustainable development). The ENP goes

beyond existing relationships to offer political association and deeper economic integration, increased mobility and more people-to-people contacts.[9]

For the states to the East, the EU has implemented a specific policy called the Eastern Partnership. Developed in 2009, the Eastern Partnership is an agreement between the EU and states such as Armenia, Azerbaijan, Belarus, Ukraine and, maybe most importantly, Georgia. While the EU argues on its own webpage that this partnership is fundamentally about trade, it mentions the Russia–Georgia war as a rationale for exerting more influence in the region.[10] Not surprisingly, Russia sees the Eastern Partnership as the EU attempting to become involved in a part of the world that it sees as their sphere of influence. The inclusion of Ukraine and Georgia into the Eastern Partnership raises red flags for Russian politicians who have long warned the EU and NATO about expanding into those countries. Not surprisingly, Russia has also started to look into developing its own partnerships in the region. Most notably, it has signed the Common Economic Space Agreement with Belarus and Kazakhstan. This is to say nothing of the Shanghai Cooperative Organization discussed elsewhere in this volume. The Common Economic Space was established in 2010 and President Putin has been adamant that the EU must formalize relations with not the states involved but the Space itself. He argues that, much like the states of the EU, Russia has surrendered sovereignty on some issues of trade to the agreement. Therefore, if the EU wants to negotiate with Russia, it must negotiate with all of the states.[11] Putin has even gone further to call for a discussion on the creation of a new formal organization, what he called the Eurasian Union, which has been met with initial positive support by potential members.[12] Such an organization, if developed, would be a powerful answer to the EU's Eastern Partnership. As opposed to an arrangement where states such as Armenia or Moldova must adhere to EU policies as if they were candidate countries without the hope of membership, they could instead find the stability and protection they are looking for within a union of their own where they would be (relative) equals. While it is unlikely Georgia would be interested in any union, formal or otherwise, with Russia, many of the other countries currently involved in the Eastern Partnership could be interested, including Ukraine. There appears to be a growing fight over the hearts and minds of the non-EU states of Eastern Europe and Eurasia between Russia and the EU. If Russia were able to move these states back into their sphere of influence, the EU would lose trading partners, control over gas lines and the buffer between it and Russia. While the EU is unwilling to include these states in any discussion of expansion, it may need to sweeten the Eastern Partnership or risk losing these states to Russian influence and all the consequences such a reality would bring.

Kaliningrad

If there were to be one physical representation of the difficulties surrounding the EU–Russian relationship, Kaliningrad would make an ideal choice. A remnant of the former Soviet Union, Kaliningrad is a small jut of land on the Baltic Sea.

Prior to the Second World War it was a German city, Konigsberg. Much of the German city was destroyed in the war and a new city has been built around it. When Kaliningrad was part of the Soviet Union it was linked to the rest of the country through the Soviet Republic of Lithuania, but since the collapse of the USSR it is an oblast of Russia completely isolated from the rest of the country. It is of key military and political importance to Russia and creates an unusual problem for the EU. The problem is quite simply that, after Lithuania achieved accession into the EU after 2004, the EU now finds itself with a part of Russia inside its borders. Militarily, Kaliningrad serves as Russia's only year round, ice free port for the Navy on the Atlantic Ocean, therefore it is of great importance for Russia's ability to exert military influence on the region. Moreover, during the early 2000s while Poland and the Czech Republic were entertaining thoughts of participating in George W. Bush's missile defence shield – ostensibly to protect against a perceived Russian threat, even if the stated purpose concerned Iran – President Putin threatened to move weapons to Kaliningrad to neutralize the usefulness of the shield.

Economically, the EU has been willing in the past to work on increasing trade with the oblast and industry has increased. In fact, for a while Kaliningrad was outpacing both the rest of Russia and the neighbouring EU states in economic development, raising concern from Russia, Poland and Lithuania. In 2011, the EU came to an agreement with Russia to allow citizens of Kaliningrad to travel 30–50 km into Poland or Lithuania without a transit visa. This agreement finally allowed the people of the oblast to travel outside of their very small geographic space freely (to a point). The visa-free travel is also allowing the citizens to spend money in other states, helping the local economies.[13] Of some concern in Russia, however, is that the Russians in Kaliningrad are already inundated with EU culture and media. While they have long been physically separated from their fellow Russians, those in Kaliningrad, with their easier access to European products, European media and Europeans themselves, are becoming separated culturally as well. As the region is of such vital geo-political importance, the last thing the government would want is for those in the oblast to lose their sense of belonging with the rest of Russia.[14] This puts Russia in a difficult situation in that Kaliningrad has been an issue of contention that the EU has now addressed, but it threatens the ability of the Russian government to use the oblast in future posturing with the EU on other issues.

Syria

No issue better illustrates the ideological divide between the EU and Russia better currently than the on-going crisis in Syria. It is possible that by the time this chapter appears in print the Syria conflict will have ended and President Assad removed from office. Even if this is the case, the long-term damage to the EU–Russia relationship on account of this crisis will remain. Since the beginning of the conflict in Syria, Russia has found itself at odds with the West and in particular Europe and the United States. Both the EU and the US have strongly condemned the violence and in particular the government crackdown first on protestors and then, as the conflict escalated, the rebel forces. While the United States, Britain and France all support greater sanctions and, potentially, intervention by the United Nations, Russia (and, it should be remembered, China) has been steadfast in its refusal to allow the Security Council to act. Russia, a long time ally and supplier of military equipment for Syria has been willing to support the Assad regime's claims that it is fighting terrorism within its borders. It was only when the government threatened the use of chemical weapons against the rebels that Russia finally warned Syria that this would be an act too far. Previous to this escalation, the Russian government had challenged the EU and the United States by arguing that those powers were supporting opposition groups without being able to fully know their goals or post-Assad plans. The EU views Russia's unwillingness to become engaged as self-interested and obstructionist while Russia views the EU as impetuous and grandstanding. Both sides argue the other is ignoring what is in the best interest of the Syrian people and are adding to the pre-existing problems. The reality is that, no matter the outcome of the conflict, the two sides will have to find common ground and work on rebuilding Syrian society. The United Nations will need to become involved in some capacity and this will require Russia's consent. Until that point, however, it appears that, unless the Syrian government radically escalates its offensive, the EU and Russia will not see eye to eye on an issue of vital geo-political importance.

This would not be the first time that the two sides have had radically different opinions on the direction of geo-politics. The EU and Russia, for example, still do not agree on the status of Kosovo as an independent state. Russia has long been a staunch ally of their fellow Slavs in Serbia, dating back to before the First World War. During the instability following the break-up of Yugoslavia, that support did not waver. It continued through to the 1999 Kosovo crises that resulted in NATO bombing Serbian targets from the air and sending peacekeepers to Kosovo to try and protect Kosavar citizens from the Serb army. Then Russian President Boris Yeltsin insisted that this peacekeeping mission was not purely a NATO exercise and demanded the inclusion of Russian troops to protect Serb citizens as well. Rather than cooperate, the Russian troops quickly took control of the local airport and severally hampered NATO's operations. While this was a NATO mission, the EU specifically became involved in the Kosovo issue in 2007. It announced that it was supporting the 'Ahtisaari Plan', which called for an independent Kosovo. When this plan moved to the UN Security Council, Russia used its veto to prevent it moving forward. Undeterred, the EU announced in 2008 that it would be sending over 1,000 'peacekeepers' to the region to complement the 10,000 NATO troops still in the country. While the NATO troops were just that, military troops, the EU peacekeepers were bureaucrats not well suited to the perils of peacekeeping. For Russia, the presence of the EU peacekeepers was obvious; they were in the country to help Kosovo declare itself independent. This is exactly what happened on 17 February 2008, when the Parliament of Kosovo declared itself independent (in violation of the Ahtisaari Plan). The EU immediately recognized the new state even though some of the member states, particularly those with ethnic minority issues such as Spain, refused to do the same. Not surprisingly Russia has also refused to recognize an independent Kosovo and without its approval Kosovo cannot gain a seat at the United Nations, a key milestone for full recognition as an independent state.

The disagreement over the future of Kosovo, much like the current Syrian conflict, illustrates the divide between the EU and Russia on foreign policy. On both issues Russia and the EU have been unable to overcome their own vested interests in a particular outcome. As a result the two sides often talk over or around one another rather than look for common goals and promote a conciliatory approach. By sticking to their initial positions the result has been gridlock and a lack of any action whatsoever. As a result, people continue to be killed in Syria and Kosovars are stuck in limbo somewhere between independence and Serbia.

Eastern Europe

If there were one area where the EU–Russia relationship has improved it would have to be Eastern Europe. In particular, the relationship between Poland and Russia has improved drastically which, by extension, has improved the overall relationship with the EU. Similarly, the tensions between Russia and Estonia, which reached their peak in 2007 after Estonia accused Russia of a cyber attack against its economic interests, has also died down. In the case of Poland, Russia's most vocal critic since its membership into the EU, a turning point came as a result of a tragedy. In 2010 a Polish Air Force airliner carrying a delegation that included the president and many top bureaucrats crashed on its way to Russia. While there was initial hostility between Poland and Russia over the cause of the crash, the Russian government and public's reaction to the tragedy has been seen as a major contributor for improved relations. There is no better illustration of this new spirit of trust than Russia's willingness to participate in discussions of a common missile defence shield centred in Eastern Europe and in particular, Poland. As mentioned in the discussion on Kaliningrad, the missile defence programme, which dates back to the presidency of George W. Bush, has been a major stumbling block between the EU, the US and Russia. Now, with a better relationship with Eastern Europe, Russia is able to participate in the discussions surrounding the future of the programme. While still not completely sold on the current programme, and there are some who remain completely opposed, Russia has remained an interested party and as long as the programme is never used against them they are willing to speak with NATO, the EU and the United States about it. Conversely, Poland and other states in Eastern Europe see a possibility to work militarily, at least at some level, with Russia. It must be emphasized that this is an important step, but only an initial one. There would still need to be a radical shift in the relationship before *either* side is completely comfortable with the programme. As Russian Deputy Defence Minister Anatoly Antonov described the negotiations in 2011:

> Today, our primary goal is to agree on mutually acceptable conditions for cooperation. If we fail to do this and NATO missiles block the capabilities of

Russia's strategic nuclear forces, we will take this factor into consideration. I believe that our response will be wide-ranging and not limited to improving our means to overcome the missile defence shield.[15]

Clearly, when it comes to Eastern Europe generally, and the missile defence shield specifically, an improvement in the relationship is positive, but there is still a long way to go.

The future of the relationship

Based on the issues outlined above, it is clear that the relationship between Russia and the EU remains complex. Because of economic and energy ties, it also means that the relationship cannot disappear entirely either. The future of the relationship is murky, however, with the first years of this Putin presidency key to the direction it will take. Behind all of the power struggles over energy and foreign policy, the current EU economic crisis shapes the relationship in the present and will continue to do so in the future. The EU was designed to be at its very core an economic powerhouse. States voluntarily sacrifice aspects of their sovereignty in exchange for economic wellbeing. The entire EU project started as a way to jump start the economies of post-war West Germany and France. Over time the model of economic union proved so lucrative that the enterprise expanded into the 27-country organization it is today. From the beginning of the European experiment until the first signs of the crisis in Greece, the experiment worked. The EU improved the economic conditions of the members, it grew in stature and relevance globally and within Europe and it was able to negotiate with non-members in a way that always placed it at an advantage. The EU always knew when entering into negotiations, whether they were with smaller economies or large powers such as Russia or the United States, that it outnumbered the other side 27 to 1 and was in a superior economic position. No country better illustrated this inequality of relationship than Russia. In the immediate post-Communist period the Russian economy was in ruins and the political system was unstable. Russia needed the European Community to support its transition to democracy and capitalism. It was in no position to dictate the terms of the PCA. For a country the size and importance of Russia, the need for assistance and the inability to negotiate as equals was a particularly difficult pill to swallow. After the Russian economy collapsed at the end of the 1990s the situation was even worse. While Russia had serious disagreements with the EU over issues of national security, human rights and trade it was not in a position to fully negotiate. It was again dependent on both monetary aid and the benefits of a trading relationship with the EU. This inequality continued until the price of oil and natural gas started to rise and the EU economy started to weaken. Even after gas prices started to fall back to earth, the EU, and in particular the common currency, the Euro, was then in crisis. On account of the necessary bailouts of the Spanish, Portuguese and Irish economies, along with the seemingly never-ending problems in Greece, the EU no longer has the ability to dictate negotiations as it once had. Russia and other states appear aware of this and are starting to change their approach to dealing with the EU. As Trenin describes:

> Buoyed by high oil prices, Russian leaders are standing tall for the first time in almost two decades. Their level of self-confidence can only be compared to the early 1970s, when the Soviet Union achieved strategic nuclear parity with the United States and the United States suffered defeat in Vietnam. Once begging for loans, Russia has now paid off its debts. Russia is sovereign at last and fiercely independent, no longer a poor ward of the West, and on the way to becoming a power on par with others. For each concession the Russians are now asked to make, they will quote a price.[16]

Trenin wrote this in 2007, before the Euro collapse, so his analysis is even more apt today. Russia now knows that in a fractured EU it is able to play the fears of the member states off one another. Rather than always dealing with the group collectively, where it is at a decided disadvantage, Russia is now able to negotiate some issues with the individual states which radically alter the power dynamic of the negotiations. As Leonard and Popescu note, 'Russia has sought to bilateralise both its deals and its disputes with EU member states, putting a strain on EU solidarity and making Russia the stronger power'.[17] This strategy also allows the Russians to pick and choose which states they want to work with, what deals they are willing to sign and further cause the EU member states to fight among themselves. For the immediate future there does not appear to be an end to the Euro crisis. Despite the bailouts in Southern Europe many questions remain. Will another southern economy, such as Italy, require a full bailout? Will the crisis impact other states such as Belgium or the Netherlands? How long will the German government and, maybe more importantly, the German people tolerate bailing out failing European economies? What if the Euro proves unworkable? In an environment with so many questions and such vulnerability the EU cannot act as it once did. The shoe is on the other foot in the Russia–EU relationship and President Putin knows it.

Fortunately for Europe, Vladimir Putin is not Dmitry Medvedev. Despite the change in power dynamics, Putin appears to see Russia's future more in the West than Medvedev. While it appears that Russia will continue to look eastward and push the Shanghai Cooperation Organization (SCO) as a means to counter the EU and NATO in Central Asia it is likely that Putin will continue to dialogue with the West and push for greater trade and political stability. The reason for this is simple, even with the SCO Russia has much to gain through a relationship with the EU. Having competition for Russia's oil and natural gas reserves is better for the price than if there was only a single buyer. Moreover, while Russia straddles two continents and shares a border with China, Afghanistan and other non-European states, many Russians who live in the urban areas of Moscow and St Petersburg see themselves as Europeans. Certainly the culture in Western Russia is more similar to Europe and Russia is an active participant in European organizations, such as the Organization for Security and Cooperation in Europe, and activities such as the European football championships and the Eurovision song contest.

Therefore, it is not possible to completely shut the door on Europe. That does not mean that Putin will ignore the opportunities to the East, quite the contrary actually, but he will make an effort to re-establish a better working relationship with the EU, although on his terms. It appears that the Russia people have already begun to be less interested in the EU generally or as it concerns Russian affairs. During the fiftieth anniversary celebrations of the EU in 2007 the BBC World Service commissioned a poll asking if the EU was a positive or negative influence in the world. Less than half of Russians responded that it was positive. Less than 20 per cent said it was a negative force. The rest saw the EU as having no influence positively or negatively.[18] Over the three-year period of 2005–07 in another study when asked to name 'Five Countries that were Friends' and 'Five Countries that were Unfriendly' to Russia the results are telling. Of the members of the EU only France in 2005 (13 per cent) and Germany in all three years (23 per cent in 2005, 22 per cent in 2006 and 24 per cent in 2007) scored above 10 per cent of respondents thinking they were friends of Russia. When looking at the unfriendly score we see Estonia receiving the highest number of respondents in 2007 (during a conflict over a war memorial) at 60 per cent. In the two previous years the Estonia percentages were 28 per cent and 32 per cent, respectively. Latvia, Lithuania and Poland also broke the 10 per cent threshold with Poland's percentage jumping from 7 per cent in 2006 to 20 per cent in 2007. Again, what is interesting is that the majority of EU states fail to significantly register on *either* scale.[19] Conversely, all of the members of the SCO registered high on the friend scale and Russians were six times more likely to respond that China was a friend than any of the East European states. For many Russians, although they may see themselves as similar to Europeans culturally, there is a limit to their interest in Europe as a political entity.

The question remains, however, where does the future of the Russian–EU relationship hold? As an enormous country that straddles both Europe and Asia, Russia is always going to be pulled in two directions. For every argument in favour of looking west there is now an equally convincing argument for looking east. This may be the biggest challenge for the relationship, even with the return to the presidency of Vladimir Putin. At the beginning of the post-Soviet era the direction of Russia's attention was obvious. To be seen as an equal to Europe meant achieving the status of a world player. Failing equality, maintaining a positive relationship with the EU ensured access to financial support and much needed trade markets. Now that has changed. With the decline of the European economy, with the rise of China as a world economic power and growing consumer of oil and the litany of problems and with disagreements and accusations that have defined the EU–Russia relationship, Europe is simply not as attractive a partner as it once was. It is also not able to influence Russia or any of its neighbours as effectively as it once did. As Hanson notes,

> the EU seeks to conduct its dealings with its neighbours on the basis that they can and should adopt European rules and norms. This approach looks increasingly divorced from reality.[20]

While the need remains for Russia and the EU to maintain a relationship – they do share a border – the reality is that Russia has already started the process of moving away from the EU in many ways. While some in the EU thought initially that Russian membership was a possibility, the reality is that was never an option. The EU requires too much sovereignty to be handed over to a supra-state bureaucracy. However, Russia has entered into the SCO and has accepted some level of cooperation, again on its terms. The emphasis on security and trade and the lack of structure found in the SCO provides Russia with what it so desperately wants – a counter to both NATO and the EU without being fully tied to other states. The EU cannot provide the level of autonomy and economic possibilities that the SCO (or even Putin's proposed Eurasia Union) can. In the SCO Russia has finally found a forum of international cooperation in which it currently feels both protected and left alone. The answer to what the future holds, then, may be more of what we see now, no matter who is President of Russia. Russia will work with its partners in the SCO for as long as that relationship is beneficial for all those involved. Russia will also concentrate on developing a working relationship with the EU on areas of common interest while countering the EU on foreign policy and other issues where their interests diverge. On large international issues they will be willing to go against the EU if necessary but also work collectively if the situation warrants. It will continue to supply Europe with energy and continue a strong trading relationship on other goods, but will be less concerned with criticism coming from Europe over issues of human rights or democratization. As the missile defence agreement illustrates, there are even areas of military cooperation that can be explored but the balance of power has shifted and Russia will not be forced into any agreements that it does not think are beneficial. By aligning itself more with countries outside of the EU, Russia frees itself from dependence on the EU whether in good times or bad. Being free from its reliance on Europe is good for the Russian economy and the Russian psyche. That said, the next question that may have to be asked in the future is: Does Russia's ties with China simply replace one problem for another? No matter what direction the EU–Russian relationship takes in the future, the Russian president and the Russian people may need to start looking for an answer to that question already. To return to the analogy at the beginning of this chapter, it appears that, while they may always be dance partners, Russia now knows that it has other suitors and its dance card is filling up.

Notes

1. M. Johns, 'Reluctant Dance Partners: Russians and the European Union', in J. L. Black and Michael Johns (eds), *From Putin to Medvedev: Continuity or Change?*, Manotick: Penumbra Press, 2009.
2. D. Trenin, 'Russia Redefines Itself and its Relations with the West', *The Washington Quarterly* Vol. 30 (2), 2007, p. 96.
3. Council of the European Union, 'EU–Russia Common Spaces – 2007 Progress Report', 7 April 2008.
4. Sabine Fischer, 'The EU and Russia: Stumbling from Summit to Summit', *Russian Analytical Digest* Vol. 26 (4), September 2007, p. 11.

5 Z. Baran, 'EU Energy Security: Time to End Russian Leverage', *The Washington Quarterly*, Vol. 30 (4), 2007, p. 132.
6 F. Proedrou, 'The EU–Russia Energy Approach under the Prism of Interdependence', *European Security*, Vol.16 (3), 2007, pp. 329–55.
7 http://www.news.bbc.co.uk/2/hi/europe/8281990.stm, accessed 2012.
8 http://www.ec.europa.eu/world/enp/policy_en.htm, accessed 2012.
9 Ibid.
10 http://www.eeas.europa.eu/eastern/index_en.htm, accessed 2012.
11 http://www.euractiv.com/europes-east/putin-promotes-eurasian-union-eu-news-513123, accessed 2012.
12 D. Peleschuk, 'Getting the Priority Straight: Is Vladimir Putin Shifting his Foreign Policy Focus to Russia's Near Abroad?', *Russia Profile*, 21 May 2012.
13 http://www.euractiv.com/justice/eu-borders-open-kaliningrad-citi-news-506852, accessed 2012.
14 L. A. Karabeshkin and D. R. Spechler, 'EU and NATO Enlargement: Russia's Expectations and Options for the Future', *European Security*, Vol.6 (3–4), 2007, p.314.
15 http://www.en.rian.ru/infographics/20110921/167000140.html, accessed 2012.
16 Trenin, p. 97.
17 M. Leonard and N. Popescu, *A Power Audit of EU–Russia Relations: Policy Paper*, London: European Council on Foreign Affairs, 2007, p.13.
18 http://www.worldpublicopinion.org/pipa/articles/views_on_countriesregions, accessed 2012.
19 Found in *Russian Analytical Digest*, Vol. 26, No. 4, 7 September 2007.
20 P. Hanson, 'On the Fringes: Russia, Turkey and the European Union', *Chatham House Briefing Paper*, July 2011, p. 10.

11 Russia and Central Asia
Does the tail wag the dog?

Jeff Sahadeo

In May 2010, Russian Federation President Medvedev received an urgent plea from Rosa Otunbaeva, Kyrgyzstan's interim leader. Otunbaeva requested Russian peacekeepers to calm an explosion of ethnic rioting that had already resulted in hundreds of deaths in the Kyrgyz Republic's restive south. Granting the request appeared as the logical culmination of a decade of increased Russian engagement in Central Asia. Over that period, the Russian Federation had engaged in numerous security treaties and energy agreements with the post-Soviet Central Asian states, with trade volume and labour migration mushrooming. Both Medvedev and past/future President Putin considered Central Asia as key to Russian power and prosperity. Flowing through Russian pipelines, the region's oil and gas underpins a 'state-led energy export model' with vital political and economic implications.[1] Russian bases and troops are present in Kazakhstan, Kyrgyzstan, and Tajikistan. Joint military and peacekeeping exercises through the Collective Security Treaty Organization, formed in 2002–03, were designed to show other regional and global powers, particularly the United States, that the region remained solidly in Russia's sphere of influence.

President Medvedev declined Otunbaeva's request. Instead, he sent extra troops only to safeguard Russia's base in Kyrgyzstan, which lay far from the rioting. Continued violence and the stream of refugees to Uzbekistan, potent threats to regional stability, reminded Russians of the limits of their influence in Central Asia. Because of its relationship to Afghanistan, where the Russian military failed so spectacularly a generation earlier, and where, now, the United States and China could exploit any Russian weakness, Medvedev could not risk deploying troops to Kyrgyzstan. The difficulty of selling such a mission to the public also likely played a role, as Russians have reacted with increased bitterness and xenophobia towards the millions of Central Asian labour migrants on their territory, attitudes promoted by a state feeding from the nationalist trough.

The Russian president's inaction highlighted the complex relationship between his country and the former Soviet states of Kazakhstan, Kyrgyzstan, Tajikistan, Turkmenistan, and Uzbekistan. As Putin moved aggressively to assert Russian regional primacy in the early 2000s, Central Asian leaders carefully and cagily exploited their resource wealth, geostrategic position, and relationships with numerous other countries interested in the region. Even before, but particularly after, 9/11 the United States and China have made strong moves to engage Central Asia, with other major powers also seeking important trade and energy relationships. The Soviet legacy nonetheless continues to offer Russia important advantages in engaging its southern neighbours. Soviet planning bound these economies, notably today in areas from pipeline politics to migration. Current Central Asian leaders are products of a Soviet education, many more comfortable in the Russian language than their own, and have continued Soviet administrative models. Putin's rise in the 2000s solidified a link between rulers who combine strong nationalist and authoritarian tendencies.

Putin has signalled his continuing interest in Central Asia and begins his third term working on macro-projects, such as Eurasian Union, designed to serve as a global counterbalance to the European Union and as an energy superstate. Central Asia retains a critical role in Putin's strategies and method of engagement with the West. Losing control of the region's energy resources and security alliances would threaten the foundation of Russian regional and global power, as not only the US and China, but India, Iran and other competitors have vied for influence on Russia's doorstep and dominion since the late nineteenth century.

The 1990s: divorce and reconciliation

The USSR's 1991 collapse drove Russia and the Central Asian republics apart. Even as the leaders of the Kazakh, Kirgiz, Tajik, Turkmen, and Uzbek Soviet Socialist Republics (SSR) desired the continued existence of the Soviet Union in some form, Russia's first president, Boris Yeltsin, turned his eyes elsewhere. Engagement with the United States and Western Europe emerged as his regime's top priority as the Russian Federation was envisioned as a Euro-Atlantic power. Continued domestic economic crises also consumed a weakening Yeltsin over the 1990s. Shunned, Central Asian leaders turned their attention inward. Former Communist Party first secretaries had suddenly become presidents of independent countries. Each sought simultaneously to consolidate personal power and build the foundation for new nation-states. Except for Tajikistan, consumed by a civil war that lasted for most of the decade, the former Communist leaders (Nursultan Nazarbaev in Kazakhstan, Askar Akaev in Kyrgyzstan, Saparmurat Niyazov in Turkmenistan, and Islam Karimov in Uzbekistan) and party structures successfully transformed themselves into 'nationalist' ones. National economic strategies sought to develop a degree of autarky, in the case of Turkmenistan and Uzbekistan, or western investment, in the case of Kazakhstan and Kyrgyzstan, to replace their dependence on Moscow's planning and goods from elsewhere in the USSR.[2] Strategies for region-wide cooperation foundered, however, on mutual suspicions as leaders struggled over issues from water rights to border demarcation.[3] Even at this low point in the relationship between Russia and Central Asia, these leaders, as they did during the Soviet era, saw Moscow as a critical arbiter in regional disputes.

By the end of the decade, as Yeltsin named Putin prime minister, leading figures in the presidential administration were beginning to see the importance and value of Central Asia. The Taliban's rise in Afghanistan prompted grave fears that Islamic extremism could spread through the former Soviet Central Asian states to Russia's more than 20 million Muslims. Poor social and economic conditions for the great majority of Central Asians added potency to extremist groups, such as the Islamic Movement of Uzbekistan, who were now operating in several countries. Russia maintained the 101st Motorized Division, a border patrol force, along the Afghan–Tajik border, with the permission of the weakened post-conflict Tajik government. Drug trafficking along that frontier had emerged as another critical concern, as deaths from needle-sharing and other drug-related issues spiked in Russia in the late 1990s. Coexisting with such threats from the south were significant opportunities. Rising energy prices stemming from increased global demand had already spurred Russia's economy after the 1998 crash.[4] As Yeltsin's team considered ways to exploit their control of Soviet pipelines, which led landlocked Central Asian states to send hydrocarbon exports through Russia, the United States and China also began to examine the region as part of broader strategies of energy diversification, as well as a frontline against the spread of Islamism from Afghanistan.

As these sands shifted, Putin exerted his own influence on Russian foreign policy. Unlike Yeltsin, he retained a strong Soviet mentality and saw Russia as a Eurasian instead of Euro-Atlantic power. Control over the Caucasus and Central Asian regions of the former USSR would presage engagement with the Middle East, South Asia, and China in what could be an effective challenge to American dominance.[5] In October 2000, Russia, Kazakhstan, Kyrgyzstan, Tajikistan, and Belarus formed a European Economic Community that created a unified customs zone. Russia increased offerings of subsidized weapons to Central Asian militaries in a prelude to efforts for tightened security agreements. Even as Putin's team worked on economic and security initiatives, the events in the United States on 11 September 2001 placed the global spotlight on Central Asia and upset efforts at Russian primacy.

9/11, energy, and the centrality of Central Asia

As the George W. Bush Administration prepared to attack Afghanistan, the hub of al-Qaeda and base of Osama Bin Laden, US diplomats and officers rapidly engaged the leaders of the post-Soviet Central Asian states. Their primary interest involved the use of military bases for aircraft, equipment, and personnel. For the new Russian president, Central Asia now became a centrepiece in his foreign policy towards the West, a pattern that would endure throughout the 2000s. Even as his closest advisors protested potential US military presence in the former Soviet space, Putin, against the backdrop of the fallen twin towers, chose to seek closer relations with the United States and NATO countries around the common goal of combating Islamic radicalism in Central Asia. His rhetoric positioned Russia as a modern, European state facing the same kinds of extremist tensions that were spreading across the developed world. Certainly, Western criticism of Russian human rights abuses in Chechnya, already muted, grew silent as Putin sought to lead discussions on common security strategies. Central Asian leaders, meanwhile, seized the opportunity to gain economic benefits as well as security from the presence of US forces after 9/11. American bases opened in Manas, Kyrgyzstan, and Karshi-Khanabad, Uzbekistan, in 2001. Putin satisfied himself, and tried to placate hawks in his administration, by pushing for an agreement that these bases would be used for supply and not military purposes, though the compromise was more likely the result of Central Asian leaders' own fears of a backlash if American troops were present in their countries. Putin quickly grew frustrated at his lack of influence as Central Asian leaders enjoyed all the blandishments of US and NATO attention.[6] Still wary of drawing themselves back into Russia's orbit, the opportunity to become integrated into Western security structures provided significant incentive for Central Asian leaders, ever more anxious about Islamist threats. In addition to supporting the invasion of Afghanistan, for the Bush administration this was an ideal moment to gain a foothold in a region they had identified as a foreign policy priority.

Anger among political and military elites in Moscow rose precipitously when it became clear that the US intended to be more than short-term visitors in Central Asia. The quick end to the Taliban regime in November 2001 gave way to an indeterminate US-led occupation of Afghanistan, with the Manas and Karshi-Khanabad bases maintained. US generals and congressional members stepped up rather than reduced their visits to the Central Asian states. Islam Karimov, along with the Kyrgyz and Tajik presidents, visited Washington in 2002. Great power rivalries in Central Asia played an important role in the quick abandonment of Putin's Western pivot, as his policy team grew increasingly cynical about the possibility of forming joint security partnerships with the US and NATO.[7] Russian support for what would be a Western-led war on terror evaporated. By spring 2002, Putin, in accordance with leading figures in the Russian general staff and other power ministries, designed a strategy to reassert Russian primacy in Central Asia.[8] Their goal was not only to maintain regional stability under a Russian umbrella and derive economic benefits for Russia, but also to use dominance in an area contested by the west to make Russia's claim as a critical geostrategic power in post 9/11 global politics.

A window of opportunity opened when the Bush administration turned its attention towards Iraq, leaving Central Asian leaders to realize that US attention could be fickle. Putin began by pushing for stronger security arrangements by means of the Collective Security Treaty Organization (CSTO) in May 2002. Russia, Kazakhstan, Kyrgyzstan, Tajikistan, Armenia, and Belarus emerged as inaugural members, with a formal treaty signed on 7 October 2002 to come into force the following year. The CSTO charter set out a 'close and comprehensive' military and foreign policy alliance, including military threats from other states, terrorism, and numerous other security threats.[9] However, the CSTO failed to live up to Putin's vision, which was to build a Russian-led alternative to NATO that would bargain collectively with the West. NATO ignored calls of the CSTO's first head, Nikolai Bordyuzha, to deal with the organization as a whole, and instead continued to work with each state bilaterally. CSTO members Kazakhstan, Kyrgyzstan, and Tajikistan enrolled in NATO's Partnership for Peace programme in 2003 and accepted Western training, arms, and equipment. Uzbek President Islam Karimov, who had kept his country out of the CSTO, declared that US troops could stay on his territory as long as they liked. Central Asian leaders displayed their strong preference for direct relations with multiple outside powers within a multi-vector foreign policy that allowed maximum room for manoeuvre. As long as Turkmenistan, who declared a foreign policy of 'neutrality', and Uzbekistan, the region's most populous state with its largest army, remained outside a pro-Russian security umbrella, the CSTO had at best limited regional effectiveness. Even as Russia signed a bilateral security agreement with Tajikistan in 2003, it pledged to withdraw its forces from the Afghan–Tajik border by 2005.

Putin's vision of using Central Asia as a centrepiece of Russia's regional and global ambitions enjoyed greater initial success in the energy and economic sectors. The Russian president saw the region as revitalizing an old Soviet strategy of using energy supplies to enforce Russian power in Europe. The USSR's subsidized hydrocarbons to the Communist states of Eastern Europe, whose planned economies were led by energy-hungry industries, successfully linked the two, in the minds of Soviet apparatchiks in Putin's administration.[10] In the 2000s, channelling Central Asian oil and gas to Europe through Russian companies and pipelines would give Russia renewed foreign policy clout. The state-led energy export model developed by the Putin administration simultaneously sought to increase its strategic significance and consolidate state power. The Russian president had already brought Gazprom, Russia's virtual monopoly natural gas company, under state control, naming future president Dmitry Medvedev as one of its leaders. But new natural gas fields in Russia would take several years to tap, and imported Central Asian gas would be significantly cheaper.[11] In meetings over 2002, the presidents of Russia and the energy-rich states of Uzbekistan, Turkmenistan, and Kazakhstan designed an 'energy security strategy' that focused on common pipeline use. For the landlocked Central Asian states, comprehensive agreements with Russia provided guaranteed buyers and supply routes, locking in benefits for their most precious resources, which would accrue directly to the respective presidents' offices. Turkmen president, Saparmurat Niyazov, saw his country's massive natural gas reserves, claimed to be among the top five in the world, as vital to the national economy and, even more importantly, regime stability and wealth. Gazprom signed an agreement in April 2003 that would see almost all of Turkmenistan's gas piped through Russia.

Putin's effort to monopolize Russia's oil industry accompanied moves to control the resource in Central Asia. In June 2002, Kazakhstan signed a fifteen-year agreement to transit at least 17.4 million tons a year of oil through Russian pipelines. The state-led energy export model drew President Putin's attention to Mikhail Khodorkovsky, one of Russia's richest men, a potential political rival, and leader of the private oil firm Yukos. Khodorkovsky was jailed in 2004 and the company's assets were sold to firms loyal to the state. Khodorkovsky's arrest clearly demonstrated the parallel tracks of Putin's strategy for increased state control over the Russian economy and society on the one hand and hydrocarbons as a foreign policy tool on the other. Oil and pipeline control was used increasingly to reward allies, from Germany in Western Europe to Belarus and Abkhazia in the former Soviet Union, and to punish adversaries, particularly Ukraine.[12] Putin's planning involved the use of Central Asian oil and gas for Russia's domestic market, so Russian oil and gas can be exported to as many countries as possible. Moscow has consistently refused to sign a European Union energy charter that would forswear politically motivated energy embargoes.

Central Asian leaders remained wary of exclusive dependence on Russia's pipeline network. Kazakh President Nazarbaev and Turkmen President Niyazov had no shortage of foreign suitors as international demand and prices rose throughout the 2000s and other global powers fretted over Russia's assertive moves in such a geo-strategically important part of the world. Construction began, in 2002, on the Baku–Tbilisi–Ceyhan pipeline, designed by an international consortium and supported by the United States. Nazarbaev and Uzbek President Karimov saw the pipeline as allowing Central Asian oil to be shipped across the Caspian Sea to Azerbaijan, and then out to Europe and the world without passing through Russia. A booming China, whose energy needs seemed to be growing exponentially, also explored partnerships with its neighbour Kazakhstan and Uzbekistan. In 2004, the Kazakhs and Chinese agreed to build a pipeline to link their two countries.[13]

In the face of global competition, Putin maintained his courtship of Central Asia, travelling across the region in October 2003. He saw the post-Soviet states as critical markets for Russian manufactured goods – Russia remained the largest trading partner for all of these countries – and a gateway to trade with the Middle East, South and East Asia. The Russian president broadened his simultaneous effort to monopolize influence and regional energy supplies, offering to invest and build hydropower stations in Kyrgyzstan and Tajikistan. The highlight of Putin's trip to Kyrgyzstan was a visit to a new Russian airbase at Kant, 40 kilometres from the US station at Manas. Housing 20 aircraft and 500 troops, the base was designed to support CSTO endeavours in Central Asia. The agreement that led to Kant was bilateral, a tacit admission by Putin that he would need to play by Central Asian leaders' rules. Strong bilateral agreements in 2003–04 were catalyzed by Central Asian leaders' frustrations over the US emphasis on human rights and liberal democratic reforms in foreign policy dealings. US criticism of a brutal 2002 crackdown on dissent in Turkmenistan led Niyazov to sign an unpublicized security arrangement with Russia at the same time as the energy deal.[14] In June 2004, increased US criticism of his human rights record, which included the torture of prisoners and activists, led Islam Karimov to sign a strategic partnership with Russia. Central Asia's status as a part of the former USSR also made its mark on the political scene in the 2004 Russian presidential elections, when Putin lamented the collapse of the Soviet Union, though he saw it as a tragedy for the Russian people, who had been accustomed to superpower status and dominance over neighbouring lands.

Central Asian domestic economies, meanwhile, continued to struggle in the early 2000s.[15] Energy revenues that flowed into presidents' offices served to bolster the strength, and the bank accounts, usually offshore, of their leaders. Kazakhstan proved a partial exception, investing in the rural economy. Social safety nets built under the Soviet Union were left to erode, and average salaries of rural populations outside of Kazakhstan were running at approximately US$10–20 monthly.[16] Regional economic integration remained a pipe dream, despite the formation of a Central Asian Cooperation Organization in 2002, which Russia joined in 2004 before Putin led a charge for a Eurasian Economic Community in 2006. Many observers believed that neglect of increasingly younger and poorer populations might drive Central Asians to Islamist organizations. Hizb ut-Tahrir, a group based in London that preaches the overthrow of secular states and the formation of an Islamic caliphate, recruited heavily in the region in the early 2000s.[17] The main tendency to emerge out of this deepening poverty, however, was labour migration to Russia as hundreds of thousands of Kazakhs, Kyrgyz, Uzbeks, and Tajiks – strict border controls lessened the numbers of Turkmen – flowed northwards, sending and receiving countries alike tried to sweep the problem under the carpet, though it emerged with a vengeance later in the decade.

Coloured revolutions

Popular discontent against post-Soviet authoritarian regimes and declining living standards erupted in the 'coloured revolutions' of 2003–05. Massive demonstrations and political machinations combined to oust leaders in Ukraine and Georgia in 2003–04. Putin and other Soviet leaders focused not on the reasons behind the discontent, but on the role of the West, particularly the United States and its Agency for International Development, in assisting protest leaders with training and money in order to install friendly governments. In 2005, revolution engulfed Kyrgyzstan following parliamentary elections widely considered fraudulent. Popular protests had been common in post-Soviet Kyrgyzstan and the political elite fractured along lines between northerners and southerners. Demonstrations against President Askar Akaev began in the south on 18 March and spread to the capital; on 24 March, Akaev fled the country and a new interim government was announced.[18] Unlike in the previous coloured revolutions, however, where pro-Western regimes emerged, the eventual president of Kyrgyzstan, Kurmanbek Bakiev, had strong ties to Moscow.

The first overthrow of a Soviet-era leader had a shock effect across the region. Uzbek President Karimov saw a Western hand behind the Kyrgyz 'Tulip Revolution' and shuttered US- and European-affiliated organizations working in the country. Soon Karimov would have his own protests to address. Unrest following the arrest of popular local businessmen accused of Islamist tendencies in Andijon exploded on 13 May 2005, with thousands occupying the town square and demanding meetings with government authorities. The government responded with deadly force: Uzbek troops killed hundreds of civilians, burying many in mass, unmarked graves.[19]

The massacre's aftermath, on the heels of the Tulip revolution, confirmed the region's move towards a Russian security orbit. Aware of Central Asian anxiety over democracy and human rights promotion of the US government, Putin played up talk of Western plots to overthrow post-Soviet regimes. Internal regime stability, always the top foreign policy priority of Central Asian presidents, now appeared to demand a strong, stable alliance with a powerful state that shared its status quo politics.[20] Unlike the US and Europe, which, trapped between a desire to keep Uzbekistan as a strategic partner and their own discourses of human rights and democratic freedoms, dithered over the response to the slaughter of unarmed civilians at Andijon, Putin announced full and unqualified support for Islam Karimov against extremists who ostensibly acted with outside help.

Karimov received support not only from Russia, but also from all members of the Shanghai Cooperation Organization (SCO), a grouping that burst onto the global scene in the 2000s. Formed on 15 June 2001 and uniting China, Kazakhstan, Kyrgyzstan, Russia, Tajikistan, and Uzbekistan, the SCO was designed with a focus on combating what China has labelled the 'three evils' – religious extremism, ethnic separatism, and international terrorism.[21] The discovery of Uzbeks and ethnic Uighurs from the restive Xinjiang province of China as fighters with the Taliban and al-Qaeda in the aftermath of 9/11 appeared to confirm the need for a regional anti-terrorist organization and security alliance. SCO members have established intelligence sharing and conducted joint military exercises. Andijon and the coloured revolutions focused on the need for protective integration, with Russia, China, and Central Asia moving together in a type of,what Julie Wilhelmsen has called, 'normative convergence' to counter perceived American unilateralism and universalism towards a neo-liberal reform.[22] Mutual support has allowed SCO leaders to position themselves as part of a larger struggle against western uniformity, later confirmed during the 2007 Bishkek summit, legitimating neglect of western criticisms of their illiberal regimes. Upset by US congressional criticism of his actions at Andijon, the Uzbek president terminated the US lease on the Karshi-Khanabad airbase, signing an enhanced Treaty of Allied Relations with Russia on 14 November 2005, the same day that US troops left the country. In May 2006, Karimov entered Uzbekistan as a full member in the CSTO.

The turmoil following the coloured revolutions blunted the US as a major player in the Central Asian energy game. Putin pressed his advantage; in 2005, Gazprom and the Russian oil company Lukoil signed 2.5 billion dollars of deals with Uzbekistan. Central Asian states' multi-vector foreign policies turned increasingly towards China. Trade between Russia, China, and Central Asia had tripled since the 1990s and the Chinese also now saw the region as both an energy supplier and export market. In 2005, China announced a four billion dollar takeover of PetroKazakhstan; Karimov signed an oil exploration deal with the China National Petroleum Corporation the following year. Even as Kazakhstan, Turkmenistan, and Uzbekistan signed an agreement to modernize and expand the Central Asia–Russia pipeline system in 2007, fears of Russian 'pipeline arrogance' festered.[23] Common membership in the SCO, however, has led members to downplay regional competition, with Chinese and Russian leaders talking of a unified 'energy club' among member states.[24]

Medvedev–Putin era

Russian policy towards Central Asia, unsurprisingly, demonstrated significant continuities between the Putin and Medvedev presidencies. Medvedev's foreign policy rhetoric, which included dashes of language promoting human rights and the rule of law, had no significant effects on relations with the region. The passage of time, and the continued global energy and geopolitical importance of Central Asia led the West – the European Union as well as the United States – back to engage leaders who, secure that the threats of the coloured revolution era had lowered, were anxious to gain legitimacy and resources from constructive engagement. Medvedev's decision not to intervene in southern Kyrgyzstan in 2010 signalled the limits of Russian power in a complicated region where the continued deterioration of the security situation, as well as an apparent NATO withdrawal in Afghanistan, looms ever larger. Even so, the continued waves of labour migrants, particularly from Kyrgyzstan, Tajikistan, and Uzbekistan, as well as pipeline politics and the tenacity of the last Soviet generation at the heights of power in Russia and Central Asia alike, demonstrate that the USSR's legacy continues to bind Russia and Central Asia.

Central Asian fears of the consequences of Russia's desire to use the region for its own economic and geopolitical ends heightened following the 2008 Russo–Georgia war. Putin and Medvedev had anticipated support from the Central Asian leaders against the truculent and pro-Western Mikheil Saakashvili. Kazakhstan, which shares a long common border with Russia and holds a significant Russian minority in the north, a region that nationalists have called to be reunited within a broader Slavic homeland, worried about setting a precedent by supporting the armed invasion of a neighbour. They prevented the issuance of a joint pro-Russia CSTO statement; the SCO too, as an organization, remained silent. China has always seen the SCO primarily as a vehicle to promote its own economic interests. China's economic clout allowed it to gain leverage in Kazakhstan, offering loans during the 2008 economic crisis as oil prices plummeted. Chinese goods, and in some cases workers on specific projects, including new highways, are increasingly common in the region. Chinese companies continue to invest in Kazakh energy ventures. According to the Kazakh energy ministry, of the 80 million tons of crude oil Kazakhstan produced in 2010, 25.7 tons were going to China.[25] Chinese interests are expanding beyond the SCO, most notably now to Turkmenistan. Niyazov's successor, Gerguly Berdymukhamedov, has pledged a multi-vector energy policy and approved a gas pipeline that now links directly to China through Uzbekistan and Kazakhstan. Russia has already agreed to pay a higher price for Turkmen gas than agreed upon in 2003, but reduced the amount of gas it purchased as the global crisis hit. Berdymukhamedov has promised the sale of gas to China above and beyond what is already promised to Russia; whether the Turkmen have adequate reserves to fulfil both obligations if the Russians resume full purchases remains unclear.[26]

The European Union has also increased its engagement of Central Asia. The EU dropped Andijon-related sanctions against Uzbek leaders for travel to member states and on arms sales in 2008 and 2009 respectively. Amnesty International and Human Rights Watch, who saw no progress in human rights since Andijon, heavily criticized these decisions.[27] Germany, which led the move to engage Uzbekistan, no doubt saw potential access to its growing gas supplies. The EU pledged to double support to Central Asia from 2009–13, but its strategy of development aid has remained unfocused and the organization remains weak in a region where leaders strongly prefer bilateral relations with heads of government.[28]

Kazakhstan's resistance to a statement approving Russia's actions in the Russo–Georgia war, even as it has tried overall to push economic cooperation with Moscow, signals the assertiveness of the one Central Asian state that has developed a diverse and dynamic economy, with – like Russia – a rising middle class. Over the 2000s, Kazakhstan has shifted from a net sending to a net receiving country of migrants, mainly from the other Central Asian states. Oil wealth has been used to pay higher salaries to civil servants, from bureaucrats to teachers, and provide price supports to farmers, which has stabilized the rural economy. The population under the poverty line is shrinking, but remains relatively high at 21 per cent.[29] Kazakh President Nazarbaev sees the country as an economic, and even sociocultural, bridge between not only Russia and China, but also Europe and Asia. Economic success, however, has not translated into political pluralism, as the government and parliament remain dominated by Nazarbaev and his allies, and journalists and opposition members are regularly harassed, intimidated, and sometimes imprisoned.

Russia still retains significant power in the region, particularly among the poorer Central Asian states of Kyrgyzstan and Tajikistan. Kyrgyz President Kurmanbek Bakiyev discovered the impact of Russian support, or lack thereof, in 2010. Bakiyev had initially curried favour with Moscow upon assuming the presidency in 2005, gaining lucrative contracts to supply subsidized oil and gas to through companies linked to his family.[30] In return, he favoured Russian companies on contracts for hydroelectricity and declared that he would close the US airbase at Manas when the lease expired in 2014. The decision, accompanied by 2 billion dollars in Russian loan guarantees, set off a furious round of lobbying for a base that American leaders considered critical to the Afghan war effort and as an important symbol of its regional power. Bakiyev's backing away from his position on Manas infuriated the Medvedev–Putin tandem. Russian television stations, widely available in Kyrgyzstan, began to report on corruption and bad governance in the Bakiyev family, and the Russian government invited leading Kyrgyz opposition figures, including the future interim president, Roza Otunbaeva, for talks. On 1 April 2010, Russia raised tariffs on petroleum exported to Kyrgyzstan, complicating its precarious economic situation.[31]

Efforts to increase electricity prices provided one important spark to mass demonstrations against the Bakiyev government, which began on 6 April 2010 and spread to Bishkek the next day. Rumours spread that the protestors had the support of the Russian government, and that many in the crowd with arms were aligned with Moscow. Demonstrators stormed the presidential residence, and exchanges of fire with government troops resulted in some 60–75 deaths. Violent protests spread across the city, leading to the destruction of many businesses linked to the Bakiyev family. The president fled to the south, and eventually out of the country. Unintended consequences of the fall of the Bakiyev regime, primarily the unleashing of ethnic violence between Kyrgyz and Uzbeks in the south, demonstrated the peril that apparent Russian intervention in Central Asia's domestic affairs in the region could unleash.[32] Medvedev's refusal to send Russian peacekeepers, when most in Kyrgyzstan believed that Russia had played a key role toppling the Bakiyev regime, lowered the country's standing among elites and public alike across Central Asia.

The Russian refusal to aid a fellow member of the SCO and CSTO calls the value of these organizations into question. The SCO made no statement on the Kyrgyz revolution or violence, and the CSTO offered only humanitarian aid. The Uzbek government expressed displeasure over the number of unwanted Uzbek refugees who crossed their border. Neither the SCO nor the CSTO has proven greater than the sum of its parts, only useful to its member states to the extent that direct domestic advantages can be derived from involvement. Putin and Medvedev see the SCO as well as the CSTO through security and military prisms, but view threats selectively. Anti-drug trafficking is one area where the CSTO has attempted to work cooperatively.[33] At times, the symbolism of the SCO as an anti-Western club appears as more important for Russia than sharing intelligence on potential anti-government forces in Central Asia. Central Asian leaders see these organizations through the prism of security for their own particular regimes, and it is unclear whether they would cooperate with a Russian-led military force in any circumstance.[34] Continued summits and military exercises, nonetheless, offer a greater chance at cooperation, if not convergence, and signal Russia as a strong, albeit – as Kyrgyzstan showed – not an unconditional, ally and supporter of present Central Asian leaders. The SCO has also allowed Russia and China to contain potential regional rivalries, and China has taken the lead on developing the SCO as an economic club. Such an emphasis poses no direct threat to Russian security, and allows both countries to present the organization as an alternative forum to Western multilateral bodies.[35]

Labour migration

Labour migration highlights at once the complications of the relationship between Russia and Central Asia and their interdependency, two decades after the USSR's collapse. Mass Central Asian migration to Russia began with the oil-fuelled construction boom of the early 2000s and continued throughout the Medvedev presidency, even over the 2008 economic crash. Millions of Kyrgyz, Tajik, and Uzbek workers have flooded cities and construction zones throughout Russia.[36] Their presence is a powerful reminder of the Soviet legacy, when Central Asia was developed as a pool for raw resources bound to the richer industrial Russian core. Migration networks that began in the Soviet era via Central Asian students, traders, and professionals continue to operate today. As birth rates remain high in Central Asia – half of Uzbekistan's population is under thirty – and economic opportunities remain scarce, with the rural economy suffering from water shortages, low procurement prices for goods, and a scarcity of employment in other sectors, Russia has emerged as critical in family and village strategies for survival and prosperity. A construction or service position in Russia can bring in about 400 dollars, over 10 times what can be earned at home. Such inequities have made Russia, after the United States, the second largest migration-receiving country in the world.

Russia and Central Asian states maintain ambiguous positions towards this migration. Russia's shrinking and ageing population necessitated migrant labour as its economy boomed. Travel for residents of the former Soviet states to Russia remains visa-free, and in 2007 processes to allow foreign migrants to gain work authorization were streamlined. At the same time, Putin introduced limits to migrant labour, particularly in sectors like private trade, where Caucasus and Central Asian merchants were ostensibly driving out ethnic Russians. Putin has exploited the Russian nationalism, if not xenophobia, that has resulted from large-scale southern migrations. Leading officials across the Russian government blame any increases in crime on migrants. Ethnic violence against 'blacks' (*chernye*)[37] and non-Slavic minorities peaked in 2008, with at least 109 race-based murders and hundreds more violent attacks on Russian streets.[38] Skinheads and anti-immigrant groups, some sponsored by leading local political figures, launch hunts for or raids on Central Asian migrants with virtual impunity. Central Asian migrants also note frequent extortion from police, who ignore blatant legal and labour violations by employers. Many Central Asians do report positive work experiences as janitors or chauffeurs, which enable them to send significant amounts of money home as they cram into apartments or live in shanty towns on the edge of the city; others, however, particularly in the construction industry, are kept in a state of virtual slave labour, their passports confiscated as they live in locked trailers in horrid conditions.[39]

As radical nationalist groups' rhetoric grew increasingly vitriolic against the state as well as 'blacks', the Russian government under Medvedev re-examined its hands-off attitude. In 2009, police and judicial authorities prosecuted racists who had murdered Central Asian and other migrants, though convictions for assaults or extortion remain extremely rare. The new mayor of Moscow, Sergei Sobyanin, and the Russian government continued to reduce the number of work permits available for migrant labourers in 2010–11, perpetuating the system where these migrants work underground, with no rights and extreme vulnerability. Putin remains extremely reluctant to crack down on nationalist groups and often resorts to rhetoric that enforces the superiority of ethnic Russians in the Russian Federation.

Central Asian governments have struggled to confront the consequences of a mass exodus to Russia. In Kyrgyzstan, Tajikistan and Uzbekistan, remittances from labour migrants have become a critical part of the national economies. In 2011, the World Bank ranked Tajikistan as the country the most dependent on migrant remittances in the world; estimates of migrant labour as a percentage of GDP range from 31 per cent (through official channels) to over 50 per cent (including the black market).⁴⁰ Kyrgyzstan ranked fifth on the list. Central Asian leaders generally ignore the issue, except to occasionally condemn murders of their nationals in Russia. It appears, nonetheless, that the Kyrgyz, Tajik, and Uzbek governments would rather have unemployed youth in Russia than their home countries. These governments have so far failed to design a strategy to employ the majority of their younger populations and their families.⁴¹ The Uzbek government subsidizes flights to Moscow through its national airline. Central Asian youth now see time abroad in Russia as a necessary part of their lives, to gain sufficient funds not only to support their families but also to buy a car, fix a house, or prepare for the expenses associated with marriage.⁴² Public pressure, particularly from Kyrgyz and Tajik families, upset at attacks of their own in Russia, is beginning to lead to efforts to negotiate greater rights and better treatment with the Russian government. Moscow, meanwhile, has used labour migrants as political tools. In November 2011, the Medvedev government rounded up hundreds of Tajik labour migrants and threatened to deport them in response to the arrest of a Russian pilot after smuggling allegations in Tajikistan. The continued importance of labour migration to both the Russian and Central Asian economies means the issue will become increasingly intertwined with other foreign policy areas.

Afghanistan and the pullout

Along with labour migration, the evolving security situation in Afghanistan is likely to dominate regional politics over the next years. The Obama Administration's increased focus on Afghanistan has led it to an intense engagement with Central Asia. In 2008, Uzbekistan agreed to act as a transport corridor for NATO supplies to Afghanistan as part of a Northern Distribution Network that also includes the other Central Asian countries, with the exception of Turkmenistan.⁴³ Sixty per cent of fuel deliveries to US forces now are shipped through Uzbekistan, even as the US administration consistently complains of the graft and corruption, as well as constantly increasing transit fees, that accompany doing business with Tashkent.⁴⁴ As US relations with Pakistan remain difficult, the Northern Distribution Network will remain critical to the US strategy of a phased drawdown from Afghanistan.

Continued insecurity in Afghanistan has cast a pall over Russia's entire policy in Central Asia. Many Russian observers have taken pleasure in NATO's Afghan struggles, and the eventual withdrawal will leave a gap that Russia could fill. The potential collapse of an Afghan government heavily dependent on foreign support could have disastrous consequences, and the outcome of previous Soviet involvement in the country will offer pause to the Putin regime.

The scale of the drug trade from Afghanistan through Central Asia has overwhelmed Russian officials. At present, Afghanistan is responsible for 90 per cent of the world's opiates, and 30 per cent of these transit Central Asia annually. Massive corruption in Tajikistan has led to reductions in drug seizures over the past five years, even as transited amounts rise.⁴⁵ Russia's greatest fear, of a spreading, mass Islamic insurgency, remains possible as long as the Afghan as well as Central Asian regimes carry a large number of unemployed, disaffected youth.

US plans to develop the Afghan and Central Asian economies through its 'New Silk Road' initiative have got off to a rocky start. The first phase of the Obama Administration's plan, to link electricity grids, remains distant.[46] Turkmenistan and Uzbekistan, whose economic strategies depend on tight border and trade controls, will not be ideal partners for a scheme that seeks open webs of trade throughout Eurasia, and Iran's opposition poses a significant roadblock.[47] Putin continues to stand on the sidelines, unwilling to cooperate with what he sees as a competitor for regional influence. For its part, Russia is moving to solidify a Central Asian buffer, providing military hardware to Kyrgyzstan under a programme entitled 'Brothers Fighting for Fixed Borders' and signing agreements to ensure Russian involvement in policing the Tajik–Afghan border.

Future

As he enters his third term as president, Putin continues to see Central Asia as a linchpin. His latest initiative involves the formation of a Eurasian Union, reviving and expanding previous failed efforts for a regional economic organization that Russia could dominate. Kazakh President Nazarbaev is an enthusiastic proponent of a preliminary customs union that would initially involve Russia, Belarus, and Kazakhstan, with Kyrgyzstan and Tajikistan considering membership. Putin aspires to create an alternative to the European Union, though the Eurasian Union's charter, with guiding rhetoric of 'freedom, democracy, and law', seems a poor fit for many regional leaders, and the institutional structure remains unclear.[48] How such a body would exist alongside the SCO remains unclear, and the likelihood of Uzbekistan joining remains slim. The Uzbeks have pulled away from the Russian orbit once more, refusing to participate in 2011 CSTO exercises.[49] Central Asian states continue to harbour deep mutual suspicions, divided by issues that vary from water rights, energy, cross-border minorities and young, sometimes aggressive, nationalisms. Regional leaders continue to court the United States, Europe, and China; Uzbekistan has longstanding ties with South Korea and has sought closer relations with Iran and Japan. New Kyrgyz President Almazbek Atambaev has fostered relations with Turkey, a country that withdrew from Central Asia in the 1990s after regional accusations that it was acting as a new 'big brother' to the young states and their largely Turkic populations.

Central Asia's energy resources, geostrategic significance, and continued young, growing, mobile populations ensure it will continue to have the eye of the world's powers. Stability will crucial once US and NATO troops withdraw from Afghanistan; the US continues to lobby furiously to keep the Manas base after 2014. As oil- and gas-hungry companies and countries court Central Asia with new pipeline initiatives and super-national organizations, the region's leaders actively develop their own projects through preferred bilateral channels. Atambaev is negotiating separately with the Uzbek and Chinese governments to build a new regional railway line.

Russia and Central Asia are locked in a complicated, mutually dependent relationship even as each plays critical roles in world politics and economics. Putin has built an energy superstate, but Russian power now operates primarily as a function of how much oil and gas it can export. Central Asia plays a critical role in supplying Russian domestic markets to allow Putin to play his energy cards on the world stage. Russia's 20 million Muslims, and millions of Muslim labour migrants from the Caucasus and Central Asia, link the regions as well. The Putin regime's actions indicate it would prefer to hold its own intelligence and strategies for itself rather than develop regional plans to counter the ostensible, still unrealized threat of Islamic radicalism. The Soviet legacy continues to bind the regions beyond common pipelines and labour migration. Substantial numbers of the current Central Asian elites received their educations in Leningrad or Moscow and share worldviews with the Russian leadership, which accounts at least in part for the common drift towards authoritarian, neo-patrimonial regimes directed tightly from the presidents' offices. Leaders still see Moscow, albeit often begrudgingly, as an 'honest broker', a sign of an enduring Soviet success where regions competed against each other for resources in the planned economy. Medvedev's refusal to commit Russian troops to the region may have blunted Moscow's authority, diluting credible threats of military intervention that might be able to support regime legitimacy. None of the Central Asian leaders feel completely confident with their regimes' longevity in these new countries with young and often poor populations who have suffered human rights abuses and widespread corruption at various levels of society and government. Riots among oil workers in Western Kazakhstan in late 2011, resulting in 17 deaths and over 100 wounded, showed that even the richest of these republics has a significant underclass that could become a force for political change. Russia needs to proceed with a carefully calibrated, bilaterally focused policy that accounts for the energy and geopolitical cards that Central Asian leaders have to play as well as the interests of China and the United States, among others. The SCO and CSTO and other potential organizations like the Eurasian Union may work as effective umbrella organizations to contain regional rivalries, but each leader, including Putin, seeks maximum flexibility in a hotspot where political winds are constantly shifting.

Notes

1 Theresa Sabonis-Helf, 'Power and Influence: Russian Energy Behavior in Central Asia', *Competition and Change* 11, no. 2, 2007, p. 200.
2 Pauline Jones Luong (ed.), *The Transformation of Central Asia: States and Societies from Soviet Rule to Independence*, Ithaca: Cornell University Press, 2004.
3 Roy Allison, 'Virtual Regionalism, Regional Structures and Regime Security in Central Asia', *Central Asian Survey* 27, no. 2, 2008, pp. 185–202.
4 Dina Rome Spechler and Martin C. Spechler, 'The Foreign Policy of Uzbekistan: Sources, Objectives and Outcomes, 1991–2009', *Central Asian Survey* 29, no. 2, 2010, p. 166.
5 Matteo Fumagalli, 'Alignments and Realignments in Central Asia', *International Political Science Review* 28, no. 3, 2007, pp. 253–71.
6 Roy Allison, 'Strategic Reassertion in Russia's Central Asia Policy', *International Affairs* 80, no. 2, 2004, pp. 1145–71
7 Lena Jonson, *Vladimir Putin and Central Asia: The Shaping of Russian Foreign Policy*, London: I. B. Taurus, 2004.

8 Jonson, pp. 98–102.
9 Andrei Kazantsev, 'Russian Policy in Central Asia and the Caspian Sea Region', *Europe–Asia Studies* 60, no. 6, 2008, p. 1077.
10 Randall Newnham, 'Oil, Carrots, and Sticks: Russian Energy Resources as a Foreign Policy Tool', *Journal of Eurasian Studies* 2, 2011, pp. 136–43.
11 Sabonis-Helf, p. 204.
12 Newnham, p. 138.
13 Julie Wilhelmsen and Geir Flikke, 'Chinese–Russian Convergence and Central Asia', *Geopolitics* 16, no. 4, 2011, p. 877.
14 Wilhelmsen, p. 876.
15 On Central Asian politics, economics, and society over the 2000s, see Dan Burghart and Theresa Sabonis-Helf (eds), *In the Tracks of Tamerlane: Central Asia's Path to the 21st Century*, University Press of the Pacific, 2005; Eric McGlinchey, *Chaos, Violence, and Dynasty: Politics and Islam in Central Asia*, Pittsburgh: University of Pittsburgh Press, 2011.
16 On the social impact of Central Asian state policies, see Jeff Sahadeo and Russell Zanca (eds), *Everyday Life in Central Asia, Past and Present*, Bloomington: Indiana University Press, 2007.
17 On Hizb ut-Tahrir, see McGlinchey and Emmanuel Karagiannis, 'Political Islam in Uzbekistan: Hizb ut-Tahrir al-Islami', *Europe–Asia Studies* 58, no. 2, 2006, pp. 261–80.
18 On the Tulip Revolution, see International Crisis Group, 'Kyrgyzstan: After the Revolution', *Asia Report*, no. 97, 4 May 2005.
19 On the Andijon events, see International Crisis Group, 'The Andijon Uprising', *Asia Briefing* no. 35, 25 May 2005.
20 Allison, 'Virtual Regionalism', p. 185.
21 On the SCO, see Jing-Dong Yuan, 'China's Role in Establishing and Building the Shanghai Cooperation Organization', *Journal of Contemporary China*, vol. 19, no. 67, 2010, pp. 855–69.
22 Wilhelmsen, p. 865; on the neo-liberal agenda, see also Allison, 'Strategic Reassertion', p. 1155.
23 Kazantsev, p. 1086
24 Wilhelmsen, p. 881.
25 'Struggle for Central Asian Energy Riches', BBC News, 3 June 2010, http://www.bbc.co.uk/news/10175847.
26 Kazantsev, p. 1080
27 'EU Removes Uzbekistan Arms Block', http://news.bbc.co.uk/2/hi/europe/8327703.stm.
28 Teemu Naarajarvi, 'China, Russia, and the Shanghai Cooperation Organization: Blessing or Curse for the New Regionalism in Central Asia', *Asia–Europe Journal*, unpublished manuscript in press.
29 Charles E. Ziegler, 'Civil society, Political Stability, and State Power in Central Asia: Cooperation and Contestation', *Democratization*, vol. 17, no. 5, 2010, p. 801.
30 Andrew Bond and Natalie Koch, 'Interethnic Tensions in Kyrgyzstan: A Political Geographic Perspective', *Eurasian Geography and Economics*, vol. 51, no. 4, 2010, pp. 531–62.
31 Bond and Koch, p. 542.
32 The post-Bakiyev government under Otunbaeva made conciliatory moves towards the minority Uzbek population in the south, which was Bakiyev's power base. Ethnic Kyrgyz leaders, feeling threatened, mounted a campaign that span into violence. Madeleine Reeves, 'A Weekend in Osh', *London Review of Books*, vol. 32, no. 13, 8 July 2010, pp. 17–18.
33 Allison, 'Virtual Regionalism', p. 187.
34 Joshua Kucera, 'Moscow Strives to Clarify Vision for Central Asian Alliance', 30 September 2011, http://www.eurasianet.org/node/64248, accessed 21 May 2012.

35 Yuan, p. 863.
36 On numbers, which are only educated guesses, see Erica Marat, 'Shrinking Remittances Increase Labor Migration from Central Asia', *Central Asia–Caucasus Analyst* vol. 11, no. 3, 2009, pp. 7–9. Estimates place the numbers of Tajiks and Kyrgyz working abroad, primarily in Russia, at about one million, and the numbers of Uzbeks closer to two million or more.
37 *Chernye*, for ethnic Russians, refers exclusively to inhabitants of the post-Soviet Caucasus and Central Asia.
38 The Sova Center, which provides detailed reports on violence and xenophobia in Russia, notes that chronic underreporting by Russian authorities means the actual numbers are likely to be significantly higher: http://www.sova-center.ru/en/xenophobia/reports-nalyses/2010/03/d18151/.
39 Human Rights Watch, 'Are You Happy to Cheat Us: Exploitation of Migrant Construction Workers in Russia', February 2009, http:/ www.hrw.org/sites/default/files/reports/ *russia0209web_0.pdf*.
40 'Tajikistan Tops Remittancy Dependency Ranking', eurasianet.org, http://www.eurasianet.org/node/64641, accessed 21 May 2012.
41 Madeleine Reeves, 'Black Work, Green Money: Remittances, Ritual, and Domestic Economies in Southern Kyrgyzsta', *Slavic Review*, vol. 71, no. 1, 2012, p. 118.
42 Reeves, p. 121.
43 Andrew C. Kuchins and Thomas M. Sanderson, 'The Northern Distribution Network: Geopolitical Challenges and Opportunities', Report of the Center for Strategic and International Studies Transnational Threats Program and the Russia and Eurasia Program, January 2010.
44 'Tashkent's Shakedown Practices Hold up NDN Traffic', *Eurasianet*, 27 February 2012.
45 'On Afghanistan's Heroin Highway, Corruption Fuels Addiction and HIV', *Eurasianet*, 9 April 2012.
46 Richard Weitz, 'Obama's New Central Asian Strategy and Its Impediments', *Central Asia Caucasus Analyst*, 25 January 2012.
47 'Northern Distribution Nightmare', *Foreign Policy*, 6 December 2011.
48 Farkhod Tolipov, 'Eurasia and Central Asia: Soviet Syndrome and Geopolitical Reversal', *Eurasianet*, 25 January 2012.
49 'Moscow Strives to Clarify Vision for Central Asian Alliance', *Eurasianet*, 30

12 Moscow's evolving partnership with Beijing
Countering Washington's hegemony

Jacques Lévesque

Twenty years after the collapse of the USSR, the course of Russia's international politics can be characterized as a tortuous and often erratic search for a new place in the post-Soviet world order. In that search, Russia's posture underwent many variations and even spectacular changes. Two of these occurred during Putin's first two terms as president. No spectacular change occurred under Medvedev, but we nevertheless witnessed significant ones that took place with Putin's acquiescence. What can we expect, therefore, in terms of continuity and change for some of Russia's big stakes in international affairs during his new tenure?

This chapter will focus on Russia's relations with China and their so-called 'strategic partnership', which will be examined and assessed here as a function of Russia's relations with the USA and as a key tell-tale sign of its quest for a place and a role in the international system best suited to its perceived interest. In this endeavour, two points must be made here to underline the relevance of such an approach. First, even if US hegemony in world affairs has declined over the past few years, Russia's view of the world remains basically Americano-centric. This is not simply a relic of the Cold War, which leads us to the second point. Even before the existence of the USSR, geopolitics was the dominant approach in Russian foreign policy and views of the world. Except for a brief period that immediately followed the dissolution of the USSR, this is still very much the case.

Based on the ups and downs of its relations with the US and the Euro-Atlantic world, five different phases in Russia's search for a place in the international system can be distinguished. Roughly speaking, the first and very short one extended from the emergence of the new Russia at the end of 1991 to the fall of 1993. The second spread from 1994 to 2001. The third began exactly in the immediate aftermath of 9/11, 2001, and faded out in 2003. The fourth, which marked a nadir in Russia–US relations, began by the end of 2004 with the extension of the 'colour revolutions' in the former Soviet space and culminated with the Russian–Georgian war of August 2008. Finally, the fifth started with Barak Obama's Administration in 2009 and its attempt at a reset of US–Russia relations.

It is against such a background that I will assess the evolving trends of the Russia–China relationship, its significance, its ambiguities, its strengths and fragilities.

Having begun in 2000, Putin's tenure as president or prime minister overlaps four of our five phases. Since the Russia–China strategic partnership began to take shape only in the second part of the nineties, the specifics of the first two phases will be sketched in a more schematic manner.

The first two phases of Russia's quest and the emergence of the partnership

From high expectations to growing disillusion

The first period of Russian foreign policy is characterized by a boundless idealism, a radicalism and a dogmatism that are often typical of revolutionary situations. Here, they are also typically Russian. If we refer to the terms of the age-old Russian debate between Slavophiles and Westernizers, the policies of Yeltsin and his first associates in 1992 represent the triumph of the most radical form of westernization in all Russian history. Their proclaimed goal was to make 'tabula rasa' not only of the USSR's political, economic and social legacy but of old Russia as well. As for new Russia's place in the world, Foreign Minister Andrei Kozyrev could not be clearer when he stated: 'Our first goal in foreign policy is to join the ranks of the civilized world.' The 'civilized world' meant the Euro-Atlantic world and nothing else.[1]

In 1992–93, Russia's foreign policy was entirely and unconditionally aligned with US positions. For instance, at the UN Security Council Russia voted in favour of sanctions against Serbia and Iraq. At that time, Russian behaviour with the New Independent States of the former Soviet Union were remarkably tolerant and restrained. Russia's relations with the 'near abroad' were officially second as a priority, clearly subordinated to the demands of the first. Kozyrev denounced 'aggressive nationalism' towards neighbouring countries as a threat to Russia's place in the 'civilized world'.[2] Here, Milosevic's Serbia, an outcast from the Western world for having disputed the borders of its former Yugoslav neighbours, was plainly a case in point.[3] It must be noted that a comparable tolerance and restraint was found in Russia itself during that period. In spite of the non-recognition of the proclaimed and de facto independence of Chechnya, the use of force to end it came only in 1994.

This first phase of Russia's foreign policy was brief. It was based on too many wild illusions to last for long. For example, Yeltsin and his initial entourage made up of militant neophytes of neo-liberalism who were convinced that the chaos expected from their 'shock therapy' would last no more than six months, and would be followed by rapid economic recovery. They expected massive economic support from the West, something bigger than the Marshall Plan.

With the disasters brought about by the shock therapy, the resurgence of the Communist Party, the rise of different nationalist movements and a change of minds among a majority of Yeltsin's former supporters in the Supreme Soviet, the radical Westernizers of the Executive were left increasingly isolated. In foreign policy, adjustments already appeared in the first half of 1993, and it is fair to say that, after the military suppression of the Supreme Soviet in September of that year, the phase of complete alignment on US policies was definitely over.

The second phase, to September 2001, is the most inconsistent in Russia's search and trial for a place in world affairs.

Until the end of Yeltsin's presidency in December 1999, he held to his aspiration to become an important partner of the US and the Euro-Atlantic world, but complaints about their disregard of Russian interests festered. Relations with states of the 'near abroad' were officially proclaimed top priority in 2000. With the return of geopolitical considerations, and military influence and considerations, Kozyrev (himself a direct reflection of the changing course) asserted that a Russian military presence had to be maintained everywhere in the post-Soviet space. An important caveat must be made here. While Russia was more or less successful in the campaigns by Ukraine, Azerbaijan, Georgia and Moldova to maintain or restore their territorial integrity, in that it obtained military bases, Moscow continued to recognize borders they all inherited from the USSR. In this respect the 'taboo' of the first phase was still in place and stayed so until the aftermath of the war with Georgia in 2008.

From 1994, Russia's long battle against NATO's eastward enlargement began. It must be stressed here that the process of NATO's completed and expected expansion to the East has been the main *constant* factor in the deterioration of Russia–US relations over the years since the end of the USSR. From the first wave that did not yet involve former Soviet republics, the largest political consensus against it existed in Russia. Even the most fervent Westernizers opposed it. Their concern had nothing to do with the renewal of the military encirclement of Russia, as argued by the communists. Neither did they see an enlarged NATO as a safeguard against the resurgence of Russia as a major power, as did moderate nationalists or 'centrists'. Their fear was the marginalization of Russia in European affairs as a result of being kept outside what was to become the most important political and security organization in Europe. Considering themselves (rather than Ronald Reagan, the Poles, or the Pope) as having played the most decisive role in ending communism in Europe, Russians felt very badly rewarded in return. NATO expansion, in fact, was interpreted in Moscow as a purposeful humiliation of Russia – losers in the Cold War.

Primakov and the beginnings of the partnership

During the first years of our second phase, Russia's relations with China stayed on the path of improvement started by Gorbachev. However, they were not yet developing as a function of its relations with the US. A turning point came in 1996 with the nomination of Yevgeny Primakov as foreign minister and the appearance of the term 'strategic partnership' to characterize these relations. In Primakov's approach, that partnership was meant to develop 'a multipolar world and the formation of a new international order'.[4] In other words, reinforcing multipolarity was the way to resist the perceived US goal of preserving the unipolar order that followed the collapse of the USSR. Even a substantial coordination of both countries' international behaviour was deemed insufficient to counter US power. Other major partners were needed for such a purpose, so Primakov looked towards India and, as a more elusive goal, even West Europe. It must be stressed that from the beginning of the strategic partnership between Russia and China, and in spite of their growing self-confidence, they carefully avoided antagonizing the US on highly touchy issues. In this respect, China has always been more prudent than Russia, the US being a vital economic partner for her. A formal alliance was never contemplated between the two partners, not only because they both wished to preserve their freedom of manoeuvre but also to avoid a confrontational posture with the US. Russia and China's top leaders have always avoided declaring that their strategic partnership was directed against the US, even though it was obviously one of its main purposes. From its inception to the present, the content of the partnership has grown substantially. But, to employ a suggestive political science term, one can say that both countries practice 'soft balancing' of US power. In this capacity, China has remained Russia's main partner, among lesser ones.

In the last years of Yeltsin's presidency, the strategic partnership with China was not yet a major goal of Russia's foreign policy. Relations with the US and other countries were conducted in an impulsive and inconsistent manner. The US-led NATO war against Serbia to expel it from Kosovo in January 1999 is a case in point. It was seen in Moscow as a dreadful confirmation of Russia's worse fears about the meaning of NATO expansion. Without any of its members under attack, the US and NATO (previously a strictly defensive alliance) bypassed the UN Security Council to avoid having to compromise with Russia on the terms and limits of an international intervention – and started a war in the centre of Europe. From Russia's perspective, that war was bound to lead sooner or later to the dismembering of a post-Yugoslav state: the very reason for which Serbia had been made the pariah of Europe. In the hours that followed the beginning of the war, Yeltsin issued empty threats. He brandished 'the danger of a new World War' and sent a few warships into the neighbourhood. But soon afterwards, in the vain hope of saving a somewhat significant role for Russia, he sent to Belgrade, not Primakov, who was then prime minister, but his predecessor, Viktor Chernomyrdin, to serve as a mediator between Serbia and NATO. The only thing Chernomyrdin could achieve was to convince Milosevic that he had no option but to accept all NATO's terms for his capitulation. No wonder there is a consensus among Russian foreign affairs analysts that the 1999 war was a major turning point in the worsening of their country's relations with the US.

Putin's first 20 months

That war was but one of many issues that drew Russia and China closer in their political views. But it is only after Putin became Acting President of Russia, on 1 January 2000, that their strategic partnership acquired more substance and consistency. One could say that on the Russian side, Primakov was its scriptwriter and Putin the producer. Such an assessment is, however, more accurate for Putin's second term, as we shall see.

The Russian National Security Concept, adopted in 2000 by presidential decree, cautioned against 'attempts to create an international order based on the domination of the United States and Western countries'. In 2001, two important landmarks were reached in structuring the strategic partnership with China. The first was the creation of the Shanghai Cooperation Organization (SCO) that became the main framework and instrument of the strategic partnership. The SCO was meant to institutionalize and build as an international organization the so-called Shanghai Group of Five. With China and Russia, the Shanghai Group consisted of Kazakhstan, Kyrgyzstan and Tajikistan: the five countries that shared Sino-Soviet borders and had been part of an agreement on the terms for a final settlement of what had been a most contentious issue between the USSR and Beijing. The three Central Asian countries were part of the Collective Security Treaty of the CIS, the military alliance led by Russia. Uzbekistan joined the SCO and later the Security Treaty. The SCO was a piecemeal success in Putin's efforts to restore Russian hegemony in former Soviet space.

The second landmark of 2001 was the conclusion of the bilateral Treaty for Good-Neighbourliness, Friendship and Cooperation between Russia and China. It did not seal a near-alliance, as was abusively said by some observers.[5] But both the treaty and the declaration establishing the SCO reflected a wide range of common views and positions on issues of international significance, stated in diplomatic language. For instance in Article 13 of the treaty the contracting parties pledged to work together 'to reinforce the central role of the United Nations as the most authoritative' world organization and to 'strengthen their cooperation' in the Security Council. Needless to say, they had already stated, more than once, their joint opposition to NATO expansion. Even if it was not explicitly said in the Declaration of the SCO, one of its major goals for preserving 'stability in the region' was to keep the US out of Central Asia. Another common military concern was reflected in the treaty's Article 12 about the 'stability of the strategic balance'. At that point in time, Russia was waging a major diplomatic battle for the preservation of the ABM Treaty that forbade the deployment of anti-missile defence. That 1972 treaty had been a cornerstone of the strategic arms limitations treaties concluded between the US and the USSR, and later Russia. Without success, the Clinton Administration had tried to persuade Russia to amend it to allow for limited deployments. The Bush Administration contemplated a US unilateral withdrawal from the treaty, but hesitated because of objections from many West European governments. The Chinese strategic arsenal being much smaller than that of Russia, Beijing had the best reasons for fully supporting the Russian stance.

The common goal of combating 'terrorism, separatism and extremism', stated in the SCO founding document referred to many issues of mutual support between Russia and China. Extremism being here a euphemism for Muslim fundamentalism, all 'three evils' applied first of all to the war in Chechnya. For China, the fight against separatism fully endorsed by Moscow had to do with Sinkiang and Tibet, but above all with Taiwan. Article 5 of the treaty, stressed that 'the Russian side opposes any form of Taiwan's independence'. Russia considers the reunification of Taiwan as a Chinese internal affair, in which no foreign power has a right to interfere.

In 2000–01, the economic content of the partnership between the two countries was weak. Neither was a major trade partner of the other. For instance, there was still no pipeline linking them and Russian oil was exported to China by rail. But the will to increase the exchange was very much in place. China was already a major buyer of Russian sophisticated weapons systems needed for the development of its naval and air forces. It included war planes, war ships and a very wide assortment of heavy and light weapons. Russian leaders saw this as crucial to regain for Russia a minimum of international economic competitiveness in an area of high technology and turn their country into something more than an exporter of raw materials, which it basically was and remains. As we know, military production was the most, if not the only, high tech efficient sector of the Soviet economy and it had been seriously shaken and threatened in the 1990s with the general collapse of the Russian economy.

The sudden and unexpected opening of the third phase in Russia's quest

Only a few weeks after the above-mentioned landmarks, the dramatic and spectacular events of 11 September 2001 shook the world and brought an entirely unexpected turn in Russian foreign policy. Putin saw a large window of opportunity opening for nothing less than a re-founding of the relationship between Russia and the US, and was the first foreign leader to express his sympathies to George W. Bush.

The Russian defence minister publicly declared that Russia would support the US war in Afghanistan as soon as it was contemplated in Washington, but added that opening military bases in Central Asia for the US was out of order. Putin overruled him only a few days later, against the wishes of most of his advisers. At the urging of the Russian leader, Kyrgyzstan, Tajikistan and even Kazakhstan offered to open military bases or facilities to US forces. Uzbekistan, eager to do it on its own, was encouraged to go ahead. China was notified but not consulted.

Putin's decision is understandable in many respects. The war in Chechnya was raging and he was not only concerned, he was *obsessed* about 'international terrorism' based on Islamic fundamentalism. He saw it as the chief cause of Russia's incapacity to win Chechnya's war. For two years, long before the US, Russian leaders had been warning the world against the threat of international terrorism. They had spoken about a wide arch of subversion and international destabilization, extending from the Philippines (with the Abu Sayaf group) through Afghanistan, Central Asia and Chechnya, up to Kosovo. Their hostility to the Taliban's regime was much stronger than Washington's. Besides arming and training Chechen rebels, Afghanistan was the only country in the world that officially recognized Chechnya's independence. Together with Iran, incidentally, Russia was supporting and sending weapons to the Northern Alliance of Ahmed Shah Massoud, who was fighting the Taliban.

These were very sound reasons for welcoming the United State's war in Afghanistan that Washington would have undertaken with or without direct Russian assistance. However, the multi-sided dimensions of the Russian military, intelligence and logistical support, and Putin's behaviour on a range of unrelated issues, reveal much more than the desired destruction of the Afghan regime.

With the deep traumatic effects of 9/11 in the US, Putin rapidly and rightly sensed that terrorism and the war on terrorism would become a central fixation of the Bush Administration's foreign policy. On that basis, he proved to be deeply convinced that a new, solid and privileged partnership could and would be built with the US. The extent and the high value of Russian assistance in the Afghan war was a way to show Washington that Russia could be a more useful partner than NATO on a very crucial American stake. As a matter of fact, NATO was not involved in the first phase of the war. In October 2001, shortly after the beginning of the Afghan war, Russia's ministries of Defence and Foreign Affairs announced the closing of the remaining Soviet military installations in Cuba and Vietnam. These were mainly radar and surveillance systems with little military value, but the timing of the move was clearly meant as a signal to Washington that Russia and the US were henceforth in the same camp.

Needless to say, all of this was most welcome by the Bush Administration. But contrary to Putin's hopes, these concessions did not end US unilateralism at the expense of Russia's most clearly stated interests. Just the opposite happened. The inclusion of the three Baltic Republics in a next phase of NATO expansion had been discussed and anticipated, but no clear commitment had yet been made by NATO or the US and fears were voiced in the Baltic capitals about an indefinite postponement of their request for membership. But no later than 6 November 2001, in a major speech given in Warsaw, George W. Bush gave the US green light for their inclusion in NATO. A month later, on 13 December, Washington issued official notice of its unilateral withdrawal from the ABM Treaty, even though there was no technical calendar that made the decision urgent.

The Russian official reactions to these two events were astoundingly subdued. Not even the slightest threat of retaliation was issued. Putin simply said that these decisions were unfortunate, behaving as if they were sequels of a bygone past. As a matter of fact, Russia's cooperation with the US continued unabated for about two years, while Putin constantly downplayed what could be seen as irritants. His persistent investment in the Russia–US relationship led Russian observers to compare him to Gorbachev who made concession after concession with the unshakable conviction that they were bound to bring a significant change in a difficult partner's behaviour – to no avail.

Not surprisingly, Chinese leaders voiced their dissatisfaction to their Russian counterparts for the lack of consultations in connection with US military bases and facilities in Central Asia by SCO members. They were also displeased and disappointed by the absence of any significant Russian reaction to the US withdrawal from the ABM Treaty.[6] Nevertheless, the partnership between the two countries was not severely damaged. Economic and trade exchanges grew. Cooperation on a wide range of issues continued alongside meetings of the SCO.

But the geopolitical dimension of the strategic partnership was losing much of its significance. One could say that the partnership endured while its strategic content diminished. Russia had always been more eager and more in a hurry than China in its desire to balance US hegemony.

Putin's will and capacity to put up with a lot from the US could not last forever. Russia's economic situation was not as desperate as it had been under Yeltsin or Gorbachev. On the contrary, thanks to soaring oil and gas prices, it was rapidly improving. Nonetheless, the 'honeymoon' between Russia and the US began to erode in 1993, but slowly. For instance, although Russia made clear that it was opposed to the war against Iraq long before it began in March, Moscow did not declare its intention to use its veto at the UN Security Council before France did.[7] For many months before that, Putin had tried unsuccessfully to obtain guarantees from Washington that would preserve options granted Russia by Saddam Hussein for the exploitation of the biggest oil reserves of Iraq. Even after the 'Rose Revolution' in Georgia in December 2003, Russian reactions were restrained in spite of US support for Saakashvili. However, a turning point was reached with the 'Orange Revolution' of December 2004 in Ukraine, the most important state in post-Soviet space after Russia. Even if Putin was aware of the internal causes of these events, his KGB professional background, the huge political and media support from the West, and the American limited organizational and financial support to leading Ukrainian protest groups convinced him that these were ultimately decisive in the upturn of events. To a considerable extent he shared the Russian view according to which the colour revolutions were 'orchestrated' from Washington. The full support of George W. Bush for a rapid admission of Georgia and Ukraine in NATO also persuaded him that the US was engaged in an all out offensive to destroy Russia's influence in the sphere of its most 'legitimate' interests (to use the Russian words). Needless to say, the promotion of democracy in these countries was not seen in Moscow as a goal in itself but as an instrument for the advancement of US and Western influence and interests at the expense of Russia.

Thus began the fourth phase in Russia's quest for the most adequate international posture to defend its interests.

The fourth phase and the full propulsion of the strategic partnership with China

As mentioned above, that fourth phase was the worst in the short history of Russia's relations with the US. Their relations deteriorated to such an extent that books have been written on 'a new Cold War'.[8] During that period the goal of reinforcing multipolarity in the world made a forceful comeback. That central goal was pursued in a renewed and multi-sided way, but the strategic partnership with China remained the keystone of Russia's approach in this respect. As far as relations with the US are concerned, the fourth of the five phases delineated on that basis ended in 2009 with the advent of the Obama Administration. Nevertheless, the momentum acquired by the partnership with China continued unabated after 2009, building on a landmark joint military exercise in 2005.

In August that year, the first joint military manoeuvres since the Sino-Soviet alliance of the 1950s were held by the two parties along the Chinese coast of Shandong, under the umbrella of the SCO. Because of their unprecedented character and size, China and Russia both presented them as opening a new era in their strategic partnership. More than 10,000 troops participated, with sophisticated Russian fighter-planes, supersonic heavy bombers Tu-95 and TU-22M, and nuclear-propelled submarines. Besides their political implication, the manoeuvres served also as a Russian promotional exhibit for the Chinese customer. Chinese purchases of Russian weapon systems increased substantially and Beijing remained the number one client of Russian military hardware. Only in 2011 was the top spot taken over by India. The joint military manoeuvres of 2005, called 'Peace Mission', were held every two years or so in different countries of the SCO. In 2007, the leaders of all the member states attended the first training sessions to involve the Central Asian members associated with the Russian-led Collective Security Treaty Organization (CSTO). Western observers spoke of the transformation of the SCO into a NATO of the East. They were just as seriously off the mark as were those who spoke of a new Cold War. The game was much more fluid, as again both Russian and Chinese leaders knew they could not sustain a large-scale competition with the US and NATO.

They could, however, challenge them on specific issues, as happened at the summit meeting of the SCO members of July 2005. The leaders unanimously demanded a timely schedule for the closure of the military bases granted to the US in Central Asia in 2001. Uzbekistan complied shortly afterwards, while Kyrgyzstan's Bakiyev, after wavering, did not live up to his pledge and as a consequence later paid a heavy price.

At the same summit of July 2005, the SCO awarded observer status within the organization to three new states. From Russia's perspective, the most important of these was India. India had been a major Soviet partner since Primakov's time, and was seen as a growing factor of potential multipolarity in world affairs. An important Primakov goal now pursued by Putin was to have Russia, India, and China working together to balance US hegemony. Given the traditional rivalry and distrust between China and India, this was not an easy task. Still, Russia has succeeded in institutionalizing regular trilateral meetings of the foreign ministers of the three countries. In official Russian documents, such as the Foreign Policy Concept, they are referred to as the 'troika'. It is safe to say that Russia's efforts contributed to a non-negligible improvement in Sino–Indian relations. Not surprisingly, China wanted to have Pakistan alongside India as an observer in the organization. Needless to say, this did not bring more political cohesion to the SCO, for Russia and China continued to set the organization's agenda and a common goal of both leaders is to reduce India and Pakistan's mutual distrust. The third country to be admitted as an observer was Iran, an obvious pole of resistance to the US eager to garner Russia and China's selective and prudent support. Besides its geopolitical purposes, the extension of the SCO was also intended to make it an important instrument of regional economic cooperation.

To get back to economic matters, the 2005 statistics of bilateral trade between Russia and China showed a dramatic increase of 38 per cent by comparison to those of 2004. With the political will to intensify them, trade relations kept growing so that by 2010 China, for the first time, became Russia's largest commercial partner, bypassing Germany. There is no symmetry here. Russia ranks eleventh as trade partner of China. When the European Union is considered as a single trade unit, as is often the case, it remains Russia's first partner.[9]

A significant development in fostering the economic relationship between the two countries took place during the phase considered here. Since the end of the 1990s, agreements were reached for the construction of a long pipeline to carry massive quantities of Russian oil from East Siberia to the Chinese oil terminal of Daqing in north-western Manchuria. In January 2003, to Chinese discontent, Russia put the project aside and opted for a much longer one, partly financed by Japan, to carry oil up to the Pacific coast near Vladivostok. This allowed Russia to have more East Asian customers and avoid a situation that could permit a single recipient to dictate prices. However, to intensify the strategic partnership with China, Russia decided in 2005 to build a branch of the projected pipeline directly to Daqing and give it priority in development. Oil began to flow in Daqing in January 2011.[10]

Anticipated weaknesses of the partnership

With the proportional diminution of weapons and the rise of oil, the share of raw materials in Russian exports to China is increasing. Western analysts go so far as to say that the economic relationship has a neo-colonial bent: backward Russia being the exploited party. Since the beginning of the partnership many, if not a majority, of Western analysts as well as Russian observers and politicians have emphasized a broad range of problems and issues potentially plaguing the relationship and threatening its viability. Most of these relate to heavy asymmetries between the two countries and it may be useful to review some of them here.

The first and most obvious one that has been a source of worries in Russia is the huge population gap between the two countries. The potential consequences of the gap seemed to be made worse by two self-reinforcing causes. The chasm keeps increasing with the dramatic and continuous decrease of the Russian population. The problem is particularly acute in regions bordering on China, as it is everywhere in under-populated Siberia, by the emigration of Russians towards the European part of the country. Highly alarmist scenarios have been evoked by nationalists in Moscow and politicians in the regions bordering China regarding massive illegal Chinese immigration. In the early 2000s assertions were heard that as many as two million Chinese 'illegals' already accounted for up to one third of the regional population. Pointing to an expected increase of immigrants from China and the growing legal and illegal trans-border trade, and Chinese investments, nationalists claimed that a de facto annexation was underway. These phobias proved to be totally unfounded. With China's cooperation, border controls were reinforced and Russian official estimations made in 2004 put the number of Chinese living in all of

Russian territory under 250,000. Moreover, the most populated parts of China are not those bordering Russia and by the end of the 2010s Japanese and South Korean investments were higher than China's one in neighbouring Russian *oblasti.*

The asymmetry in the content of economic exchanges between China and Russia and the size of their economies is a source of concern for the Russian leaders. But it does not necessarily weaken their relationship, as is often argued. Russia is basically a raw materials provider in its trade with all developed countries and not only with China. Reinforcing political relations with the USA or Europe would not solve the problem, which is a Russian one. As for the 'neo-colonial' bent of the economic relationship, Russia is careful in preserving the diversity of its oil customers as we have seen. The building of a gas pipeline has been discussed between Russia and China for more than four years. It is still held up by a persistent stalemate in gas price negotiations. Russia refuses China's demand (based on reasons of proximity) for a price that would be less than half that paid by Europe.

The growing economic Chinese presence in Central Asia is certainly more disturbing for Putin, given his key preoccupation with preserving Russia influence in the former Soviet space. In 2009, for the first time, China's turnover trade in post-Soviet Central Asia (taken as a whole) exceeded that of Russia. Moscow is partly responsible for this situation. Its tergiversations in negotiating oil and gas contracts with China facilitated less complicated Chinese deals with Kazakhstan, Turkmenistan and Uzbekistan. Until then, most gas and oil from Central Asia had to go through, or be sold to, Russia. This was a legacy of the USSR that was bound to end, one way or the other. Displeased as they have been by such an evolution, Russian leaders probably preferred that US and Western consortia did not take the lion's share.

There is a key reason as to why Russia came to terms with China's growing influence in Central Asia. Until now, and very skilfully, China has deferred to the primacy of Russian geopolitical interests in the region. Contrary to the US, it recognizes the Russian lead and deals with it. It has never sought to detach any of its members. It has not required military bases or facilities in Central Asia. This is consistent with what is generally held as China's priorities: the sustained growth of its economy, stability in the neighbouring areas while keeping a low profile on geopolitical issues.

Given all the warnings that have been made over the years about the shallowness and the impending erosion of the partnership between China and Russia, its resilience is striking. It has even constantly gained in scope and substance since 2004–05. This has continued during the fifth and last phase of Russia's tortuous relations with the US.

One could say that this last phase began in the first months of Obama's presidency in 2009 – one year after Medvedev became president of Russia. It can be characterized as a search for a new modus vivendi between the two countries. A peak of their bad relations had occurred a few months before, with the war between Georgia and Russia in August 2008 and it is important to stress what was then at stake in order to better understand what was to follow.

The meaning of the Russian–Georgian war

Both Georgia's and Russia's actions leading to the war are directly related to the anticipated recognition of Kosovo's unilateral declaration of independence of February 2008 by the US and a majority of NATO members. In 2007, together with China, Russia opposed any Security Council decision that would have infringed on Resolution 1214 that explicitly referred to Serbia's territorial integrity after the 1999 war, at Russia's insistence. Since 2006, Putin had warned that any recognition of Kosovo's independence could lead to similar Russian behaviour with the so-called 'frozen conflicts' in former Soviet space. Not surprisingly, only Georgia was explicitly targeted. Saakashvili was challenging Russia on a wide range of issues and had vowed to restore the territorial integrity of Georgia, blocked by Moscow.

A decisive event occurred before the war and the subsequent Russian formal recognition of South Ossetia and Abkhazia's long-standing de facto independence by Moscow. At the NATO summit in Bucharest in April 2008, Bush failed to obtain the Membership Action Plan (MAP) for Georgia and Ukraine because of opposition from Germany, France and Italy. However, against all expectations and with strong insistence he succeeded in obtaining as compensation a formal NATO declaration stating that both countries would eventually become members, without any specific agenda. Immediately after the summit, without a formal recognition of their de facto independence, Putin sent a directive authorizing direct contacts between different Russian ministries and their Abkhazian and South Ossetian counterparts. In retrospective, this can be seen as a successful provocation. Indeed, overestimating and betting on the strength of his exceptional relation with George W. Bush, whose term was to end four months later, Saakashvili ordered a military offensive in South Ossetia. Of course, he could not imagine the US going to war with Russia to stop a massive military retaliation. But he expected no less than a major international crisis and confrontation, sufficient to compel Russia to negotiate a solution to the Georgian unfrozen conflicts.

Despite hidden US and Western irritation with Saakashvili's behaviour, an international crisis did occur. Emergency meetings of NATO and the European Union took place, but with very limited sanctions and threats of further ones that never came. Bogged down in Iraq as well as in Afghanistan, where it was in need of Russian help, the US could not press their European allies to do more.

These events demonstrated that NATO had reached the borderlines of overcommitment. It could do very little for a country that had been officially promised membership six months earlier. As a result, this experience (that vindicated West European reticence) spelled the end of NATO enlargement in the former Soviet space at least for the foreseeable future. That boosted the self-confidence of the Russian leaders and facilitated their exploration of a possible modus vivendi with Washington after the accession of Obama.[11]

The fifth phase: a new trend in Russia–US relations together with a growing partnership with China

As early as one month after Obama's investiture, Vice President Biden spoke of the White House's desire to 'press the reset button' in US–Russia relations. The reset became the buzzword characterizing the evolution of the relationship in the following years. Up to 2012, it indeed underwent a significant improvement. Observers spoke of 'reconciliation'. The term is not too strong to stress the contrast with the four preceding years. But it understates Russian prudence and suspicion inherited from that period.

The reset produced four major results. The first was the new START treaty signed in April 2010 that was very advantageous and symbolically important for Russia's status in world affairs. It provided for a substantial reduction of the ceilings of nuclear strategic weapons. Since Russia did not have the means to keep up with the former ones, the treaty preserved the last vestige of military parity between the two countries. It was, however, made precarious by US projects to develop anti-missile defences that could eventually neutralize much of the Russian nuclear dissuasion capacities. To appease these constantly voiced Russian fears, Washington proposed negotiations with Russia for a joint European missile defence. The second result of the reset was Russia's acceptance of the proposal and the process thus initiated. Yet, one year later, Russia's inability to obtain binding guarantees on the number and potential capacities of American anti-missile systems contributed to a souring of the improved relations. A third result was a clear Russian concession. Until then, together with China, it had refused to endorse any new round of UN sanctions against Iran. In June 2010 Moscow adhered to UN sanctions. The last, but not the least, result was a very substantial increase of Russian support to the US and NATO war effort in Afghanistan, as it had done in 2001. Highly appreciated as this is in Washington, it was not really a Russian concession. In the few preceding years, Russian leaders had been rather pleased to see the US stalemated in Afghanistan. But after Obama set a deadline for the beginning of a US withdrawal and for the termination of its combat operations in 2014, the Russian perspective has changed completely. Although the return of the Taliban to power in Kabul would be a political disaster for the US, Russian leaders know that it would be a much greater catastrophe for them.

The improvement of relations with the US, together with Medvedev's liberal profile in internal as well as foreign affairs, misled many Russian analysts and pundits to believe that the time and opportunity had come for reconsidering the value of the strategic partnership with China. Indeed, Medvedev spoke of the US also as a strategic partner (that was not new) and of their improving relationship as an open-ended process. Official documents and declarations spoke of a 'multi-vector' foreign policy as well as of multipolarity.

Questioning the merits of the partnership with China was not new in Russia. This time though, it involved more important newspapers and more members of the academic establishment. Traditional warnings were amplified, based on recent statistical projections. It was emphasized that in 2010 the Chinese GDP was nearly five times the Russian one, while China had surpassed Japan as the second world economy and was expected to outstrip the US in 2025. Even a military imbalance was stressed, comparing the 2011 Chinese military budget of US$143 billion to the Russian one of US$76 billion. Political analysts argued that with the observable decline of US hegemony in the world, multipolarity was already a fact of life and that the best way to preserve or reinforce it was to 'go West' and side with the US to balance China's growing power. In an article written in 2011, the deputy director of the prestigious Institute of International Trade and International Relations (IMEMO) said more or less the same thing, in more prudent and diplomatic terms.[12] He advocated the institutionalization of 'a new triangular strategic dialogue' between Russia, China and the US to address global problems.

Even if Medvedev was the favourite Russian leader for Obama and other Western statesmen, he did not neglect China – quite the contrary. In January 2011, at the opening of the fifth round of 'China–Russia Strategic Security Talks' conducted by the Russian Security Council Secretary and his counterpart, Medvedev declared, as if to reassure his Chinese guest, that China was Russia's 'closest partner, a position that will never be changed'.[13] As prime minister, Putin remained very much involved in the promotion of the relationship. On the background of China's onset as the first trade partner of Russia in 2010, the Russian leaders and their counterparts pledged to raise the exchanges, from a turnover of $60 billion in 2010 to $100 billion in 2015 and $200 billion in 2020. At the same time, through a 'Modernization Partnership Agreement', efforts are being made to combine the respective economic strengths of both countries to reinforce high tech production and exchanges. Many experts in Russia are convinced that its problem is not with technological and scientific capacities but with its weaknesses in translating them into industrial production; an ability that China has acquired. On that basis, joint projects are foreseen in both countries.[14] Of course, results remain to be seen.

On the political side, a new significant and potentially important international grouping was formally launched in June 2009, when Medvedev hosted the first summit of BRIC (standing for Brazil, Russia, India, China) in Ekaterinburg. BRIC can be seen as an extension of the 'troïka' (Russia, China, India) and as a success of Russian diplomacy. It is meant to be the group of the most important emerging economies in the world, comprising over 40 per cent of the world population and taking a major and rapidly growing share of its economy. In order to give it a worldwide four-continental dimension, the Brasilia summit of 2010 decided to take in South Africa as a fifth member.

The goal of BRICS is nothing less than using the collective influence of its members for reshaping the geometry of the changing world order. The first concerns of its members are about reforming the global financial architecture of institutions considered to be more favourable to the US and the European Union. For instance, they support an increase of the voting rights of China and India at the IMF and press for the reform of its governance. The New Delhi summit of March 2012 insisted on the primary role of the G-20, rather than that of the G-7 as the forum for global economic governance. To a lesser degree, BRICS also addresses international political issues. Russia and China support a larger place and role at the UN Security Council for the three other members (without giving the specifics, for obvious reasons). The Delhi summit of 2012 expressed a community of views on Syria and its opposition to sanctions against Iran that go beyond those approved by the Security Council in 2010.

The efficiency of BRICS in reshaping the world order is far from established. Given the enormous diversity of its members' interests, the political cohesion of the group is very weak and BRICS's effectiveness is more virtual than actual. It is relevant here as an indicator of the persistence of Russia's goal of balancing US hegemony in world affairs during the period under consideration.

A multi-level partnership and Putin's return

The international groupings promoted by Russia for that purpose can be seen as a four-floor house or construction. If we rank each grouping according to the level of its members' political cohesion on international issues, we have on the ground floor the Russia–China partnership, on the second floor the SCO, on the third floor the 'troïka', and BRICS on the fourth floor. In Russian perspective, the strategic partnership with China is the basis and the core of that construction. Indeed, in joint official declarations during Medvedev's presidency, Russia and China pledged to coordinate their positions in all these groupings specifically, besides the UN Security Council.

While Medvedev was pursuing 'the reset' with optimism, Putin kept a low profile on related issues. His aversion to enforced regime changes leading to an increase of US or NATO influence, led him to criticize the position taken by Russia at the Security Council on Libya. He could have prevented it had he wished to do so. He was certainly in favour of pursuing the reset as far as possible, but given his previous experience he was probably more sceptical than Medvedev on the chances of having it on many of Russian terms. However much he wished for such a reset, he was not prepared to put the strategic partnership with China on the backburner.

In February 2012, during his campaign for the presidential election, Putin published a lengthy article on foreign policy issues in which he raised the topic of Russian–Chinese relations. He did it forcefully, as if he was challenging arguments made against it. Three sentences deserve to be quoted here in their full length. He wrote:

> First of all, I am convinced that China's economic growth is by no means a threat, but a challenge that carries colossal potential for business cooperation and a chance to catch the Chinese wind in the sails of our economy. ... Second, China's conduct on the world stage gives no grounds to talk about aspirations to dominance. The Chinese voice in the world is indeed growing ever more confident, and we welcome that, because Beijing shares our vision of the emerging equitable world order.[15]

These words were not simply electoral grandiloquence as some pundits suggested at the time. Recent events speak to the contrary. Medvedev's first official trip out of the former Soviet space after becoming president in 2008 (before the reset) was to China. Putin's first one in 2012 was to Germany and France. But he had made an earlier and explicit rebuff to the US and Obama. Initially, Obama had planned to host NATO and a G-7 (G-8 with the Russian backseat) summits consecutively in May in Chicago. Out of diplomatic courtesy for the Russian president he later decided to separate them and host the G-8 in Camp David. Putin decided not to go to the meeting (a first time event) and sent Medvedev in his place. For Putin it was a way to underline the greater importance of the G-20 that he attended in June in Mexico, where he had his first meeting with Obama as president.

In the meantime, he had made an official visit to China in April, before the regular summit of the SCO. There, he could take advantage of the noiseless Chinese dissatisfaction with the beginnings of a major reinforcement of US military presence in different bases in East Asia, explicitly meant to counterweight China's influence. Hu Jintao and Putin emphasized the importance of their country's partnership with special reference to their will to increase its military component. Prior to his arrival in China, Putin had made an overstatement, speaking for the first time of the two partners as 'strategic *allies*'.

Conclusion

Looking at Russia's quest for a place and role in world affairs over a twenty-year retrospective, it seems safe to say that its first preference would have been to stand alongside the US and the Western world. This comes out clearly from the first and third phases skimmed over here. For most of the second phase, that goal was pursued with increasing frustration. So, it might be said that it was present for 10 out of 20 years. Even the fourth phase might be seen as its prudent revisiting. In such a perspective, the strategic partnership with China can be seen as a fall back position.

That said, the strategic partnership with China has proved much more enduring than generally expected. This does not mean that it is bound to gain momentum. Even as it stands now, it is in no way an impediment to a considerable and open-ended improvement of Russia's relations with the US and Europe. This option is open for Moscow. However, in its negotiations with Washington and Europe as a whole, Russia is now a very tough and demanding partner. It has not always been so and there have been many lost opportunities. For a significant and lasting improvement, at least some of Russia's terms will have to be met. Some of them could be met without big and unwarranted compromises from Washington and its allies. A single example may be given here. In the context of the renewed support given to the US and NATO in their war effort in Afghanistan, Moscow proposed formal meetings and discussions between NATO and the CSTO. Preferring to deal bilaterally with its members, Washington refused so as not to give legitimacy to the CSTO as an instrument of Russian hegemony in Central Asia.

As mentioned above, at the beginning of 2009, Russia felt stronger and more self-confident in exploring a new modus vivendi with the US. Since the end of 2011, the situation looks somewhat different for both internal and international reasons. Putin's staunch fight against advocates of a complete regime change in Syria (with the more discreet support of China) has much to do with the entirely unexpected and unprecedented wave of demonstrations that took place against his regime, in autumn 2011, when he announced his new bid for the presidency. He not only saw but also publicly alluded to an American hand in the Moscow events. To be sure his opposition to an internationally supported overthrow of the Syrian regime preceded the Russian events and it is based on obvious geopolitical considerations, as it would only reinforce Saudi Arabian and US influence in the Middle East at the expense of Russia and Iran.

This is simply to say that besides the turn of international events, the evolution of Russia's political regime, one way or the other, will certainly impact on the ups and downs of its relations with both the US and China. Fallback position or not, the vicissitudes of Moscow's relationship with Beijing will continue to have wide-ranging ripple effects on global affairs, and itself be shaped by the course of Moscow's relationship with Washington.

Notes

1 Kozyrev also said: 'Our country must follow the example of the Eastern European countries whose purpose is to belong to the world of democracy, to enter the European Community and NATO, briefly speaking, to participate in the life of the civilized world.'
2 See his article for *Krasnaia zvezda*, 26 November 1992.
3 When Russia's Supreme Soviet adopted a resolution in 1992 declaring illegal and void Khrushchev's cession of Crimea to Ukraine in 1954, Yeltsin immediately declared that the government would entirely ignore it. This was in spite of the major dispute with Ukraine concerning the property of the Black Sea Fleet.
4 This was the title of the joint declaration that followed a meeting of Yeltsin and Jiang ZeMin on 23 April 1997.
5 Such assessments were based for instance on an interpretation of Article 8 that stated: 'The contracting parties shall not enter into any alliance or be a party to any bloc ... that could be seen as threatening by the other one.'
6 See, Bobo Lo, *Axis of Convenience*, Washington: Brookings Institution, 2008, p. 51.
7 This is the background of Condoleezza Rice's famous 'punish France, ignore Germany, forgive Russia', 13 April 2003. It is one of the few 'rewards' that Putin got during that period of time.
8 See for example Mark Mackinnon, *The New Cold War: Revolutions, Rigged Elections and Pipeline Politics in the former Soviet Union*, Toronto: Random House, 2007.
9 Trade with China accounts for 9.6 per cent of Russian foreign trade.
10 The Pacific branch is scheduled for completion in 2014.
11 That self-confidence took Russia too far after the end of the war when they decided to formally recognize the independence of South Ossetia and Abkhazia instead of returning to the status quo ante. Not only China, but also all CSTO members, proved to be more consistent than Russia in their pledge to oppose separatism and refused to endorse the Russian move.

12 See Vasili Mikheev, 'Russia–China: "Reloading" the Relationship', *Russian Politics and Law*, 49, no. 6, November–December 2011, pp. 74–93.
13 Quoted by Yu Bin, 'China–Russia Relations', *Comparative Connections*, May 2011, pp.137–45.
14 See Yu Bin, ibid., January 2012, pp.129–38.
15 *Moskovskie Novosti*, 27 February 2012.

13 Defence innovation and Russian foreign policy

Frederic LaBarre

For 70 years, communist totalitarianism shielded from view much of Russia's defence developments, which required the creation of Sovietology as a new field of political and analytical enquiry. Sovietology was a difficult craft because it involved making assumptions about a system that depended on secrecy and isolation for survival. Consequently, Sovietologists had to generate knowledge by extrapolating on scarce and incomplete information.

A by-product of this predisposition is the belief that every little change in Russia is politically significant. While this may be true in some cases, significance has often been constructed by analysts, journalists and pundits alike, comfortable in considering Russia in a Cold War light. The perception that Russia is not a status quo power endures, and the responsible analyst must take into account that Russia is built on paradoxes. Russia's attachment to defence innovation has often been perceived as ominous.

David Glantz, Dale Herspring, Pavel Baev, Roger McDermott, Keir Giles and Marcel de Haas, as well as this author,[1] have commented on the process of reform since 1992, seeking to detect changes in policy through the transformation of the armed forces. Others, like Pavel Felgenhauer and Alexander Golts, highlighted the ludicrous attachment to large armed forces as the Russian state struggled with its finances. Between the two types, we can see the competing notions of transformation, modernization, innovation and reform. The terms are neither synonymous, nor do they complement each other.

This chapter argues that the Russian defence innovation efforts represent one of those paradoxes. The task of the Ministry of Defence and of the armed forces of the Russian Federation is to ensure the security of the country. The collapse of the Soviet Union did not translate into a crisis of national security for the Russian state that was left in its wake, save for the crises in the Caucasus. It can be postulated here that the cost of maintaining a four-million-strong army in permanent high-readiness status was one of the principal factors leading to the collapse of the USSR. Yet, paradoxically, it partly made the USSR what it was. This leads to another paradox: while the re-establishment of the prestige of Russia as a great power is dependent upon the armed forces, a balanced and sustainable structure must also be generated, which requires embracing reform.

To understand the input of defence innovation as a support for Russian foreign policy, we must distinguish it from the notion of 'reform'. In the Russian experience, reform refers to the human aspect of administrative and organizational transformation. It is a process that finds its source in the foreign policy components of *perestroika*; when the separation of border troops, the KGB and the Interior Ministry troops from the mainstream armed forces helped the Soviet Union meet disarmament thresholds. Since then it is summed up by a race to reduce troop numbers.[2]

Research and development is not synonymous with innovation, rather they contribute to it. For the purpose of this chapter we define innovation as the R&D efforts of a state and technological improvements applied to new systems. In the context of reduced troop numbers, it becomes the driver for modernization. R&D not only costs resources, its results must be integrated in the force structure renewal plans. Because the force structure was 'under reform' between 1992 and 2002, and because adequate funding for new equipment did not manifest itself until 2007, achieving a credible conventional capability meeting the requirements of Russian policy has been laborious.

Russia's relative weakness has been exacerbated by alleged foreign policy setbacks, such as the political and economic isolation of some of Russia's traditional client states (e.g. Iraq, Libya and Syria), the persistent enlargement of NATO and difficult relations with some of the USSR's former Soviet Republics (the Baltic States and the South Caucasus come to mind). The manner in which Russia has met these challenges has revealed a critical gap in its foreign policy toolbox. Diplomatically, Russia is still a respected member of some of the most prestigious 'clubs': a permanent member of the UN Security Council, member of the OSCE, the G8 and the G20, it has also created security and trade regimes for its own region. Yet, these levers are insufficient to shape international behaviour and institutions in Russia's interests.

When Russia cannot influence, it must compel. But the arsenal at its disposal is depleted. Save for low-level pressure such as that generated by cyber-assaults,[3] the denial of energy to customers, and the high-level pressure contained in its dwindling but still significant – – thanks to the New START signed with the United States in 2010 – nuclear arsenal, there is very little that Russia can do supported by the credible deterrent (or compellent) of conventional weapons.

Supporting foreign policy by a capable and actionable conventional force has been a luxury for Russia. But the urgency of developing the appropriate policy levers emerged with the struggle against terrorism, and intensified when NATO welcomed new members from the former Soviet Union in 2004. NATO's continued appetite for new members resonates deeply in Moscow. When the wire was tripped by Georgia's attack on Tskhinvali in August 2008, Russia reacted with all its might and all its craft, and at the cost of temporary opprobrium, scored a number of foreign policy successes. First, the attack communicated unequivocally to the Alliance that it should cease the process of enlargement. Second, the action took place in such a way as to discredit Georgia, disqualifying her from membership. Third, it served a stern warning to Ukraine regarding any NATO membership ambitions it might harbour.

Without suggesting that Russian policy will henceforth be buttressed by force, the Russian leadership was reassured by its military success for two reasons. First, the military tool had functioned well enough; second, it validated the tried and tested Soviet method of developing military options in the service of precise political objectives.[4] This may have worked well to compel Georgia, but is clearly insufficient when it comes to larger powers or Alliances.

The first part of this text will trace the 'genealogy' of the first 15 years of reform after the collapse of the USSR. It will summarize the efforts undertaken and highlight the timing of the more significant events that may have spurred innovation efforts. The second part attempts to measure the significance of R&D and its real-world applicability in the last five years. Lastly, we try to explain the motivation behind the process of modernization.

Overview of post-soviet reform and innovation

Reform and innovation under Yeltsin, 1992–2000

There were only 'reforms' during the Yeltsin period, and no innovation in the sense defined above. The transformation that took place focused more on macro-management of the defence budget and human resources, a combination of challenges unique to Russia. The pressures exercised by the transition to a civil society meant that central political authorities had to balance competing demands for resources within the bureaucracy. Since peoples' livelihood depended on employment in the state's security apparatus, the omnipresent danger of revolt weighed heavily on Yeltsin's mind. According to Shlykov, the strength of the army personnel was cut in half between 1992 and 1994, but the interior security services grew exponentially; no doubt by the transfer of laid-off defence personnel.

One way out of the dilemma of choosing between fiscal austerity and human resource stability was a middle road involving transforming the armed forces from a large, unmanageable behemoth to a smaller, more nimble and more affordable force structure. Implementation began in 1996 with the recruitment of contract soldiers, with the aim, eventually, of putting an end to conscription.[5]

Chris Donnelly, former Special Advisor to the NATO Secretary General for Central and Eastern Europe provides a theoretical glimpse of the challenges of post-Soviet defence reform By his account there are three stages: the first stage is force reductions; the second stage is one of institutional fragmentation and anarchy; and the third stage is procurement system breakdown.[6] Russia, like many of the larger Warsaw Pact countries, experienced all three stages in the last 20 years. Yeltsin's tenure saw the first two stages take place.

The first stage of reform was precipitated by the loss of ideological rationale and Russia's dismal economic situation. In this stage, mostly between 1992 and 1994, the spirit of intra-security sector rivalry came to a head and the ensuing fight for control of resources threatened effective central (if not civilian) control of the armed forces. Stage two of the process – institutional anarchy, also called the era of 'too many cooks'[7] – coincided with the first Chechen war (1994–96), and highlighted the danger of pursuing drastic personnel cutbacks in a context of regional instability. Consequently, the evacuation of the word 'reform' from the official vocabulary was a significant victory for the military because it meant that the haemorrhage of personnel (and capability) would cease. As one analyst put it:

> Due to the centrality of the military institution in the history of the Russian state, there has been no decisive impetus in favour of military reform from Russian society and the political class ... Actually, many Russians believe that a radical reform of the army would present a serious risk to national security.[8]

A comment made in the Russian press in 1995 reveals the true preferences of the Russians,

> if we don't have the money to feed the soldier and to provide an apartment for the officer, all talk about reform is worthless. If we had the same economic resources as the Americans, we wouldn't be needing ... reform'.[9]

Implicit in the statement is not only the aversion to change, but the constant reference to the American force structure as a benchmark. It also marks the beginning of the end of structural reform in the Russian armed forces. By that time, reform had become a derisive term, seldom mentioned in official policy circles, '... although political leaders and the MoD went on to pay lip service to it until 2002 ...'.[10]

Reform and innovation under Putin, 2000–08

The arrival on the scene of Vladimir Putin in December 1999 signalled both the end of institutional anarchy and that the intelligence services had prevailed. The return to centralization, of control and order, took place just in time to avert the third stage of the crisis of post-Soviet defence reform, i.e. the collapse of the procurement system.

The 1998 collapse of the rouble reinvigorated the export of defence equipment. This had a paradoxical effect on the relationship between industry and the armed forces. Until then, Russia's defence manufacturing had been living on borrowed time, surviving off meagre subsidies from a state that did not have the revenue to purchase new equipment. From 1998, however, the national defence sector has continued to thrive while the armed forces it is supposed to supply have continued to decline. Louis-Marie Clouet estimated that Russian arms exports had tripled in nine years, from US$2 billion in 1998 to US$7 billion in 2007. However, 70 per cent of the revenue of the 20 biggest Russian firms came from exports in 2004.[11]

Rosoboronexsport (ROE) was created in November 2000 as a response to the fratricidal institutional competition of the 1990s. The fusion of the PromExport and Rosvooruzhenie defence industrial agencies into ROE created the conditions of monopolization of the defence industry into a clearinghouse that became indistinguishable from the foreign policy of the state.[12] Privatization and re-nationalization aimed at greater control and income generation.[13]

While ROE activities alleviated the budgetary pressures that subsidizing national design bureaus caused, it also gave it the right of 'life or death' over them.[14] By monopolizing the defence industry, ROE also killed off the incentive for R&D that would have made every individual design bureau more attractive (and costly) to its clients. ROE effectively divorced innovation from the defence reform it should have served. Not surprisingly, a year after the creation of ROE, Minister of Defence Sergei Ivanov declared that what was now needed was 'not reform, but modernization'.[15]

The Russian defence industry was now expected to conduct its own R&D and *give* equipment to the Russian armed forces.[16] Since the defence industry barely met market expectations for its more demanding clientele, there were few resources or time available to conduct R&D.[17] Still, personnel cuts meant that a credible conventional capability would have to embrace quality over quantity.[18]

While a smaller, more agile force structure may be less expensive, it is also insufficient for the defence of a territory as large as Russia's. Simultaneously, a series of foreign policy setbacks – the inclusion of former Soviet Republics in NATO, the Kosovo air war, the unilateral decision of the United States to withdraw from the ABM Treaty in 2002 – illustrated Russia's weakness and became the catalyst for modernization.

As Steven Rosefielde has argued, Russia's understanding of power is based on its capacity to coerce and compel. To this, we could add 'within reason'. At present, Russia cannot carry out its ambitions beyond the reach of its petro-diplomacy. And because the stakes are not worth annihilation, nuclear brinksmanship is useless. This means that the creation of a capable conventional force to support its foreign policy objectives is more necessary than ever, because Russia cannot modulate its response between the two extremes of cyber attacks and nuclear attacks.[19]

Under Putin's first administration as president, there was a valiant attempt at linking readiness and capable human resources. The 'Pskov Experiment' entailed turning the 76th Airborne Division (Spetsnaz) from a conscripted to a contracted soldiery in 2003. There were several objectives to this initiative. First, it was aimed at reassuring the population that its youth would not be sent to any Caucasus hot spot. Second, it started from the point of permanent readiness and attempted to bring an incentive for continued service by raising the pay level of the contract soldier. While theoretically this would have achieved the desired effect – capability and readiness – the experiment turned sour when soldiers would not re-enlist after their contract ended.[20] While this was clearly a symptom of the new-found economic freedom that Russian society afforded (troop numbers in conscript and contract form kept declining),[21] it was also a consequence of the inadequacy of the equipment.

The Russian government had tried its best to stimulate R&D mainly by strengthening the legal regime around intellectual property rights, trade and competition.[22] Around 2005, several sources noted that 40–60 per cent of the defence *budget* was devoted to R&D.[23] Sources from the Centre for Analysis of Strategies and Technologies (CAST) indicate rather a percentage of defence *procurement* (the so-called state defence orders which exclude operations and maintenance costs). The confusion may come from the fact that there is no official definition of procurement in the national budget.[24] In any event, the CAST calculations show that R&D was at its highest in 2005, when it represented some 35 per cent of the procurement budget. Even so, Pavel Baev notes that,

> [w]hile there are useful designs for weapon systems of a new generation, the Russian Army remains unable to make use of them not due to the lack of funds but primarily because such systems require a higher level of military organization ... This kind of modernization would require a different quality of manpower from thoroughly trained and motivated soldiers to well-educated and computer-literate officers to dynamic and innovative thinking generals.[25]

Thus Vladimir Putin's first tenure as president of Russia ended with Russia's international resurgence, but little technological innovation.[26] Meanwhile, Russia's foreign policy difficulties continued, and became intolerable at the April 2008 NATO Summit in Bucharest, where, in the presence of the Russian president, it was declared that Ukraine and Georgia would one day be NATO members.[27]

Innovation in the Medvedev era

The period between April 2007 and April 2008 was a watershed for Russian foreign policy. It is then that 'Russia's return' was felt more keenly. First, this was manifested by the cyber attacks aimed at Estonia in the wake of the removal of the 'Bronze Soldier'. Misha Glenny has convincingly argued that Russian interests (but not necessarily military or ordered by the Kremlin) were behind the campaign that crippled Estonian networks for several days.

Simultaneously, Russia flexed its political muscle by engaging in petro-brinkmanship, since the price of crude had created a windfall of revenue for the Russian state that year. Unwisely, the subsequent budgets were planned on the assumption that the price of crude would go on rising. With revenue coming in from oil and gas, trade in armaments and foreign direct investment, Russia was able to pay off the majority of its foreign debt, releasing it from pressure by the Club of Rome. Even with all these advantages, Russia did not appear to be taken as a serious international actor.

Russia made a return to capital expenditure projects aimed at modernizing the Russian armed forces in 2007. But, as Yazbeck has observed, even a one-to-one replacement of obsolete equipment failed to maintain the level of capability of the force structure. Equipment was becoming obsolete faster than it could be replaced and much faster than R&D solutions could be applied. Since much of the procurement spending up to 2005 had gone to R&D, this was paradoxical:

Even though the defence industry has been in failure for the past ... years and already was backward technologically during the late Soviet epoch, it still contains 75% of Russia's Research, Development, Test and Evaluation capacity.[28]

R&D is not only a function of modernization; it must also be aimed at eventual integration into innovative products. If design bureaus are propelled into free-market competition in a context in which the only advantage is to have a captive underdeveloped clientele, then the incentive to carry out R&D and apply it in the field will be non-existent. R&D data is nevertheless an important indicator of the degree to which Russia's conventional forces are becoming more 'modern' and 'capable'.

R&D as an indicator of innovation

Until 2005, R&D amounted to 40–60 per cent of government defence orders (GOZ) or procurement (not the whole defence budget). In 2009, Yazbeck noted that this amount had dropped to 30 per cent.[29] R&D figures are very scarce, and difficult to interpret. For example, CAST estimates Russian armed forces procurement in billion USD in Table 13.1.

To identify the shift from R&D to actual procurement requires knowing the value of the GOZ, and the quantity devolved in procurement. CAST analysts take their figures from official Russian sources. Yazbeck, however, has estimated – using the same definition of procurement – that the amount of defence R&D for 2009 was rather US$4.9 billion (using the 2009 exchange rate between roubles and USD at 31:1).[31]

There is a further discrepancy in the figures for Russia's 2009 defence budget. The Stockholm International Peace Research Institute (SIPRI) claims it stood at US$53.3 billion (1.7 trillion roubles), whereas Yazbeck estimated it as US$37.8 billion (1.2 trillion roubles).[32] Keith Hartley, the renowned defence management expert, has estimated defence R&D figures as being very close to that of Yazbeck's.[33] An average between Yazbeck and CAST's estimations gives a good approximate figure.

Finding consistent, robust reporting about Russian equipment purchases is a daunting task, as has been acknowledged by the SIPRI and even by CAST analysts. Russian defence procurement and R&D estimations are complicated by the

Table 13.1 Russian procurement 2005–10 (US$bn)[30]

State defence orders (GOZ)	2005	2006	2007	2008	2009	2010
New weapons	4.0	4.3	5.7	8.1	8.0	10.5
Repair and upgrade	0.4	1.8	2.3	2.9	2.4	2.1
R&D	2.2	2.7	3.8	3.7	3.9	3.6
Total procurement	6.6	8.7	11.8	14.7	14.3	16.1
Arms exports	6.1	6.5	7.6	8.4	8.5	10.0

Defence innovation and Russian foreign policy 209

lack of definitions from one source to another and by the Russian government's opaque accounting standards. A valiant attempt has been made by the Swedish FOI, amalgamating several methodologies. Although different methodologies showed similar overall trends, they did not show proximate results.[34]

Julian Cooper, of Birmingham University (UK) and SIPRI, has been the preferred source for Yazbeck and possibly for Hartley. We use his figures to show the overall trends in Russian defence R&D in Table 13.2.[35]

The Battelle Group's *2011 Global R&D Funding Forecast* corroborates trends where 'the economies of China, Korea, India, Russia and Brazil, and their investments in R&D, are expanding at rates substantially higher than that of the US, Japan and Germany'.[36] In particular, Russian Defence Ministry sources have stated that procurement funding would triple by 2013,

> from 487 billion rubles (US$16.3 bln) in 2010 to 574 bln (US$19.2 bln) in 2011, 726 bln (US$24.3 bln) in 2012, and up to 1,160 billion ($38.8 bln) in 2013 ... The increase in spending is attributed to additional procurement – While actual spending on R&D will also double, from the current US$3.5 billion to US$6.5 billion, the share of R&D in the budget is expected to fall from the current 22% to 16% in 2013 indicating that most of the growth will be invested in operations and procurement. The share of procurement spending is expected to almost triple between 2010 and 2013, growing from 13% in 2010 (US$2.1 billion) to 14% in 2013 (US$5.4 billion).[37]

R&D spending has taken place amid important fiscal challenges brought on by the world economic crisis, and despite the now structural socioeconomic challenges that Russia faces – an aging population, brain drain, massive emigration and the perception of low quality of workmanship.

Figure 13.1 shows the determination of the Russian government in pursuing innovation; at the very moment that the Russian defence budget was plummeting in 2010, hitting a low of US$48 billion in early 2011, R&D had begun to grow at a rapid pace. As the defence budget picked up again in 2011, the R&D contributions levelled off and the procurement plan started rising. Must we conclude that the fruits of R&D were being fielded? Not necessarily. As the Battelle market study shows, the equipment to perform R&D is *old*; 37 per cent of the R&D equipment pool is 25 years old on average.[38] To compound matters, the amount of young graduates entering the ranks of the R&D field remains low, as veteran researchers continue to age. As a result, Russia suggests it is relatively weak in terms of technical capability.[39]

Table 13.2 2007–12 R&D with procurement against Russian defence budget (US$bn)

	2007	2008	2009	2010	2011	2012
Applied R&D	3.9	4.1	4.0	4.0	5.4	5.7e
Procurement	11.8	14.7	14.3	16.1	17.5e	20.0e
Defence budget	45.9	50.9	53.3	52.6	48.9	53.4e

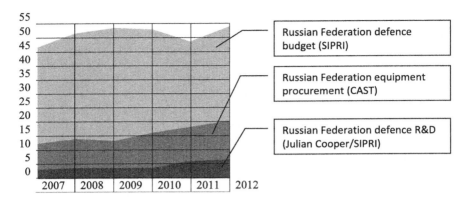

Figure 13.1 Trends of R&D and procurement, relative to defence budget (US$bn)

This suggests that even if the R&D production of the last few years is integrated into the defence industry's production, there is a strong likelihood that the quality will not yield equipment that corresponds to the government's requirements (i.e. match NATO equipment in quality).[40] There are two reasons for this. First, there is little evidence of symbiosis between the 1,134 technical universities and the defence industry. The R&D work of academics does not correspond to what the defence factories should apply in the field. This was already evident in 2005, when the military industrial complex was seen as unable to develop large-scale production of high-tech weaponry.[41]

Confirmation of this came from the highest levels in 2010, when President Dmitry Medvedev inaugurated the Skolkovo Complex to stimulate R&D. This may be reflected by the higher levels of expenditures in Figure 13.1. Simultaneously, however, Russia aimed at implementing an ambitious state armaments programme (GPV) worth US$169 billion during 2007–15.[42] As we can see from Figure 13.1, the defence budget dropped, but the procurement schedule kept on track, or improved, in 2011. This could be on account of a transfer of funding away from defence and directly towards the military industrial complex, possibly to stimulate R&D funding.[43] Yazbeck supposes that the first five years of the GPV were dedicated to R&D, but since 2011 funding is directed at procurement.[44]

Dale Herspring sees this change of funding allocation as proof that innovation is *ad hoc*, and not necessarily planned, but still aimed at shaping capable, ready and affordable forces.[45] Rather, we would suggest it is because the plan did not meet expectations. Yazbeck, for instance, shows that the economic assumptions underlying GPV-2015 were unrealistic, and that the objectives have had to be pushed back in an amended GPV-2020 plan. With moderate defence funding (2.5–2.7 per cent of GDP), the Russian Federation can achieve its GPV objectives of achieving a force structure that is 70 per cent modern by 2020.[46]

In 2008, tectonic changes took place in the highest echelons of the defence structure. In June 2008, Anatoly Serdyukov, a civilian and financial expert, became

Minister of Defence, replacing Sergei Ivanov, who was promoted to Deputy Prime Minister. Simultaneously General Nikolai Egorovich Makarov replaced General Baluevsky as Chief of the General Staff. In July 2008, the Russian officer corps was reduced by half. Previously, there were 52 government procurement agencies in Russia. This was reduced to 1. The 65 military education institutions were reduced to 10.[47] Rather than a return to the spirit of 'reform' of the Yeltsin era, it expresses the exasperation of the higher political class with administrative stagnation. The GPV-2015's lacklustre performance was being blamed on the armed forces' General Staff.

With these changes, the Russian government still hoped to have it all: 'efficient, self-financing, state of the arts, mass weapons production'.[48] But the Military Industrial Commission (MIC), whose comparative advantage lies in affordability and access to markets shunned by large Western companies, has been privatized in the hope of spurring innovation from within. But this has failed because, once privatized, the MIC has had to cater to clients' wishes at a rebate; most of the sales in armaments merely kept the Russian defence companies' heads above water while Russia itself could not afford *any* weapons, let alone modern ones.[49] This has had two consequences: it led to MIC dependence on foreign clients, which means that production cannot keep up with the Russian demand,[50] and it has led the defence procurement budget to be oriented on inapplicable R&D for too long, divorcing the declining capacity from the real needs of the MIC.[51] According to Blank,

> As the Russian government still cannot meet modern budgetary-industrial challenges, and defence economic structures remain pre-modern nonmarket institutions, military modernization occurs in a vacuum that cannot sustain such projects ...[52]

When the Russian government began to procure armaments from its own MIC, therefore, the weaponry it got was merely the same design that Russian defence companies clients were getting. In other words, it tended to consecrate the technological gap of Russian defence relative to the rest.

The Russian context of R&D, the creation of new platforms, the ability of industry to meet demand, and the usual socioeconomic challenges delay, if not prevent, the modernization of conventional forces. The longer this situation endures, the further behind Russian defence technology will fall, and the further behind Russian foreign policy will stand in the concert of great powers. At this point, it has three options. The first is to give up on the idea of materiel quality, and resort to purchasing quantity, ignoring technological innovation, as Rosefielde has argued.[53] This does not resolve the MIC's now chronic incapacity to meet production expectations.

The second option is to rely on foreign input in R&D and production. The sale of the *Mistral* class warship to the Russian Navy by the French government is an example of this option. But even this solution does not provide the Russian government with the expected capability before 2020, partly because of the inflation increase brought on by higher oil and gas prices, which, ironically, the Russian state depends on to fund its security.[54]

The third option is a mix of increased defence spending with option two. This would involve greater expenditure and greater integration and partnerships with other countries' military industries. Prior to his re-election, President Putin vowed not only to modernize the Russian military, but also to bring it in line with fifth generation weaponry at the cost of US$772 billion over a decade.[55] Russia's deepening defence integration with countries like India[56] (which graduates twice as many college students as China), and its newly-acquired taste for Western-procured platforms, is commitment of funds which represents a mere US$21 billion increase of the defence budget annually. Has Russia opted for a 'third way'?

It would represent an important change in Russian cooperation attitudes; for a proud people, and political elite for whom appearances are important, engaging in partnerships where Russia is the dependent party is rare, and requires great courage. Of course, the Russians are renowned for their courage and resilience, but they also have a very acute memory. So it is surprising to see them engage in the sort of defence-binging that helped spell the ruin of the Soviet Union.

This elicits the question 'why'? Here we may venture a hypothesis that has less to do with the West than with the East. Over the last few years, the Russian–Chinese relationship, at first sustained by the commerce of natural resources and weaponry, has cooled. Deliveries to China are rarer because that country produces its own weapons under licence. China has also sought to diversify its energy resources to maintain its economic growth. The fact that this growth is as disquieting to India as it is to Russia may have propelled them towards each other, and would explain the feeling of urgency manifested by the Russian government at generating a credible conventional counterweight.

Conclusion

In November 2011, General Makarov made a presentation on the progress made on GPV-2020. His threat assessment was that of an 'upsetting of the balance of military forces' and of 'Russia being outstripped by Western technology'.[57] This does not mean that Russia fears the *West*; Makarov could be referring to the emergence of competitors in the East. In fact, the geographic challenges highlighted refer to 'uncontrolled migration' from the Far East, and territorial disputes with Japan, in addition to Arctic pretensions from various countries. The assessment here is that it will still be a long time before Russia develops the kind of conventional structure that can support any level of foreign policy ambition outside its 'near-abroad'.

Writing in 2009, Jan Leijonhielm *et al.* concluded,

> The Russian military industry is capable of supporting regional Great Power ambitions ... but it is not likely by its own efforts to produce all the weapons and materials necessary to allow the Armed Forces to conduct modern warfare. If the capacity for research, development and production is not considerably improved, the defence industrial complex will find it increasingly hard to support great power ambitions in the long run ...[58]

We in the West often forget that Russia is a country with more than a dozen neighbours straddling two and possibly three civilizations. Of course, the experience of the twentieth century also weighs heavily on the Russian mind. The intention is apparently to support the foreign policy of the Russian Federation, so that it does not have to rely on the unusable (its nuclear arsenal) or double-edged tools (cyber- and petro-coercion). The Russo–Georgian war strengthened the Russian conviction that, if need be, the measured application of overwhelming force brought positive foreign policy results; namely, stopping the enlargement of NATO to include Georgia and Ukraine, thereby turning the Black Sea into a NATO lake.

Russia aims to be big enough and capable enough quickly to maintain its dominion over the near-abroad and possibly to affect outcomes well beyond, a tall order in the best of circumstances, and with a doubtful outcome.[59] This study reveals that innovation started only in the last half decade or so, and was preceded by reforms which aimed at making Russian defence financially sustainable, not more capable. Various analysts have shown that the ROE public–private partnership has helped Russian defence industry survive and prosper, but not to innovate.

Furthermore, its dependence on foreign clientele means that there is no possibility of developing the critical force structure needed for credible conventional deterrence of either NATO or China. In turn that means that for some time still, Russia will remain without appropriate foreign policy levers should its interests require them. In consequence, the Kremlin has chosen to purchase quality en masse by looking to the West, much to the irritation of the Russian defence industry.[60]

While such circumstances may spur a domestic MIC-based commitment to real R&D and applicable innovation, this 'industrial' rapprochement reveals that the Russians may be more wary of their Eastern neighbours than their Western ones. Meanwhile, the West has little to fear from the Russians technologically speaking. But the strategic shift taking place may be an opportunity to finally draw Russia closer in the spirit of cooperation, as its own socioeconomic shortcomings force it to be more transparent and conciliatory towards its Western neighbourhood.

Notes

1 See Frederic LaBarre, 'Russian Military Reform: An Overview', *Baltic Defence Review*, 5, 2001, as well as 'The Sources of Russian Neo-Mercantilism', in J. L. Black and M. Johns (eds), *From Putin to Medvedev: Continuity or Change?*, Manotick: Penumbra Press, 2009, and 'Sustainable Armor Capability for Small Powers: The Case of Georgia in the August War' *Baltic Security and Defence Review*, 11, 2009.
2 Vitaly Shlykov, 'Military Reform and its Implication for the Modernisation of the Russian Armed Forces', in Jan Leijonhielm and Fredrick Westerlund (eds), *Russian Power Structures: Present and Future Roles in Russian Politics*, FOI Report 2437-SE, Stockholm: FOI, 2007, pp. 56–65.
3 Presentation by Misha Glenny to the Rideau Club, Ottawa, 16 March 2012, on cyber criminality and international relations.
4 Ghulam Dastagir Wardak (ed.), *The Voroshilov Lectures. Materials from the Soviet General Staff Academy*, vol. 1: *Issues of Soviet Military Strategy*, Washington, DC: National Defence University Press, 1989, p. 55. According to Wardak's notes, Soviet strategy is 'a system of scientific information about the characteristics of contemporary wars, the forms and types of their execution, the structure of Armed Forces and the preparation of the state

for war. It also includes the field of practical action of the political leadership and the high military command with respect to the preparation of the Armed Forces and their deployment to foil enemy aggression and achieve political aims in war'.
5 *Nevasimaia gazeta*, 22 August 1996.
6 Chris Donnelly, 'Reform Realities', in Teddy Winkler and Istvan Gyarmati (eds), *Post-Cold War Defence Reform*, London and Washington: Brassey's, 2002, pp. 36–9.
7 Richard Sakwa, *Russian Politics and Society*, 2nd edition, London: Routledge, 1997.
8 Andrew Liaropoulos, 'The Russian Defence Reform and Its Limitations', *Caucasian Review of International Affairs*, 2:1, winter 2008, p. 46.
9 *Moskovskie Novosti*, 31 July–6 August 1995, quoted in Shlykov, 'Military Reform and Its Implications…' p. 62.
10 Vitaly Shlykov, 'Military Reform and its Implications…', p. 60.
11 Louis-Marie Clouet, 'Rosoboronexport: Fer de Lance de l'Industrie russe de l'Armement', *Russie.NEI.Visions*, no. 22, Paris: Institut Français des Relations internationales (IFRI), September 2007, p. 5.
12 Ibid., pp. 5–6. See also Frederic LaBarre, 'The Sources of Russian Neo-Mercantilism', in *From Putin to Medvedev: Continuity or Change?*, pp. 105–6.
13 Stephen Blank, *Rosoboroneksport: Arms Sales and the Structure of Russian Defence Industry*, Carlisle, PA: Strategic Studies Institute of the US Army War College, January 2007, pp. 11–12.
14 Clouet, 'Rosoboronexport', p.7.
15 Vitaly Shlykov, 'Military Reform and Its Implications…', p. 62.
16 Vitaly Shlykov, 'Military Reform and Its Implications…', pp. 41–2.
17 Clouet, 'Rosoboronexport', p. 7; 70 per cent of exports go to China and India. See also Blank, *Rosoboroneksport…*, p. 42.
18 Andrew Liaropoulos, 'The Russian Defence Reform…', pp. 44–5.
19 Carolina Vendil Pallin, 'The Role of the Military in Russian Foreign Policy', in *EU–Russia Review*, 8 October 2008, p. 117.
20 Carolina Vendil Pallin, *Russian Military Reform: A Failed Experiment in Defence Decision Making*, London: Routledge, 2009, p. 160.
21 'Russian Defence Policy', http://www.russiandefpolicy.wordpress.com/2011/01/12/ accessed 18 March 2012.
22 Steven Rosefielde, 'Russian Rearmament: Motives, Options and Prospects', in Jan Leijonhielm and Fredrick Westerlund (eds), *Russian Power Structures: Present and Future Roles in Russian Politics*, p. 79; and also Dale Herspring, *Putin's Russia: Past Imperfect, Future Uncertain*, 3rd edition, New York: Rowman and Littlefield, 2007, p. 183.
23 Pavel K. Baev, *Russian Energy Policy and Military Power: Putin's Quest for Greatness*, London: Routledge, 2008, p.16; Jan Leijonhielm, Jan T Knopf, Robert L Larsson, Ingmar Oldberg, Wilhelm Unge and Carolina Vendil Pallin, 'Russian Military Capability in a Ten-Year Perspective: Problems and Trends in 2005', *FOI Memo 1396*, Stockholm: FOI, June 2005, p. 7; and notes taken at the presentation by a Russian naval officer PfP Fellow of the NATO Defence College, Rome, June 2005. R&D figures dropped steeply in 2009 as a result of the economic crisis and the desire to focus more on procurement; see T. Yazbeck, *The Russian Economy and Resources Available for Military Reform and Equipment Modernization*, DRDC CORA TM 2010-192, Ottawa: Defence R&D of Canada, September 2010, p. 18.
24 *Russian Defence Industry and Arms Trade: Facts and Figures*, Moscow: CAST, 2011, p. 11, http://www.cast.ru.
25 Pavel Baev, *Russian Energy Policy…*, p. 16.
26 Marcel de Haas, *Russia's Military Reforms: Victory after Twenty Years of Failure?*, Clingendael Paper no. 5, November 2011, p. 35.
27 NATO Summit Declaration, 3 April 2008, http://www.nato.int.
28 Blank, *Rosoboroneksport*, pp. 55 and 72.
29 Yazbeck, *The Russian Economy and Resources Available…*, p. 22.

Defence innovation and Russian foreign policy 215

30 *Russian Defence Industry and Arms Trade* (CAST), pp. 11–12.
31 Yazbeck, *The Russian Economy and Resources Available…*, p. 21.
32 SIPRI, Military Expenditure of Russia 1988–2010, http:// www.sipri.se; ibid., p. 21.
33 Keith Hartley, 'Defence R&D: Data Issues', *Defence and Peace Economics*, 17:3, June 2006, p. 172.
34 Bengt-Göran Bergstrand, *Economic and Military Expenditures Trends since 1990 for the Russian Federation and for EU and NATO*, FOI Memo 3203, Stockholm: FOI, May 2010.
35 Julian Cooper, *Military Expenditure in the Three-year Federal Budget of the Russian Federation, 2008–10*, p. 13; ibid., *Military Expenditure in the Russian Federal Budget, 2010–2013*, p. 3, http://www.sipri.org.
36 Battelle Group, *2011 Global R&D Funding Forecast*, December 2010, p. 24, http://www.battelle.org.
37 *Russia to Triple Defence Spending by 2013*, 14 October 2010, http://www.defence-update.com/20101014_russian_defence_budget.html.
38 Battelle Group, *2011 Global R&D Funding Forecast*, p. 31.
39 Battelle Group, *2011 Global R&D Funding Forecast*, p. 30. On a scale of 1–5 (weak to strong), Russia scored 2.0 for the year 2010, but is expected to score 2.1 in 2015, putting it at the lowest rank.
40 Fredrik Westerlund, 'Russian Science: In Peril but out of Focus', *RUFS Briefing 8*, Stockholm : FOI, 2010.
41 Jan Leijonhielm, *et al.*, 'Russian Military Capability in a Ten-Year Perspective: Problems and Trends in 2005', p. 17.
42 Yazbeck, *The Russian Economy and Resources Available…*, p. 19.
43 Yazbeck, *The Russian Economy and Resources Available…*, p. 10.
44 Yazbeck, *The Russian Economy and Resources Available…*, p. 20.
45 Herspring, *Putin's Russia …* 3rd edition, p. 174.
46 Yazbeck, *The Russian Economy and Resources Available…*, p. 23; Blank, *Rosoboroneksport*, p. 28.
47 Stephen Wagran and Dale Herspring, *Putin's Russia: Past Imperfect, Future Uncertain*, 4th edition, New York: Rowman and Littlefield, 2010, pp. 267–80.
48 Steven Rosefielde, 'Russian Rearmament: Motives, Options and Prospects', p. 77.
49 *Russian Defence Industry and Arms Trade* (CAST), p. 12.
50 Yazbeck, *The Russian Economy and Resources Available…*, p. 27. To meet the GPV-2015 objectives, for example, 30 new planes per year must be delivered every year until 2015, double the current rate of delivery.
51 Blank, *Rosoboroneksport*, p. 39. For example, the research side looks at nanotechnology, biometrics, directed energy weapons which industry is not yet capable of fielding.
52 Blank, *Rosoboroneksport*, pp. 33–4.
53 Steven Rosefielde, 'Russian Rearmament: Motives, Options and Prospects', p. 81.
54 Yazbeck, *The Russian Economy and Resources Available…*, p. 30.
55 Fred Weir, 'Fearing West, Putin Pledges Biggest Military Buildup Since Cold War', *Christian Science Monitor*, 21 February 2012, online at: http://www.csmonitor.com/World/Europe/2012/0220/Fearing-West-Putin-pledges-biggest-military-buildup-since-cold-war.
56 Battelle Group, *2011 Global R&D Funding Forecast*, pp. 26, 29.
57 I am grateful to Ruslan Pukhov from CAST for forwarding me a copy of this presentation.
58 Jan Leijonhielm, Jakob Hedenskog, Jan T.Knoph, Robert L. Larsson, Ingmar Oldberg, Roger Roffey, Maria Tisell and Fredrik Westerlund, *Russian Military Capability in a Ten-Year Perspective: Ambitions and Challenges in 2008*, FOI Report 2759, Stockholm: FOI, February 2009, p. 25.
59 Marcel De Haas, *Russia's Military Reforms…*, p. 32.
60 Marcel De Haas, *Russia's Military Reforms…*, p. 26.

Concluding remarks

J. L. Black

Whereas almost all of our authors make it plain that Russia has changed enormously over the last two decades, they caution that problems once endemic to the old Soviet Union have not all gone away. Putin's remark in 2005 to the effect that the collapse of the USSR was 'the greatest geopolitical catastrophe of the 20th century' rang true then to a great many Russians. Although the statement has been abused badly over the years, used out of context to suggest wrongly that Putin wanted to resurrect the USSR, few would deny that the precipitous collapse of the USSR left millions of people dangling with none of the economic or social safeguards to which they were long accustomed. In 1992 the new Russia's economy was in tatters, the country had no foreign policy, no allies, and no reasonably sufficient means of defence. In short, Russia stood naked on the world arena. The optimism that existed in spite of those grave circumstances soon fell by the wayside as the economic situation actually worsened, NATO expanded eastward, and civil war burst out in Chechnya. An inner circle of unelected former KGB and military operatives, known as the *siloviki*, wielded economic and political power hand-in-hand with media and industry barons generally know as the Oligarchs.

Much changed and much remained the same in Vladimir Putin's first eight years as president, 2000–8, and Dmitry Medvedev's four-year interregnum, 2008–12. For one thing, Russia's experiment with capitalism took firm root, though with mixed fortunes and heavy dependence on the energy sector and government. The government now has revenue to cover its spending, and usually a surplus; the country has international partnerships, among them the Shanghai Cooperation Organization, the Collective Security Treaty Organization, and a wide range of economic based multi-lateral agreements. Towards the end of 2011 the way was finally cleared for Russia's entry into the World Trade Organization in the spring of 2012.

There are recurring dilemmas. Ethnic tensions appear to be on the rise, political power beyond the presidency has fallen into the hands of a single party, and the socially discontented and political opposition are losing forums in which to express their dissatisfaction. Medvedev's final six months as president, in which there were chaotic parliamentary and presidential election campaigns, both with virtually foregone conclusions, were symptomatic of how far Russia has come since 1992, and how far it still has to go. That said, the citizenry seems to have become politically and socially active after a decade of quiescence.

As the year 2012 unfolded in Russia, judgements abounded on the effectiveness of 'tandem' governance during Medvedev's term as president, that is, the unusual practice of political power shared equally (in theory at least) by president and prime minister even though the Russian Constitution allocates considerably more power to the president than it does to the head of government. That is why we decided to finalize our essays after the presidential election of 2012 and use the results of that election as a vantage point from which to assess the direction Russia has been heading since 2009, and project beyond that to the extent possible.

The last few months of Medvedev's presidency were exciting ones. In addition to, and partly a consequence of, the furore over electoral legitimacy, a number of political reforms were introduced. These included a return to the direct election of governors in the regions, greatly simplified procedures for creating political parties and putting forward candidates for the presidency, and an expressed intention on the part of the authorities to treat opposition in a more civilized manner than they had been in the past. Time will tell on this one.

In foreign affairs, the positions Russia has taken to rising tensions in Syria and the potential of nuclear research in Iran set Moscow apart from Brussels and Washington and serve as symbolic of new/old divides. The Kremlin's foreign ministry sees great danger in the 'Libya approach' to international conflict resolution, vociferously resents the missile defence projects set for Europe, and worries about the long term consequences for Russia of both the 'Arab Spring' and NATO's forthcoming withdrawal from Afghanistan. In the latter case, the concern was primarily over the dramatic increase in the flow of drugs from Afghanistan into Central Asia and from there into Russia, but they also knew that the Taliban was not likely to be defeated fully and would try again to spread their cause into Central Asia after NATO left. Linked with the on-going violence in Russia's North Caucasus, circumstances in Central Asia therefore could turn age-old concerns about the 'soft underbelly' of Russia's strategic defence into a major calamity.

Overall, the practical and strategic shift to the east by Moscow's foreign ministry is palpable, but the western option remains a desired ambition. Although long-standing differences remain, the road to normalization may lie primarily in muting the lingering Cold War rhetoric that burst so easily to the surface for domestic political ends – on both 'sides'.

At home, the date of 24 September 2011, when the Tandem announced its formal continuation to a United Russia Congress is mentioned by most of our contributors as a turning point – and rightly so. That moment ended parlour guessing games about the presidency in Russia at least for the next six years; it also bore witness to the Tandem's belief that its system was durable and workable. Putin and Medvedev's popularity was still solidly tangible, but their assertion of unwavering mutual support was then, and is now, running a little thin.

Whereas the event of 24 September 2011 saw talking heads popping up everywhere on Russian (and Western) television, intoning about causes and implications of the Putin–Medvedev decision, it was greeted with 'so what?' on the streets of Moscow.[1] That apparent indifference – or cynicism – did not last long, as subsequent street demonstrations revealed.

Perhaps the best forewarning came from the 80 year-old originator of *perestroika* (where the transition started), M. S. Gorbachev. A few days before the Congress noted above, the ex-Soviet president warned about the danger of a return to Brezhnev-like stagnation and called for a new *perestroika*. He described the Duma election a Potemkin village and cautioned that the 'monarch-like' powers of the presidency could lead Russia to a dead end within five to six years.[2] Concerns that the Tandem's decision was timed primarily to boost the United Russia's sagging popularity, and Putin's admission that the switch had been planned years ago tainted any residual notion that Medvedev had grown into the presidency.

The essential issues at home, however, are still the connected questions of corruption and the economy, political stability, and the potential for upheaval. The Russian Federation is a work in progress; it is still going through a vibrant transitional stage in its short post-Soviet history. Time will tell where that transition leads.

As events unfold, we hope that the papers included here provide a useful starting point for studies of 'Russia after 2012'.

Notes

1 This editor happened to be in Moscow at the time, LB.
2 Gorbachev, 'Chtoby idti vpered, nuzhno izmenit' sistemu', *Moskovsky komsomolets*, 21 September 2011.

Appendix 1
Russian Federation parliamentary and presidential election results, 1993 to 2012

J. L. Black

State Duma election results, 12 December 1993

- Parties, movements and associates eligible to offer candidates = 93
- Parties that satisfied all criteria to have names on ballots = 13
- Eligible voters = 106 million; Turnout = 59 percent
- 225 seats based on proportional representative by parties; 225 are single constituency; parties must earn 5 percent of votes cast to earn seats in the Party side of the State Duma.

		Seats by		
Election results	%	Party	Single	Seats
Liberal Democratic Party of Russia	23.0	59	11	70
Russia's Choicer	15.4	40	56	96
Communists	12.5	32	33	65
Women of Russia	8.1	21	4	25
Agrarians	7.8	21	26	47
Yabloko	7.8	20	13	33
Russian Unity	6.7	18	9	27
Democratic Reform	4.1			
Civic Union in the Name of Stability	1.9			
The Future of Russia	1.2			
Ecological Movement –Cedar	0.7			
Dignity and Compassion	0.7			
Against all	4.7			

Referendum "Yeltsin" constitution was held the same day, with 58 percent approval.

State Duma election results, 17 December 1995

- Parties, movements and associations eligible to offer candidates = 266
- Parties and Blocs finally registered to have names on ballots = 43
- Eligible voters = 104 million; Turnout = 65 percent.

		Seats by		
Election results	%	Party	Single	Seats
Communists	22.3	99	58	157
Liberal Democratic Party Of Russia	11.2	50	1	51
Our Home is Russia	10.2	45	10	55
Yabloko	6.9	31	14	45
Women of Russia	4.6	0	3	3
Working Russia	4.5	0	1	1
Congress of Russian Communities	4.3	0	5	5
Party of Sviatoslav Fedorov	3.9	0	1	1
(Russia's) Democratic Choice	3.8	0	9	9
Agrarian Party	3.8	0	20	20
Power to the People	1.6	0	9	9
Other parties	–	0	17	17
Independents	–			77
Against all	2.7			

State Duma election results, 20 December 1999

- Parties and blocs finally registered to have names on ballot = 26
- Eligible voters = 106 million; turnout = 61.85 percent.

		Seats by		
Election results	%	Party	Single	Seats
Communist Party	24.3	67	43	110
Unity (*Medved* – Bear)	23.3	64	10	76
Fatherland—All Russia	13.33	37	29	62
Union of Right-Wing Forces	8.52	24	5	29
Yabloko	5.93	16	5	22
LDPR (Zhirinovskii Bloc)	5.98	17	0	17
Communists. Working People of Russia For the Soviet Union	2.22			
Women of Russia	2.04			
Party of Pensioners	1.95			
Our Home is Russia	1.19			
Russian Party for the Protection of Women	0.80			
Stalin Bloc – for the USSR!	0.61			
Social Democrats (Gorbachev)	0.08			
And 13 others against all	3.30			

State Duma election results, 7 December 2003

- Parties and blocs finally registered to have names on ballot = 23
- Eligible voters = 106 million; turnout = 55.75 percent.

Election results	%	Seats by Party	Single	Seats
United Russia	37.57	120	102	222
Communist Party	12.61	40	11	51
LDPR (Zhirinovsky)	11.45	36	1	37
Rodina (Motherland)	9.02	29	8	37
Yabloko	4.30		4	4
Union of Right-Wing Forces	3.97		3	3
Agrarian Party	3.64		3	3
Pensioners' Party	3.09		1	1
Russia's Revival	1.88		3	3
People's Party	1.20		16	16
Independents				74
				450
Against all	4.70			

State Duma election results, 2 December 2007[1]

- All seats based on proportional representation by parties; parties must achieve 7 percent of votes cast to earn seats
- Eligible voters = 109,145,517; Turnout = 63.78 percent
- Two parties, the Greens and Peace and Unity were declared ineligible at the last moment because their lists contained too many false names
- "Against all" category eliminated from ballot.

Party	% of votes	No. of votes	Seats
United (One) Russia	64.3	44,714.241	315
Communist Party of Russia	11.57	8,046,886	57
Liberal Democratic Party of Russia	8.14	5,660,823	40
Just (Fair) Russia[2]	7.74	5,383,639	38
Agrarian Party	2.30	1,600,234	0
Yabloko	1.59	1,108,985	0
Civil Force	1.05	733,604	0
Union of Right Forces (SPS)	0.96	699,444	0
Patriots of Russia	0.89	615,417	0
Social Justice Party	0.22	154,083	0
Democratic Party of Russia	0.13	89,780	0

State Duma election results, 4 December 2011

- Parties still needed 7 percent of votes cast to earn seats
- Parties with 5–6 percent of votes will get one seat; 6–7 percent will get two seats
- On 20 June 2011, Medvedev submitted a bill to the State Duma lowering the ceiling to 5 percent. The bill was adopted by the Federation Council in October and will be in effect for the 2016 Duma elections
- The Duma elected in 2011 will sit for five years, rather than the four years allocated to previous sessions
- On 30 September, only seven parties were declared eligible
- Votes cast = 65,774,462; Turnout = 60.21 percent.

Party	% of votes	No. of votes	Seats
United (One) Russia Party	49.32	32,379,135	238
Communist Party of Russian Federation	19.19	12,599,507	92
A Just (Fair) Russia	13.24	8,695,522	64
Liberal Democratic Party of Russia	11.67	7,664,570	56
Yabloko	3.43	2,252,403	
Patriots of Russia	0.97	639,617	
Right Cause	0.60	392,806	

Source: Central Electoral Commission's final report t, *Interfax*, 9 December 2011.

* * *

Presidential elections, 16 June, 13 July 1996

- Eligible voters = 108.4 million; turnout = 69.8 percent
- Victor had to win 50 percent of votes cast and 50 percent of eligible voters must vote for election to be considered valid
- This and subsequent elections to 2012 were for four-year terms.

Name	Votes (millions)	%
First round		
B. N. Yeltsin	26,665.495	35.28
Gennady Zyuganov	24,211,686	32.03
Aleksandr Lebed	10,974,736	14.52
Grigorii Yavlinsky	5,550,752	07.34
Vladimir Zhirinovsky	4,311,479	05.70
Svyatoslav Fedorov	699,158	00.92
M. S. Gorbachev	386,069	00.51
4 others	–	
Against all	1,163,921	–

Name	Votes (millions)	%
Second round		
Yeltsin	40,208,384	
Zyuganov	30,113,306	
Against all	3,604,550	

Presidential elections, 26 March 2000

- Eligible voters = 108 million; turnout = 68.74 percent.

	%	Votes
Vladimir Putin	52.90	39,740,434
Gennadii Zyuganov	29.21	21,928,471
Grigorii Yavlinskii	5.80	4,351,452
Aman Tuleev	3.07	2,217,361
Vladimir Zhirinovsky	2.72	2,026,513
Konstantin Titov	1.47	1,107,269
Ella Pamfilova	1.01	758,967
Stanislav Govorukhin	0.44	328,723
Yury Skuratov	0.43	319,189
Aleksei Podberezkin	0.13	98,177
Umar Dzhabrailov	0.10	78,498
Against all	1.88	1,414,673

Presidential elections, 14 March 2004

- Eligible voters = 108 million; turnout = 64.3 percent.

	%	Votes
Vladimir Putin	71.2	49,565,238
Nikolai Kharitonov (CPRF)	13.7	9,513,313
Sergei Glazov (Rodina)	4.1	2,850,063
Irina Khakamada (SPS)	3.9	2,671,313
Oleg Malyshev	2.1	1,405,315
Sergei Mironov	0.7	524,304
Against all	3.7	2,396,219

Presidential election, 2 March 2008

- Eligible voters = 107,222,016; turnout = 69.71 percent
- "Against all" category eliminated from ballot.

	%	Votes
Dmitry Medvedev	70.28	52,530,712
Gennady Zyuganov	17.72	13,243,550
Vladimir Zhirinovsky	9.35	6,988,510
Andrei Bogdanov	1.30	968,344
Invalidated votes	1.36	1,015,533

Presidential election, 4 March 2012

- Eligible voters = 108 million; turnout = 65.34 percent (71,701,665)
- This election was for a six-year term
- The "against all" category eliminated from ballot.

	%	Votes
Vladimir Putin	63.60	45,602,075
Gennady Zyuganov	17.18	12,318,353
Vladimir Zhirinovsky	6.22	4,458,102
Sergei Mironov	3.85	2,763,935
Mikhail Prokhorov	7.98	5,722,798

Notes

1 These figures were published in Russia on 10 December 2008; later official government website figures have all the percentages higher because only the four parties with over 7 percent were included in the distribution of seats.
2 Just Russia included as well Rodina, the Pensioners Party, and Russia's Revival

Appendix 2
Russian Federation's international alliances, associations, and organizations

J. L. Black

Integrating organizations to the East: memberships and (dates) of entry

1   Commonwealth of Independent States (CIS), was formed in December 1991 by Armenia, Azerbaijan, Belarus, Kazakhstan, Kyrgyzstan, Moldova, Russia, Tajikistan, Turkmenistan, and Uzbekistan.
    Ukraine signed the original agreement and has always participated, but its parliament has not yet ratified membership in the CIS.
    Georgia joined in 1993, left the Council of Defence Ministers (06), and declared its withdrawal altogether in August 2008.
    Uzbekistan "suspended" its membership on 28 June 2012.
    Turkmenistan changed its status to Associate Member in 2005.
    HQ = Minsk, Belarus.
2   Shanghai Cooperation Organization (SCO), was formed as Shanghai Five in 1996. *Chartered* as SCO in 2001: Russia (96), China (96), Kazakhstan (96), Kyrgyzstan (96), Tajikistan (96), Uzbekistan (01).
    Official Observer States: Mongolia (04), India (05), Pakistan (05), Iran (05), Afghanistan (2012).
    Unofficial Observer States: Turkmenistan (07), Azerbaijan (07).
    Dialogue Partners: Sri Lanka (10), Belarus (10), Turkey (2012).
    Bids for full membership by Iran (2007 and 2008), India (2010) and Pakistan (2006 and 2011), under a moratorium that was lifted for the Astana Summit, June 2011, were vetoed by China at that summit. Iran is not eligible because it is currently under sanctions set by the UN.
    Population of participants combined = one half of world's population.
    It is primarily a political and economic organization, with a business council, an energy club, a research and educational centre (Yekaterinburg), a joint environmental protection agency, and a disaster management centre (Krasnoyarsk). The SCO organizes anti-terrorist training operations.
    Energy links: SCO includes major energy producers (RF, Kazakhstan, Uzbekistan, Turkmenistan (by contract), Iran, and major energy customers, China and India).

Afghanistan links: SCO established an Afghanistan Contact Group in 2007, at the specific request of President Karzai, and has an anti-drug trafficking office in Kabul; RF also has a permanent "drug enforcement" office in Kabul; cooperates with CSTO (see below) on anti-drug-trafficking.

HQ = Beijing, China.

3 Collective Security Treaty Organization (CSTO), was founded within the CIS in 1992, with nine members; six confirmed in 1999.

Chartered in October 2002: Russia (02), Armenia (02), Belarus (02), Kazakhstan (02), Kyrgyzstan (02), Tajikistan (02); Uzbekistan (06); Uzbekistan "suspended" its membership on 28 June 2012.

Presidency rotates; the current Secretary General (since 2008) is a Russian, Nikolai Bordyuzha.

It is primarily a military organization, has a Peacekeeping Corps (07) with a mandate to be deployed anywhere on the territory of members' states, with permission of the host; it conducts military exercises, is compiling a joint data bank on drug trafficking in the region, and (with SCO) has a permanent anti-drug trafficking program. Members train their officers in Russian Military academies and purchase weapons from Russia at domestic rates. As of December 2011, each member has the right to veto the siting of foreign military bases on each other's territories.

HQ = Moscow, Russia.

i   These two bodies have official UN status as regional organizations.
ii SCO and CSTO have detailed and ratified agreements for cooperation on security matters, organized crime, drug trafficking, and anti-terrorism.
iii RF Foreign Minister Lavrov has, since 2006, regularly proposed collective cooperation between the CSTO and NATO in Afghanistan, i.e. that, in matters related to security and Afghanistan, NATO should deal with the CSTO as a collective organization rather than bilaterally with each member. NATO equally consistently rejected this idea until September 2010 when General Secretary Rasmussen called for greater cooperation with regional organizations in the Afghanistan conflict.
iv In addition to a shared need to counter political challenges to the status quo at home, and mutual struggles against drug trafficking, terrorism, separatism, and religious extremism, their members are held together by:
    a gas and oil pipelines and long-term energy contracts
    b huge cross-border investments in infrastructure (roads, airports); large-scale joint manufacturing enterprises – e.g. Russia–Uzbekistan Chkalev aviation industry
    c education and culture (Eurasia university system is shaping up), and Russian language TV.

4 Moscow–Beijing–New Delhi Axis is a concept proposed first by Russian Foreign Minister Yevgeny Primakov in the mid-1990s. Formalized in 2005,

the three heads of state, defence ministers, foreign affairs ministers, and economic ministers now hold regularly scheduled meetings and issue joint communiqués. (See also BRICS, below).
5   The Customs Union between Russia, Belarus, and Kazakhstan came into effect on 1 January 2010, and evolved into a Common Economic Space as of 1 January 2012. Kyrgyzstan opted to join in April 2011. Tajikistan and Ukraine are considering accession.
   i   On 12 November 2011 the prime ministers of all CIS countries signed an agreement to establish the CIS Common Economic Space, essentially a free-trade zone.
   ii On 18 November 2011, the presidents of Russia, Kazakhstan, and Belarus signed an agreement to create the Eurasian Single Economic Space, a basis for a future Eurasia Union.
   iii A Eurasian Economic Commission, with some 180 trade and economc functions allocated to it, was ratified by all three states before the end of November 2011. It replaced the Customs Union on 1 January 2012.

6   The Union State of Belarus and Russia was officially created by treaty in April 1997 and took its final shape by treaty in December 1999. This odd creation by Presidents Yeltsin and Lukashenka has a state council, a council of ministers, and an elected two-house parliament, with 75 deputies from Russia and 28 from Belarus. The Union State has its own State Secretary and its own annual budget, provided mainly by Russia. It has no authority over either country.

Other relevant organizations with active Russian membership

Eurasia Economic Community: founded 2000.
Chartered in 2001: Russia (01), Belarus (01) Kazakhstan (01), Kyrgyzstan (01), Tajikistan (01), Uzbekistan (06);
Observer States: Ukraine (02), Armenia (03), Moldova (03).
(see above, under Customs Union).

Organization of Central Asian Cooperation (OCAC): Kazakhstan (91), Kyrgyzstan (91), Turkmenistan (91 – withdrew 94); Tajikistan (98), Russia (04); *Observer States*: Georgia, Turkey, Ukraine;
Associate Member: Turkmenistan (07).

Organization of the Islamic Conference: founded in the 1960s, this body has 57 members; Russia was admitted as full member in 2005.

Russia's global and Western-oriented associations

United Nations: As the successor state to the USSR, the Russian Federation holds a permanent (veto-wielding) seat on the United Nations Security Council (UNSC).

PACE (Parliamentary Assembly of the Council of Europe): The Russian Federation acceded to the PACE on 28 February 1996. Although the credentials of Russia's delegation were challenged subsequently over the conflict in Chechnya and, more recently, in Georgia, it has remained an active member.

BRICS: The term originated, apparently, with a Goldman Sachs Report in 2003 that listed Brazil, Russia, India, and China as the four most quickly developing economies in the world. BRIC leaders began meeting regularly in 2006 and held their first summit in 2009. The BRIC invited South Africa to join in late 2010 and its membership was made official during a BRIC (now BRICS) summit in China, April 2011. BRICS foreign ministers also hold meetings, usually scheduled just prior to a major international summit such as the G8, where they set out economic priorities and goals in common. See also Moscow–Delhi–Beijing axis, above.

Quartet on the Middle East: Established in 2002 on the initiative of the prime minister of Spain, the Quartet consists of a representative from the United Nations, the European Union, the United States, and Russia. Its mandate, clearly unsuccessful thus far, is conflict resolution in the Middle East.

NATO–Russia Council: Formed on 28 May 2002, the council's tasks are limited specifically to "areas of mutual interest" outlined clearly in a declaration that day by the heads of NATO countries and the Russian Federation. The council replaced the NATO–Russia Permanent Joint Council (PJC), which was established in 1997 with the first Russian envoy to NATO arriving in March 1998. Russia severed relations with NATO in 1999 when the Alliance opened its bombing campaign against Serbia and only began sending its envoy to Brussels again in May 2000.

Arctic Council: Formally established by the Ottawa declaration in 1996.

Permanent members: Canada, Denmark/Greenland/Faroe Islands, Finland, Iceland, Norway, Sweden, Russia, and USA.

Permanent Observers: France, Germany, Netherlands, Poland, Spain, and the UK. It also has nine International Organizations and 11 NGOs represented, but no permanent Secretariat or HQ.

Gas Exporting Countries Forum (GECF): Sometimes referred to as the GasOPEC, it started in 2009, though the first official ministerial meeting was held in Iran in 2010. A Russian was elected its first president.

Members: Algeria, Bolivia, Egypt, Equatorial Guinea, Iran, Libya, Nigeria, Qatar, Russia, Trinidad and Tobago, and Venezuela.

Observer States: Kazakhstan, Netherlands, Norway.

HQ is in Doha, Qatar.

World Trade Organization (WTO): Russia applied for membership in the WTO in 1993, was promised admission by President Clinton in 1997, as quid pro quo for Boris Yeltsin's acquiescence on the first wave of NATO expansion, and by every US president since. In May and June 2011, the G8 and the G20 supported Russia's entry into the 153-member body by the end of the year. The final roadblock, Georgia's veto, was surmounted in November 2011 when a Swiss-brokered deal was agreed to by both parties. The final decision was reached in Geneva on 16 December. Russia is scheduled to become the WTO's one-hundred-and-fifty-fourth member on 15 June 2012.

Current arms control agreements

START (Strategic Arms Reduction Treaty) was signed by Presidents Obama and Medvedev in Prague on 8 April 2010 and came into effect on 26 January 2011. START (sometimes referred to as START III) replaced the USSR–USA ABM Treaty, signed in 1972 and abrogated unilaterally by the USA in December 2001, earlier START agreements, and the SORT (Strategic Offensive Reductions Treaty), signed by Presidents Bush and Putin in May 2002.

NPT (Nuclear Non-Proliferation Treaty), now includes 189 states, among them nuclear-armed states Russia, the United States, the United Kingdom, France, and China. Nuclear-armed non-signatories are India, Pakistan, and presumed North Korea and Israel.

CTBT (Comprehensive Test Ban Treaty), approved by the UN General Assembly in 1996, now has 153 ratified members, including Russia, but is not yet in force because over 40 states have signed but not ratified. Among these latter are the United States, China, Iran, and Israel. India, Pakistan, and North Korea have not signed.

INF (Intermediate-Range Nuclear Forces Treaty), signed by the USSR and the USA in 1987, eliminated nuclear and conventional ground-based ballistic and evasive missiles (500–5,500 km range). Russia is threatening to withdraw because China is building such missiles, and the US and NATO are building a missile shield for Europe.

Proposed and in-limbo European arrangements

In abeyance:
CPA (EU–RF Cooperation and Partnership Agreement), was adopted in 1997 and came up for renewal in 2007. Renewed on an annual basis until 2009, it passed out of force in 2010. The CPA was complicated by the fact that Russia never ratified an Energy Charter signed by Russia and the EU and, as far as the EU was concerned, integral to the CPA.

CFE (Conventional Forces in Europe Treaty), was adopted in 1990 by NATO and the Warsaw Pact to limit conventional forces on their mutual border regions. The CFE was amended in 1992 to take into account the dissolution of both the Warsaw Pact and the USSR, and again in 1999 to account for NATO expansion. Russia ratified, NATO members did not. Russia withdrew unilaterally in 2007, and NATO withdrew in 2011.

Desultory discussion: The Pan-European Security Treaty proposed by Medvedev during a speech delivered in Berlin in 2008 was submitted to the EU, NATO, and the US in November 2009. Little has been heard of it since, and European missile defence is now a major point of contention between the US and NATO on the one hand, Russia on the other.

Organizations that Russia is partially excluded from

EU (European Union): The EU has been expanding exponentially since the collapse of the USSR and now has 27 member states, five official candidate members, and three potential candidates. Although Russia is not a member, the EU is Russia's main trading partner. Together with 10 other countries, Russia is a member of the EU's Northern Dimension Initiative, which promotes cooperation between the Baltic and Arctic countries, with an emphasis on environmental issues. Russia is also a beneficiary of the EU's TACIS (Technical Assistance to the CIS) project, especially in connection with nuclear safety programs.

NATO (North Atlantic Treaty Organization): NATO has been expanding more rapidly even than the EU since the collapse of the USSR, mostly eastward. It now has 28 member states. NATO's Partnership for Peace (PfP) program, ostensibly to prepare countries for membership, started in early 1994 and soon included all former Warsaw Pact countries and several former Soviet republics. Russia reluctantly joined late in that year. Preparation for membership was assigned to MAP (Membership Action Plan). Currently Georgia and Ukraine have applied to MAP, over strong Russian objections. The question of Russian membership crops up from time to time, but to date the idea has few proponents on either "side." See also NATO–Russia Council, above.

Index

There will be no separate entry for Vladimir Putin or Dmitry Medvedev. For details on both, see subject entries.

Abkhazia 142,156, 172, 195
ABM Treaty 188, 190, 206, 229
Afghanistan 143, 144, 163, 167, 169, 170, 175, 179–80, 189, 190, 195, 196, 199, 217, 226
Agency for Strategic Initiatives (ASI) 112
A Just Russia Party 6, 79, 81
Akaev, Askar 168, 173
Alferov, Zhores 105
All-Russian Civic Forum 107
Al-Queda 169, 174
Andijon 173–6
Antonov, Anatoly 161
Arab Spring 15, 16, 217
Arbatov, Aleksei 128
Arctic 125, 139, 147, 212
Armed Forces, Chapters 8 and 13 *passim*; conscription 204; contract troops (kontraktniki) 125, 127, 128; procurement 108, 126, 127, 130, 204, 207–11; reform 121–9, 130–3, 202–6, 211, 213; weaponry 210–12
Armed Forces, Military Bases; Armenia 90, 158, 170, 225–7; foreign 167, 169, 170, 174, 176, 180, 189, 192, 194, 199; Russian 126, 144, 172, 186
arms control 188, 206; START 143, 196, 203, 229,
arms sales 176
Atambaev, Almazbek 180

Bakiev, Kurmanbek 173
Baltic States 157, 190, 203, 230
Baluevsky, Yuri 211
Baranets, Viktor 123
Barrett, Craig R. 105
Baturina, Elena 76, 113
Belarus 16, 90, 158, 169, 170, 172, 180, 225–7
Belkovsky, Stanislav 107, 109, 111

Berdymukhamedov, Gerguly 175
Biden, Joseph 149, 196
Boehner, John 144
Brezhnev, Leonid 94, 103, 218; Brezhnevian 42, 49
BRIC (BRICS) 112, 197–8, 228
Browder, William 113
Burmatov, Vladimir 65
Bush, George W. 143, 159, 161, 189, 190, 191, 195, 229; Bush Administration 141, 142, 169, 170, 188, 190

Central Asia, Chapter 11, *passim*; 163, 188–92, 194, 199, 217, 227
Chaika, Yury 107, 110, 114, 116
Chernomyrdin, Viktor 187
China, Chapter 12, *passim*; 68, 112, 115, 139, 140, 148, 150–1, 155, 160, 163, 167–8, 169, 180–1, 212–3, 225–6; BRICS 112, 197–8, 228; economics 91, 93, 97, 99, 142, 145–6, 172, 209; SCO 164–5, 174–5, 177
Chirikova, Evgeniia 80
Chirikova, Lidia 79
Chubais, Anatoly 105, 109
Chuichenko, Konstantin 112
Churov, Vladimir 50
Civil Platform 11
Clinton, Hillary 150
Clinton, William 228; Clinton Administration 188
Cold War 139–41, 148, 157, 202, 217
Collective Security Treaty Organization (CSTO) 170–2, 174, 175, 177, 180–1, 192, 199, 226
Commonwealth of Independent States (CIS) 90, 99, 188, 225, 227
Communist Party of the Russian Federation (CPRF/ KPRF) 6, 10–12, 43, 79, 81, 185, 220–3

Index

Constitution 4, 11, 25, 27, 44, 51, 101, 217; Constitutional Court 21, 24–5
Corruption, Chapter 7, *passim;* in education 58, 64, 65; in government 6, 14, 27, 42, 47–9, 52, 53, 79, 145, 149, 179, 181, 218; in law enforcement 29, 31, 33–4; in military 122–6, 129, 130
Council on Human Rights; Presidential 32, 76
Court System, Chapter 2, *passim*
Crawley, Edward F. 115
Crime 24, 26–8, 31, 34, 35, 89, 91, 99, 103, 107, 109, 112–13; *see also* Corruption
Criminal Code(s) 26–9, 112
Customs Union 180, 227

demographic issues *see* population
demokratizatsiia 42, 43
Dmitrienko, Dmitry 49
Dneprov, Edward 62
Dvorkin, Vladimir 124

Easton, David 14
Economy, Chapter 6, *passim*; oil and gas industry 4, 14, 77, 89, 90, 93, 98, 142, 145, 155–6, 158, 162, 163, 167, 171, 172, 175, 176, 180–1, 194, 226; pipelines 155–6, 167, 169, 171, 172, 174, 175, 180, 181, 193, 194, 226; 'shock therapy' 111, 185; tax collecting 13, 28, 32, 90, 94, 98, 99, 103, 106, 112; *see also* modernization
Education, Chapter 4, *passim*
Estonia 90, 157, 161, 164, 207
European Court of Human Rights (ECHR) 20, 25, 34
European Neighbourhood Policy (ENP) 157, 158
European Union (EU), Chapter 10, *passim*

Federation (Federal) Assembly 46
Federation Council 25, 46, 76, 103, 222
Fedotov, Mikhail 32
foreign policy, Russia relations with; Belarus 16, 169, 170, 180; BRICS 112, 197, 198; China, Chapter 12, *passim;* 146, 148, 150, 151, 164, 165, 174, 177; European Union, Chapter 10, *passim*; India 139, 142, 151, 168, 187, 192, 197, 212; Iran 144, 147, 168, 192; Iraq 191, 203; Israel 139; Japan 139, 212; Kazakhstan 106, 158, 167, 169, 170, 174–6, 189; Middle East 139; Ukraine 158, 172, 203; United States 106, 139, 141–5, 151, 159–61, 168, 169, 196–8, 203, 206

Gazprom 4, 105, 115, 156, 171, 174
Germany 93, 98, 108, 140, 145, 156, 164, 172, 176, 193, 195, 199, 209, 228
glasnost 3, 43, 74, 102, 109
Gorbachev, M.S. 3, 4, 16, 42, 43, 53, 102, 103, 109, 121, 141, 186, 190, 191, 218
Grigoriev, Leonid 108
Guriev, Sergei 48

Hale, Henry 8, 13
healthcare 51, 58, 77, 81, 82, 94, 102, 107
Herspring, Dale R. 121, 202, 210
Hu Jintao 199
Human Development Index 14, 91
human rights 25, 30, 31, 33, 34, 78, 148, 149, 157, 165, 169, 172, 174, 176, 181
Huntingdon, Samuel 4

Iakovleva, Iana 27
immigration 106, 193, 167, 175, 176, 178, 179, 181
India 57, 91, 93, 94, 112, 139, 142, 151, 155, 168, 187, 192, 197, 209, 212, 225, 228, 229
Iraq War 142, 191, 195
Ivanov, Sergei 206, 211

Japan 58, 91, 93, 139, 140, 145, 180, 193, 194, 197, 209, 212
Jowitt, Ken 42
Judicial System *see* Court System

Kaliningrad 158–9, 161
Kandaurov, Dmitry 132
Karimov, Islam 168, 170–4
Kasparov, Gerri (Garry) 11
Kasyanov, Mikhail 9, 11
Kazakhstan, Chapter 11, *passim;* 188, 189, 194, 225–8
Khakamada, Irina 76, 223
Khodorkovsky, Mikhail 19, 32–4, 103, 171
Konovalov, Aleksandr 26
Kornberg, Roger 105
Kosovo 154, 160, 161, 187, 189, 195, 206
Kozak, Dmitri 46
Kryshtanovskaia, Olga 110
Kudrin, Aleksei 8, 11
Kyrgyzstan, Chapter 11, *passim;* 188, 189, 192, 225, 226–7

labour 65, 167, 177–9, 181
Laden, Osama bin 169
Latvia 78, 90, 157, 164
law enforcement agencies 21, 26, 31, 32, 34, 110, 112; Investigatory Committee 27, 34; Ministry of the Interior (MVD) 29, 30, 34, 108, 112, 114, 116, 203
Lebedev, Platon 19, 33
Liberal Democratic Party of Russia 6, 10, 79, 81, 219, 220–2
Libya 148, 198, 203, 217, 228
Lipset, Seymour Martin 57
Lithuania 90, 157, 159, 164
Lukashenka, Aleksandr 16, 227
LUKoil 174
Luzhkov, Yuri 113

McFaul, Michael 106, 149, 150
Magnitsky, Sergei 29, 33
Makarov, Nikolai Ye 126–8, 131, 211, 212
March of Millions 8
Marxism-Leninism 61, 62, 64, 102
Matviyenko, Valentina 76
media 6, 20, 34, 45, 80, 103, 107, 111, 113, 114, 116, 148, 159, 191, 202, 216; social media 3, 8, 11, 15, 49, 50, 111
Meshalkin, Valeri 63
migration *see* immigration
military *see* armed forces
Milosevic, Slobodan 185, 187
Mironov, Sergei 10, 223, 224
modernization, Chapter 7, *passim*; 7, 29, 59; *see also* economics
Morshchakova, Tamara 32
Moses, Joel 48, 78

Nabiullina, Elvira 81
Nashi 113
national projects 58, 66, 150–1
nationalism 16, 81, 178, 180, 185
Navalny, Aleksei 3, 5, 8, 11, 12, 16, 50, 80, 113
Nazarbaev, Nursultan 168, 172, 176, 180
Nazarov, Aleksandr 113
Nemtsov, Boris 11
NGOs 30, 31, 34, 35, 149; Amnesty International 176; Human Rights Watch 176
Niyazov, Saparmurat 168, 171, 172, 175
North Atlantic Treaty Organization (NATO) 144, 150, 160, 161, 163, 165, 169–71, 175, 179, 180, 187, 190, 192, 195, 196, 198, 199, 210, 217, 226, 228, 229; NATO expansion 142, 143, 147, 158, 186, 188, 190, 191, 203, 206, 207, 213, 216, 230
Northern Distribution Network 179
Nurgaliev, Rashid 30

Obama, Barack 142–4, 149, 194–7, 199, 229; Obama Administration 142, 143, 149, 179, 180, 184, 191
oligarchs 74, 103, 107, 216
Orange Revolution 7, 9, 16, 148, 191
Organization for Security and Cooperation in Europe (OSCE) 6, 80, 203
Other Russia 11
Otunbaeva, Rosa 167, 176
Ovcharova, Lilia 15

Pakistan 179, 192, 225, 229
Paleev, Mikhail 27
Pamfilova, Ella 76, 223
Parfenov, Leonid 11
Parliamentary Assembly of the Council of Europe (PACE) 80, 228
Partnership and Cooperation Agreement (PCA) 154, 155, 162
Pavlovsky, Gleb 111
People's Freedom Party 113
perestroika 3, 42, 43, 102–4, 109, 203, 218
Petrov, Nikolai 49
Poland 157, 159, 161, 164, 228
political system, Chapter 1, *passim*
Polyakov, Leonid 53
Popescu, Nicu 16, 163
population 15, 26, 77, 91, 173, 176–9, 193, 197, 209
Primakov, Yevgeny 186, 187, 192, 226
Prokhorov, Mikhail 10, 11, 224
Public Chamber 26, 76, 102, 112, 114, 126
Pushkov, Aleksei 149
Pussy Riot 15, 35, 80

Radchenko, Vladimir 26
Radzikhovsky, Leonid 45
Reagan, Ronald 141, 186
regions, Chapter 3, *passim*
religion 45; Islam 142, 143, 169, 170, 173, 179, 181, 188, 189, 227
Remington, Thomas 13
Right Cause Party 222
Rogozin, Dmitry 130
Romney, Mitt 147

Saakashvili, Mikheil 175, 191, 195
Sadovnichy, Viktor 66
Sakwa, Richard 3

Satarov, Georgyi 33
Savchenko, Mikhail 49
Scharpf, Fritz W. 13
Schwarzenegger, Arnold 110
Serdyukov, Valery 108, 122, 123, 126, 129, 210
Shanghai Cooperation Organization (SCO) 155, 158, 163–5, 174, 175, 177, 180, 181, 188, 190, 192, 198, 199, 216, 225, 226
Shurygin, Vladislav 123
siloviki 103, 111, 113, 114, 216
skinheads 178
Skolkovo Innovation Centre 105–7, 109–12, 115, 210
Slipchenko, Vladimir 131
Sobchak, Anatoly 12
Sobchak, Ksenia 12, 80
Sobyanin, Sergei 113, 178
Sorochkin, Aleksandr 108
South Ossetia 142, 156, 195
Soviet Union 3, 4, 16, 43, 59–63, 73, 78, 82, 91, 93, 94, 102, 103, 140–1, 157, 158, 171, 173, 188, 194, 216; *see also* Union of SSRs
Stalin, J.V. 113
Starovoitova, Galina 76
State Council 64
State Duma, Chapter 1, *passim*; 35, 46, 47, 49, 50, 76, 78–80, 103, 114, 116, 149, 218, 219–22
Stepashin, Sergei 103
Strategy-31 11
Subbotin, Sergei 49
Surkov, Vladislav 104, 106, 109
Syria 147, 150, 159–61, 198, 200, 203, 217

Tajikistan, Chapter 11, *passim*; 90, 110, 188, 189, 225–7
Taliban 169, 170, 174, 189, 196, 217
terrorism 24, 46, 142, 160, 169, 174, 188, 189, 190, 203
Titov, Aleksei 16, 223
Tocqueville, Alexis de 47, 53
Torshin, Aleksandr 25, 26
Transparency International 104, 110, 114, 115
Tsyganok, Anatoly 124
Turkmenistan 90, 167, 168, 171, 172, 174, 175, 179, 180, 194, 225, 227

Udaltsev, Sergei 10
Ukraine 6, 7, 9, 90, 142, 148, 155, 156, 158, 172, 173, 186, 191, 195, 203, 207, 213, 225, 227, 230
Unified Energy System (UES) 105
Union of Soviet Socialist Republics (USSR) *see* Soviet Union
United Nations 74, 75, 161, 227, 228; United Nations Security Council (UNSC) 103, 156, 160, 185, 187, 188, 191, 195, 198, 203, 227
United Russia Party, Chapter 1, *passim*; 47, 48, 77, 79, 80, 81, 110, 149, 217, 218, 221
United States of America 93, 106, 139, 140, 141, 143, 145, 149, 150, 159, 160, 163, 167–9, 173, 178, 180, 181, 188, 203, 206, 228, 229; Re-Set xi, xvi, 143, 144, 145, 149, 150, 184, 196, 198
Uzbekistan, Chapter 11, *passim*; 90, 188, 189, 192, 194, 225, 226, 227

Vekselberg, Viktor 105
Vinogradoff, Paul 43

wars; Afghanistan 143, 144, 169, 170, 175, 179, 180, 189, 190, 195, 196, 199, 217; Chechnya 45, 52, 121, 142, 154, 169, 185, 188, 189, 216, 228; Georgia 123, 127, 142, 147, 156–7, 158, 175, 176, 184, 194, 195, 203, 213; Iraq *see* Iraq War; Yugoslavia (including Kosovo conflict) 160, 185, 187, 206
women, Chapter 5, *passim*
World Trade Organization (WTO) 115, 144, 151, 216, 228

Yabloko 219–22
Yavlinsky, Grigory 222
Yeltsin, Boris 3, 4, 33, 44, 74, 78, 81, 103, 104, 121, 141, 145, 148, 154, 160, 168, 169, 185–7, 191, 204, 211, 219, 222, 223, 227, 228
Yevdokimov, Yuri 49
Yukos 32, 45, 171

zastoi 42, 43, 49
Zhirinovsky, Vladimir 7, 81, 221–4
Zorkin, Valery 25, 33
Zyuganov, Gennady 4, 6, 7, 10, 12, 222–4